D1737467

ADVANCES IN CONFIGURAL FREQUENCY ANALYSIS

Methodology in the Social Sciences
David A. Kenny, Founding Editor
Todd D. Little, Series Editor

This series provides applied researchers and students with analysis and research design books that emphasize the use of methods to answer research questions. Rather than emphasizing statistical theory, each volume in the series illustrates when a technique should (and should not) be used and how the output from available software programs should (and should not) be interpreted. Common pitfalls as well as areas of further development are clearly articulated.

SPECTRAL ANALYSIS OF TIME-SERIES DATA
Rebecca M. Warner

A PRIMER ON REGRESSION ARTIFACTS
Donald T. Campbell and David A. Kenny

REGRESSION ANALYSIS FOR CATEGORICAL MODERATORS
Herman Aguinis

HOW TO CONDUCT BEHAVIORAL RESEARCH OVER THE INTERNET:
A BEGINNER'S GUIDE TO HTML AND CGI/PERL
R. Chris Fraley

PRINCIPLES AND PRACTICE OF STRUCTURAL EQUATION MODELING, SECOND EDITION
Rex B. Kline

CONFIRMATORY FACTOR ANALYSIS FOR APPLIED RESEARCH
Timothy A. Brown

DYADIC DATA ANALYSIS
David A. Kenny, Deborah A. Kashy, and William L. Cook

MISSING DATA: A GENTLE INTRODUCTION
Patrick E. McKnight, Katherine M. McKnight, Souraya Sidani, and Aurelio José Figueredo

MULTILEVEL ANALYSIS FOR APPLIED RESEARCH: IT'S JUST REGRESSION!
Robert Bickel

THE THEORY AND PRACTICE OF ITEM RESPONSE THEORY
R. J. de Ayala

THEORY CONSTRUCTION AND MODEL-BUILDING SKILLS: A PRACTICAL GUIDE
FOR SOCIAL SCIENTISTS
James Jaccard and Jacob Jacoby

DIAGNOSTIC MEASUREMENT: THEORY, METHODS, AND APPLICATIONS
André A. Rupp, Jonathan Templin, and Robert A. Henson

APPLIED MISSING DATA ANALYSIS
Craig K. Enders

ADVANCES IN CONFIGURAL FREQUENCY ANALYSIS
Alexander von Eye, Patrick Mair, and Eun-Young Mun

Advances in
Configural Frequency
Analysis

■ ■ ■ ■ ■ ■ ■ ■ ■

Alexander von Eye
Patrick Mair
Eun-Young Mun

Series Editor's Note by Todd D. Little

THE GUILFORD PRESS
New York   London

© 2010 The Guilford Press
A Division of Guilford Publications, Inc.
72 Spring Street, New York, NY 10012
www. guilford. com

Printed in the United States of America

This book is printed on acid-free paper.

Last digit is print number: 9   8   7   6   5   4   3   2   1

Library of Congress Cataloging-in-Publication Data

Eye, Alexander von.
    Advances in configural frequency analysis / Alexander A. von Eye,
Patrick Mair, and Eun-Young Mun.
        p. cm. — (Methodology in the social sciences)
    Includes bibliographical references and index.
    ISBN 978-1-60623-719-9 (hardcover: alk. paper)
    1. Psychometrics.   2. Discriminant analysis.   I. Mair, Patrick.   II. Mun,
Eun-Young.   III. Title.
    BF39.E93 2010
    150.1'519535—dc22

                                                            2010005255

Series Editor's Note

When you see the acronym CFA, you, like me, may be conditioned to think confirmatory factor analysis. This authoritative assemblage by von Eye, Mair, and Mun will change your conditioned response. Now when you see CFA, you'll know that it might refer to an equally powerful analytic technique: configural frequency analysis. Like its continuous variable acronym, CFA is a useful and potent inferential tool used to evaluate the expected patterns in two-way to multiway cross tabulations of frequencies. Remember your two-way frequency tables from your first undergraduate introduction to statistics? In that course, you were taught to calculate the expected value of each cell and then calculate a simple chi-squared test to see if the whole table deviated from the expected pattern. When you have some ideas about what is going on with your data, such approaches to frequency tables are pretty dissatisfying, right? Well . . . be dissatisfied no more. Much as confirmatory factor analysis revolutionized how we examine the covariations between two or more continuous variables, configural frequency analysis revolutionizes how we examine the cross-tabulation of two or more count variables.

CFA models allow you to identify and test for cell configurations in your data that are either consistent with or contrary to your hypothesized patterns (the types and antitypes of CFA). These models are flexible and powerful enough to allow you to control for potential covariates that might influence your observed results. They can address questions of moderation and mediation. They can be applied longitudinally. They can include predictive models. In fact, the variations in how CFA models can be used indicate that CFA models have matured to the level of a general multipurpose tool for analyzing categorical data.

von Eye, Mair, and Mun have written a masterfully balanced book. They have provided a resource that is ideal for both the uninitiated and the CFA expert. The novice will learn precisely why and how CFA can unlock the mysteries of categorical data. The expert will find a state-of-the-science reference for all the new developments and advanced extensions that have emerged in the literature on CFA over the last decade or so. Given that this authorial team has been significantly responsible for many of those new developments, you'll feel well connected to the "source" of knowledge.

The accolades from reviewers of this book are uniform in their appreciation. I'm confident you'll join the chorus of appreciation when you tell your colleagues and students about this wonderful resource.

TODD D. LITTLE
University of Kansas
Lawrence, Kansas

Preface

Configural Frequency Analysis (CFA; Lienert, 1968; von Eye, 2002a) is a method for the analysis of bi- or multivariate cross-classifications of categorical variables. In contrast to such methods as log-linear modeling, which express results mostly in terms of relationships among variables, CFA allows one to look for effects at the level of individual cells, or groups of cells, in a table. The patterns of categories that define a cell, that is, the cell indices, are called *configurations*. CFA identifies those configurations that contradict hypotheses because they contain more cases than expected. These configurations are called *type-constituting*. CFA also allows one to find those configurations that contain fewer cases than expected. These configurations are called *antitype-constituting*. Configurations that constitute neither a type nor an antitype contain as many cases as expected.

The number of cases that are expected for each cell is determined by specifying a CFA base model. The base model includes all effects that are not of interest to the researcher. If the base model is rejected—this is the precondition for CFA types and antitypes to emerge—those effects that the researchers are interested in identifying exist in the form of types and antitypes. This is a textbook on CFA that serves three purposes:

1. Introduction to CFA and review of existing concepts and approaches
2. Introduction and application of new CFA methods
3. Illustration of computer applications

The book begins with an introduction and review of methods of CFA proposed earlier. Readers not familiar with CFA will benefit from this introduction (Chapter 1 of this book). Readers who need more detail may find it useful to review introductory textbooks on the topic of CFA (von Eye, 2002a) or overview articles (e.g., von Eye & Gutiérrez Peña, 2004).

The second purpose involves the presentation, discussion, and application of recently proposed methods of CFA, and the introduction of new methods. Recently introduced methods include CFA of rater agreement (von Eye & Mun, 2005). This method, presented in Chapter 2, allows one to look at those configurations that indicate agreement between raters and to answer the question whether each of these constitutes a CFA agreement type (as one would expect if there is strong agreement). Similarly, one can ask whether configurations that indicate discrepant judgments constitute CFA agreement antitypes (as one would also expect if there is strong agreement). To complement the analysis of rater agreement, one can also look at agreement antitypes and disagreement types (the emergence of either of these may constitute a surprising result).

Also recently discussed, but not in the context of a broader text, is the use of covariates in CFA (Glück & von Eye, 2000). In this book, in Chapter 4, the discussion focuses on the role that covariates play for the detection of types and antitypes.

Configural prediction models are among the more widely discussed models of CFA (P-CFA). In Chapter 5 of this book, we focus on various designs of P-CFA and the corresponding interpretation of types and antitypes. It is shown that there is no a priori correspondence between P-CFA and logistic regression. However, by way of considering higher order interactions, corresponding models can be created. Still, whereas logistic regression relates variables to each other, the types and antitypes of P-CFA relate predictor patterns and criterion patterns to each other.

There are two topics in the chapter on P-CFA that have not been discussed before in the context of CFA. One is CFA of predicting end points; the other is CFA of predicting trajectories. Also new is the discussion of options of graphical representations of P-CFA results.

In the following chapters, a new approach to CFA is introduced. So far, CFA involved performing the five steps outlined in Chapter 1, which required performing just one CFA run and the interpretation of the resulting types and antitypes. The new approach involves performing more than one run of CFA, the comparison of results from these runs, and the interpretation of types and antitypes from one of the runs, depending on the results of the comparison. This new approach opens the doors to answering questions that were previously not accessible with CFA.

The first application of this new approach is CFA of mediation hypotheses (Chapter 6). Here, four CFA runs are needed that, in part, mimic the mediation regression models proposed by Baron and Kenny (1986). These runs allow researchers to determine (1) where mediation takes place in a cross-classification, and (2) the type of mediation (i.e., complete vs. partial). One interesting result of CFA of mediation is that, in the same table, complete mediation may be found for some configurations, partial for others, and no mediation for the rest of the configurations. A second application of this new approach to

CFA can be found in Auto-Association CFA (Chapter 7). Here, researchers can ask (1) whether types or antitypes exist at all, and (2) which of the possible relationships between two or more series of measures and covariates are the reasons for the types and antitypes to emerge.

Similarly, in CFA moderator analysis, at least two models are run. The first does not include the moderator. The cross-classification is, thus, collapsed across all categories of the moderator variable. The second includes the moderator. If the type and antitype patterns differ across the categories of the moderator, the hypothesis that moderation takes place is supported, at the level of individual configurations. Again, moderation may be supported for some configurations but not others, so that an analysis at the level of individual configurations will almost always lead to a more detailed picture of the processes that take place than an analysis at the level of variables. Chapter 8, on Moderator CFA, also contains the discussion of special topics such as the analysis of hypotheses of moderated mediation, and the graphical representation of configural moderator results.

A third application of this new methodology is presented in Chapter 9, on the validity of types and antitypes. It is proposed that types and antitypes can be considered valid if they can be discriminated in the space of variables that had not been used for the search of the types and antitypes. Here, at least two runs are needed. The first involves CFA. The second involves estimating a MANOVA, discriminant analysis, or a logit model.

In Chapter 10, two types of Functional CFA (F-CFA) are presented. First, F-CFA helps identify the role that individual configurations play in the identification of types and antitypes. F-CFA identifies phantom types and antitypes, that is, configurations that stand out just because other configurations stand out. F-CFA is, therefore, a tool of use when one suspects that the mutual dependence of CFA tests leads to the identification of invalid types and antitypes. The second flavor of F-CFA concerns the role played by the effects of log-linear models for the explanation of types and antitypes. F-CFA can be used to isolate the effects that carry types and antitypes. Each of the two versions of F-CFA can require multiple CFA runs.

Coming back to CFA models that require only one run, two new models allow one to explore hypotheses concerning repeatedly measured variables (Chapter 11). Specifically, intensive categorical longitudinal data have been elusive to CFA, thus far. Intensive longitudinal data involve many observation points. Instead of declaring bankruptcy under Chapter 11, we propose using the concept of runs. In a series of scores, runs are defined by the frequency and length of series of scores that share a particular characteristic (same score, ascending, etc.).

The second new approach to analyzing intensive longitudinal data involves configural lag analysis. This method of CFA allows one to identify those configurations that occur more (or less) often than expected after a particular time lag, that is, for example, after 1 day, 2 days, a week, etc.

Another topic that has never been discussed in the context of CFA concerns fractional factorial designs (Chapter 12). These designs are incomplete in that only a selection of all possible configurations is created. This strategy has the advantage that the table to be analyzed can be much smaller than the table that contains all possible configurations. In other words, for a table of a given size, the number of variables that can be analyzed simultaneously can be much larger when fractional factorial designs are used. The price to be paid for this advantage is that not all higher order interactions can be independently estimated. A data example illustrates that CFA of fractional factorial designs can yield the same results as CFA of the complete table.

The third major purpose of this text is to provide the illustration of computer applications. Three applications are presented in Chapter 13. Each of these uses programs that can be obtained free of charge. The first application involves using a specialized CFA program. The second involves using the cfa package in a broader programming environment, R. The third application involves using ℓEM, a general purpose package for the analysis of categorical data.

This book targets four groups of readers. The first group of readers of this book knows CFA, finds it useful and interesting, and looks forward to finding out about new developments of the method. The second group of readers of this book has categorical data that need to be analyzed statistically. The third group is interested in categorical data analysis per se. The fourth group of readers of this book considers data analysis from a person-oriented perspective interesting and important. This perspective leads to far more detailed data analysis than aggregate-level analysis, at the level of variables.

The reader of this book can come from many disciplines in the social and behavioral sciences (e. g., Psychology, Sociology, Anthropology, Education, or Criminal Justice). Our collaboration with colleagues in medical disciplines such as Pharmacology and Nursing has shown us that researchers in these disciplines can also benefit from using CFA for the analysis of their data. Naturally, researchers in the field of Applied Statistics will notice that many of the concepts that are discussed in this text add interesting elements to person-oriented research and to data analysis, in general, and that the application of CFA involves interesting facets that go beyond those covered by well-known procedures.

Acknowledgments

This book involved the intensive collaboration of three authors who are separated by frequent flyer miles and red-hot Internet connections. The first author is deeply indebted to Patrick and Eun-Young for putting up with his desire of presenting new materials in textbook format. This book shows that it can be done. Nobody is perfect. Still, please blame all mistakes and blunders only on the first author.

We are greatly indebted to C. Deborah Laughton, the best publisher of research methods and statistics books The Guilford Press could possibly hire. Having worked on other books with her before, we had no doubt that, with her, this book would be in the best hands. Professional and human in one person—hard to find and fun to collaborate with.

We also appreciate Todd Little's expertly and scholarly feedback and the suggestions from the reviewers: Michael J. Cleveland, The Methodology Center, The Pennsylvania State University; Mildred Maldonado-Molina, Health Policy Research, University of Florida, Gainesville; and Paula S. Nurius, School of Social Work, University of Washington.

We would also like to thank our families and friends from around the globe for letting us disappear to be with our computers, work over weekends and at night, and take naps at daytime (EYM and PM insist on making the statement that this part applies only to the first author, who was napping when this was written).

Contents

1

Introduction

Configural Frequency Analysis (CFA) is a method for the analysis of multivariate cross-classifications (contingency tables). The motivation for this book is to present recent exciting developments in the methodology of CFA. To make sure readers are up to date on the basic concepts of CFA, Chapter 1 reviews these concepts. The most important include (1) the CFA base model and its selection, (2) the definition and interpretation of CFA types and antitypes, and (3) the protection of the nominal level of the significance threshold α. In addition, this first chapter presents sample questions that can be answered by using the existing tools of CFA as well as questions that can be answered by using the new tools that are presented in this book. Throughout this book, emphasis is placed on practical and applied aspects of CFA. The overarching goal of this chapter — and the entire book — is to illustrate that there is more to the analysis of a multivariate cross-classification than describing relationships among the variables that span this cross-classification. Individual cells or groups of cells stand out and identify where the action is in a table. CFA is the method to identify those cells.

This chapter provides an introductory review of Configural Frequency Analysis (CFA), a method of categorical data analysis originally proposed by Lienert (1968). A textbook on CFA is von Eye (2002a), and for an article-length overview, see von Eye and Gutiérrez Peña (2004). CFA allows one to focus on individual cells of a cross-classification instead of the variables that span this cross-classification. Results of standard methods of categorical data analysis such as log-linear modeling or logistic regression are expressed in terms of relationships among variables. In contrast, results from CFA are expressed in terms of configurations (cells of a table) that are observed at different rates than expected under some base model. We begin, in this section, with an example. Section 1.1 presents sample questions that can be answered by using the CFA methods known so far and, in particular, the new methods discussed in this book. Section 1.2 introduces the five decision-making steps that researchers take when

TABLE 1.1. Cross-Classification of Depression, Happiness, Stress, and Emotional Uplifts in 123 First-Time Internet Users

Depression	Happiness	Stress	Uplifts 1	Uplifts 2
1	1	1	6	5
1	1	2	5	0
1	2	1	4	27
1	2	2	12	10
2	1	1	10	5
2	1	2	19	10
2	2	1	2	4
2	2	2	1	3

applying CFA. Section 1.3 presents a slightly more technical introduction to the methods of CFA.

Before going into conceptual or technical detail, we illustrate the type of question that can be asked using CFA as it is known so far. CFA is a method that allows one to determine whether patterns of categories of categorical variables, called configurations, were observed more often than expected, less often than expected, or as often as expected. A configuration that contains more observed cases than expected is said to constitute a CFA type. A configuration that contains fewer observed cases than expected is said to constitute a CFA antitype.

For the first example, we use data from a study on the effects of Internet use in individuals who, before the study, had never had access to the Internet (L. A. Jackson et al., 2004). In the context of this study, 123 respondents answered questions concerning their depression, feelings of stress, happiness, and the number of emotional uplifts they experienced within a week's time. For the following analyses, each of these variables was coded as 1 = below the median and 2 = above the median for this group of respondents (minority individuals with below-average annual incomes). Crossing these variables yields the $2 \times 2 \times 2 \times 2$ given in Table 1.1.

The Pearson X^2 for this table is 91.86. Under $df = 11$, the tail probability for these data is, under the null hypothesis of independence of the four variables that span this table, $p < 0.01$. The null hypothesis is thus rejected. The standard conclusion from this result is that there is an association among Depression, Happiness, Stress, and Emotional Uplifts. However, from this result, one cannot make any conclusions concerning the specific variables that are associated with one another (i.e., that interact). In addition, based on this result, one cannot make any conclusions concerning the occurrence rate of particular patterns of these four variables.

To answer questions of the first kind, log-linear models are typically applied. A log-linear model that describes the data in Table 1.1 well includes all main effects and the two-way interactions between Stress and Uplifts, Happiness and Uplifts, and Depression and Happiness. The likelihood ratio $X^2 = 15.39$ for this model suggests no significant overall model – data discrepancies ($df = 8; p = 0.052$).

To answer questions of the second kind, one uses CFA. These questions are qualitatively different from the questions answered using such methods as X^2, log-linear modeling, or logistic regression. The questions that CFA allows one to deal with operate at the level of individual cells (configurations) instead of the level of variables. As will be illustrated later, when we complete this example, CFA allows one to examine each individual pattern (cell; configuration) of a two- or higher-dimensional table. For each configuration, it is asked whether it constitutes a CFA type, a CFA antitype, or whether it contains as many cases as expected. A base model needs to be specified to determine the expected cell frequencies. In the next section, we present sample questions that can be answered by using CFA.

1.1   Questions That CFA Can Answer

In this section, we first discuss the questions that can be answered by using the methods of CFA known so far. The methods presented in this book allow one to address a large number of new questions. A selection of these questions is given, beginning with Question 6. The first five questions review previously discussed tools of CFA (von Eye, 2002a).

1. Do the observed cell frequencies differ from the expected cell frequencies? Counting and presenting frequencies are interesting, in many cases. For example, during the Olympic Games, news reports present medal counts to compare participating nations. However, the interpretation of observed frequencies often changes when expected frequencies are considered. For example, one can ask whether the number of medals won by a country surprises when the size of the country is taken into account when estimating the expected number of medals. Methods of CFA allow one to make statistical decisions as to whether an observed frequency differs from its expected counterpart. Naturally, expected frequencies depend on the characteristics of the CFA base model, discussed in Section 1.2. If a cell contains significantly more cases than expected, it is said to constitute a CFA type. If a cell contains significantly fewer cases than expected, it is said to constitute a CFA antitype.

2. Is there a difference between cell counts in two or more groups? A large number of empirical studies are undertaken to determine whether gender differences exist, whether populations from various ethnic backgrounds differ from one another, and when and in which behavioral domain development can be detected. For these and similar questions, multi-group CFA has been developed. The base model for this method is saturated in all variables that are used for the comparison. However, it proposes that the grouping variable is independent of the variables used for comparison. Discrimination types can, therefore, result only if a pattern of the variables used for comparison is observed at disproportional rates in the comparison groups.

3. Are there configurations whose frequencies change disproportionally over time? A large number of CFA methods has been devoted to the analysis of longitudinal data. New methods for this purpose are also proposed in this book (see Chapters 5, 6, and 7). Temporal changes can be reflected in shifts between patterns, constancy and change in means or slopes, temporal predictability of behavior, or constancy and change in trends. Whenever a configuration deviates from expectation, it is a candidate for a type or antitype of constancy or change.

4. Are patterns of constancy and change group-specific? Combining Questions 2 and 3, one can ask whether temporal or developmental changes are group-specific. For example, one can ask whether language development proceeds at a more rapid pace in girls than in boys, or whether transition patterns exist that show that some paranoid patients become schizophrenic whereas others stay paranoid. The base model for the group comparison of temporal characteristics is saturated in the temporal characteristics, and proposes independence between temporal characteristics and the grouping variable. Patterns that are observed disproportionally more often than expected based on group size are candidates for discrimination types (of constancy and change).

5. How are predictor variables related to criterion variables? One of the main tenets of CFA application is that relationships among variables are not necessarily uniform across all categories (or levels) of these variables. For example, a medicinal drug may have effects that are proportional to dosage. However, it may not show additional benefits if a stronger than the prescribed dose is taken, and deleterious effects may result if even stronger doses are used. Prediction CFA allows one to determine which patterns of predictor variables can be predicted to be followed above expectation by particular patterns of criterion variables, thus constituting prediction types. Accordingly, prediction antitypes are constituted by predictor

configurations for which particular criterion configurations are observed less often than expected. The present book presents new prediction models for CFA (Chapter 5).

The following sample questions are new in the array of questions that can be addressed using CFA methods:

6. Does rater agreement/disagreement exceed expectation for particular combinations of rating categories? Coefficients of rater agreement such as Cohen's κ (Cohen, 1960) allow one to make summary statements about rater agreement beyond chance. CFA models of rater agreement allow one to test hypotheses concerning, for instance, the weights raters place on rating categories (von Eye & Mun, 2005). CFA allows one to examine individual cells in agreement tables and ask whether there is agreement or disagreement beyond expectation in individual cells. One possible outcome is that raters agree/disagree more often than expected when they use the extreme categories of a rating scale. Chapter 2 presents methods of CFA of rater agreement.

7. Can structural zeros be taken into account in CFA? Many cross-tabulations contain cells that, for logical instead of empirical reasons, are empty. These cells contain structural zeros. In this book, methods are reviewed that allow one to blank out cells with structural zeros. In addition, it is discussed that particular designs systematically contain structural zeros. An algorithm is proposed for the detection of such cells (Chapter 3).

8. Can the effects of covariates on the results of CFA be assessed? In Chapter 4, methods for the accommodation of continuous as well as categorical covariates are discussed and illustrated.

9. Do particular characteristics of series of measures result in types or antitypes? In many contexts, characteristics of series of measures are used to predict an outcome. For example, one can ask whether a series of therapeutic steps will cure a neurotic behavior, or whether a series of evasive maneuvers can prevent a car from sliding into an elephant. In these cases, the series is used to predict an outcome. In other series, a starting point is used to predict a trajectory. CFA applications assume that the relationships that allow one to predict outcomes or trajectories can be described at the level of configurations. Sections 5.2 and 5.3 present CFA methods for the prediction of end points and trajectories.

10. Which configurations carry a mediation process? Standard methods for the analysis of mediation hypotheses are based on regression methods.

As such, they imply the assumption that the relationships among variables are the same over the entire range of admissible scores (Baron & Kenny, 1986; MacKinnon, Fairchild, & Fritz, 2007; von Eye, Mun, & Mair, 2009). In a fashion analogous to Prediction CFA, Mediation CFA proceeds under the assumption that predictive and mediated relationships are carried by configurations of variable categories instead of all categories. Mediation CFA, therefore, attempts to identify those patterns that support mediation hypotheses. A second characteristic that distinguishes Mediation CFA from standard mediation analysis concerns the nature of a mediation process. Based on CFA results, it may not only be that some configurations support mediation hypotheses whereas others do not, it is very well possible that the same table can support the hypothesis of complete or full mediation for some configurations, the hypothesis of partial mediation for others, and the null hypothesis for still a third group of configurations. More detail on mediation models is presented in Chapter 6.

11. Which configurations carry a moderator process? The relationship between two variables, A and B, is considered "moderated" if it changes over the range of admissible scores of a third variable, C. Here again, CFA assumes that the relationship between A and B may better be described at the level of configurations than the level of parameters that apply to the entire range of possible scores. In the context of CFA, it may be the case that a type or antitype exists for one category of C but not for another. Moderator CFA helps identify those types and antitypes (Chapter 8).

12. Is mediation the same or different over the categories of potential moderator variables? If a mediation process exists for a particular category of a variable that was not considered when Mediation CFA was performed, it may not exist for another category of that variable. Alternatively, if, for a particular category of that variable, a mediation process is complete, it may be partial for another category. In general, whenever the characteristics of a mediation process vary with the categories of a variable that was not considered when Mediation CFA was performed, this variable can be viewed as moderating the mediation. Section 8.4 presents CFA methods of analysis of moderated mediation.

13. Can we identify configural chains? Chains of events imply that three or more time-adjacent events predict one another. A configural chain implies that categories of time-adjacent observations co-occur more often (chain type) or less often (chain antitype) than expected. Section 6.3 discusses configural chain models in the context of CFA mediation models.

14. Are there types and antitypes beyond auto-association? In longitudinal

data, auto-associations are often the strongest associations. Because they are so strong, they may mask other relationships that can be of interest. Auto-association CFA (Chapter 7) allows one to identify types and antitypes that are caused by variable relationships other than auto-associations.

15. Are types and antitypes distinguishable in variables other than those used to establish the types and antitypes? This question concerns the validity of types and antitypes. The results of CFA are important in particular if types, antitypes, as well as nonsuspicious configurations can be discriminated in the space of variables that were not used in CFA. That is, one may ask whether members of types and antitypes also differ in those other variables (ecological validity) or, alternatively, if membership in types and antitypes can be predicted from a second set of variables (criterion-oriented validity). Chapter 9 discusses how to establish validity in the context of CFA.

16. Can phantom types and antitypes distort the results of CFA? As is well known, multiple tests on the same data usually are, to a certain degree, dependent, increase the risk of capitalizing on chance, and types and antitypes may emerge only because other types and antitypes emerged. In CFA, in particular CFA of small tables, the results of examining individual cells can affect the results of examining other cells. Therefore, strategies are being proposed to reduce the chances of misclassifying cells as type- or antitype-constituting. Section 10.1 (Functional CFA I) discusses and compares two strategies.

17. What effects in a table explain types and antitypes? Types and antitypes result when a base model does not describe the data well. Making the model increasingly complex results in types and antitypes disappearing. Section 10.3 (Functional CFA II) presents, discusses, and compares two strategies for the parsimonious identification of those effects that explain types and antitypes.

18. Can CFA be used to analyze intensive longitudinal data? Walls and Schafer (2006) discussed the situation in which data are so complex that standard methods of analysis cannot easily be applied any more. In longitudinal research, the consideration of a cross-classification of responses from different observation points in time can come quickly to an end when the resulting table becomes so large that sample size requirements become prohibitive. In this book (Chapter 11), two methods are proposed for the analysis of intensive longitudinal data. The first of these methods, CFA of Runs, analyzes the characteristics of series of data as repeated events instead of the data themselves. The second, CFA of Lags, analyzes long time

series of data collected on individuals. It allows one to answer questions concerning the typical sequence of responses from one observation to the next, the second next, and so forth.

19. Is it possible to analyze fractional designs with CFA? There are two reasons why fractional, that is, incomplete, designs are of interest in categorical data analysis. The first reason is based on the Sparsity of Effects Principle. This principle states that most systems are run by main effects and interactions of a low order. Higher order interactions are, therefore, rarely of importance. Second, if many variables are completely crossed, tables can become so large that it is close to impossible to collect the necessary data volume. Therefore, fractional factorial designs have been discussed. In this book (Chapter 12), we apply fractional designs in the context of CFA. In a comparison of a fractional table with the completely crossed table, it is illustrated, using the same data, that the use of fractional designs can yield results that differ only minimally or not at all from the results from the complete table.

These and a number of additional questions are addressed in this book. Many of the questions are new and have never been discussed in the context of CFA before. Chapter 2 begins with the presentation and illustration of CFA of rater agreement.

1.2   The Five Steps of CFA

CFA has found applications in many disciplines, for example, medical research (Koehler, Dulz, & Bock-Emden, 1991; Spielberg, Falkenhahn, Willich, Wegschneider, & Voller, 1996), psychopathology (Clark et al., 1997), substance use research (K. M. Jackson, Sher, & Schulenberg, 2008), agriculture (Mann, 2008), microbiology (Simonson, McMahon, Childers, & Morton, 1992), personality research (Klinteberg, Andersson, Magnusson, & Stattin, 1993), psychiatry (Kales, Blow, Bingham, Copeland, & Mellow, 2000), ecological biological research (Pugesek & Diem, 1990), pharmacological research (Straube, von Eye, & Müller, 1998), and developmental research (Bergman & El-Khouri, 1999; Bergman, Magnusson, & El-Khouri, 2003; Mahoney, 2000; Martinez-Torteya, Bogat, von Eye, & Levendosky, 2009; von Eye & Bergman, 2003).

The following paragraphs describe the five decision-making steps researchers take when applying CFA (von Eye, 2002a).

1. *Selection of a base model and estimation of expected frequencies*: A CFA base model is a chance model that indicates the probability with which a

configuration is expected to occur. The base model takes into account those effects that are NOT of interest to the researcher. If deviations between the expected and the observed cell frequencies are significant, they reflect, by necessity, the effects that are of interest to the researcher. Most CFA base models are log-linear models of the form $\log \hat{m} = X\lambda$, where $\hat{m}$ is the array of model frequencies, X is the design matrix, and λ is the parameter vector[1]. The model frequencies are estimated so that they reflect the base model. For example, a typical CFA base model specifies independence between categorical variables. This is the main effect model, also called the model of variable independence. Types and antitypes from this model suggest that variables are associated. Another base model, that of Prediction CFA (see Section 5.1.2), specifies independence between predictor variables and criterion variables and takes all possible interactions into account, both within the group of predictors and within the group of criteria. Types (antitypes) from this model indicate which patterns of predictor categories allow one to predict the patterns of criterion categories that occur more often (less often) than expected with respect to the base model. Base models that are not log-linear have also been proposed (for a classification of log-linear CFA base models, see von Eye, 2002a; more detail follows in Section 1.3).

2. *Selection of a concept of deviation from independence*: Deviation from a base model can come in many forms. For example, when the base model proposes variable independence, deviation from independence can be assessed by using measures that take into account marginal frequencies. However, there exist concepts and measures that do not take into account marginal frequencies. The corresponding deviation measures are termed marginal-dependent and marginal-free (Goodman, 1991; von Eye & Mun, 2003; von Eye, Spiel, & Rovine, 1995). An example of a marginal-dependent measure that is based on Pearson's X^2 is the Φ-coefficient. Φ measures the strength of association between two dichotomous variables, that is, the degree of deviation from the base model of independence between these two variables. Measures that are marginal-free include the odds ratio, θ. Marginal-dependent and marginal-free measures can give different appraisals of deviation from a base model. So far, most CFA applications have used marginal-dependent measures of deviation from a model. Marginal-free measures have been discussed in the context of CFA-based group comparison (von Eye et al., 1995).

---

[1]Note that, although here and in the following equations the expression "log" is used, log-linear modeling employs the natural logarithm for calculations. In many software manuals, for example, SPSS, we find the abbreviation "ln". In other manuals, for example SAS and R, "log" is used to indicate the natural logarithm, and "log10" is used to indicate the logarithm with base 10.

3. *Selection of a significance test*: A large number of significance tests of the null hypothesis that types or antitypes do not exist has been proposed for CFA (for an overview, see von Eye, 2002a). These tests differ in that some are exact, others are approximative. These tests also differ in statistical power and in the sampling schemes under which they can be employed. Simulation studies have shown that none of these tests outperforms other tests under all of the examined conditions (Indurkhya & von Eye, 2000; Küchenhoff, 1986; Lindner, 1984; von Eye, 2002a, 2002b; von Eye & Mun, 2003; von Weber, Lautsch, & von Eye, 2003b; von Weber, von Eye, & Lautsch, 2004). Still, simulation results suggest that the tests that perform well under many conditions include, under any sampling scheme, Pearson's X^2, the z-test, and the exact binomial test. Under the product-multinomial sampling scheme, the best-performing tests include Lehmacher's exact and approximative hypergeometric tests (Lehmacher, 1981).

4. *Performing significance tests under protection of* α: CFA can be applied in both exploratory and confirmatory research. In either case, typically, a large number of tests is conducted. The number of significance tests performed is generally smaller in confirmatory CFA than in exploratory CFA. In either case, when more than one significance test is performed, the significance level, α, needs to be protected. The classical method for α protection is the Bonferroni procedure. This method can suggest rather conservative decisions about the existence of types and antitypes. Therefore, beginning with Holm's procedure (Holm, 1979), less prohibitive methods have been proposed.

5. *Interpretation of types and antitypes*: The interpretation of types and antitypes uses five types of information. First is the meaning of the configuration, which is determined by the meaning of the categories that define a configuration. For example, in a table that cross-tabulates smoking status, age, and gender, we may find that female adolescents who smoke cigarettes are found more often than expected. The second type of information is the base model. For example, when the base model distinguishes between predictor and criterion variables, types and antitypes have a different interpretation than when this distinction is not made. The third type of information is the concept of deviation from expectation. The fourth type is the sampling scheme (e.g., multinomial vs. product-multinomial), and the fifth type is external information that is used to discriminate among types and antitypes (from each other and from the configurations that constitute neither types nor antitypes). This information and the discrimination are not part of CFA itself. Instead, this

information is used in follow-up tests that are intended, for example, to establish the validity of CFA types and antitypes (see Chapter 9 of this book).

In this book, we focus on CFA applications that use marginal-dependent measures of deviation, and multinomial sampling. In addition, we use only a small selection of significance tests and procedures for α protection. Therefore, these issues will not be pursued in detail in any of the data examples (see von Eye, 2002a). Instead, we discuss the questions in detail that can be answered with CFA, and the corresponding base models.

In the following paragraphs, we present two data examples. The first rounds out the analysis of the data on Internet use in Table 1.1 by performing a CFA. The second example presents a complete CFA of a different data set.

Data Example 1: Based on the X^2 analysis of the data in Table 1.1, we concluded that associations exist among Depression, Happiness, Stress, and Emotional Uplifts. However, the analysis did not allow us to go into any detail that would describe where exactly in the cross-classification the correspondence can be found and what form it assumes. In the following paragraphs, we use CFA to provide a more detailed description of the data in Table 1.1. We first make the decisions required in the five steps of CFA.

1. *Selection of base model*: In the above null hypothesis, it was stated that the four variables, Depression, Happiness, Stress, and Emotional Uplifts, are unrelated to one another. The base model that corresponds to this hypothesis is that of variable independence. In log-linear modeling terms, the base model is $\log \hat{m} = \lambda^{Depression} + \lambda^{Happiness} + \lambda^{Stress} + \lambda^{Uplifts}$. This is also the model that underlies the Pearson X^2 test. Types from the present analysis indicate correspondence beyond expectation. Antitypes also indicate correspondence, but with the effect that the configurations that constitute the antitypes are observed less often than expected.

2. *Concept of deviation from independence*: In the present example, we note that none of the variables is uniformly distributed (the marginal frequencies are 69 for Depression = 1 and 54 for Depression = 2; 60 for Happiness = 1 and 63 for Happiness = 2; 63 for Stress = 1 and 60 for Stress = 2; and 59 for Uplifts = 1, and 64 for Uplifts = 2). In our analysis, we take the marginal distributions into account (CFA based on odds ratios would be a case in which marginal distributions are not taken into account). Therefore, we use marginal-dependent measures of deviation from independence (see Section 1.3).

3. *Selection of significance test*: We use the z-test. This test is known to perform well when samples are reasonably large, which is the case in the

present example. We protect α using the Holland-Copenhaver procedure (Holland & Copenhaver, 1987). For more detail on significance tests and the protection of α, see Section 1.3 or von Eye (2002a).

4. *Performing significance tests under protection of α*: The estimation of expected cell frequencies, protection of α, and the identification of types and antitypes can be preformed with the programs discussed in Chapter 13. Table 1.2 displays the results of a CFA of the data in Table 1.1.

5. *Interpretation of types and antitypes*: The results in Table 1.2 show a clear picture. Types are constituted by Configurations 1 2 1 2, and 2 1 2 1. This indicates that particular patterns of responses occurred more often than expected. The sole antitype is constituted by Configuration 1 1 2 2. It indicates that one pattern of responses occurred less often than expected. More specifically, the first type, 1 2 1 2, suggests that more first-time Internet users than expected simultaneously exhibit below average scores in Depression, above average scores in Happiness, below average scores in Stress, and above average scores in Emotional Uplifts. Clearly, this pattern is plausible (and the fact that this pattern was observed more often than expected speaks to the validity of the four scales). The second type, 2 1 2 1, suggests that more first-time Internet users than expected simultaneously exhibit above average scores in Depression, below average scores in Happiness, above average scores in Stress, and below average scores in Emotional Uplifts. There is a strong element of plausibility to this result too.

The sole antitype, 1 1 2 2, suggests that fewer first-time Internet users than expected simultaneously exhibit below median scores in Depression, below median scores in Happiness, above median scores in Stress, and above median scores in Emotional Uplifts. A pattern with these scores would be highly implausible. Evidently, it was not observed at all ($m_{1122} = 0$).

None of the other configurations was observed more (or less) often than expected under the assumption of independence among the four variables that span the cross-classification. The associations among the four variables are, thus, carried by just three local associations[2]. The term *local association* is introduced in more detail in the context of the next data example.

Data Example 2: In a study on the development of aggression in adolescence (Finkelstein, von Eye, & Preece, 1994), 114 adolescents (67

---

[2]The log-linear model that explains the data well ($LR - X^2 = 11.93; df = 7; p = 0.10$) contains the three bivariate interactions Depression × Happiness, Depression × Stress, and Stress × Emotional Uplifts.

TABLE 1.2. CFA of Depression, Happiness, Stress, and Emotional Uplifts in 123 First-Time Internet Users

Configuration DHSU	m	$\hat{m}$	z	p	Type/Antitype
1111	6	8.269	−.789	.21499847	
1112	5	8.970	−1.326	.09248374	
1121	5	7.876	−1.025	.15275226	
1122	0	8.543	−2.923	.00173423	Antitype
1211	4	8.683	−1.589	.05600484	
1212	27	9.419	5.729	.00000001	Type
1221	12	8.269	1.297	.09726839	
1222	10	8.970	.344	.36549411	
2111	10	6.472	1.387	.08273513	
2112	5	7.020	−.762	.22289023	
2121	19	6.164	5.170	.00000012	Type
2122	10	6.686	1.282	.09997573	
2211	2	6.795	−1.840	.03291632	
2212	4	7.371	−1.242	.10717321	
2221	1	6.472	−2.151	.01574287	
2222	3	7.020	−1.517	.06459447	

girls) indicated, at age 13, whether they were, in their own opinion, above or below average in verbal aggression against adults (V) and in physical aggression against peers (P). The variables V and P were coded as 1 = low (below median) and 2 = high (above median). Gender (G) was coded as 1 = male and 2 = female. The cross-classification $V \times P \times G$ was analyzed under the main effect base model of standard, first order CFA, that is, the log-linear model $\log \hat{m} = \lambda + \lambda^V + \lambda^P + \lambda^G$. CFA used the binomial test (marginal-dependent), and protected α, using the Holland-Copenhaver procedure. Table 1.3 shows the results.

The $LR - X^2$ for the base model is 733.19 ($df = 4$; $p < 0.01$), indicating significant discrepancies between the base model and the data. We thus can expect types and antitypes to emerge. The resulting types and antitypes indicate local associations among the three variables that were crossed. The term *local association*, introduced by Havránek and Lienert (1984), indicates that the association among the variables manifests only in a selection of category patterns (configurations), in the form of types and antitypes. Those configurations that do not emerge as types and antitypes contain frequencies that do not deviate from the expectation that was formulated by the base model of variable independence.

Table 1.3 shows that CFA yields two types and one antitype. The first type, constituted by Cell 1 1 1, suggests that more boys than expected report low verbal aggression against adults and also low physical aggression

TABLE 1.3. First Order CFA of the Cross-Classification of Verbal Aggression against Adults (V), Physical Aggression against Peers (P), and Gender (G)

Configuration VPG	m	$\hat{m}$	p	Type/Antitype
111	28	15.5746	.00127984	Type
112	11	10.9254	.53681743	
121	10	17.9254	.02218115	
122	8	12.5746	.10690979	
211	11	15.5746	.13097985	
212	3	10.9254	.00382328	Antitype
221	18	17.9254	.53188666	
222	25	12.5746	.00059501	Type

against peers. The second type is constituted by Cell 2 2 2. This type suggests that the other end of the spectrum is occupied by girls. More girls than expected report high verbal aggression against adults and also high physical aggression against peers.

The sole antitype (Cell 2 1 2) suggests that fewer girls than expected report high verbal aggression against adults but low physical aggression against peers.

The types and antitypes in this example show that associations among the three variables exist that span Table 1.3. A log-linear model that describes these data well is $[V,P][P,G][G]$. For this model, we calculate the likelihood ratio $LR - X^2 = 1.21$ ($df = 2$; $p = 0.55$). This model indicates that verbal aggression against adults and physical aggression against peers are associated with each other. Surprisingly, verbal aggression against adults is unrelated to adolescent gender. In contrast, physical aggression against peers is gender-specific. While interesting and interpretable, this description of the data is less detailed than the one provided by CFA. In addition, the CFA results suggest that gender plays a major role in the interpretation of these data. Both types and the antitype are gender-specific.

The results in Tables 1.2 and 1.3 are typical of CFA results in several respects:

1. CFA tables are interpreted, in virtually all cases, only after the base model is rejected. A rejected base model is not a guarantee that types and antitypes will result. However, if the base model describes the data well, there is no need to search for types and antitypes that indicate the location of significant discrepancies between model and data.

2. Only a selection of cells emerges as type- and antitype-constituting. The remaining cells do not deviate from the base model. Types and antitypes, thus, indicate where, in the table, the action is.

3. Although, in Tables 1.2 and 1.3, the largest two cells constitute types and the smallest constitute antitypes, this is not always the case. We will encounter tables in which small size cells constitute types. The main reason for this observation is that CFA focuses on discrepancies from expectation instead of sheer size (zero order CFA being the only exception; see von Eye, 2002a). Even relatively small cells can contain more cases than expected, and relatively large cells can contain fewer cases than expected.

A large number of CFA models and applications has been proposed (Lautsch & von Eye, 2000, 2003, 2005; von Eye, 2002a). Current development of CFA and, thus, this book focus on CFA models that allow researchers to approach data with research questions that are similar to those asked in variable-oriented research. Examples of such models include mediator models (see Chapter 6). For example, researchers ask whether the predictive relationship between two variables is mediated by a third variable. Results state that the relationship is either not mediated, partially mediated, or fully mediated (Baron & Kenny, 1986; Kenny, 2005). Using CFA, one can determine which of the configurations in particular carry the partial or full mediation (von Eye, 2008a; von Eye, Mun, & Mair, 2009). In general, CFA results are formulated at the level of configurations, that is, patterns of variable categories, instead of the level of variables.

In the following sections and chapters, those elements of CFA are introduced that are needed for the new and the advanced CFA models discussed in this text. In the remainder of this book, these models are introduced and illustrated by using empirical data.

1.3   Introduction to CFA: An Overview

The following introduction into the method of CFA focuses on (1) frequentist CFA models and (2) base models that can be expressed by using the general log-linear model $\log \hat{m} = x\lambda$. The two main reasons for not elaborating on other approaches such as Bayesian CFA (Gutiérrez Peña & von Eye, 2000; von Eye, Schuster, & Gutiérrez Peña, 2000) or non-log-linear base models (von Eye, 2004a) are that (1) the newer methods discussed in this book were all formulated in the context of frequentist CFA, and (2) they all use frequentist log-linear methods for the estimation of expected cell frequencies. Corresponding Bayesian models still need to be formulated. The following introduction is selective in that it emphasizes those elements of CFA that are needed in the later chapters. More detail can be found in the existing literature (e.g., von Eye, 2002a; von Eye & Gutiérrez Peña, 2004).

The Data Situation: Consider d categorical variables. For log-linear modeling or CFA, these variables are crossed to span a contingency table with $R = \prod_{i=1}^{d} c_i$ cells, where c_i is the number of categories of the ith variable. The frequency with which cell r was observed is m_r, and the frequency that was estimated for cell r is $\hat{m}_r$, with $r = 1, \ldots, R$.

Cell Probabilities and Significance Tests: The probabilities of the R cell frequencies depend on the sampling scheme (von Eye & Schuster, 1998; von Eye et al., 2000) and the base model. In most cases, sampling is multinomial, and we obtain

$$P(M_1 = m_1, \ldots, M_R = m_R | N, \pi_1, \ldots, \pi_R) = \frac{N!}{m_1!, \ldots, m_R!} \sum_{r=1}^{R} \pi_r^{m_r},$$

with and $\sum p_i = 1$ and $\sum m_r = N$. It follows that the frequency M_r is binomially distributed, with

$$P(M_r = m_r | N, \pi_r) = \frac{N!}{m_r!(N - m_r)!} \pi^{m_r}(1 - \pi)^{N - m_r}.$$

Therefore, to test hypotheses about a particular cell, one can use the binomial distribution, and one applies the exact binomial test

$$B_{N,p}(m) = \sum_{j=0}^{m} \frac{N!}{j!(N - j)!} p^j (1 - p)^{N-j},$$

with $0 \leq m \leq N$, and p is estimated from the sample. If $Np \geq 10$ (Osterkorn, 1975), the standard normal

$$z_r = \frac{m_r - Np_r}{\sqrt{Np_r q_r}}$$

provides a good approximation, where p_r is the estimate of π_r, $q = 1 - p$, and r indicates that the test is being performed for the rth cell. Usually, p is estimated from the data, and we obtain the estimate $p = \hat{m}/N$. Alternative tests include, for instance, the X^2 and the Freeman-Tukey deviate.

These tests are still applicable when sampling is product-multinomial. Lehmacher's hypergeometric test requires product-multinomial sampling. This test starts from the well-known relation

$$X_r = \frac{m_r - \hat{m}_r}{\sqrt{\hat{m}_r}} = N(0, \sigma)$$

for $df = 1$. When the model fits, $\sigma^2 < 1$ (Christensen, 1997; Haberman, 1973). To replace the term in the denominator, Lehmacher derived the exact variance. It is

$$\sigma_r^2 = Np_r[(1 - p_r) - (N - 1)(p_r - \tilde{p}_r)],$$

where p is the same as for the binomial test. Lehmacher's test requires that p be estimated, based on a main effect model. To illustrate the estimation of $\tilde{p}$, consider a table that is spanned by three variables. For this case, the estimate is

$$\tilde{p}_{ijk} = \frac{(m_{i..} - 1)(m_{.j.} - 1)(m_{..k} - 1)}{(m - 1)^d},$$

where i, j, and k index the categories of the three variables ($d = 3$) that span the table. Using the exact variance, $\sqrt{\hat{m}_r}$ can be replaced by the standard normal

$$z_{L,r} = \frac{m_r - \hat{m}_r}{\sigma_r}.$$

Because $p > \tilde{p}$, Lehmacher's z will always be larger than X. To prevent non-conservative decisions Kuchenhoff (1986) has suggested using a continuity correction.

A residual measure that was discussed only recently in the context of CFA (von Eye & Mair, 2008b) is the *standardized Pearson residual*, r_i. This measure is defined as

$$r_i = \frac{m_i - \hat{m}_i}{\sqrt{\hat{m}_i(1 - h_i)}},$$

where i goes over all cells of the table, m_i is the observed cell frequency of Cell i, $\hat{m}_i$ is the estimated expected frequency for Cell i, and h_i is the ith diagonal element of the well-known *hat matrix*,

$$H = W^{1/2}X(X'WX)^{-1}X'W^{1/2}.$$

The elements w_{ii}, which are the elements of the diagonal matrix W, are the estimated expected cell frequencies, $\hat{m}_i$. The standardized Pearson measure r_i has the following interesting characteristics:

1. If $m_i = \hat{m}_i$, no standard error can be estimated. This is typically the case when an observed cell frequency is exactly estimated, for example in a saturated model, or when Cell i is blanked out. Each of these cases is possible in CFA applications and will not affect the validity of the solution.

2. If one of the variables is dichotomous, corresponding cells can come with exactly the same standardized Pearson residual. This characteristic is discussed in more detail in Section 10.2.

The Null Hypothesis in CFA: In CFA, individual cells are examined. For Cell r, a test is performed under the null hypothesis $H_0 : E[m_r] = \hat{m}_r$. This null hypothesis states that Cell r does not constitute a type or an antitype. If, however, Cell r constitutes a CFA type, the null hypothesis is rejected because (using the binomial test for an example)

$$B_{N,\pi_r}(m_r - 1) \geq 1 - \alpha,$$

or, in words, the cell contains more cases than expected. If Cell r constitutes a CFA antitype, the null hypothesis is rejected because (again using the binomial test)

$$B_{N,\pi_r}(m_r) \leq \alpha.$$

This indicates that Cell r contains fewer cases than expected.

α **protection**: In standard application of CFA, many cells are examined. In fact, in exploratory CFA applications, typically, all cells of a table are examined. In confirmatory CFA applications, this number can be smaller because only those cells are examined for which a priori hypotheses exist concerning the existence of types and antitypes. In either case, significance tests are dependent (Krauth, 2003; von Weber, Lautsch, & von Eye, 2003a); the topic of dependence of tests will be taken up again in Section 10.1). In addition, large numbers of tests carry the risk of capitalizing on chance, even if α is selected to be small. For these two reasons, CFA application routinely comes with protection of the significance level α.

The most popular procedure for α protection is the *Bonferroni* method. It requires that the sum of all α values not exceed the nominal α, or $\sum_r \alpha_r \leq \alpha$, and that all α_r be equal, or $\alpha_r = \alpha^*$, for all $r = 1, \ldots, R$. The protected α that fulfills both conditions is $\alpha^* = \alpha/R$.

Holm's (1979) procedure does not use the second of these two conditions. Instead, the number of tests is taken into account that was performed before the current one. One obtains the protected

$$\alpha_r^* = \frac{\alpha}{R - i + 1},$$

where i numbers the tests, and $i = 1, \ldots, R$. This procedure requires the test statistics to be ranked in descending order, and the tests are performed in order. As soon as the first null hypothesis survives, the procedure is concluded. The first α^* is the same under the Bonferroni and the Holm procedures. Beginning with the second test, Holm's procedure is less conservative than the Bonferroni procedure. For the last, that is, the Rth test, the Holm-protected $\alpha^* = \alpha$.

As another alternative to Bonferroni's procedure, Holland and Copenhaver (1987) proposed the protected

$$\alpha_r^* = 1 - (1 - \alpha)^{\frac{1}{R-i+1}}.$$

This procedure is slightly less conservative than Holm's procedure.

When tables are small, that is, the number of cells (configurations) is small, tests can become completely dependent (see von Weber et al., 2003a). When tables are large, dependency is less of a problem. However, as Krauth (2003) showed, tests never become completely independent. When tables are large, the risk of capitalizing on chance increases. Therefore, protection of α is routine in CFA applications.

The CFA Base Model: A CFA base model must fulfill the following four criteria (von Eye, 2004a; von Eye & Schuster, 1998):

1. *Uniqueness of interpretation of types and antitypes*: It is required that there be only one reason for the existence of types and antitypes. For example, in Prediction CFA (P-CFA; see Chapter 5), types and antitypes must emerge only if relationships between predictors and criteria exist, but not because of relationships among the predictors or among the criteria.

2. *The base model contains only, and all of, those effects of a model that are not of interest to the researcher*: If, under this condition, types and antitypes emerge, they reflect, by necessity, the relationships the researcher is interested in. In the example of P-CFA, the base model takes into account all main effects and interactions among the predictors and all main effects and interactions among the criteria. The model is thus saturated within both the predictors and the criteria, and types and antitypes can emerge only if relationships among predictors and criteria exist.

3. *Parsimony*: A CFA base model must be as parsimonious as possible (see Schuster & von Eye, 2000).

4. *Consideration of sampling scheme*: This criterion has a number of technical implications. Specifically, the marginals of those variables that were observed under a product-multinomial sampling scheme must be reproduced. Therefore, the CFA base model must contain the effects that allow one to reproduce these marginals. This applies accordingly if multivariate product-multinomial sampling took place. By implication, base models that do not contain these effects are not admissible (von Eye & Schuster, 1998). Under standard multinomial sampling there are no constraints concerning the specification of base models.

TABLE 1.4. Sample Base Models for the Four Variables A, B, C, and D

Base Model	Log-Linear Representation
Global Models	
Zero order	$\log \hat{m} = \lambda$
First order	$\log \hat{m} = \lambda + \lambda^A + \lambda^B + \lambda^C + \lambda^D$
Second order	$\log \hat{m} = \lambda + \lambda^A + \lambda^B + \lambda^C + \lambda^D + \lambda^{AB} + \lambda^{AC} + \lambda^{AD} + \lambda^{BC} + \lambda^{BD} + \lambda^{CD}$
Regional Models	
P-CFA[a]	$\log \hat{m} = \lambda + \lambda^A + \lambda^B + \lambda^C + \lambda^D + \lambda^{AB} + \lambda^{CD}$
Predicting D	$\log \hat{m} = \lambda + \lambda^A + \lambda^B + \lambda^C + \lambda^D + \lambda^{AB} + \lambda^{AC} + \lambda^{BC} + \lambda^{ABC}$
Predicting A	$\log \hat{m} = \lambda + \lambda^A + \lambda^B + \lambda^C + \lambda^D + \lambda^{BC} + \lambda^{BD} + \lambda^{CD} + \lambda^{BCD}$

[a]For P-CFA, A and B are considered predictors, and C and D are considered criterion variables.

There are two groups of CFA base models. The first includes most of the original CFA models (Krauth & Lienert, 1973). It is called the group of *global CFA base models*. These models do not distinguish between variables of different status. By implication, there is no grouping of variables in predictors and criteria or dependent and independent variables. There is not even the separation of groups of variables that are related to one another. All variables have the same status. This group of models has its parallel in exploratory factor analysis, correspondence analysis, or in multidimensional scaling. These methods also consider all variables of the same status.

Global CFA base models are structured in a hierarchy. In ascending order, the lowest order model is that of zero order CFA (Lienert & von Eye, 1984). This model takes no effect into account whatsoever. Therefore, types and antitypes suggest only that the distribution in a table is not uniform. Specifically, a type suggests that a cell contains more cases than the average cell, and an antitype suggests that a cell contains fewer cases than the average cell. In zero order CFA, the average cell contains N/t cases, where t is the number of cells in the cross-classification. Because of this characteristic, types and antitypes from zero order CFA have also been called configural clusters.

The next higher level in the hierarchy of CFA base models is constituted by first order CFA. This model takes the main effects of all variables into account. Types and antitypes can, therefore, emerge only when associations (interactions) among variables exist. These interactions can be of any order. Unless every configuration in a table constitutes a type or antitype, these associations are termed local (Havránek & Lienert, 1984).

First order CFA is followed by second order CFA. This base model takes, in addition to all main effects, all first order interactions into account, that is, all pair-wise interactions. Types and antitypes emerge only when interactions in triplets or larger groupings of variables exist. Second order CFA is interesting because it allows one to identify effects that go, in their order, beyond the effects considered in factor analysis, correspondence analysis, or multidimensional scaling. If types or antitypes emerge, the results of factor analysis or correspondence analysis can be considered incomplete.

Higher order global base models of CFA can be considered. To the best of our knowledge, there has been no application of such higher order CFA models.

The second group of CFA base models is called *regional*. The base models in this group distinguish between groups of variables. Most prominent in this group is the base model of Prediction CFA (P-CFA) which distinguishes between predictor and criterion variables. This book presents many extensions and developments of P-CFA (see, e.g., Chapter 5).

To illustrate the base models that are used in CFA, we use the four variables *A*, *B*, *C*, and *D*. In Table 1.4, we present the base models for zero order, first order, and second order CFA. In addition, we present the base model for P-CFA, for which we declare variables *A* and *B* predictors and *C* and *D* criteria.

Table 1.4 displays all interactions that are taken into account in these six sample base models. Types and antitypes will emerge only if those terms (main effects or interactions) exist that are not part of the base model. CFA methods for the identification of the terms that explain types and antitypes are introduced in Chapter 10.

Data Example 3: For the following data example, we use data from the Finkelstein et al. (1994) aggression study again (see Data Example 2, Section 1.2). We ask whether there are gender differences in the development of physical aggression against peers from the age of 11 to the age of 15. To answer this question, we perform a two-group analysis. For this analysis, we cross the two measures of Physical Aggression against Peers, observed in 1983 and in 1987 (*P83* and *P87*; dichotomized at the grand median) with Gender (*G*; 1 = males and 2 = females). The base model represents a regional CFA model. It specifies that there are no relationships between *P83* and *P87* on one side and *G* on the other. However, *P83* and *P87* can be associated in the form of an auto-association. The base model is, thus,

$$\log \hat{m} = \lambda + \lambda_i^{P83} + \lambda_j^{P87} + \lambda_{ij}^{P83,P87} + \lambda_k^{G}$$

TABLE 1.5. 2×2 Cross-Classification for Two-Group CFA Testing

Configurations $P1P2$	Groups		Row Totals
	I	II	
ij	$a = m_{ijA}$	$b = m_{ijB}$	$A = m_{ij}$
All others combined	$c = m_{.A} - m_{ijA}$	$d = m_{.B} - m_{ijB}$	$B = m - N_{ij}$
Column Totals	$C = m_{.A}$	$D = m_{.B}$	N

The design matrix for this base model is

$$X = \begin{pmatrix} 1 & 1 & 1 & 1 & 1 \\ 1 & 1 & 1 & -1 & 1 \\ 1 & 1 & -1 & 1 & -1 \\ 1 & 1 & -1 & -1 & -1 \\ 1 & -1 & 1 & 1 & -1 \\ 1 & -1 & 1 & -1 & -1 \\ 1 & -1 & -1 & 1 & 1 \\ 1 & -1 & -1 & -1 & 1 \end{pmatrix}.$$

The first column vector in this design matrix represents the constant of the base model. The following three column vectors specify the main effects of the variables $P83$, $P87$, and G. The last column vector specifies the interaction between $P83$ and $P87$. This base model can be contradicted only if relationships exist between the grouping variable, Gender, and the development of physical aggression against peers. These relationships are reflected in interactions among Gender and the two aggression variables, specifically, $[P83, G]$, $[P87, G]$, and $[P83, P87, G]$. Therefore, if types and antitypes emerge, they speak to the question of whether developmental patterns of aggression against peers are gender-specific.

This two-group CFA does not examine individual cells. Instead, it compares the two groups in each pair of configural patterns of the variables that are used to discriminate between the two groups. To perform such a pair-wise comparison, a 2×2 table is created in which the frequencies of the pattern under study are compared with each other with respect to the aggregated frequencies of all remaining patterns. This is illustrated in Table 1.5. The groups are labeled A and B, and the example uses two variables, $P1$ and $P2$, to compare these groups.

Table 1.6 shows results of this analysis. For this analysis, the z approximation of the binomial test and Holm's procedure of α protection were used. Sampling was multinomial.

The results in Table 1.6 show that only those boys and girls differ

TABLE 1.6. Two-Group CFA of the Cross-Tabulation of Physical Aggression against Peers in 1983 × Physical Aggression against Peers in 1987 × Gender

Configuration P83P87G	m	z	p	Type/Antitype
111	14			
112	18	1.341	.090	
121	10			
122	15	.691	.245	
211	10			
212	15	.691	.245	
221	5			
222	27	−2.613	.004	Discrimination Type

from each other whose physical aggression against peers is high at both assessments. Specifically, significantly more girls than boys report themselves as engaging in high physical aggression against peers both at age 11 and at age 15.

It is interesting to compare these results with those obtained from log-linear modeling. The most parsimonious log-linear model that describes these data is the main effect model ($LR - X^2 = 9.30$; $df = 4$; $p = 0.054$). Adding any of the two-way interactions improves the model only to a non-significant degree. For example, adding the $P83 \times P87$ interaction, as is done in the base model for two-group CFA, yields $LR - X^2 = 7.57$ ($df = 3$; $p = 0.056$). This improvement over the main effect model is nonsignificant ($\Delta X^2 = 1.73$; $\Delta df = 1$; $p = 0.188$). To give another example, adding the $P83 \times G$ interaction yields $LR - X^2 = 6.12$ ($df = 3$; $p = 0.106$). The improvement over the main effect model is not significant either ($\Delta X^2 = 3.18$; $\Delta df = 1$; $p = 0.075$). This applies accordingly when the third two-way interaction, $P87 \times G$, is added. In sum, log-linear modeling suggests that G, $P83$, and $P87$ are independent of one another. In contrast, based on the results from two-group CFA, we can state that gender differences exist in the development of physical aggression against peers, specifically for those at the higher end of the spectrum of aggression from age 11 to age 15. Two-group CFA will be used again, in Section 8.3.

1.4 Chapter Summary

CFA is a method for the statistical evaluation of individual cells or groups of cells in cross-classifications of two or more variables. For each cell, it is determined whether it contains about as many cases as expected, or more or fewer cases. Cells that contain more cases than expected are said to constitute CFA types. Cells that contain fewer cases than expected are said to constitute CFA antitypes. Application of CFA proceeds in the five steps (1) selection of base model and estimation of expected cell frequencies; (2) selection of concept of deviation from independence; (3) selection of significance test; (4) performing of significance tests under protection of α; and (5) interpretation of resulting types and antitypes.

Most important for the interpretation of types and antitypes is the selection of a suitable base model. The same type or antitype can come with interpretations that differ, depending on the effects that are taken into account in the base model. Also depending on the specification of the base model, the same cell can vary in whether it constitutes a type, an antitype, or contains the expected number of cases.

In this book, two sets of new base models for CFA are introduced. The first follows the tradition of CFA development by specifying base models that lead to particular interpretations of types and antitypes. This applies, for example, to the types and antitypes of rater agreement or disagreement that are discussed in Chapter 2. The second set involves specifying series of base models that, taken together, allow one to answer more complex questions.

2
Configural Analysis
of Rater Agreement

To illustrate the focus that CFA places on individual cells instead of aggregate-level appraisals of characteristics of cross-classifications, Chapter 2 introduces CFA of rater agreement. In contrast to such measures as κ, which present general statements about agreement beyond chance, CFA allows researchers to identify four groups of cells. The first includes cells that represent agreement beyond chance, that is, cells that constitute agreement types. These types can be found only in the diagonal of an agreement table. The same applies to cells that constitute agreement antitypes, which indicate less agreement than expected. In contrast, disagreement types can surface in any of the off-diagonal cells, and so can disagreement antitypes. The flexibility of the method of CFA is illustrated by the possibility of using different base models, by presenting (1) the standard base model of rater independence, which is also used to calculate κ, (2) an analogue to the well-known equal weight agreement model (Tanner & Young, 1985), as well as (3) a base model (a quasi-independence model) that focuses exclusively on the disagreement cells. Examples apply CFA of rater agreement to data on the assessment of qualification and fit of job applicants.

2.1 Rater Agreement CFA

So far, exploratory applications of CFA scouted cross-classifications with the goal of finding types and antitypes, with no constraints concerning the location in the table on which to focus. CFA of rater agreement can proceed in a different way. In agreement tables, particular cells indicate agreement, and other cells indicate disagreement. CFA of rater agreement can focus on either or both (von Eye & Mun, 2005, 2006). To introduce agreement tables, consider two raters, A and B, who use the three categories 1, 2, and

TABLE 2.1. Agreement Table of Two Raters' Judgments

| | | Rater B Rating Categories | | |
		1	2	3
	1	m_{11}	m_{12}	m_{13}
Rater A Rating Categories	2	m_{21}	m_{22}	m_{23}
	3	m_{31}	m_{32}	m_{33}

3 to judge objects. The agreement table of these raters' judgments is given in Table 2.1 (see von Eye & Mun, 2005, 2006).

The interpretation of the frequencies, m_{ij}, in the cross-classification in Table 2.1 is straightforward: Cell 1 1 contains the number of instances in which both Rater A and Rater B use Category 1; Cell 1 2 contains the number of instances in which Rater A uses Category 1 and Rater B uses Category 2, and so forth. The cells with indexes $i = j$ with $i, j = 1, \ldots, 3$ contain the numbers of incidences in which the two raters use the same category. These cells are called *agreement cells*. All other cells, which have indexes $i \neq j$, are called *disagreement cells*.

When exploring cross-classifications of two (or more) raters, one has a number of options concerning the selection of cells to examine (von Eye & Mun, 2006). The *coefficient of raw agreement* focuses on the agreement cells and expresses degree of agreement as the proportion of all judgments that can be found in the agreement cells. Cohen's (1960) κ and Brennan and Prediger's (1981) κ_n are *proportionate reduction in error* measures (see Fleiss, 1975). These measures ask whether the number of observed instances of disagreement is below the expected number. If all agreement cells are taken into account, this corresponds to asking whether the diagonal cells contain more cases of agreement than predicted from a base model. When applying CFA of rater agreement, one can focus on the diagonal cells, looking, for example, for agreement types. However, one can also examine off-diagonal cells, looking, for example, for disagreement antitypes (see von Eye & von Eye, 2005). Alternatively, CFA can examine each cell in the table, looking for patterns of types and antitypes. In more general terms, significant deviations from base models can suggest that the two raters

1. agree more often than expected; if $E[m_{ii}] > E_{ii}$, Cell ii constitutes an *agreement type*;

2. agree less often than expected; if $E[m_{ii}] < E_{ii}$, Cell ii constitutes an *agreement antitype*;

3. disagree more often than expected; if $E[m_{ij}] > E_{ij}$ (for $i \neq j$), Cell ij constitutes a *disagreement type*; and

4. disagree less often than expected; if $E[m_{ij}] < E_{ij}$ (for $i \neq j$), Cell ij constitutes a *disagreement antitype*.

In the following paragraphs, we present von Eye and Mun's (2006) four base models for the exploration of rater agreement. These models differ in the assumptions made concerning the agreement cells. The first two models are based on the assumptions of zero order and first order CFA. These models do not make any particular assumptions that would single out agreement or disagreement cells. It is simply assumed that the frequency distribution in these cells follows the base models. For zero order CFA, the base model proposes that no effects exist. The log-linear model for this base model was used to define Brennan and Prediger's (1981) κ_n, an alternative to Cohen's κ (1960). For first order CFA, the base model is that of rater independence. This base model was used for Cohen's κ. The third model considered here was proposed by Tanner and Young (1985) for explanatory analysis of agreement tables. This model proposes that raters place equal weights on the agreement cells. The fourth model is specific for the exploration of disagreement cells. This model blanks out the agreement cells and searches for types and antitypes in the disagreement cells. The following paragraphs describe these four models in more detail.

First Order CFA of Rater Agreement: In the present context, the base model of first order CFA proposes independence among the d raters whose judgments are crossed. Specifically, the model proposes, for d raters,

$$\log \hat{m} = \lambda + \sum_{ij} \lambda_{ij}^{Rater},$$

where $\hat{m}$ is the estimated expected frequency, λ is the intercept, and the λ_{ij}^{Rater} are the parameters for the rater main effects.

CFA of agreement tables does not attempt to achieve overall model fit. Instead, it examines individual cells and asks whether the CFA null hypotheses must be rejected. If a null hypothesis is rejected, it suggests an agreement type or antitype, or a disagreement type or antitype. The typical result for agreement tables includes a number of agreement types and a number of disagreement antitypes. Data examples follow below.

Zero Order CFA of Rater Agreement: Cohen's κ has been criticized for a number of reasons, one of which stands out and is discussed here. This criticism of Cohen's κ is known as marginal dependence (for a discussion of this characteristic, see von Eye & von Eye, 2008). This characteristic indicates that if (1) the marginal probabilities are not uniformly distributed and (2) at least one off-diagonal cell has a probability greater than zero, κ has an asymptotic maximum of less than unity. As a result, a comparison of κ values can be problematic. As a consequence of this characteristic, κ can indicate low levels of agreement beyond chance although a vast proportion of judgments matches exactly. The reason for this pattern of results is that large frequencies in diagonal cells can conform with expectation as specified in the main effect model, in particular if the marginals differ from each other.

To deal with these problems, Brennan and Prediger (1981) proposed using the log-linear null model as the base model for κ instead of the main effect model of rater independence. This model is $\log \hat{m} = \lambda$. The resulting measure of rater agreement, κ_n, does not suffer from these two criticized characteristics of Cohen's κ.

In the context of configural exploration of rater agreement, the same discussion can be carried out. Types and antitypes from first order CFA do not necessarily reflect the largest or smallest numbers of agreements, because these numbers can conform with the expectancy that is based on the model of rater independence. In contrast, when Brennan and Prediger's (1981) null model is used, deviations indicate that particular configurations of rating categories were observed more often (types) or less often (antitypes) than estimated by the null model. This implies that cells emerge as constituting types if they contain significantly more cases than the average cell, and cells emerge as constituting antitypes if they contain significantly fewer cases than the average cell.

Tanner and Young's (1985) Equal Weight Agreement Model as a CFA Base Model: To introduce Tanner and Young's (1985) equal weight agreement model (also called the null-association agreement model; Schuster, 2001), we use the sample case of the two raters, A and B. The model assumes that the parameters for the interaction between Rater A and Rater B, $A \times B$, are all zero. In this respect, this model is identical to the base models for Cohen's κ, Brennan and Prediger's κ_n, and first order CFA. However, to model agreement, Tanner and Young's model, which is equivalent to Aickin's (1990) constant predictive probability model, specifies an equal weight parameter for the diagonal cells, that is, the agreement cells. For two raters, the model can be formulated as the log-frequency model

$$\log \hat{m} = \lambda + \lambda^A + \lambda^B + \delta_{ij}\xi,$$

where δ_{ij} is the vector that contains the weights, the subscripts ij are used to indicate that these weights are placed on the agreement cells, and ξ is the parameter that is estimated for this vector. This model can be adapted for the case of more than two raters (von Eye & Mun, 2005).

Schuster (2001) showed that the expression $\exp(2\xi)$ has a simple odds-ratio interpretation that reflects the degree of agreement. This interpretation is

$$\exp(2\xi) = \frac{m_{ii}m_{jj}}{m_{ij}m_{ji}}.$$

Thus, ξ can be compared to Cohen's κ.

In the present context, we are less interested in the overall degree of agreement. Instead, we ask whether types and antitypes exist that contradict the equal weight agreement model. If such types and antitypes can be identified, they indicate local associations. Just as with zero order and first order CFA of rater agreement, these associations suggest systematic patterns in the joint frequency distribution of the raters. When Tanner and Young's model is used, however, types and antitypes indicate that the hypothesis of equal weights in the agreement cells allows one to explain only part of the variation in the cells of the agreement table.

Quasi-Independence Model for the Exploration of Disagreement: For example, in the context of rater training, it can be important to know where raters disagree. Disagreement beyond chance may lead to additional training or redefining categories of rating scales. A CFA model that is suited for the exploration of disagreement cells is the log-linear quasi-independence model. For two raters, this model is

$$\log \hat{m} = \lambda + \lambda^A + \lambda^B + \sum_k \lambda_k,$$

where the first three terms on the right-hand side of the equation are the same as in the first order CFA base model. The summation term describes the vectors needed to blank out the agreement cells. In the typical case, J such vectors are needed in a model, with J being the number of rating categories, and $k = 1, \ldots, J$. Types that result from this model indicate disagreement beyond chance, and antitypes indicate lack of disagreement beyond chance (for adaptations of coefficients of agreement to questions concerning disagreement, see von Eye & von Eye, 2005).

It is important to realize that types and antitypes of disagreement that result from the model of quasi-independence differ from those that result from the first order CFA base model. Both models assume independence between raters. However, whereas the first order CFA model estimates expected cell frequencies taking into account all cells, including the agreement cells, the quasi-independence base model estimates expected cell frequencies under exclusion of the agreement cells. Thus, types and antitypes of disagreement describe patterns of disagreement instead of judgments in general.

2.2 Data Examples

In the following paragraphs, we present two data examples. The first involves data from two raters. The second involves data from three raters.

Data Example 1: In the following example, we analyze data from a study on the agreement of raters on the qualification of job applicants in a large agency in the United States[1]. A total of 466 interview protocols was examined by two evaluators, A and B. Each evaluator independently indicated on a six-point ordinal scale the degree to which an applicant was close to the profile specified in the advertisement for the position, with 1 indicating very good match and 6 indicating lack of match. We analyze the cross-classification of the judgments of the two raters under the following four base models:

1. Null model: $\log \hat{m} = \lambda$;

2. Main effect model of rater independence: $\log \hat{m} = \lambda + \lambda^A + \lambda^B$;

3. Equal weight agreement model: $\log \hat{m} = \lambda + \lambda^A + \lambda^B + \delta_{ij}\xi$; and

4. Quasi-independence model for the exploration of rater disagreement: $\log \hat{m} = \lambda + \lambda^A + \lambda^B + \sum_k \lambda_k$.

Matrix X shows the vectors needed for each of these base models:

---

[1]Thanks go to Neal Schmitt for making these data available. Note that the data used here are from the same data set as the ones used by von Eye and Mun (2006). However, in the present example, different raters are used.

$$
X = \left(
\begin{array}{c|ccc|ccc|c|cccccc}
1 & 1 & \cdots & 0 & 1 & \cdots & 0 & 1 & 1 & 0 & 0 & 0 & 0 & 0 \\
1 & 0 & \ddots & 0 & 1 & \ddots & 0 & 0 & 0 & 0 & 0 & 0 & 0 & 0 \\
1 & 0 & & 0 & 1 & & 0 & 0 & 0 & 0 & 0 & 0 & 0 & 0 \\
1 & 0 & & 0 & 1 & & 0 & 0 & 0 & 0 & 0 & 0 & 0 & 0 \\
1 & 0 & & 1 & 1 & & 0 & 0 & 0 & 0 & 0 & 0 & 0 & 0 \\
1 & -1 & \cdots & -1 & 1 & \cdots & 0 & 0 & 0 & 0 & 0 & 0 & 0 & 0 \\
1 & 1 & \cdots & 0 & 0 & \cdots & 0 & 0 & 0 & 0 & 0 & 0 & 0 & 0 \\
\hline
1 & 0 & \ddots & 0 & 0 & \ddots & 0 & 1 & 0 & 1 & 0 & 0 & 0 & 0 \\
1 & 0 & & 0 & 0 & & 0 & 0 & 0 & 0 & 0 & 0 & 0 & 0 \\
1 & 0 & & 0 & 0 & & 0 & 0 & 0 & 0 & 0 & 0 & 0 & 0 \\
1 & 0 & & 1 & 0 & & 0 & 0 & 0 & 0 & 0 & 0 & 0 & 0 \\
1 & -1 & \cdots & -1 & 0 & \cdots & 0 & 0 & 0 & 0 & 0 & 0 & 0 & 0 \\
1 & 1 & \cdots & 0 & 0 & \cdots & 0 & 0 & 0 & 0 & 0 & 0 & 0 & 0 \\
\hline
1 & 0 & \ddots & 0 & 0 & \ddots & 0 & 0 & 0 & 0 & 0 & 0 & 0 & 0 \\
1 & 0 & & 0 & 0 & & 0 & 1 & 0 & 0 & 1 & 0 & 0 & 0 \\
1 & 0 & & 0 & 0 & & 0 & 0 & 0 & 0 & 0 & 0 & 0 & 0 \\
1 & 0 & & 1 & 0 & & 0 & 0 & 0 & 0 & 0 & 0 & 0 & 0 \\
1 & -1 & \cdots & -1 & 0 & \cdots & 0 & 0 & 0 & 0 & 0 & 0 & 0 & 0 \\
1 & 1 & \cdots & 0 & 0 & \cdots & 0 & 0 & 0 & 0 & 0 & 0 & 0 & 0 \\
\hline
1 & 0 & \ddots & 0 & 0 & \ddots & 0 & 0 & 0 & 0 & 0 & 0 & 0 & 0 \\
1 & 0 & & 0 & 0 & & 0 & 0 & 0 & 0 & 0 & 0 & 0 & 0 \\
1 & 0 & & 0 & 0 & & 0 & 1 & 0 & 0 & 0 & 1 & 0 & 0 \\
1 & 0 & & 1 & 0 & & 0 & 0 & 0 & 0 & 0 & 0 & 0 & 0 \\
1 & -1 & \cdots & -1 & 0 & \cdots & 0 & 0 & 0 & 0 & 0 & 0 & 0 & 0 \\
1 & 1 & \cdots & 0 & 0 & \cdots & 1 & 0 & 0 & 0 & 0 & 0 & 0 & 0 \\
\hline
1 & 0 & \ddots & 0 & 0 & \ddots & 1 & 0 & 0 & 0 & 0 & 0 & 0 & 0 \\
1 & 0 & & 0 & 0 & & 1 & 0 & 0 & 0 & 0 & 0 & 0 & 0 \\
1 & 0 & & 0 & 0 & & 1 & 0 & 0 & 0 & 0 & 0 & 0 & 0 \\
1 & 0 & & 1 & 0 & & 1 & 1 & 0 & 0 & 0 & 0 & 1 & 0 \\
1 & -1 & \cdots & -1 & 0 & \cdots & 1 & 0 & 0 & 0 & 0 & 0 & 0 & 0 \\
1 & 1 & \cdots & 0 & -1 & \cdots & -1 & 0 & 0 & 0 & 0 & 0 & 0 & 0 \\
\hline
1 & 0 & \ddots & 0 & -1 & \ddots & -1 & 0 & 0 & 0 & 0 & 0 & 0 & 0 \\
1 & 0 & & 0 & -1 & & -1 & 0 & 0 & 0 & 0 & 0 & 0 & 0 \\
1 & 0 & & 0 & -1 & & -1 & 0 & 0 & 0 & 0 & 0 & 0 & 0 \\
1 & 0 & & 1 & -1 & & -1 & 0 & 0 & 0 & 0 & 0 & 0 & 0 \\
1 & -1 & \cdots & -1 & -1 & \cdots & -1 & 1 & 0 & 0 & 0 & 0 & 0 & 1 \\
\end{array}
\right)
$$

Matrix X contains four blocks of vectors. The first consists of one constant vector of 1s, in the first column. This column is all that is needed for the null model. This base model proposes a uniform distribution for the entire agreement table. The second block contains the 10 vectors needed for the main effects of the two raters. Each rater used six rating categories. Therefore, five effects coding vectors are needed per rater to capture the main effects of the two raters. The main effect model for rater independence, which is also used to calculate Cohen's κ, uses the constant vector and the main effects vectors. The third block consists of just one column. This is the vector that is added to the first two blocks for Tanner and Young's equal weight agreement model. Using this vector, it is proposed that the diagonal cells are different from the rest of the table, and that the weights of the diagonals cells are the same. Differential weight agreement models have been discussed also (for an overview, see von Eye & Mun, 2005). The fourth block contains the six vectors needed to blank out the diagonal cells of the agreement matrix. To obtain the quasi-independence model, this block of vectors is added to the first two.

In the following paragraphs, we report the results for the four models. For each of the analyses, we use the z-test and the Holland-Copenhaver procedure of α protection. Table 2.2 displays the results for the CFA that used the null model for a base model. The $LR - X^2$ for this model is 808.8 ($df = 35; p < 0.01$). We expect many types and antitypes to emerge.

As is characteristic of zero order CFA, the cells with the large frequencies constitute types, and the cells with the small frequencies constitute antitypes. In Table 2.2 cells with frequencies above 28 constitute types, and cells with frequencies less than 5 constitute antitypes. As far as rater agreement is concerned, we note that Configurations 2 2, 3 3, 4 4, and 5 5 constitute types. Configurations 1 1 and 6 6 fail to constitute types. We conclude that, when the number of judgments is the only main indicator of agreement, with no reference to expected rates of agreement other than the average number of judgments, the two raters agree beyond chance in the middle segment of the evaluation scale, but not when it comes to the extreme scores. In addition, many of those configurations constitute types that indicate stronger disagreement by just one scale point. With just a few exceptions, configurations that indicate disagreement between the two raters constitute antitypes.

Table 2.3 displays the results for first order CFA, which uses the base model of rater independence. This is the same base model as the one used for Cohen's κ. The $LR - X^2$ for this model is 297.27 ($df = 25; p < 0.01$). This model is significantly better than the null model ($\Delta X^2 = 511.53; \Delta df = 10; p < 0.01$). Still, it fails to explain the frequency distribution in the agreement

TABLE 2.2. Zero Order CFA of Job Interview Protocol Evaluation Data

Configuration AB	m	$\hat{m}$	z	p	Type/Antitype
11	5	12.944	−2.2081	.013618	
12	6	12.944	−1.9302	.026793	
13	2	12.944	−3.0419	.001175	Antitype
14	0	12.944	−3.5978	.000160	Antitype
15	0	12.944	−3.5978	.000160	Antitype
16	0	12.944	−3.5978	.000160	Antitype
21	11	12.944	−.5404	.294444	
22	29	12.944	4.4626	.000004	Type
23	34	12.944	5.8523	.000000	Type
24	7	12.944	−1.6522	.049244	
25	1	12.944	−3.3199	.000450	Antitype
26	0	12.944	−3.5978	.000160	Antitype
31	3	12.944	−2.7640	.002855	Antitype
32	29	12.944	4.4626	.000004	Type
33	56	12.944	11.9671	.000000	Type
34	43	12.944	8.3538	.000000	Type
35	3	12.944	−2.7640	.002855	Antitype
36	0	12.944	−3.5978	.000160	Antitype
41	1	12.944	−3.3199	.000450	Antitype
42	9	12.944	−1.0963	.136466	
43	36	12.944	6.4082	.000000	Type
44	73	12.944	16.6921	.000000	Type
45	32	12.944	5.2964	.000000	Type
46	1	12.944	−3.3199	.000450	Antitype
51	0	12.944	−3.5978	.000160	Antitype
52	2	12.944	−3.0419	.001175	Antitype
53	4	12.944	−2.4861	.006458	Antitype
54	30	12.944	4.7405	.000001	Type
55	36	12.944	6.4082	.000000	Type
56	4	12.944	−2.4861	.006458	Antitype
61	0	12.944	−3.5978	.000160	Antitype
62	0	12.944	−3.5978	.000160	Antitype
63	1	12.944	−3.3199	.000450	Antitype
64	0	12.944	−3.5978	.000160	Antitype
65	2	12.944	−3.0419	.001175	Antitype
66	6	12.944	−1.9302	.026793	

TABLE 2.3. First Order CFA of Job Interview Protocol Evaluation Data

Configuration AB	m	$\hat{m}$	z	p	Type/Antitype
11	5	.558	5.9469	.000000	Type
12	6	2.092	2.7016	.003451	
13	2	3.710	−.8879	.187295	
14	0	4.268	−2.0660	.019415	
15	0	2.064	−1.4368	.075388	
16	0	.307	−.5540	.289805	
21	11	3.519	3.9876	.000033	Type
22	29	13.197	4.3499	.000007	Type
23	34	23.403	2.1904	.014247	
24	7	26.923	−3.8396	.000062	Antitype
25	1	13.021	−3.3314	.000432	Antitype
26	0	1.936	−1.3913	.082072	
31	3	5.751	−1.1472	.125656	
32	29	21.567	1.6007	.054725	
33	56	38.245	2.8711	.002045	Type
34	43	43.996	−.1501	.440337	
35	3	21.279	−3.9626	.000037	Antitype
36	0	3.163	−1.7785	.037660	
41	1	6.524	−2.1626	.015285	
42	9	24.464	−3.1264	.000885	Antitype
43	36	43.382	−1.1208	.131192	
44	73	49.906	3.2691	.000539	Type
45	32	24.137	1.6004	.054756	
46	1	3.588	−1.3663	.085927	
51	0	3.262	−1.8060	.035456	
52	2	12.232	−2.9255	.001719	Antitype
53	4	21.691	−3.7985	.000073	Antitype
54	30	24.953	1.0104	.156153	
55	36	12.069	6.8887	.000000	Type
56	4	1.794	1.6470	.049778	
61	0	.386	−.6215	.267134	
62	0	1.448	−1.2035	.114385	
63	1	2.569	−.9788	.163849	
64	0	2.955	−1.7190	.042808	
65	2	1.429	.4775	.316512	
66	6	.212	12.5566	.000000	Type

table. Therefore, again, we expect many types and antitypes to emerge.

The base model used by first order CFA takes rater main effects into account. In other words, this base model (1) accounts for raters' differential use of rating categories and (2) proposes independence of the two raters' ratings. Based on these expectations, we note that, now, each of the six agreement cells constitutes a type. The expected cell frequencies for Configurations 1 1 and 6 6 are small. Therefore, interpretation has to proceed with caution for these two configurations. The antitypes in Table 2.3 present an interesting picture also. Only (but not all) cells with disagreement by two or more rating categories constitute antitypes (Configurations 2 4, 2 5, 3 5, 4 2, 5 2, and 5 3). Judgment discrepancies larger than two rating categories occurred rarely (Configurations 2 5 and 5 2) or not at all (Configurations 1 6 and 2 6). In addition, large discrepancies were not expected to occur very often. Thus, antitypes did not emerge for these configurations (e.g., Configurations 1 6 or 2 6).

The results of the CFA that uses the Tanner and Young (1985) equal weight agreement model for a base model are given in Table 2.4. The $LR-X^2$ for this model is 205.41 ($df = 24$; $p < 0.01$). This represents a significant improvement over the first order CFA base model ($\Delta X^2 = 91.86$; $\Delta df = 1$; $p < 0.01$). Still, it fails to explain the frequency distribution in the agreement table. Therefore, again, we expect types and antitypes to emerge. If types and antitypes emerge for the diagonal, that is, the agreement cells, they indicate the agreement cell configurations that deviate from the expectation that is based on the equal weight hypothesis.

The results in Table 2.4 show that only one agreement type is left. It is constituted by Configuration 6 6. It suggests that the two raters agree more often than expected under the equal weight agreement model in the extreme category, 6, that describes a job candidate as not matching the advertized job profile. All other agreement cells contain observed frequencies that differ from expectation only randomly. The remaining four types suggest that disagreement by one scale unit occurs more often than expected. In contrast, disagreement by more than one scale unit is particularly unlikely when one of the raters uses rating Category 5 (Antitypes 2 5, 3 5, and 5 3).

The results of the CFA with the base model that blanks out the agreement cells are given in Table 2.5. The $LR - X^2$ for this model is 158.77 ($df = 19$; $p < 0.01$). This represents a significant improvement over the first order CFA base model ($\Delta X^2 = 138.50$; $\Delta df = 6$; $p < 0.01$). Still, this model also fails to explain the frequency distribution in the agreement table. Therefore, we expect types and antitypes to emerge. From this model, types and antitypes cannot emerge for the diagonal cells, because they were blanked out. Types and antitypes thus indicate where, in particular, disagreement differs from

TABLE 2.4. CFA of Job Interview Protocol Evaluation Data; Base Model Is the Equal Weight Agreement Model

Configuration AB	m	$\hat{m}$	z	p	Type/Antitype
11	5	1.749	2.4577	.006992	
12	6	2.014	2.8088	.002486	
13	2	3.231	−.6850	.246668	
14	0	3.611	−1.9004	.028691	
15	0	2.022	−1.4221	.077496	
16	0	.371	−.6094	.271116	
21	11	3.588	3.9133	.000046	Type
22	29	28.581	.0784	.468772	
23	34	17.433	3.9679	.000036	Type
24	7	19.484	−2.8282	.002341	
25	1	10.911	−3.0004	.001348	Antitype
26	0	2.004	−1.4155	.078454	
31	3	5.186	−.9597	.168591	
32	29	15.704	3.3553	.000396	Type
33	56	66.283	−1.2631	.103277	
34	43	28.161	2.7963	.002585	
35	3	15.770	−3.2157	.000651	Antitype
36	0	2.896	−1.7018	.044395	
41	1	5.677	−1.9630	.024822	
42	9	17.193	−1.9759	.024082	
43	36	27.587	1.6018	.054599	
44	73	81.106	−.9001	.184031	
45	32	17.266	3.5460	.000196	Type
46	1	3.171	−1.2191	.111401	
51	0	3.322	−1.8227	.034176	
52	2	10.061	−2.5413	.005522	
53	4	16.143	−3.0222	.001255	Antitype
54	30	18.042	2.8154	.002436	
55	36	26.577	1.8277	.033795	
56	4	1.855	1.5744	.057701	
61	0	.478	−.6914	.244666	
62	0	1.448	−1.2031	.114461	
63	1	2.323	−.8679	.192735	
64	0	2.596	−1.6112	.053572	
65	2	1.454	.4531	.325227	
66	6	.702	6.3217	.000000	Type

TABLE 2.5. First Order CFA of Job Interview Protocol Evaluation Data; Agreement Cells Blanked Out

Configuration AB	m	$\hat{m}$	z	p	Type/Antitype
11	5	—	—	—	
12	6	1.319	4.0769	.000023	Type
13	2	2.686	−.4184	.337831	
14	0	2.849	−1.6878	.045724	
15	0	1.028	−1.0140	.155290	
16	0	.119	−.3448	.365108	
21	11	2.726	5.0121	.000000	Type
22	29	—	—	—	
23	34	20.208	3.0680	.001077	Type
24	7	21.435	−3.1178	.000911	Antitype
25	1	7.737	−2.4220	.007718	
26	0	.895	−.9459	.172096	
31	3	4.977	−.8862	.187747	
32	29	18.118	2.5566	.005284	
33	56	—	—	—	
34	43	39.143	.6165	.268783	
35	3	14.128	−2.9606	.001535	Antitype
36	0	1.634	−1.2783	.100579	
41	1	5.190	−1.8392	.032943	
42	9	18.893	−2.2759	.011424	
43	36	38.481	−.4000	.344592	
44	73	—	—	—	
45	32	14.733	4.4987	.000003	Type
46	1	1.704	−.5392	.294873	
51	0	1.976	−1.4055	.079930	
52	2	7.191	−1.9359	.026442	
53	4	14.648	−2.7821	.002701	
54	30	15.537	3.6693	.000122	Type
55	36	—	—	—	
56	4	.649	4.1616	.000016	Type
61	0	.132	−.3631	.358275	
62	0	.480	−.6927	.244243	
63	1	.977	.0229	.490879	
64	0	1.037	−1.0182	.154292	
65	2	.374	2.6578	.003933	
66	6	—	—	—	

the assumption of rater independence when agreement is not taken into account.

Table 2.5 shows that six disagreement types and two disagreement antitypes emerged. The types are constituted by Configurations 1 2, 2 1, 2 3, 4 5, 5 4, and 5 6. Each of these types suggests that disagreement by just one scale unit is more likely than expected under the base model. The two antitypes are constituted by Configurations 2 4 and 3 5. They suggest that particular deviations between the two raters by more than two scale units are very unlikely for categories in the middle range.

Data Example 2: In the second data example, we analyze data that involve three raters (see von Eye & Mun, 2005). Three psychiatrists reviewed the depression diagnoses of 163 inpatients. For each patient, it was determined whether a diagnosis of 1 = not depressed, 2 = mildly depressed, or 3 = clinically depressed can be supported. For the CFA of the cross-classification of three psychiatrists' judgments, we use the base model of independence. Labeling the three psychiatrists with A, B, and C, we thus use the base model

$$\log \hat{m} = \lambda + \lambda^A + \lambda^B + \lambda^C.$$

For the CFA, we use the z-test and protect α by using the Holland-Copenhaver procedure. Table 2.6 displays the CFA results.

Table 2.6 suggests that the three psychiatrists' diagnoses are not independent. Five types emerge, but no antitype. The types are constituted by Configurations 1 1 1, 1 1 2, 1 2 2, 2 2 1, and 2 2 2. The first and the last of these types suggest that the psychiatrists agree more often than expected on the diagnoses "no depression" and "mild depression". The diagnosis "clinical depression" was also observed more often than expected (and it was stated more often than any of the other diagnosis patterns), but not significantly more often than expected.

Also observed more often than expected were three disagreement patterns. These types suggest that certain patterns of disagreement by just one scale point occur more often than expected under the base model of independence of psychiatrists' diagnoses.

One important aspect of the analysis of the data in Table 2.6 is that the sample is relatively small for CFA. Many of the expected cell frequencies are very small. Therefore, the types that are based on particularly small expected cell frequencies ($m_{ijk} < 0.5$) can be interpreted only with caution. An increase in sample size can be recommended.

TABLE 2.6. CFA of Depression Diagnoses Given by Three Psychiatrists

Configuration ABC	m	$\hat{m}$	z	p	Type/Antitype
111	4	.271	7.1633	.000000	Type
112	3	.422	3.9714	.000036	Type
113	6	4.215	.8692	.192374	
121	2	.244	3.5559	.000188	Type
122	1	.379	1.0076	.156830	
123	3	3.794	−.4076	.341788	
131	2	1.694	.2354	.406967	
132	2	2.635	−.3910	.347900	
133	17	26.346	−1.8209	.034311	
211	0	.068	−.2603	.397322	
212	1	.105	2.7558	.002928	
213	2	1.054	.9216	.178357	
221	1	.061	3.8028	.000072	Type
222	1	.095	2.9391	.001646	Type
223	1	.948	.0529	.478903	
231	0	.423	−.6507	.257616	
232	0	.659	−.8116	.208516	
233	4	6.587	−1.0079	.156760	
311	0	.766	−.8750	.190798	
312	1	1.191	−.1749	.430579	
313	3	11.909	−2.5815	.004918	
321	0	.689	−.8301	.203253	
322	1	1.072	−.0693	.472363	
323	8	10.718	−.8302	.203226	
331	0	4.785	−2.1874	.014357	
332	4	7.443	−1.2620	.103478	
333	96	74.429	2.5004	.006203	

2.3   Chapter Summary

CFA of rater agreement allows one to explore cross-classifications of judgments of two or more raters, with the goal of identifying those patterns that indicate agreement or disagreement beyond the rate expected with reference to the base model.   Instead of summarizing degree of rater agreement in a single coefficient, CFA allows one to identify those patterns of agreement and disagreement that stand out as beyond expectation. The standard base model for CFA of rater agreement proposes rater independence. Types and antitypes from this base model indicate patterns of judgments that occur more or less frequently than expected. More complex base model as well as base models that reflect particular hypotheses can be specified. Weights can be taken into account, and there can be a focus on selections of cells, for example cells that contain cases of rater disagreement.

3

Structural Zeros in CFA

Zeros in cross-classifications come in two forms. The first involves cells for which no case was observed but, theoretically, for example, in a larger sample, cases could have been observed. Zero counts typically pose no problem (unless there are so many that parameter estimation or the estimation of a CFA base model becomes impossible). The second form of zeros in a table involves cells for which it is impossible to find cases. The zero counts in these cells are called structural zeros. A classical example is the table that crosses location of cancer and gender. In this table, for obvious reasons, the cell "female and prostate cancer" cannot contain anybody. Chapter 3 discusses various ways in which structural zeros can occur. Some of these ways are design-specific. It is shown how these zero cells can be identified. The chapter also shows how the CFA base model can be reformulated to take into account the presence of structural zeros. It is illustrated that ignoring structural zeros can lead to antitypes with no interpretation. It is also illustrated that the number of structural zeros can have an effect on the complexity of CFA base models that can be estimated. In a data example, data from an experiment in cognitive psychology are reanalyzed.

In this chapter, issues concerning zeros in cross-classifications are discussed. Zeros can come in various forms. In Section 3.1, we introduce the distinction between empirical and structural zeros, and we talk about blanking out structural zeros. In Section 3.2, we discuss the case in which structural zeros are the result of design and data coding. Some of the strategies to deal with zeros can also be applied to solve other problems (Section 3.1). In both sections, the focus is on concepts and applications in the context of CFA (von Eye & Mun, 2007). Methods of estimation have been discussed elsewhere (see Birch, 1963; Bishop, Fienberg, & Holland, 1975; Fienberg, 1970; Haberman, 1973, 1974).

3.1   Blanking Out Structural Zeros

Cross-classifications often contain cells with zero frequencies. For example, in Table 2.2, 9 of the 36 cells did not show a single case. With only one exception (Cell 6 4), each of these cells would have contained cases in which the two raters disagreed by three or more scale units. Although disagreement by this many scale points is, theoretically, possible, it did not occur in this study. Zero counts with this characteristic are termed *empirical zeros*.

In contrast, cells can exist that are characterized by *structural zeros*. These are cells that are empty for logical or design reasons. Consider the cross-classification of Location of Cancer and Gender. In this table, the configuration "Prostate Cancer" and "Female" cannot contain cases, for obvious reasons. A table with structural zeros is called *structurally incomplete*. Tables can contain both empirical and structural zeros.

When it comes to estimating expected cell frequencies for log-linear models or for CFA, empirical and structural zeros must be treated differently. Empirical zeros usually pose no problems (unless there are too many empirical zeros or entire variable categories were never observed, that is, when marginal counts are zero). The estimation procedure generates the probabilities for these cells, and, based on this estimate, valid expected frequencies can be calculated. In contrast, when zero observation cells are structural, it would be a mistake to place a portion of the probability mass into these cells. The effect would be that, for this empty cell, there is an automatic deviation that will be held against the model. The probability of being in this cell is misestimated. In addition, for the remaining cells, there is not enough of the probability mass left, and the probability of being in any of the remaining cells will, on average, be underestimated. This will be held against the model too. As a result, the model that is needed to describe the data will, in many cases, end up being unnecessarily complex.

Therefore, two strategies are pursued, depending on the nature of zeros in a table. When a zero is empirical, either no corrective measure is taken at all, or a small constant is added to each cell. This second option is called *invoking the Delta option*. There is no general agreement on the magnitude of the constant Delta. Some software packages automatically add 0.5 to each of the t cells in a table. The effect of this measure is that the sample size is artificially increased by $0.5t$. Often, a model that would not converge before the Delta option is invoked will converge with Delta. One possible consequence of this strategy is that, again, models that fit the data are more complex than necessary, given the data structure, because most of the overall goodness-of-fit measures are sensitive to sample size, in particular the ones that are based on X^2. Another problem with the Delta option is that it is *ad hoc*, and the magnitude of the constant is arbitrary. Therefore, Bayesian methods have been discussed for estimation as alternatives to standard maximum likelihood methods (see Agresti, 2002).

When zeros are structural, the cells that contain these zeros must be blanked out, to prevent the estimation algorithm from placing probability mass into these cells. Blanking out a cell is easily done by adding a column vector to the design matrix in which the blanked-out cell is given a 1, and all other cells are given zeros.

In addition to distinguishing between empirical and structural zeros, a distinction must be made between the term *declaring cells structural zeros* and the superordinate term of *blanking cells out*. The former is based on the existence of logically impossible patterns. Cells that show these patterns are *blanked out*. Blanking out, however, can be used for purposes other than specifying structural zeros. As was done for the analysis in Table 2.5, cells can be blanked out when they are not part of the data structure of interest. In Table 2.5, the focus was on disagreement cells. Therefore, all agreement cells had been blanked out.

One important implication of blanking cells out in CFA concerns the number of cells that are subjected to CFA tests and, thus, the protection of the significance threshold, α. When s cells are blanked out, the number of CFA tests is reduced by s, and the maximum number of CFA tests becomes $t - s$. The protected significance threshold for the $t - s$ tests is, therefore, less extreme than for the CFA of the table with t cells. Implications for power are obvious.

The number of cells that can be blanked out is limited, for two reasons. First, if too many cells are blanked out, the degrees of freedom can become negative. In most cases, each cell that is blanked out reduces the degrees of freedom by one. Second, the blanked-out cells can change the structure of a table such that estimation of expected cell frequencies is no longer possible. In CFA applications, neither problem is frequent.

Data Example 1: The following example uses data from an experiment on information processing (Hussy, 1991). 118 individuals played the game Mastermind on the computer. The time needed to make a decision in each trial was coded as 1 = up to 10 sec; 2 = between 10 and 20 sec; and 3 = more than 20 sec. In addition, a fourth category was used with 4 = problem solved. The players had up to eight trials to solve a problem. For the following example, we analyze the cross-classification of Trials 7 and 8. The cross-classification of the four categories of decision making contains three structural zeros. These zeros can be found in Configurations 4 1, 4 2, and 4 3. They indicate that those respondents who solved the problem in

Trial 7, or before, cannot register a nonzero decision-making time for Trial 8. Configuration 4 4 contains those cases that solved the problem before Trial 8 and therefore do not log a problem-solving time in Trial 8.

We approach the data by using two CFA base models. The first is that of independence between the two trials. Types and antitypes can, under this model, emerge if a particular amount of time needed to make a decision at Trial 7 is associated with a particular amount of time needed in Trial 8. This base model, which is that of a first order CFA, ignores the fact that the cross-classification of decision-making categories contains three structural zeros. The second base model includes vectors for the three structural zeros. Let the decision-making variables be labeled as $T7$ and $T8$. Then, the base model that disregards the structural zeros is

$$\log \hat{m} = \lambda + \lambda^{T7} + \lambda^{T8}.$$

Under consideration of the structural zeros, this model becomes the nonstandard

$$\log \hat{m} = \lambda + \lambda^{T7} + \lambda^{T8} + \sum_{k} \lambda^{S_k},$$

where the last term indicates the vectors used to specify the structural zeros (one per structural zero). The design matrices for these two models are

$$X = \begin{pmatrix}
1 & 0 & 0 & 1 & 0 & 0 & 0 & 0 & 0 \\
0 & 1 & 0 & 1 & 0 & 0 & 0 & 0 & 0 \\
0 & 0 & 1 & 1 & 0 & 0 & 0 & 0 & 0 \\
-1 & -1 & -1 & 1 & 0 & 0 & 0 & 0 & 0 \\
1 & 0 & 0 & 0 & 1 & 0 & 0 & 0 & 0 \\
0 & 1 & 0 & 0 & 1 & 0 & 0 & 0 & 0 \\
0 & 0 & 1 & 0 & 1 & 0 & 0 & 0 & 0 \\
-1 & -1 & -1 & 0 & 1 & 0 & 0 & 0 & 0 \\
1 & 0 & 0 & 0 & 0 & 1 & 0 & 0 & 0 \\
0 & 1 & 0 & 0 & 0 & 1 & 0 & 0 & 0 \\
0 & 0 & 1 & 0 & 0 & 1 & 0 & 0 & 0 \\
-1 & -1 & -1 & 0 & 0 & 1 & 0 & 0 & 0 \\
1 & 0 & 0 & -1 & -1 & -1 & 1 & 0 & 0 \\
0 & 1 & 0 & -1 & -1 & -1 & 0 & 1 & 0 \\
0 & 0 & 1 & -1 & -1 & -1 & 0 & 0 & 1 \\
-1 & -1 & -1 & -1 & -1 & -1 & 0 & 0 & 0
\end{pmatrix}.$$

The first of the two column blocks in this design matrix contains the vectors for the first order CFA base model. The second block, added to the first for the second CFA run, contains the three vectors that are used to specify the position of the structural zeros in the table. Table 3.1 displays the results from both CFA runs.

The $LR - X^2$ for the first model is 44.36 ($df = 9$; $p < 0.01$). This base model is, thus, rejected, and we expect types and antitypes to emerge. The $LR - X^2$ for the second model is 21.26 ($df = 6$; $p < 0.01$). The improvement of the second model over the first is significant, with $\Delta LR - X^2 = 23.10$ ($\Delta df = 3$, $p < .01$). Still, it is possible that, for both models, types or antitypes emerge.

Table 3.1 shows the expected picture. In the upper panel — it displays the results from the standard first order CFA model — the estimated expected frequencies for Cells 4 1, 4 2, and 4 3 are greater than zero. These frequencies should have been placed in Cell 4 4 because, in a model that takes main effects into account, the marginals must be reproduced. As a result, the model-data discrepancies under the model without consideration of the three structural zeros are overestimated, and the overall $LR - X^2$ for the first model is exaggerated. In contrast, the base model that does take the three structural zeros into account distributes no probability mass over the empty cells, that is, over the structural zeros. This can be seen in the lower panel of Table 3.1. The overall $LR - X^2$ for this model is, therefore, significantly smaller. In addition, the right panel shows that the estimated expected frequency in Cell 4 4 corresponds perfectly with the observed one. This is natural, considering that for decision-making Category 4, at Trial 8, only one frequency was observed. (The subtable that contains this cell is locally saturated, with $df = 0$.)

CFA from both of these analyses shows one type in common, constituted by Cell 1 1. This type suggests that significantly more participants than expected make their decisions in 10 sec or less, both in Trials 7 and 8.

3.2   Structural Zeros by Design

In this section, we discuss a situation in which structural zeros result from coding and design (von Eye & Mun, 2007). We first introduce the method of differences in categorical longitudinal data analysis, and discuss the relationship of this method to polynomials in growth trajectory models. We then present an algorithm for the detection of structural zeros that are part of designs when difference variables are cross-tabulated.

3.2.1   Polynomials and the Method of Differences

Structural zeros by design can result when researchers and data analysts use the *method of finite differences*. This method goes back to Newton (see

TABLE 3.1. CFAs of Decision-Making Categories in Trials 7 and 8, without (Upper Panel) and with (Lower Panel) Consideration of Structural Zeros

Configuration T7T8	m	$\hat{m}$	z	p	Type/ Antitype
11	22	11.429	3.1271	.000883	Type
12	9	9.412	−.1342	.446615	
13	7	12.437	−1.5417	.061573	
14	2	6.723	−1.8215	.034269	
21	4	9.429	−1.7679	.038537	
22	9	7.765	.4433	.328771	
23	15	10.261	1.4796	.069488	
24	5	5.546	−.2319	.408294	
31	8	11.429	−1.0142	.155247	
32	10	9.412	.1917	.423972	
33	15	12.437	.7268	.233684	
34	7	6.723	.1070	.457413	
41	0	1.714	−1.3093	.095215	
42	0	1.412	−1.1882	.117382	
43	0	1.866	−1.3659	.085993	
44	60	1.008	4.9708	.000000	Type
11	22	12.035	2.8723	.002038	Type
12	9	9.912	−.2895	.386089	
13	7	13.097	−1.6848	.046013	
14	2	4.956	−1.3277	.092132	
21	4	9.929	−1.8817	.029942	
22	9	8.177	.2878	.386746	
23	15	10.805	1.2761	.100962	
24	5	4.088	.4508	.326069	
31	8	12.035	−1.1632	.122373	
32	10	9.912	.0281	.488787	
33	15	13.097	.5257	.299536	
34	7	4.956	.9183	.179234	
41	0	—	—	—	
42	0	—	—	—	
43	0	—	—	—	
44	60	6.000	.0000	.500000	

TABLE 3.2. First and Higher Differences for Series of Six Values for the Polynomial $y = 5 + 4x + x^2 + 0.9x^3$

X	0	1	2	3	4	5	6
$f(X)$	5	10.9	24.2	50.3	94.6	162.5	259.4
Δ_j	5.9	13.3	26.1	44.3	67.9	96.9	
$\Delta_{2,k}$	7.4	12.8	18.2	23.6	29		
$\Delta_{3,l}$	5.4	5.4	5.4	5.4			
$\Delta_{4,m}$	0	0	0				

Swade, 2002). It can be used to calculate derivatives of series of real-valued numbers. In a fashion parallel to quotients that are used in calculus to determine derivatives of functions, differences between adjacent scores show specific lawfulness. For example, the signs of the differences indicate whether a curve goes up or down.

A number of variants of the method of differences exists. To introduce the method, we use *finite ascending differences*. Other variants can be used to analogous effects. Consider a series of I measures, X, with values x_i and $i = 1, \ldots, I$. Then, the Method of Finite Ascending Differences (MFAD) calculates *first differences* by subtracting from each score the score before, beginning with the second, or $\Delta_{1,j} = x_{j+1} - x_j$, for $j = 1, \ldots, I-1$. The MFAD calculates second differences by subtracting from each first difference the previous first difference, also beginning with the second, or $\Delta_{2,k} = \Delta_{1,k+1} - \Delta_{1,k}$, for $k = 1, \ldots, I-2$, and so forth.

The relationship of differences to polynomials is as follows. If a series of measures was created by a polynomial of lth order, with $l \leq I - 1$, the lth differences are constant, and all higher order differences are zero. An artificial data example is given in Table 3.2. In the first line of the body of the table, the values of the third order polynomial $y = 5 + 4x + x^2 + 0.9x^3$ are given, for values of X from 0 to 6, in steps of 1. In the following rows, the table shows the first, second, third, and fourth differences. The third differences are constant, and the fourth differences are zero.

Figure 3.1 depicts the series of the raw scores (circles), first differences (triangles), second differences (pluses), and third differences (x's; bottom curve). Evidently, with increasing order, the differences become smaller, and the third differences are constant.

For the following paragraphs, we need to take into account that the application of CFA requires that all variables (except covariates, see Chapter 4) be categorical. In addition, the exact value of parameter estimates is rarely of interest. Therefore, researchers tend to categorize scores and, in the present context, parameter estimates. When polynomials are used, the

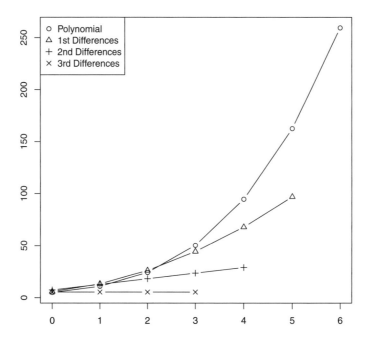

FIGURE 3.1. First, second, and third differences for a third order polynomial.

parameter score of zero is a natural cutoff point. Consider, for example, first order polynomials (or straight regression lines). A positive slope parameter indicates that the scores, over the observed series, increase. A negative slope parameter indicates that the scores decrease. Slope parameters of exactly zero practically never occur. Therefore, for the following discussion, we focus on increases or decreases, or, in more general terms, on positive versus negative polynomial parameters. Focusing on the signs of such parameters, one can classify series of scores using the transformation (Lienert & Krauth, 1973a, 1973b),

$$\Delta = \begin{cases} 0, & \text{if } \Delta < 0 \\ 1, & \text{if } \Delta > 0. \end{cases}$$

This transformation suggests that a difference is assigned a 0 if $\Delta_j = x_{j+1} - x_j < 0$, and a 1 if $\Delta_j = x_{j+1} - x_j > 0$. This transformation can be applied to differences of any order as well as to polynomial parameters. Alternative transformations, including those that allow for no change, have also been discussed (for an overview, see von Eye, 2002a; for a critique of dichotomization, see McCallum, Zhang, Preacher, & Rucker, 2002).

In particular, in the analysis of repeated observations, researchers often ask questions concerning patterns of change, where change is defined using descriptors of the shape of series of observations. To answer these questions, researchers cross dichotomized variables of the kind just introduced. More specifically, researchers cross the transformed variables that indicate first and higher differences. In the following paragraphs, we present a data example.

Data Example 2: For the following example, we use data from the study on the development of aggression in adolescents (Finkelstein et al., 1994) again. In this study, 47 boys and 67 girls in the United Kingdom were asked to respond to an aggression questionnaire in 1983, 1985, and 1987. The average age in 1983 was 11 years. One of the dimensions of aggression examined in this study was Aggressive Impulses (*AI*). In the present example, we analyze the development of *AI* in 1983, 1985, and 1987.

In this analysis, the same single variable was observed three times. For this series, two measures of first differences can be calculated ($\Delta_{1,1} =$ Time 2 − Time 1, and $\Delta_{1,2} =$ Time 3 − Time 2) and one measure of second differences ($\Delta_{2,1} = \Delta_{1,2} - \Delta_{1,1}$). Each of these measures is Δ-transformed as described above. From this transformation, three dichotomous variables result. Crossed, these three variables span a $2 \times 2 \times 2$ contingency table with cell indices 0 0 0, 0 0 1, 0 1 0, 0 1 1, 1 0 0, 1 0 1, 1 1 0, and 1 1 1. Using these indices, a decrease is indicated by 0 and an increase is indicated by 1. Table 3.3 displays this cross-classification for the present data.

We now perform a first order CFA which uses the log-linear main effect model for a base model. The z-test was used, along with the Holland-Copenhaver procedure of α protection. For the base model, we calculate an $LR - X^2$ of 88.36 ($df = 4$; $p < 0.01$). Types and antitypes can be expected to emerge.

Table 3.3 shows that CFA identified two types and two antitypes. The first type is constituted by Configuration 0 1 1. This pattern describes an initial decrease in aggressive impulses that is followed by an increase. This pattern is characterized by a positive quadratic trend, as is indicated by the 1 for the second difference. The second type is constituted by Configuration 100. It shows just the opposite curvature. It describes an initial increase in aggressive impulses that is followed by a decrease. It thus has a negative quadratic trend, which is indicated by the 0 for the second difference.

From the perspective of the present discussion of "structural zeros by design", the two antitypes are most interesting. The first antitype suggests that not a single adolescent showed a decrease from Time 1 to Time 2 that is followed by an increase from Time 2 to Time 3 and, overall, a negative quadratic trend (Configuration 010). The second antitype suggests that no

TABLE 3.3. CFA of First and Second Differences of Aggressive Impulses, Observed Three Times

Configuration $\Delta_{1,1}, \Delta_{1,2}, \Delta_{2,1}$	m	$\hat{m}$	z	p	Type/Antitype
000	20	22.241	−.4751	.317344	
001	13	13.470	−.1280	.449076	
010	0	14.505	−3.8085	.000070	Antitype
011	26	8.785	5.8084	.000000	Type
100	36	20.733	3.3529	.000400	Type
101	0	12.557	−3.5435	.000197	Antitype
110	15	13.521	.4021	.343810	
111	4	8.189	−1.4639	.071616	

one showed an initial increase, followed by a decrease in combination, for an overall positive quadratic trend (Configuration 101). Interestingly, this is not a surprise at all. It is logical that nobody showed these patterns. The difference pattern of the first antitype describes a ∪-shaped curve that is, simultaneously, ∩-shaped. The difference pattern of the second antitype describes a ∩-shaped curve that is, simultaneously, ∪-shaped. Neither is logically possible. Because of this pattern of contradictory shapes, the cells 0 1 0 and 1 0 1 are empty by definition. Nobody can possibly show this pattern. Therefore, these cells must be declared structural zeros.

As was described above, two vectors need to be added to the design matrix to blank out these two cells. The design matrix for the extended base model thus becomes

$$X = \begin{pmatrix} 1 & 1 & 1 & 0 & 0 \\ 1 & 1 & -1 & 0 & 0 \\ 1 & -1 & 1 & 1 & 0 \\ 1 & -1 & -1 & 0 & 0 \\ -1 & 1 & 1 & 0 & 0 \\ -1 & 1 & -1 & 0 & 1 \\ -1 & -1 & 1 & 0 & 0 \\ -1 & -1 & -1 & 0 & 0 \end{pmatrix}.$$

For the extended base model, we calculate an $LR - X^2$ of 25.39 ($df = 2$; $p < 0.01$). This model is significantly closer to the data than the original base model, but it still fails to describe the data well. Types and antitypes are, therefore, expected to emerge. Table 3.4 gives the CFA results. As before, the z-test was used, and the Holland-Copenhaver procedure of α protection. Note that, for the present CFA, the first protected α is $\alpha^* = 0.0085$ instead of $\alpha^* = 0.0064$, because six CFA tests are performed instead of eight

TABLE 3.4. CFA of First and Second Differences of Aggressive Impulses, Observed Three Times; Cells 0 1 0 and 1 0 1 Declared Structural Zeros

Configuration $\Delta_{1,1}, \Delta_{1,2}, \Delta_{2,1}$	m	$\hat{m}$	z	p	Type/Antitype
000	20	27.886	−1.4934	.067667	
001	13	17.234	−1.0198	.153910	
010	0	—	—	—	
011	26	13.880	3.2531	.000571	Type
100	36	23.880	2.4801	.006567	Type
101	0	—	—	—	
110	15	19.234	−.9653	.167190	
111	4	11.886	−2.2874	.011085	

in Table 3.3. Cells with structural zeros are not part of the testing routine and, thus, the number of tests is smaller.

For the extended base model, we obtain only two types. These types are the same as in Table 3.3. What used to be antitypes are now structural zeros, with zero probabilities.

3.2.2 Identifying Zeros That Are Structural by Design

In this section, we describe von Eye and Mun's (2007) algorithm for the identification of zeros that are structural by design. This algorithm is applicable when a cross-classification is spanned by variables that result from dichotomizing first and higher order differences. Variables that reflect more than one order of differences must span the same table. When researchers cross dichotomous variables that reflect patterns of differences of different orders, they analyze the linear, quadratic, cubic, etc. elements of series of measures simultaneously. Crossing such variables has the effect that all possible combinations of curvature patterns are included in the table. Unfortunately, all impossible combinations are included also. An empirical data example of a table with two impossible patterns was analyzed in Tables 3.3 and 3.4. Before describing the algorithm for the identification of structural zeros in this type of cross-classification, we present a definition of impossible patterns.

Definition: Combinations of categories of differences from different orders are impossible if the lower order patterns suggest a different curvature than the higher order patterns.

We now ask how impossible patterns can be identified. The following iterative procedure examines all candidate patterns for contradictory description of orientation. Patterns are candidates if they indicate a change in orientation (from 0 to 1 or vice versa). There is no need to consider patterns that show either zero differences or no change in orientation. Let $\Delta_{1,j}$ and $\Delta_{1,j+1}$ be the first differences between the adjacent measure pairs x_{j+1} and x_j, and x_{j+2} and x_{j+1}, for $j = 1, \ldots, I - 1$, and $\Delta_{2,k}$ the second difference, that is, $\Delta_{1,k+1} - \Delta_{1,k}$. Let $\Delta = 0$ indicate a decrease and $\Delta = 1$ indicate an increase in scores. Iteratively, the algorithm proceeds in two steps:

• Step 1: Compare each pair of first differences $\Delta_{1,j}$ and $\Delta_{1,j+1}$ with the corresponding second difference $\Delta_{2,k}$. If both $\Delta_{1,j} \neq \Delta_{1,j+1}$ and $\Delta_{1,j+1} \neq \Delta_{2,k}$, then the pattern is impossible. To give an example, consider the pattern 1 0 at a given difference level in combination with a 1 at the following level. This pattern is impossible. The second of the first differences would indicate a negative orientation, whereas the second difference would indicate a positive orientation. Accordingly, the pattern 0 1 at a given level cannot be combined with a 0 at the next higher level. If a pattern is identified as impossible, proceed to the next pattern. If a pattern is impossible, all other patterns that could be combined with the impossible pattern are impossible also.

• Step 2: Proceed to the next pair of differences, and start over, at Step 1. Continue until all patterns of differences are compared.

This procedure can be applied to difference patterns of all levels. If a researcher decides to skip levels, the procedure can be adjusted. Specifically, if a 1 at the following level renders a difference pattern impossible, a 0 at the next higher level renders it impossible also. For example, pattern 1 0 at level k cannot go with $\Delta = 0$ at level $k + 2$. For example, for x values of $-10, -5, 0$, and 5, one obtains the difference pattern 1 0 1 for the three first differences, 0 1 for the two second differences, and 1 for the sole third difference. The first differences signs indicate an initial increase that is followed by a decrease and then an increase. The second differences signs indicate that the rate of change is initially decelerated and, in later phases, accelerated. The third difference indicates an increase in acceleration. This pattern of differences is possible. In contrast, consider the series 9, 15, 10, 6. For this sequence, the first differences pattern is 1 0 0, the second differences pattern is 0 1 and, for the corresponding third difference, we calculate $\Delta = 1$, thus indicating a $\cap$-shaped trend. For this series, a zero for the third difference would be impossible.

Data Example 3: For the following example, an artificial data set was created using QuattroPro, and processed using SYSTAT. A series of four scores was created, using QuattroPro's uniform random number generator

TABLE 3.5. Cross-Tabulation of Three First and Two Second Differences (Artificial Data, 1,000 Cases; All Zeros in the Frequency Table Are Structural Zeros)

T2T1[a]	T3T2	T4T3	S21	S32 0	S32 1
0	0	0	0	7	13
0	0	0	1	8	9
0	0	1	0	0	59
0	0	1	1	0	55
0	1	0	0	0	0
0	1	0	1	213	0
0	1	1	0	0	0
0	1	1	1	69	57
1	0	0	0	69	69
1	0	0	1	0	0
1	0	1	0	0	211
1	0	1	1	0	0
1	1	0	0	55	0
1	1	0	1	60	0
1	1	1	0	14	9
1	1	1	1	12	9

[a]$T2T1$ indicates the sign of the first difference between measures $T1$ and $T2$ (1 = increase; 0 = decrease), $T3T2$ indicates the sign of the first difference between measures $T2$ and $T3$, etc.; $S21$ indicates the sign of the second difference of $T2T1$ and $T3T2$, etc.

RAND. The data set includes 1,000 cases. For the following illustration, the three first differences and the two second differences were calculated. None of these turned out to be constant. This is as expected, considering the random nature and the ratio scale level of the scores. The first and the corresponding second differences were transformed into 0–1 patterns, with 0 indicating differences ≤ 0 and 1 indicating differences > 0. Crossed, the resulting dichotomous variables span a contingency table with $2^5 = 32$ cells. This cross-tabulation is given in Table 3.5. Each of the possible patterns in this table was observed more than once. Each impossible pattern has, naturally, a frequency of zero. The variables are labeled $T1$, $T2$, $T3$ and $T4$. The first differences are labeled $T2T1$ for the difference between the second and the first scores, $T3T2$ for the difference between the third and the second scores, and $T4T3$ for the difference between the fourth and the third scores. $S21$ is the label for the difference between the second and the first of the first differences, and $S32$ indicates the difference between the third and the second of the first differences.

TABLE 3.6. Search for Structural Zeros in a 2^5 Cross-Classification That Is Spanned by Three First and Two Second Differences: Four Sample Patterns

Differences Level[a]		Pattern Compared	Overall Decision for Pattern
1st Differences	2nd Differences	1st vs. 2nd Differences	
<u>0 0</u> 0	<u>0</u> 0	0 0 - 0 possible	
0 <u>0 0</u>	0 <u>0</u>	0 0 - 0 possible	Possible
<u>0 0</u> 1	<u>0</u> 0	0 0 - 0 possible	
0 <u>0 1</u>	<u>0</u> 0	0 1 - 0 impossible	Structural Zero
0 <u>0 1</u>	<u>0</u> 1	0 0 - 0 possible	
0 <u>0 1</u>	0 <u>1</u>	0 1 - 1 possible	Possible
<u>0 1</u> 1	<u>0</u> 0	0 1 - 0 impossible	Structural Zero
0 <u>1 1</u>	0 <u>0</u>	1 1 - 0 impossible	Structural Zero

[a]Underlined numbers indicate the pair of the first and the second differences being examined at each step.

To illustrate the algorithm described above, we now discuss the four scenarios from this table. Table 3.6 shows the four decision scenarios that can occur when deciding whether a pattern that includes difference from levels k and $k + 1$ must be treated as a structural zero. The rows of Table 3.6 can be read as follows. We discuss the four possible scenarios.

Scenario 1: From the pattern of first differences (three left columns), we take the first two elements (e.g., 0 0, in the first row), and compare them to the first element of the second difference pattern (0, in the first row). If the second element of the first differences is equal to the sole element of the second differences pattern, the shape of the curve can be described in a compatible way using the MFAD approach, and we can move on to the next elements of the same row. In the present case, we compare the second two elements of the first differences pattern (0 0) in the first row and compare this change pattern with the second element of the second differences pattern (0, in the first row). If these two patterns are compatible, we are ready to make a decision on the first change pattern, that is, 0 0 0 - 0 0. If all comparisons indicate that the patterns of the first and the second differences are compatible, the entire pattern is possible. If any one pattern is incompatible, that is, impossible, we treat the entire pattern as a structural zero. In general, whenever the sign pattern at level k is constant, any combination with sign patterns at the $k+$ first level of differences is possible.

Scenario 2: The second configuration in Table 3.6 (0 0 1 - 0 0) shows that, for some patterns, the two comparisons can result in conflicting conclusions. In this case, the *impossible* supersedes the *possible*, and the pattern is treated as a structural zero. Table 3.5 shows that Pattern 0 0 1 - 0 0 was, indeed, not observed.

Scenario 3: In the third pair of rows, the two comparisons for the Pattern 0 0 1 - 0 1 suggest the same conclusion, although the sign patterns in the pair are not constant. In this case, all comparisons show that the pattern is *possible*, and the pattern can contain cases. Table 3.5 shows that Pattern 0 0 1 - 0 1 was observed 59 times. It should be noted that all comparisons need to be made only if, before the last comparison, there is none that would suggest an *impossible* pattern.

Scenario 4: The last pair of rows (Pattern 0 1 1 - 0 0) shows why this is the case. As soon as a pattern is identified as *impossible*, the subsequent comparisons are unnecessary.

Once a pattern is impossible at one level, all following patterns, taking higher order differences into account, will also be impossible. If, however, a pattern is possible at a given level, the following patterns, taking higher order differences into account, can be either possible or impossible.

Of the 32 cell patterns in the present example (Tables 3.5 and 3.6), 14 are impossible. The log-linear main effect model that ignores the structural zeros has 26 degrees of freedom. The model that takes the structural zeros into account has 12 degrees of freedom. Only the latter is conceivable as a valid base model for CFA.

In the present example, third differences can be calculated also. Taking the third differences into account results in a table with 64 cells. This table contains 46 structural zeros. The log-linear main effect model for this table has 57 degrees of freedom when the structural zeros are ignored, and 11 degrees of freedom when the structural zeros are taken into account and one column vector is inserted into the design matrix for each of them.

CFA based on the MFAD approach is attractive because it allows one to examine change and variations in change from the perspectives of pattern analysis and person orientation. However, in the complete crossing of difference patterns from different levels of finite differences, a large number of structural zeros will always and systematically result. In many cases, structural zeros are not problematic, and software such as ℓEM, Splus, or SYSTAT will allow one to take them into account. However, four issues need to be considered.

First, structural zeros lead to incomplete designs. Therefore, design matrices become nonstandard, and the interpretation of log-linear parameters can be complicated (Mair, 2007; Mair & von Eye, 2007).

Second, the models that can be fitted will have to be less complex than the number of variables and the size of the cross-classification would allow otherwise. The reason for this is that the number of degrees of freedom available for modeling incomplete tables is smaller than for complete tables of the same size. Therefore, data analysis, in particular modeling such data, may end up in nonfitting models. In the context of CFA application, the reduced number of degrees of freedom has the consequence that not all CFA base models may be possible or admissible. For example, the base model of second order CFA requires that all first order associations be taken into account. If, because of a large number of structural zeros, parameters cannot be estimated, the CFA base model that includes these parameters cannot be applied.

The third issue is that signs of differences come with a priori probabilities that do not necessarily correspond with the marginal proportions (see von Eye, 2002a). If researchers wish to take these a priori probabilities into account, additional vectors need to be included in the design matrix. Each of these vectors costs one degree of freedom. The complexity of possible log-linear models or CFA base models is thus reduced even more. In addition, the option of including covariates (see Chapter 4) becomes increasingly remote.

A fourth issue inherent in the analysis of difference scores is that differences of raw scores that come with measurement error can be unreliable (Lord & Novick, 1968). It was shown by von Eye (1982) that reliability is not always low. Instead, it varies with (1) the reliability of the individual measures and (2) retest reliability. Differences from Rasch-scaled scores and from physiological measures tend to have better measurement characteristics. The same typically applies to rank differences.

3.3   Chapter Summary

Structural zeros are zero frequencies in cells for which it is impossible that cases can be found. Reasons are largely logical or technical. An example of a logical reason is the case in which no females are found with prostate cancer. Technical is the case in which up-and-down patterns of signs of differences cannot co-occur. Structural zeros are in contrast to empirical zeros, which simply indicate that no case was found but that, under different conditions, cases could have been found with the profile indicated for a cell with a zero count.

If zeros are structural, one must make sure that cells in which they occur do not constitute antitypes. To prevent this from happening, one can blank out these cells and apply the CFA base model to the table with one or more cells blanked out. Implications of this methodology include that (1) the number of CFA tests performed to a table with structural zeros is smaller than the number of CFA tests for a complete table and, therefore, (2) the procedure used to protect α will always result in a less extreme adjusted significance threshold.

An algorithm is presented that allows one to identify structural zeros that occur for technical reasons ("by design"). A third implication is that the number of CFA base models that can be employed can be limited when the number of structural zeros is large.

4
Covariates in CFA

Covariates are defined as variables that may have an effect on the observed outcomes without being under control of the experimenter. Chapter 4 discusses continuous covariates. Categorical covariates are discussed later in the book, in the chapter on Moderator CFA (Chapter 8). It is shown how the CFA base model can be modified to take continuous covariates into account. In a fashion analogous to the number of structural zeros (Chapter 3), the number of covariates has the potential of curtailing the complexity of the CFA base model that can be estimated. A data example is given on the development of aggression in adolescence in which physical pubertal progress, a continuous covariate, is taken into account.

4.1   CFA and Covariates

A covariate is a variable that (1) may be predictive of the outcome variable and (2) is not controlled in the process of data collection. Depending on context, covariates are viewed as independent variables, as confounding variables, or as causes of dependent measures. In the analysis of categorical variables, the dependent variable is given by the logarithms of the frequencies of a cross-classification, $\log \hat{m}$. Covariates, therefore, are variables that possibly help explain the $\log \hat{m}$ (see also Section 7.2).

When covariates are categorical, they can be crossed with the variables that are of key interest in a study. If this is possible (sample size limitations may prevent researchers from doing this because, with each new variable, the cross-classification increases in size by a factor given by the number of categories of the new variable), covariates are not distinguishable from the variables of key interest, unless they play a different role in the base model (see section on structural zeros). For example, to eliminate the effects of covariates on the emergence of types and antitypes, researchers may specify the base model such that it (1) is saturated in the covariates and (2) takes into account all associations among covariates and the variables of key interest. Types and antitypes will emerge from a base model having these characteristics only if they are caused by the variables of key interest and their interactions.

In contrast, when covariates are continuous, they cannot be used as variables that span a cross-classification. To be able to take continuous covariates into account without categorizing them, researchers proceed as follows. First, the expectancy (mean) of the covariate is determined for each cell of the table. Then, the resulting vector of means is inserted into the design matrix of a log-linear model or a CFA base model. This can be done with one or more covariates, degrees of freedom permitting. Each covariate thus represents an investment of one degree of freedom.

The downside of this procedure is obvious. The design matrix, which may have included orthogonal contrast vectors, will no longer be orthogonal. Instead, effect vectors will be correlated. Typically, the mean vectors of several continuous covariates will also be correlated. Thus, the resulting design matrix is nonstandard, and parameter estimates will not be independent.

The procedure of taking categorical covariates into account is routine in CFA applications. Therefore, we focus, in this chapter, on continuous covariates. From the perspective of a CFA user, an important issue concerns the nature of covariates. On the one hand, if the covariates are hypothesized to explain the data, one can first perform a CFA based on the design matrix without the covariates. In a second step, covariates are added to the base model in the first step, and CFA is performed based on the thus extended base model. If the resulting pattern of types and antitypes changes, it must be due to the covariates' main effects, the interactions among the covariates, and the interactions of the covariates with the variables of the original base model.

Let the original base model be $\log \hat{m} = X\lambda$. Then, the extended base model that includes the covariates is

$$\log \hat{m} = X\lambda + C\lambda_c,$$

where X is the design matrix of the original base model and λ is the corresponding parameter vector. X represents the key variables of a study. C is the matrix that contains the mean vectors of the covariates and λ_c the corresponding parameter vector.

On the other hand, if the researchers wish to focus on types and antitypes that emerge solely from the key variables and their interactions but not from the covariates, the associations between covariates and key variables can be taken into account, so that the extended base model becomes

$$\log \hat{m} = X\lambda + C\lambda_c + A\lambda_a,$$

where matrix A contains the vectors for the associations among covariates and key variables, and λ_a is the corresponding parameter vector. Including the matrix A in the base model is conceptually equivalent to adjusting for effects of covariates in the examination of predictor-outcome relationships in variable-oriented research.

Data Example: In the following example, we use data from the Finkelstein et al. (1994) study on the development of aggression in adolescence again. 47 boys and 67 girls in the United Kingdom were asked to respond to an aggression questionnaire in 1983, 1985, and 1987. Their average age in 1983 was 11 years. One of the dimensions of aggression examined in this study was Aggressive Impulses (AI). In the present example, we analyze the development of AI from 1983 to 1987.

In the present analysis, two first differences of AI are calculated ($\Delta_{1,1}$ = Time 2 − Time 1, and $\Delta_{1,2}$ = Time 3 − Time 2) and one second difference ($\Delta_{2,1} = \Delta_{1,2} - \Delta_{1,1}$). Each of these differences is dichotomized into 0-1 scores as described above, with 0 indicating a decrease and 1 indicating an increase in score. Thus, three dichotomous variables result. Crossed, these three variables span a $2 \times 2 \times 2$ contingency table with cell indices 0 0 0, 0 0 1, 0 1 0, 0 1 1, 1 0 0, 1 0 1, 1 1 0, and 1 1 1. Table 3.4 displays this cross-classification for the present data, along with a CFA that takes the two structural zeros in Cells 0 1 0 and 1 0 1 into account (see Chapter 3). For the purposes of the present chapter, we ask whether the progress that the adolescents had made in the stages of physical pubertal development in 1983, that is, at the beginning of the study, measured in units of Tanner scores, allows one to predict the trajectory types found in Table 3.4. If pubertal stage in 1983 is hypothesized to predict the developmental trajectories of aggressive impulses assessed three times from 1983 to 1987, in 2-year intervals, the two types in Table 3.4 disappear. Alternatively, new types or antitypes can emerge, or only one of the two types disappears. Table 4.1 displays the results from Table 3.4 again, in its upper panel. In its lower panel, it shows the results for the base model that includes the average Tanner scores in the design matrix as a covariate.

For the results in the right-hand panel of Table 4.1, a first order CFA was performed that includes the Tanner stage score means in 1983 as a covariate in an additional column vector (see below). The z-test was used, and the Holland-Copenhaver procedure of α protection. For this extended base model, we calculate a value of 1.917 ($df = 1; p = 0.17$). This $LR - X^2$ is so small that it is impossible for types and antitypes to emerge.

TABLE 4.1. CFA of First and Second Differences of Aggressive Impulses, Observed Three Times; Cells 0 1 0 and 1 0 1 Declared Structural Zeros without Covariate (Upper Panel) and with Covariate (Lower Panel)

Configuration $\Delta_{1,1}, \Delta_{1,2}, \Delta_{2,1}$	m	$\hat{m}$	z	p	Type/Antitype
000	20	27.886	−1.4934	.067667	
001	13	17.234	−1.0198	.153910	
010	0	—	—	—	
011	26	13.880	3.2531	.000571	Type
100	36	23.880	2.4801	.006567	Type
101	0	—	—	—	
110	15	19.234	−.9653	.167190	
111	4	11.886	−2.2874	.011085	
000	20	22.212	−.4693	.319445	
001	13	10.788	.6733	.250375	
010	0	—	—	—	
011	26	26.000	.0000	.500000	
100	36	36.000	.0000	.500000	
101	0	—	—	—	
110	15	12.788	.6184	.499993	
111	4	6.212	−.8873	.187445	

Not surprisingly, Table 4.1 (lower panel) shows no type or antitype. Evidently, the residual distribution in the bottom panel of Table 4.1 can be explained by the covariate vector. The design matrix for the extended base model is

$$
X = \begin{pmatrix}
1 & 1 & 1 & 0 & 0 & 1.4 \\
1 & 1 & -1 & 0 & 0 & 1.4 \\
1 & -1 & 1 & 1 & 0 & 0 \\
1 & -1 & -1 & 0 & 0 & 1.8 \\
-1 & 1 & 1 & 0 & 0 & 1.5 \\
-1 & 1 & -1 & 0 & 1 & 0 \\
-1 & -1 & 1 & 0 & 0 & 1.6 \\
-1 & -1 & -1 & 0 & 0 & 1.6
\end{pmatrix}.
$$

In this design matrix, the first two column vectors represent the contrasts for the first differences. The third vector represents the contrast for the second differences.

The following two vectors are used to declare Cells 0 1 0 and 1 0 1 structural zeros. The last vector contains the Tanner score means for each of the eight cells.[1]

One explanation for the disappearance of the two types can be found in the correlation of the covariate with the dependent measure. The last column vector in the extended design matrix correlates with the observed frequencies, m, to $r_{cm} = 0.71$. Even more extreme, the last vector correlates with the $\log m$ vector to $r = 0.90$. Thus, it can be said that physical pubertal development in 1983 is predictive of the developmental trajectory of aggressive impulses over the following 4 years. The smaller part of the variance that physical pubertal development and the frequency vector share is explained by the first five columns of the design matrix. However, the correlation between the last vector in X and the residuals in the left-hand panel of Table 4.1, that is, the correlation $r_{c,m-\hat{m}}$ is still 0.42. Table 4.1 shows that taking this covariation into account makes the two types disappear.

4.2   Chapter Summary

Covariates are variables that are not under control of the experimenter but potentially can help explain the outcome. In CFA, covariates play the role of explaining the pattern of types and antitypes in an analysis. In CFA applications, continuous covariates can be made part of the design matrix. Categorical covariates can be crossed with the variables that are used for CFA. Alternatively, categorical covariates can be used as grouping variables in multi-group designs. Categorical covariates, when used as grouping variables or factors, have the effect that the cross-classification under study becomes larger. The number of cells increases by a factor that is given by the number of categories of the covariate. Therefore, categorical covariates tend to reduce the power of the cell-wise CFA tests.

---

[1]It is important to note that, in the current design matrix, the middle four cells, 0 1 0, 0 1 1, 1 0 0, and 1 0 1, are fully identified under the extended base model, that is, the model that takes the structural zeros into account. Therefore, any entries in the middle for coordinates of the last vector in this design matrix will yield the same results. Readers are invited to try, for example, the column vector 1 1 100 100 100 100 7 7. As far as the other four cells, 1 1 1, 1 1 0, 1 1 0, and 1 1 1, are concerned, the entries used in the last vector will function as an interaction between the first difference scores and the second difference scores. Thus, the continuous covariate, in this example, functions as if it were a categorical covariate. This situation is likely to occur when a table has only a small number of cells and when there are just a few degrees of freedom. Readers are invited to also try the column vector 1 1 0 0 0 0 0 0.

5

Configural Prediction Models

Prediction models, for example, logistic regression, are among the better-known models in the analysis of categorical variables. These models, again, relate variables to one another. In contrast, CFA prediction models, presented in Chapter 5, relate patterns of predictor categories to patterns of criterion categories. Results from logistic regression and Prediction CFA (P-CFA) are not comparable, for two reasons. First, whereas logistic regression operates at the level of variables, P-CFA operates at the level of configurations. Second, in most logistic regression models, higher order interactions among predictors and criteria are set to zero. In contrast, in P-CFA, these interactions can be causes for types and antitypes to emerge. The detailed comparison of logistic regression and P-CFA in Chapter 5 shows that P-CFA base models can be adjusted to yield results that are comparable with those of logistic regression or, in general, logit log-linear models. Models with one or more predictors and one or more criteria are presented and applied. Chapter 5 also presents two new special cases. In the first, models of P-CFA are used to predict the end point of a series. The second special case is that methods of P-CFA are used to predict a trajectory. The base models of P-CFA share two characteristics. First, they are saturated in the predictor variables (all possible relationships among the predictors are taken into account) and they are saturated in the criterion variables. Second, P-CFA base models propose independence of predictors from criteria. Because of these characteristics of P-CFA base models, prediction types and antitypes can emerge only if relationships among predictors and criteria exist, at the level of configurations. Chapter 5 concludes with a discussion of new methods of graphically representing results of P-CFA.

In this chapter, we discuss variable-level and configural prediction models (von Eye, Mair, & Bogat, 2005). We introduce these models by first comparing configural prediction models with models of logistic regression and with standard, continuous-variable ordinary least squares (OLS) regression. Then, we present configural models in more detail.

Variable-oriented prediction models, in the bivariate case, regress one variable, Y, onto another, X. In standard, continuous-variable OLS regression, results are expressed in terms of regression coefficients that indicate the number of steps that are taken on Y after a one-unit step on X. When models from the family of general linear models are used, the model equation is of the form $Y = X\beta + \varepsilon$, where Y is the array of observed scores, X is the design matrix that contains, for instance, the scores on the predictor variables, vector β contains the regression parameters, and ε is the array of residuals. If Y contains the scores of one variable and X contains one predictor, the model is called *simple regression*. If X contains more than one predictor, the model is called *multiple regression*. For example, if Y is regressed on two predictors, X_1 and X_2, the regression model is $Y = \beta + X_1\beta_1 + X_2\beta_2 + \varepsilon$. If Y contains the scores on more than one dependent variable, the model is called *multivariate regression*.

Unless piece-wise regression models are estimated (for sample applications, see von Eye & Schuster, 1998), or the regression model is restricted to be valid for a selected range of scores only, researchers assume that the regression equation is valid over the entire range of admissible scores on X. This issue will be taken up again when we discuss configural mediation models, in Chapter 6.

When the outcome variable is categorical, similar parameters can be estimated. Using the log-linear representation of logistic regression with categorical variables, the general model is, as before, $\log \hat{m} = X\lambda$. If one categorical outcome variable, Y, is regressed onto two categorical predictor variables, X_1 and X_2, the logistic regression model (or logit log-linear model) can be expressed as

$$\log \hat{m} = \lambda + \lambda_i^{X_1} + \lambda_j^{X_2} + \lambda_{ij}^{X_1 X_2} + \lambda_k^{Y} + \lambda_{ik}^{X_1 Y} + \lambda_{jk}^{X_2 Y},$$

where the subscripts index the parameters, and the superscripts indicate the variables using terms of standard log-linear models. Logit log-linear models and logistic regression models are equivalent and are used interchangeably in this chapter. Later, in this chapter, logistic regression models will be discussed in more detail.

The log-linear logistic regression model shown above estimates parameters for each predictor and for each criterion variable. In addition, all interactions among the predictors are estimated as well, and at least all two-way interactions between individual predictors and the criterion. Typically, $(k-1)(l-1)$ parameters are estimated for the interaction between a predictor with k categories and a criterion with l categories. The interpretation of these parameters depends on the definition of the effects in the design matrix. Parameters that are estimated based on effects coding can lead to a different interpretation than when they are estimated based on dummy coding. In contrast, overall model fit does not depend on type of coding.

The *configural approach* differs from both, standard and logistic regression. Specifically, instead of relating variables to one another, the configural approach asks whether particular configurations stand out because they contain more or fewer cases than one would expect under a particular base model. In the present context, this model is a prediction base model. As with all CFA base models, the prediction base model contains only those variable relationships the researcher is not interested in. So, here, the base model contains all relationships that are not part of a prediction. These are (1) all main effects and interactions on the predictor side and (2) all main effects and interactions on the criterion side.

If types or antitypes emerge, the predictive relationship must exist, at least locally, that is, for the configurations that constitute the *prediction types* and the *prediction antitypes*. A prediction type suggests that, given a particular predictor category configuration, a particular criterion category configuration was observed more often than expected. A prediction antitype suggests that, given a particular predictor category configuration, a particular criterion category configuration was observed less often than expected. In brief, instead of interpreting parameters of prediction models, users of CFA interpret the category patterns of those cells that constitute types and antitypes.

In the following sections, various prediction models are introduced and explained, all in comparison to logistic regression models (von Eye & Bogat, 2005; von Eye et al., 2005).

5.1   Logistic Regression and Prediction CFA

In this section, we first review logistic regression. This is followed by a discussion of Prediction CFA (P-CFA).

5.1.1   Logistic Regression

Logistic regression is a method for the prediction of binary outcomes[1] (for overviews, see, e.g., Agresti, 2002; Christensen, 1997, 2005; Lawal, 2003). Examples of such outcomes include political voting (respondent votes vs.

---

[1]In Section 5.1.1, we focus on binary outcome variables. That is, the sole outcome variable has two categories. The arguments used in this chapter apply accordingly when the outcome variable has more than two categories, or when more than one outcome variable is analyzed in the same model.

does not vote), hiring decision (applicant is hired vs. is not hired), and caseness (meeting vs. not meeting criteria for a clinical diagnosis). Now, let the two outcome categories of the criterion variable, Y, be labeled with 1 and 0, with probabilities $Pr(y = 1) = p$ and $Pr(y = 0) = 1 - p$. The odds of being in category $y = 1$ are $p/(1 - p)$. The logarithms of odds are termed *log-odds* or *logits*, $\log(p/(1 - p))$.

Now, in logistic regression, one predicts the logits from one or more predictors. A linear model of the log odds can be expressed as

$$\log\left(\frac{p}{1 - p}\right) = \beta_0 + \sum_{k=1}^{K-1} \beta_k x_k,$$

where K is the number of parameters and x_k is the kth design matrix vector. This is a straightforward extension of OLS regression and represents a generalized linear model with a logit link function. The probabilities are, then, estimated to be

$$p = \frac{exp(\beta_0 + \sum_{k=1}^{K-1} \beta_k x_k)}{1 + exp(\beta_0 + \sum_{k=1}^{K-1} \beta_k x_k)},$$

and

$$1 - p = \frac{1}{1 + exp(\beta_0 + \sum_{k=1}^{K-1} \beta_k x_k)}.$$

In practice, most logistic regression models can be estimated by using either analytic modules for logistic regression or log-linear modeling. The advantage of log-linear models lies in their generality. Every logistic regression model can equivalently be expressed in terms of log-linear models. However, log-linear models are more flexible than logistic regression models in terms of specifying the relationships between predictors and outcome variables.

Table 5.1 presents sample models in the log-linear bracket notation, in the logit model notation, and using the shorthand logit symbol. In the table, the variables X and Z are the predictors, and the variable Y is the criterion.

The first model in Table 5.1 proposes that (1) the criterion is unrelated to the two predictors, X and Z, and (2) the two predictors are associated with each other. A violation of this model would indicate that the predictors are related to the criterion. P-CFA, which will be elaborated below, can use this model as a base model. It is important to note that each of the models in Table 5.1 contains the association between the predictors, X and Z. The association between predictors is not part of a standard regression model in the context of the General Linear Model.

TABLE 5.1. Logistic Regression (Logit) and Log-Linear Models for the Predictors, X and Z, and the Criterion Variable, Y

Log-Linear Bracket Notation[a]	Logistic Regression (Logit Model)	Logit Symbol
Model 1: $[Y]$, $[XZ]$	β_0	$(-)$
Model 2: $[XY]$, $[XZ]$	$\beta_0 + \lambda_i^X$	(X)
Model 3: $[YZ]$, $[XZ]$	$\beta_0 + \lambda_k^Z$	(Z)
Model 4: $[XY]$, $[YZ]$, $[XZ]$	$\beta_0 + \lambda_i^X + \lambda_k^Z$	$(X + Z)$
Model 5: $[XYZ]$	$\beta_0 + \lambda_i^X + \lambda_k^Z + \lambda_{ik}^{XZ}$	$(X * Z)$

[a]Throughout this text, the bracket notation for interactions, for example, $[X, Y, Z]$ or $[XYZ]$, and the ANOVA-like notation, $X \times Y \times Z$, are used interchangeably.

The second model proposes that (1) Predictor X is associated with the criterion, Y, (2) Predictor Z is unrelated to the criterion, and (3) the two predictors are associated with each other. The third model proposes that (1) only the second predictor, Z, is associated with Y, (2) the first predictor, X, is unrelated to the criterion, and (3) the two predictors are associated with each other. Models 2 and 3 can also be used as base models for P-CFA (this is illustrated in Chapter 6, on mediation analysis).

The fourth model proposes that each of the predictors, X and Z, is associated with the criterion, and (2) the two predictors are associated with each other. The fifth model in Table 5.1 proposes that, in addition to the propositions made by Model 4, the triple interaction between the two predictors and the criterion exists, thus proposing, for example, that the relationship between X and Y varies with the categories of Z (that is, an interaction of XZ with Y). Unless constraints are placed on parameters, this model is fully saturated. As such, it has no degrees of freedom left and model fit is perfect (and not testable). Therefore, Model 5 is not a suitable base model for P-CFA because it takes all possible predictor-criterion relationships into account. In contrast, Model 4 can be used for P-CFA if the hypothesis is entertained that prediction types and antitypes are based on the triple interaction $[X, Y, Z]$ (see the discussion of Figure 5.1).

The log-linear model that is equivalent to a standard logistic regression model contains the following terms:

1. the main effect of the dependent variable;

2. the main effects of all independent variables;

3. the two-way interactions of all independent variables with the dependent variable; and

TABLE 5.2. Observed and Expected Frequencies for the Logistic Regression of Penalty (*P*) on Race of Victim (*V*) and Race of Defendant (*D*)

Configuration VDP[a]	Observed	Estimated	Std. Res.
1 1 1	593	592.416	0.024
1 1 2	14	14.584	−0.153
1 2 1	284	284.585	−0.035
1 2 2	38	37.416	0.095
2 1 1	25	25.584	−0.115
2 1 2	1	0.416	0.905
2 2 1	272	271.415	0.035
2 2 2	23	23.584	−0.120

[a]Penalty (*P*: 1 = no death penalty; 2 = death penalty), Race of Victim (*V*: 1 = black; 2 = white), and Race of Defendant (*D*: 1 = black; 2 = white).

4. all interactions among the independent variables. These terms are included because the model makes no assumptions about the relationships among the independent variables. The model is, thus, saturated in the predictors.

5. (if desired) three- and higher-way interactions between two or more predictors and the sole dependent variable, *X*.

Based on this definition and the examples in Table 5.1, the log-linear model specification for the dependent variable, *Y*, and the *K* independent variables, X_i, for $i = 1, \ldots, K$, is

$$\log \hat{m} = \lambda_0 + \lambda^Y + \sum_{i=1}^{K} \lambda_i^{X_i} + \sum_{i=1}^{K} \lambda_i^{YX_i} + \sum_{i<j} \lambda_{ij}^{YX_iX_j} + \cdots + \sum_{i,j,\ldots,K} \lambda_{i,j,\ldots,K'}^{X_iX_j\ldots}$$

with $i \neq j$, where the λ terms refer to all parameters that are estimated for a model term. Analogous models can be specified for the case in which more than one criterion variable is modeled simultaneously. In many cases, researchers set those terms to zero in which the interactions of predictors are related to the criterion.

Results of logistic regression are interpreted, using information from R^2 equivalents, odds ratios, confidence intervals of parameter estimates, goodness-of-fit and lack-of-fit tests, and significance tests of the effects of individual predictor variables (parameters).

Data Example 1: The following data example presents a reanalysis of the data that were published by the *New York Times* on January 8, 2003. For

1,311 murder cases in Maryland that were recorded from 1978 to 1999, the relationships among Race of Victim (V), Race of Defendant (D), and Penalty (P) were examined. The two race variables were coded as 1 = black and 2 = white; the penalty variable was coded as 1 = no death penalty issued and 2 = death penalty issued. In the following analysis, we use logistic regression to determine whether the two race variables allow one to predict penalty. The log-linear model that corresponds to the logistic regression model in which P is predicted from D and V is

$$\log \hat{m} = \lambda_0 + \lambda^P + \lambda^D + \lambda^V + \lambda^{DP} + \lambda^{VP} + \lambda^{DV}.$$

The equivalent logit (logistic regression) model is $\lambda_0 + \lambda^P + \lambda^D + \lambda^V$. Including the three-way interaction, $P \times D \times V$, would have resulted in a saturated model. Using the ℓEM software package (Vermunt, 1997), the results shown in Tables 5.2 and 5.3 were created. Table 5.2 shows, from left to right, the labels for the patterns; the observed cell frequencies; the expected cell frequencies from the above logistic regression model; and the standardized residuals, which are defined as

$$\text{std. res.} = \frac{\text{observed} - \text{estimated}}{\sqrt{\text{estimated}}}.$$

The overall goodness-of-fit of the logistic regression model is excellent, with $LR - X^2 = 0.65$ ($df = 1$; $p = 0.42$). The parameter estimates are summarized in Table 5.3.

The tests of the main effect parameters do not need to be interpreted in detail. The reason for this is that, in log-linear models, lower order terms are of lesser interest when higher order terms are significant. In the present model, two of the three two-way interactions are significant. The first of these, $[V, D]$, indicates that the victim and the defendant are more likely to be of the same race. This result may be interesting in itself. However, it is not of critical importance for the question asked with the logistic regression model, that is, the question concerning the prediction of penalty from race of victim and race of defendant.

The more interesting results can be found in the bottom two rows of Table 5.3. We find that race of defendant, but not race of victim, is statistically significantly related to penalty. This result contradicts the main conclusion proposed by the *New York Times*. According to this conclusion, victim's race is pivotal to the death penalty (2003, p. A12). In the next section, we ask whether P-CFA can shed additional light on these data.

5.1.2   Prediction CFA

In this section, we first cover models that include one criterion variable. We then move to models with multiple criterion variables.

TABLE 5.3. Log-linear Parameter Estimates for the $[VD]$, $[VP]$, $[DP]$ Model for the Data in Table 5.2

Label	Parameter Estimate	se	z^a
Constant (Threshold)	3.68		
Race of Victim (V)	.90	.08	11.11*
Race of Defendant (D)	−.83	.09	−9.14*
Penalty (P)	1.54	.08	18.44*
$V \times D$	.77	.05	14.26*
$V \times P$	−.10	.07	−1.52
$D \times P$	.42	.08	5.39*

^{a} *$p < 0.05$.

P-CFA with One Criterion Variable

In contrast to logistic regression, Prediction CFA (P-CFA) aims at identifying those cells of a cross-classification that stand out because they contradict a base model. The base model needs to be specified such that the cells that stand out (outlandish cells) can be interpreted as intended. When applying P-CFA, researchers are interested in relationships among predictors and criteria, at the level of individual categories. Therefore, the P-CFA base model is specified as follows. P-CFA base models

1. are saturated in the predictors; and

2. are saturated in the criteria; but they propose

3. independence of criteria and predictors.

In different words, a P-CFA base model takes all possible effects into account except those that relate predictors to criteria. If this model is contradicted, predictor-criteria relationships must exist. P-CFA identifies those configurations that carry predictor-criterion relationships.

   Consider again the death penalty data example used in the last section. In this example, Penalty (P) was predicted from Race of Defendant (D) and Race of Victim (V). Logistic regression suggested that Race of Defendant is a significant predictor, but Race of Victim is not. The log-linear model used for logistic regression was

$$\log \hat{m} = \lambda_0 + \lambda^P + \lambda^D + \lambda^V + \lambda^{DP} + \lambda^{VP} + \lambda^{DV}.$$

In contrast, the log-linear base model used for P-CFA is

$$\log \hat{m} = \lambda_0 + \lambda^P + \lambda^D + \lambda^V + \lambda^{DV}.$$

TABLE 5.4. Design Matrix for Saturated Model of the Cross-Classification of the Variables D, V, and P (Effect Coding); Column for Constant Is Implied

D	V	P	$D \times V$	$D \times P$	$V \times P$	$D \times V \times P$
1	1	1	1	1	1	1
1	1	-1	1	-1	-1	-1
1	-1	1	-1	1	-1	-1
1	-1	-1	-1	-1	1	1
-1	1	1	-1	-1	1	-1
-1	1	-1	-1	1	-1	1
-1	-1	1	1	-1	-1	1
-1	-1	-1	1	1	1	-1

The possible terms that are omitted in this base model are, in bracket notation, $[D, P]$, $[V, P]$, and $[D, V, P]$. Each of these three terms contains the criterion variable, P, and at least one of the predictors. Therefore, if cells in the P-CFA of the data in Table 5.2 emerge as constituting types or antitypes, they suggest that D, V, or both are related to P, and they can be interpreted as prediction types and prediction antitypes.

To explain the difference between logistic regression and P-CFA in more detail, consider the design matrix of the saturated log-linear model of the three dichotomous variables, D, V, and P, in Table 5.4.

The last three columns in Table 5.4 are not part of the base model of P-CFA. These are the columns for the effects that relate the criterion variable, P, to the predictors, D and V, and the interaction between D and V. The last column indicates the three-way interaction. This column is not part of the logistic regression model or the P-CFA base model. In logistic regression, the highest order interaction is typically set to zero. It implies interactions between the predictors and the criterion. Unless the log-linear logistic regression model is nonhierarchical, including this interaction in the model results in a saturated model. In P-CFA, this interaction is not part of the base model because it is part of the effects that can lead to types and antitypes. The columns for the effects of $D \times P$ and $V \times P$ are part of the logistic regression model.

Prediction types and antitypes from P-CFA suggest that predictor-criterion interactions exist, at the level of individual configurations. The topic of comparing logistic regression with P-CFA is taken up again in the context of Table 5.8 and in Sections 5.1.3 and 6.1.

In the following paragraphs, we use the death penalty data again and illustrate the application of CFA. Two base models of CFA will be computed. The first is that of standard, first order CFA, that is, the base model of variable independence. The model contains the effects that are specified in

TABLE 5.5. First Order CFA of the Maryland Death Penalty Data

Configuration DVP	m	$\hat{m}$	z	p	Type/Antitype
111	593	441.843	7.1911	.000000	Type
112	14	28.603	−2.7305	.003162	Antitype
121	284	430.674	−7.0677	.000000	Antitype
122	38	27.880	1.9166	.027645	Type
211	25	152.671	−10.3327	.000000	Antitype
212	1	9.883	−2.8257	.002359	Antitype
221	272	148.812	10.0983	.000000	Type
222	23	9.633	4.3065	.000008	Type

the first three columns of the design matrix in Table 5.4.

The second base model is that of P-CFA. The model includes the first four columns of this design matrix. The results from the first order CFA base model are summarized in Table 5.5. The z-test and the Holland-Copenhaver procedure of α protection were used. The overall $LR - X^2$ of 389.10 ($df = 4$; $p < 0.01$) suggests that large discrepancies exist, and we expect types and antitypes to emerge.

The results in Table 5.5 suggest that each cell constitutes either a type or an antitype. Instead of interpreting these four types and four antitypes in detail, we now ask whether the data reflect a predictor-criterion relationship. The P-CFA base model that allows one to answer this question is

$$\log \hat{m} = \lambda_0 + \lambda^P + \lambda^D + \lambda^V + \lambda^{DV}.$$

This model is saturated in the predictors (interaction $[D, V]$), and can be contradicted only if one or more of the interactions $[D, P]$, $[V, P]$, and $[D, V, P]$ exist. Table 5.6 summarizes results.

As for first order CFA, the z test and the Holland-Copenhaver procedure were used. The overall $LR - X^2$ of 35.95 ($df = 3$; $p < 0.01$) is significantly below the one from first order CFA. However, it still indicates that model-data discrepancies exist. Therefore, we again expect types and antitypes to emerge. P-CFA yields one antitype and one type. The antitype suggests that it can be predicted, for black defendants who are accused of having murdered a black victim, that it is less likely than chance that the death penalty will be issued. In contrast, the type suggests that it can be predicted, for black defendants who are accused of having murdered a white victim, that it is more likely than chance that the death penalty will be issued. None of the remaining configurations reflects a significant predictor-criterion relationship. These results suggest that race of victim

TABLE 5.6. P-CFA of the $D \times V \times P$ Cross-Classification

Configuration DVP	m	$\hat{m}$	z	p	Type/Antitype
111	593	570.094	.9593	.168696	
112	14	36.906	−3.7705	.000081	Antitype
121	284	302.422	−1.0593	.144720	
122	38	19.578	4.1636	.000016	Type
211	25	24.419	.1175	.453219	
212	1	1.581	−.4619	.322061	
221	272	277.064	−.3042	.380476	
222	23	17.936	1.1957	.115902	

is of importance, thus partially supporting the headline of the *New York Times* article, according to which "death penalty found more likely when victim is white" (2003, p. A12). However, based on the present analysis, this conclusion seems to apply only if the defendant is black. When the defendant is white, no configuration contradicts the assumption of independence between the two predictors and the criterion.

From this result, we conclude that the interaction between D and V explains a large part of the deviation from independence in Table 5.5. The remaining two outlandish cells are the only indicators of the predictive relations in the $D \times V \times P$ cross-classification.

It is interesting to note that neither the logistic regression model nor the P-CFA base model include the three-way interaction, $D \times V \times P$. Including this term in the logistic regression model leads to a saturated model. Still, it can be tested whether the parameter for this interaction is significant. The software package ℓEM calculates 0.14 for the parameter, 0.90 for its standard error, and 0.82 for z. This result indicates that the three-way interaction is not significant ($p = 0.37$). We thus conclude that the interaction between race of defendant and race of victim does not help one predict who is more likely to be issued the death penalty.

To probe further whether the weak three-way interaction has any effect on the results of P-CFA, we run the model again. However, this time, we add the three-way interaction to the base model. The new model is

$$\log \hat{m} = \lambda_0 + \lambda^P + \lambda^D + \lambda^V + \lambda^{DV} + \lambda^{DVP}.$$

This model is nonhierarchical (see Mair & von Eye, 2007) because it sets the parameters of the interactions $[D, P]$ and $[V, P]$ to zero. This model can be contradicted only if one or both of these two-way interactions exist. Table 5.7 displays the results of this constrained P-CFA model (we call it constrained because the number of effects is reduced that can cause

TABLE 5.7. Constrained P-CFA of the $D \times V \times P$ Cross-Classification

Configuration DVP	m	$\hat{m}$	z	p	Type/Antitype
111	593	582.101	.4517	.325727	
112	14	24.899	−2.1842	.014472	
121	284	285.914	−.1132	.454943	
122	38	36.086	.3186	.375021	
211	25	23.086	.3983	.345202	
212	1	2.914	−1.1212	.131111	
221	272	282.899	−.6480	.258492	
222	23	12.101	3.1332	.000865	Type

types and antitypes). The z-test and the Holland-Copenhaver procedure were used again. The overall $LR - X^2$ of 16.00 ($df = 2$; $p < 0.01$) for the constrained P-CFA base model is significantly below the one for the unconstrained P-CFA base model shown in Table 5.6. We thus know that the three-way interaction does explain a significant portion of the variation in the table, when the two-way interactions D × P and V × P are not taken into account. The type-antitype pattern is, therefore, bound to change.

Taking into account the three-way interaction $D \times V \times P$ in a non-hierarchical P-CFA base model results in just one type. This type suggests that if both the defendant and the victim are white, the death penalty is issued with greater probability than expected. This result differs strongly from the one from a P-CFA in which none of the predictor-criterion interactions is taken into account, in Table 5.6. Researchers will have to make a decision as to which of the results, the one in Table 5.6 or the one in Table 5.7, to retain. We see no reason why, in the present example, the three-way interaction should be excluded from causing types and antitypes to emerge. We, therefore, retain the results from Table 5.6. Note that the results in Tables 5.6 and 5.7 both contradict the conclusion published in the *New York Times* (2003).

Alternative Configural Prediction Models

We now introduce and compare alternative P-CFA base models. For the sake of simplicity, we use the case of two predictors and one criterion again. Let $P1$ and $P2$ be the predictors, and C the criterion. Then, four base models of P-CFA can be depicted as in Figure 5.1 (von Eye et al., 2005).

The P-CFA base model in the left panel of Figure 5.1 is that of standard P-CFA. It includes the smallest number of model terms and is, therefore, the most likely to yield types and antitypes. Specifically, it only includes

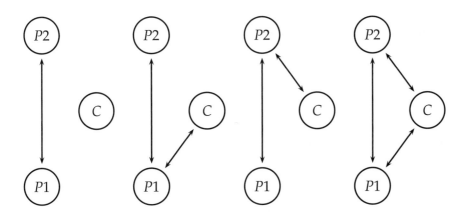

FIGURE 5.1. Four P-CFA base models.

the main effects of all variables as well as the interaction between the two predictors. A sample application of this model was given in Table 5.6. The associations among the predictors and the criterion are not taken into account. Therefore, this model can be contradicted in the form of types and antitypes only if predictor-criterion relationships exist. These relationships can be of any order. This model is parallel to the one that includes all vectors in the left panel of the design matrix in Table 5.4.

The P-CFA base model in the second panel of Figure 5.1 adds the interaction between $P1$ and C to the first base model. This model can be contradicted only if (1) the association between the first predictor, $P1$, and the criterion, (2) the three-way interaction, or (3) both exist. This model is parallel to the one that includes all vectors in the left panel and the first vector in the right panel of the design matrix in Table 5.4. Similarly, the base model in the third panel can be contradicted only if (1) the interaction between the second predictor, $P2$, and the criterion, (2) the three-way interaction, or (3) both exist. This model is parallel to the one that includes all vectors in the left panel and the second vector in the right panel of the design matrix in Table 5.4. Finally, the last panel of Figure 5.1 depicts the P-CFA base model that contains all two-way interactions. Under this model, types and antitypes can emerge only if the three-way interaction among the three variables $P1$, $P2$, and C exists. This model can be called the second order P-CFA base model. This model is parallel to the one that includes all vectors in the left panel and the first two vectors in the right panel of the design matrix in Table 5.4. With the exception of the standard P-CFA model in the first panel of Figure 5.1, none of these prediction models has been discussed in the CFA literature thus far.

TABLE 5.8. A Comparison of Logistic Regression Models and P-CFA Base Models for the Two Predictors, $P1$ and $P2$, and the Criterion, C

Logistic Regression Model		P-CFA Base Model in Log-Linear Notation	Optional Term for P-CFA Base Model
Logit Notation	Log-Linear Notation		
$\beta_0 + \beta_1 P1$	$[P1][P2][C]$ $[P1, C]$	$[P1][P2][C]$ $[P1, P2][P2, C]$	$[P1, P2, C]$
$\beta_0 + \beta_2 P2$	$[P1][P2][C]$ $[P2, C]$	$[P1][P2][C]$ $[P1, P2][P1, C]$	$[P1, P2, C]$
$\beta_0 + \beta_1 P1 + \beta_2 P2$	$[P1][P2][C]$ $[P1, P2][P1, C]$ $[P2, C]$	$[P1, P2, C]$ $[P1, P2]$	$[P1, P2, C]$
$\beta_0 + \beta_1 P1 + \beta_2 P2 + \beta_3(P1, P2)$	$[P1][P2][C]$ $[P1, P2][P1, C]$ $[P2, C][P1, P2, C]$	$[P1, P2, C]$ $[P1, P2]$	

Table 5.8 contains a comparison of logistic regression models and P-CFA base models. All of the models depicted in Figure 5.1 are included. Not all of the models are hierarchical. This applies in particular to the P-CFA base models that contain the additional, optional term (see the last column of the table). This term is part of the base model if only the lower order interactions among the predictors and the criterion are of interest. It is important to realize that the log-linear regression models are specified with the goal of model fit. In contrast, the CFA base models are specified under the expectation that they will be rejected. Rejection of a properly defined CFA base model implies that the effects of interest exist.

One may ask when a researcher would apply the base models that are shown in the second, third, and fourth panels of Figure 5.1 (these are the first, second, and third models in Table 5.8, respectively). There are two reasons for applying these base models. First, these models can be used to assess the relative importance of individual predictor-criterion relationships. In most CFA applications, this importance is not expressed in terms of magnitude of parameters or in terms of significance of parameters. Instead, it is expressed in terms of types and antitypes that emerge or disappear when a particular effect is added to a base model, or removed from it. Second, these models are of importance in the context of testing configural mediation hypotheses. This issue will be discussed in detail in Chapter 6. The issue of comparing the models of logistic regression and P-CFA is taken up again in Section 5.1.3.

TABLE 5.9. Design Matrix for the Saturated Model for the $P \times C1 \times C2$ Cross-Classification (Constant Vector Implied)

P	$C1$	$C2$	$P \times C1$	$P \times C2$	$C1 \times C2$	$P \times C1 \times C2$
1	1	1	1	1	1	1
1	1	-1	1	-1	-1	-1
1	-1	1	-1	1	-1	-1
1	-1	-1	-1	-1	1	1
-1	1	1	-1	-1	1	-1
-1	1	-1	-1	1	-1	1
-1	-1	1	1	-1	-1	1
-1	-1	-1	1	1	1	-1

P-CFA with Multiple Criterion Variables and Multiple Predictors

In most empirical data analyses, more than one predictor and more than one criterion are analyzed simultaneously. For instance, one can ask whether gender and SES predict employment status and income bracket. For this kind of design, P-CFA base models can also be specified. In addition, the definition of a base model for P-CFA that was given earlier applies here without change. That is, the P-CFA base model is saturated in the predictors, saturated in the criteria, and proposes independence between predictors and criteria. We now give two examples of P-CFA with multiple criteria.

One Predictor, Multiple Criterion Variables: In the first example with multiple criterion variables, we specify the base model for one predictor, P, and the criterion variables, C1 and C2 (all three variables dichotomous). The design matrix for the saturated model for the $P \times C1 \times C2$ cross-classification appears in Table 5.9.

The P-CFA base model for the $P \times C1 \times C2$ cross-classification is, according to the above definition,

$$\log \hat{m} = \lambda + \lambda^P + \lambda^{C1} + \lambda^{C2} + \lambda^{C1,C2},$$

where the single superscripts indicate main effects, and the double superscript indicates a two-way interaction. The corresponding vectors can be found in the first, second, third, and sixth columns in Table 5.9. This model contains none of the terms that would relate the predictor, P, to the criteria, C1, and C2. These are the terms $\lambda^{P,C1}$, $\lambda^{P,C2}$, and $\lambda^{P,C1,C2}$. These are also the only terms that could possibly be included in addition to the base model. Therefore, as is the case in all P-CFA base models, prediction types and antitypes can emerge only if predictor-criterion relationships exist.

Alternative models are conceivable. For example, if researchers are

TABLE 5.10. Design Matrix for the Saturated Model for the $P1 \times P2 \times C1 \times C2$ Cross-Classification (Constant Vector Implied)

Main Effects				2-Way Interactions						3-Way Interactions				4-Way Int.[a]
1	1	1	1	1	1	1	1	1	1	1	1	1	1	1
1	1	1	-1	1	1	-1	1	-1	-1	1	-1	-1	-1	-1
1	1	-1	1	1	-1	1	-1	1	-1	-1	1	-1	-1	-1
1	1	-1	-1	1	-1	-1	-1	-1	1	-1	-1	1	1	1
1	-1	1	1	-1	1	1	-1	-1	1	-1	-1	1	-1	-1
1	-1	1	-1	-1	1	-1	-1	1	-1	-1	1	-1	1	1
1	-1	-1	1	-1	-1	1	1	-1	-1	1	-1	-1	1	1
1	-1	-1	-1	-1	-1	-1	1	1	1	1	1	1	-1	-1
-1	1	1	1	-1	-1	-1	1	1	1	-1	-1	-1	1	-1
-1	1	1	-1	-1	-1	1	1	-1	-1	-1	1	1	-1	1
-1	1	-1	1	-1	1	-1	-1	1	-1	1	-1	1	-1	1
-1	1	-1	-1	-1	1	1	-1	-1	1	1	1	-1	1	-1
-1	-1	1	1	1	-1	-1	-1	-1	1	1	1	-1	-1	1
-1	-1	1	-1	1	-1	1	-1	1	-1	1	-1	1	1	-1
-1	-1	-1	1	1	1	-1	1	-1	-1	-1	1	1	1	-1
-1	-1	-1	-1	1	1	1	1	1	1	-1	-1	-1	-1	1

[a]The order of the effects is: $P1$, $P2$, $C1$, $C2$, $P1 \times P2$, $P1 \times C1$, $P1 \times C2$, $P2 \times C1$, $P2 \times C2$, $C1 \times C2$, $P1 \times P2 \times C1$, $P1 \times P2 \times C2$, $P1 \times C1 \times C2$, $P2 \times C1 \times C2$, $P1 \times P2 \times C1 \times C2$

interested only in predictor-criterion relationships that manifest at the level of one-way interaction, the higher order interactions must be included in the base model. In the present example, the P-CFA base model then becomes nonhierarchical, and is

$$\log \hat{m} = \lambda + \lambda^P + \lambda^{C1} + \lambda^{C2} + \lambda^{C1,C2} + \lambda^{P,C1,C2},$$

thus omitting only the terms $\lambda^{P,C1}$ and $\lambda^{P,C2}$ from the saturated model. Types and antitypes can then emerge only if one or both of these effects exist.

Two Predictors, Two Criterion Variables: In the second example with multiple criterion variables, we specify the base model for two predictors, $P1$ and $P2$, and two criteria, $C1$ and $C2$ (all four variables dichotomous). The design matrix for the saturated model for the $P1 \times P2 \times C1 \times C2$ cross-classification appears in Table 5.10.

The standard P-CFA base model for the $P1 \times P2 \times C1 \times C2$ cross-classification is, according to the above definition of P-CFA base models,

$$\log \hat{m} = \lambda + \lambda_i^{P1} + \lambda_j^{P2} + \lambda_k^{C1} + \lambda_l^{C2} + \lambda_{ij}^{P1,P2} + \lambda_{kl}^{C1,C2}.$$

The design matrix vectors for this model can be found in the columns for the four main effects in Table 5.10, and in the first and the last columns among the two-way interaction terms. None of the terms that link predictors and criteria is included in this model. These are the interactions $[P1, C1]$, $[P1, C2]$, $[P2, C1]$, $[P2, C2]$, $[P1, P2, C1]$, $[P1, P2, C2]$, $[P1, C1, C2]$, $[P2, C1, C2]$, and $[P1, P2, C1, C2]$, that is, all interactions not included in the P-CFA base model.

Alternative models can be specified as indicated in Figure 5.1. If researchers are interested only in predictor-criterion relationships at the level of two-way interactions, all three-way and higher order interactions must be included in the base model. Types and antitypes can then emerge only if two-way interactions exist.

Data Example 2: One Predictor, Two Criterion Variables: The following example uses data from a longitudinal project on intimate partner violence (Bogat, Levendosky, von Eye, & Davidson, 2006). A sample of 204 women responded, in yearly intervals, to questions concerning the frequency with which they suffered violence perpetrated by intimate partners. In addition, they filled out a questionnaire that was administered to assess the degree to which they showed symptoms of posttraumatic stress disorder (PTSD scale for battered women; Saunders, 1994). 62% of the respondents were Caucasian, 25% African American, and 13% of other or mixed racial backgrounds. At the beginning of the study, the women were, on average, 27 years of age.

For the following analyses, we use the information regarding violence assessed at the first wave and PTSD assessed at the second and third observation points. We ask whether initial violence allows one to predict PTSD 1 and 2 years later. Violence was scored as 1 = did not experience violence and 2 = did experience violence. PTSD was scored as 1 = symptoms below the clinical cutoff and 2 = symptoms above the clinical cutoff. The questions concerning both violence and PTSD were formulated such that they covered the period since the interview, that is, the year before the interview. In the following sections, we abbreviate violence as V, PTSD at Time 2 as $P2$, and PTSD at Time 3 as $P3$.

In a first analysis, we perform a standard, first order CFA. The base model for this analysis is

$$\log \hat{m} = \lambda + \lambda^V + \lambda^{P2} + \lambda^{P3},$$

where the superscripts indicate the variables whose main effects are part of the base model. For the CFA, the z-test and the Holland-Copenhaver procedure of α protection were used. Table 5.11, with violence at Time 1 (V: 1 = did not experience intimate partner violence; 2 = did experience

TABLE 5.11. First Order CFA of Violence at Time 1 (V) × PTSD at Time 2 ($P2$) × PTSD at Time 3 ($P3$) Cross-Classification

Configuration $VP2P3$	m	$\hat{m}$	z	p	Type/Antitype
111	65	27.663	7.0990	.000000	Type
112	3	10.989	−2.4100	.007976	Antitype
121	12	31.739	−3.5037	.000229	Antitype
122	3	12.609	−2.7060	.003405	Antitype
211	20	40.328	−3.2010	.000685	Antitype
212	7	16.021	−2.2537	.012108	Antitype
221	49	46.271	.4013	.344114	
222	45	18.381	6.2086	.000000	Type

violence), and PTSD at Times 2 and 3 ($P2$ and $P3$: 1 = PTSD symptoms below clinical cutoff; 2 = PTSD symptoms above clinical cutoff), presents results. The goodness-of-fit of the base model is poor ($LR - X^2 = 117.86$; $df = 4$; $p < 0.01$). We thus expect types and antitypes to emerge.

The results in Table 5.11 show that, with only one exception, each configuration constitutes a type or an antitype. Instead of interpreting each of these in detail, we ask whether the association between the two criterion variables, $P2$ and $P3$, accounts for a portion of these deviations from independence. To answer this question, we add the interaction between these two variables to the main effect model. The resulting base model is that of a P-CFA with one predictor and two criteria,

$$\log \hat{m} = \lambda + \lambda^V + \lambda^{P2} + \lambda^{P3} + \lambda^{P2,P3},$$

where the double-superscripted term indicates the interaction that is now part of the base model. For the following P-CFA, we used the z-test and the Holland-Copenhaver procedure again.

For this base model, we calculated the $LR - X^2 = 87.78$ ($df = 3$; $p < 0.01$). This model is significantly better than the base model for the first order CFA in Table 5.11 ($\Delta LR - X^2 = 30.08$; $\Delta df = 1$; $p < 0.01$). Still, it must be rejected, and we can expect types and antitypes to emerge. P-CFA results appear in Table 5.12.

The first prediction type (constituted by Configuration 1 1 1) suggests that more women than expected can be predicted to show, 1 and 2 years later, PTSD symptoms below the clinical cutoff when they were not exposed to intimate partner violence during the first observation period. The following two antitypes (constituted by Configurations 1 2 1 and 1 2 2) suggest that women were less likely than expected to show PTSD symptoms in the clinical range during the second observation period or during both

TABLE 5.12. First Order CFA of Violence at Time 1 (V) × PTSD at Time 2 ($P2$) × PTSD at Time 3 ($P3$) Cross-Classification

Configuration $VP2P3$	m	$\hat{m}$	z	p	Type/Antitype
111	65	34.583	5.1722	.000000	Type
112	3	4.069	−.5298	.298129	
121	12	24.819	−2.5731	.005040	Antitype
122	3	19.529	−3.7404	.000092	Antitype
211	20	50.417	−4.2838	.000009	Antitype
212	7	5.931	.4388	.330410	
221	49	36.181	2.1311	.016541	Type
222	45	28.471	3.0978	.000975	Type

years when they were not exposed to intimate partner violence during the first observation period. The third antitype (Configuration 2 1 1) suggests that victims of intimate partner violence are less likely than expected to show below clinical level PTSD symptoms both 1 and 2 years later. The second and the third types (Configurations 2 2 1 and 2 2 2) suggest that violence during the first observation period allows one to predict above clinical level PTSD symptoms in victims either 1 year later or both 1 and 2 years later.

Data Example 3: Two Predictors, Two Criterion Variables: In the following example, we illustrate multiple, multivariate P-CFA with two predictors and two criterion variables. We use data from the intimate partner violence project again. Specifically, we use severe violence from Time 1 ($V1$) and Time 2 ($V2$), and PTSD from Time 2 ($P2$) and Time 3 ($P3$). The cross-classification $V1 \times V2 \times P2 \times P3$ is analyzed under the P-CFA base model

$$\log \hat{m} = \lambda + \lambda^{V1} + \lambda^{V2} + \lambda^{V1,V2} + \lambda^{P2} + \lambda^{P3} + \lambda^{P2,P3},$$

where the double-superscripted terms indicate two-way interactions. For P-CFA, we use the z-test again along with the Holland-Copenhaver procedure.

For the P-CFA base model, we calculate the $LR - X^2 = 114.5$ ($df = 9$; $p < 0.01$). The model is thus rejected, and we can expect types and antitypes to emerge. P-CFA results appear in Table 5.13. The predictors are Violence at Time 1 and Time 2 ($V1$ and $V2$: 1 = did not experience intimate partner violence; 2 = did experience violence), and the criteria are PTSD at Times 2 and 3 ($P2$ and $P3$: 1 = PTSD symptoms below clinical cutoff; 2 = PTSD symptoms above clinical cutoff)

TABLE 5.13. Multivariate P-CFA of the Predictors, Violence at Time 1 ($V1$) and Time 2 ($V2$), and the Criteria, PTSD at Time 2 ($P2$) and Time 3 ($P3$)

Configuration $V1V2P2P3$	m	$\hat{m}$	z	p	Type/Antitype
1111	82	62.083	2.5277	.005740	
1112	7	7.304	−.1125	.455231	
1121	47	44.554	.3665	.357011	
1122	13	35.059	−3.7255	.000097	Antitype
1211	3	7.083	−1.5342	.062484	
1212	3	.833	2.3735	.008811	
1221	0	5.083	−2.2546	.012078	
1222	11	4.000	3.5000	.000233	Type
2111	0	7.917	−2.8137	.002449	Antitype
2112	0	.931	−.9651	.167253	
2121	12	5.681	2.6509	.004014	Type
2122	7	4.471	1.1963	.115791	
2211	0	7.917	−2.8137	.002449	Antitype
2212	0	.931	−.9651	.167253	
2221	2	5.681	−1.5445	.061236	
2222	17	4.471	5.9258	.000000	Type

Table 5.13 shows three prediction types and three prediction antitypes. The first antitype is constituted by Configuration 1 1 2 2. It indicates that it is very unlikely that women who do not experience severe violence during either observation period suffer from PTSD symptoms in the clinical range during both observation years. The first prediction type (constituted by Configuration 1 2 2 2) indicates that women who did not experience violence initially but experienced severe violence at Time 2 can be predicted to report PTSD symptoms in the clinical range for both observation periods. In contrast, women who experienced severe violence at Time 1 or both Times 1 and 2 are very unlikely to report PTSD symptoms below the clinical cutoff at Times 2 and 3 (Antitypes 2 1 1 1 and 2 2 1 1). The next type (constituted by Configuration 2 1 2 1) suggests synchronous effects. Women who experienced severe violence at Time 1 and no violence at Time 2 can be predicted to report high levels of PTSD at Time 3, that is, for the second observation period. Finally, the last type (constituted by Configuration 2 2 2 2) shows that for women who reported experiencing intimate partner violence for both observation periods, it can be predicted that they also suffer from clinical-level PTSD symptoms, at both Time 2 and Time 3.

The specification of the logistic regression model that corresponds to the above multiple, multivariate P-CFA base model is not straightforward. As always, the logistic regression model would include all main effects, the interactions among the predictor variables, and associations among predictor and criterion variables. In the present example, this way of specifying the logistic regression model would yield

$$\log \hat{m} = \lambda \quad + \quad \lambda^{V1} + \lambda^{V2} + \lambda^{P2} + \lambda^{P3} + \lambda^{V1,V2} + \lambda^{V1,P2} + \lambda^{V2,P2}$$
$$+ \quad \lambda^{V1,P3} + \lambda^{V2,P3} + \lambda^{P2,P3}.$$

This model does also contain the interaction between the two criterion variables, P2 and P3. If of importance, and if a sufficient number of degrees of freedom is available, the higher order interactions among predictors and criteria can be made part of the model also. For example, the interactions $V1 \times P2 \times P3$ and $V2 \times P2 \times P3$ may be made part of the model, which then will be

$$\log \hat{m} = \lambda \quad + \quad \lambda^{V1} + \lambda^{V2} + \lambda^{P2} + \lambda^{P3} + \lambda^{V1,V2} + \lambda^{V1,P2} + \lambda^{V2,P2}$$
$$+ \quad \lambda^{V1,P3} + \lambda^{V2,P3} + \lambda^{P2,P3}$$
$$+ \quad \lambda^{V1,P2,P3} + \lambda^{V2,P2,P3}.$$

Other models are conceivable. Note that many general purpose statistical programs (e.g., SYSTAT 12.0) are unable to process logistic regression models with more than one criterion variable under the generalized linear model or regression modules. When this is the case, the multivariate logistic regression models can be expressed in terms of log-linear models and processed by using standard log-linear modeling modules or logit log-linear modules. One possible logit model for the present example would involve specifying [P2] and [P3] as dependent variables and [V1] and [V2] as factors without including them in the model-building step. Alternatively, multivariate logistic regression models can be analyzed by using software programs that test simultaneous equations and have the capacity of analyzing categorical dependent measures (e.g., M*plus*). Either of these approaches, however, deals with relationships among variables instead of testing hypotheses concerning individual configurations.

5.1.3 Comparing Logistic Regression and P-CFA Models

In this section, we resume the comparison of models of logistic regression and P-CFA. For this comparison, we again use the log-linear model notation because both, logistic regression models and P-CFA base models, can be expressed in terms of log-linear models.

Both, logistic regression models and P-CFA base models, focus on the relationships among the criterion and the predictor variables. Effects that are not of interest are either set to zero (logistic regression) or included in the base model (P-CFA). More specifically, *models of logistic regression* take into account

1. the main effects of all variables in the model;

2. all possible interactions among the predictors in the model (this includes all higher order interactions); the model is thus saturated in the predictors;

3. all possible interactions among the criterion variables; the model is thus saturated in the criterion variables; and

4. all first order interactions between predictors and criteria.

Occasionally, researchers also consider

5. three-way and higher order interactions among predictors and criteria.   Examples of such interactions include the three-way interactions among two predictors and one criterion variable, the three-way interactions among one predictor and two criterion variables, and the four-way interactions among two predictor and two criterion variables.

6. In addition, researchers occasionally include covariates in the model.

In most logistic regression models, the highest order interaction, that is, the interaction that includes all predictor and all criterion variables, is not taken into account. This is done for a number of reasons, which include (1) the desideration of parsimony, (2) lack of hypotheses that would necessitate consideration of an interaction of the highest order, and (3) the *sparsity of effects principle* (see, e.g., Wu & Hamada, 2000), which suggests that interactions of a high order are rarely needed to explain data (this principle is taken up again in Chapter 12). The hierarchical model that includes the highest order interaction is always saturated. *P-CFA base models* take into account

1. the main effects of all variables in the model; and

2. all possible interactions among the predictors in the model (this includes all higher order interactions); the model is thus saturated in the predictors;

3. all possible interactions among the criterion variables; the model is thus saturated in the criterion variables; and, possibly

4. covariates.

However, the typical P-CFA base model will not take into account any of the interactions that link predictor and criterion variables. Therefore, prediction types and antitypes will, by necessity, reflect local interactions among predictors and criteria. To determine which interactions, in particular, cause the P-CFA types and antitypes to emerge, researchers have to search and identify those interactions that are and those that are not needed as causes for the prediction types and antitypes. Methods for this search are described in Chapter 10, on functional CFA.

The comparison of the effects that will, at the end of analysis, be interpreted as describing the relationships among predictors and criteria shows that logistic regression and P-CFA differ in two important aspects. First, logistic regression considers only the effects specified in the model, at the expense of possible other effects. Unless parameters are constrained, non-hierarchical or nonstandard models are specified, or researchers are willing to live with a saturated model, only a selection of all possible predictor-criterion relations is considered. In contrast, P-CFA typically considers all possible predictor-criterion relations. Even the highest order interactions are practically never excluded from possibly causing types and antitypes to emerge. These effects can be excluded by making them part of the P-CFA base model (see data examples in Tables 5.6 and 5.7). Because of this difference between logistic regression and P-CFA, results are rarely fully comparable. Later, in this chapter, we discuss options to make the logistic regression model and the base model for P-CFA parallel.

The second major difference between logistic regression and P-CFA is that the results of analysis of logistic regression are interpreted at the variable level, whereas the results of P-CFA are interpreted at the level of individual configurations.

To illustrate the differences between the models of logistic regression and P-CFA, consider the case in which two predictors, $P1$ and $P2$, are related to two criterion variables, $C1$ and $C2$. One logistic regression model for these four variables is

$$\log \hat{m} = \lambda \quad + \quad \lambda^{P1} + \lambda^{P2} + \lambda^{C1} + \lambda^{C2} + \lambda^{P1,P2} + \lambda^{C1,C2} + \lambda^{P1,C1} + \lambda^{P1,C2}$$
$$+ \quad \lambda^{P2,C1} + \lambda^{P2,C2} + \lambda^{P1,C1,C2} + \lambda^{P2,C1,C2}.$$

This model focuses on the four first order and two second order interactions among predictor and criterion variables, and sets the remaining third order interactions among the predictors and the criteria to zero. These are the interactions $[P1, P2, C1]$, $[P1, P2, C2]$, and $[P1, P2, C1, C2]$. Any of these can be made part of the model, if desired. In contrast, the standard base model of P-CFA is, for the same four variables,

$$\log \hat{m} = \lambda + \lambda^{P1} + \lambda^{P2} + \lambda^{C1} + \lambda^{C2} + \lambda^{P1,P2} + \lambda^{C1,C2}.$$

Based on this model, prediction types and antitypes can be caused by any of the predictor-criteria interactions. This includes the first order interactions that standard logistic regression includes as well as the higher order terms that are typically not part of that model.

If the interactions that are not considered in logistic regression are not of interest in P-CFA either, they can be made part of the base model. In the present example, the base model then becomes

$$\log \hat{m} = \lambda + \lambda^{P1} + \lambda^{P2} + \lambda^{C1} + \lambda^{C2} + \lambda^{P1,P2} + \lambda^{C1,C2} + \lambda^{P1,P2,C1} + \lambda^{P1,P2,C2}.$$

This base model can be considered parallel to the above logistic regression model.

5.2 Predicting an End Point

In many domains of research, end points are of interest. Examples of end points include the outcomes of training, therapy, punishment, drug use, job interviewing, alcohol consumption, untreated diseases, and marriage proposals. Similarly, teleological discussions concern end points of development. In many instances, end points are categorical. For example, a candidate is hired, a marriage proposal is accepted, a contract is signed, or a therapy is successful. When an end point is categorical, CFA can be a powerful method to predict the end point from concurrent and earlier events. The typical situation is that a number of predictors exists. These predictors can be repeated observations, classification variables, or concomitant variables.

Let the end point be denoted by E, and the antecedent or concurrent events by $P_1, P_2, \ldots, P_m$. Then, the P-CFA base model that allows one to determine which category of the end point is predicted to occur or not to occur with greater-than-chance probability includes the following terms:

1. Main effects of all variables; and

2. All possible interactions among the predictor variables.

The corresponding log-linear base model is

$$\log \hat{m} = \lambda + \lambda_i^E + \sum_j \lambda_j P_j + \sum_{jk} \lambda_{jk}^{P_j P_k} \ldots,$$

where the double-subscripted terms indicate two-way interactions, and the "..." indicates that all possible interactions among predictors are taken into account. The model is thus saturated in the predictor variables. If this model is rejected and types and antitypes emerge, relationships among predictors and the series of antecedent events must exist.

Data Example 4: To illustrate this model, we use data from the intimate partner violence project again. In the following data example, we ask whether longitudinal patterns of violence (here, we use any violence; this is in contrast to the severe violence observations we use in Chapter 6) over a span of 3 years allows one to predict PTSD in the following year. The following variables are used for this example:

- *Predictors*: Intimate partner violence, observed in three consecutive years (*DV1, DV2, DV3*), each scored as 1 = absent and 2 = present; and

- *End point*: Clinical-level PTSD in Year 4, scored as 1 = absent and 2 = present.

The P-CFA base model for the prediction of PTSD from a history of violence is

$$\log \hat{m} = \lambda \ + \ \lambda_i^{PTSD} + \lambda_j^{DV1} + \lambda_k^{DV2} + \lambda_l^{DV3} + \lambda_{jk}^{DV1,DV2} + \lambda_{jl}^{DV1,DV3}$$
$$+ \ \lambda_{kl}^{DV2,DV3} + \lambda_{jkl}^{DV1,DV2,DV3}.$$

As with all P-CFA base models, this model is saturated in its predictors. It can be contradicted only if the trajectory of intimate partner violence is related to the outcome, *PTSD*. Specifically, types and antitypes can emerge only if one or more of the following interactions exist: $[DV1, PTSD]$, $[DV2, PTSD]$, $[DV3, PTSD]$, $[DV1, DV2, PTSD]$, $[DV1, DV3, PTSD]$, $[DV2, DV3, PTSD]$, $[DV1, DV2, DV3, PTSD]$. These are the interactions that relate one or more of the violence indicators to the outcome, PTSD. Note that, as in the context of Section 5.1.1 on logistic regression and prediction CFA, the equivalent logit or logistic regression model can be specified by declaring $[DV1]$, $[DV2]$, and $[DV3]$ factors. The base model fails to describe the data well ($LR - X^2 = 28.54$; $df = 7$; $p < 0.01$). Therefore, we anticipate that types and antitypes may emerge. For the following CFA, we use the z-test and the Holland-Copenhaver procedure for the protection of α. Table 5.14 summarizes the CFA results.

Two types emerged from this analysis. These types indicate that two trajectories are more likely than expected to result in PTSD. The first type is constituted by Configuration 2 1 2 2. It indicates that women who first are

TABLE 5.14. Predicting-the-End-Point P-CFA of PTSD from 3 Years of Intimate Partner Violence (*V*1, *V*2, and *V*3); End Point is *PTSD* Diagnosis

Configuration V1 V2 V3 PTSD	m	$\hat{m}$	z	p	Type/Antitype
1111	99	88.074	1.1643	.122155	
1112	14	24.926	−2.1885	.014316	
1121	7	8.574	−.5374	.295497	
1122	4	2.426	1.0102	.156211	
1211	12	13.250	−.3434	.365648	
1212	5	3.750	.6455	.259302	
1221	4	3.118	.4997	.308635	
1222	0	.882	−.9393	.173779	
2111	13	12.471	.1499	.440415	
2112	3	3.529	−.2818	.389048	
2121	2	5.456	−1.4795	.069498	
2122	5	1.544	2.7811	.002709	Type
2211	16	16.368	−.0909	.463796	
2212	5	4.632	.1708	.432184	
2221	6	11.691	−1.6645	.048010	
2222	9	3.309	3.1287	.000878	Type

able to leave a violent relationship but then, later, engage in another one are more likely than chance to show signs of elevated PTSD, 1 year after having entered the second violent relationship. The second type, constituted by Configuration 2 2 2 2, indicates that women who are consistently in violent relationships, for 3 years, show, 1 year later, signs of elevated PTSD. All of the remaining configurations suggest that the presence or absence of PTSD cannot be predicted from the other patterns of intimate partner violence, over 3 years.

To compare the predicting-the-end-point P-CFA with log-linear modeling results, we attempt to find a parsimonious model for the data in Table 5.14. One such model includes all main effects and the interactions [*V*1, *V*2], [*V*1, *V*3], [*V*2, *V*3], [*V*1, *PTSD*], and [*V*3, *PTSD*]. For this model, we calculate $LR - X^2 = 10.42$ ($df = 7$; $p = 0.17$). This model suggests that the three-way interaction among the three predictor variable makes no contribution to explaining the data (and, thus, the types and antitypes). In addition, it suggests that, whereas intimate partner violence at T1 and T3 is related to PTSD at T2, it is unrelated to PTSD. While well-fitting and (maybe) interpretable, the results of this analysis suggest conclusions that differ from those suggested by CFA. In addition, this model does not allow one to talk about trajectories except that violence at one point in time is associated with violence at the following or the second next point in time.

5.3 Predicting a Trajectory

Predictions of trajectories are of importance in many respects. Given a particular point in development, one might be interested in the most (or least) likely course of subsequent development. For example, the study of pubertal physical development allows one to distinguish between early, on-time, and late maturers. Individuals in these groups can, possibly, be predicted to differ greatly in cognitive and social developmental patterns. Similarly, when an adolescent has experimented with marijuana, can it be predicted that this individual develops into a user of hard drugs?

P-CFA allows one to predict pathways of development or, in more general terms, trajectories. Based on an event or a status in time, the frequencies of trajectories can be counted and compared with expectancies. Consider the categorical variable, P, and a series of subsequent, repeated observations of an outcome variable, Y. Then, the base model that allows one to examine trajectories in Y includes the following terms:

1. Main effects of all variables; and

2. All possible interactions among the repeated observations of Y.

This model is thus saturated in the outcome variables. It can be contradicted only if relationships between P and the repeatedly observed Y variable exist.

Data Example 5: In the following example, we use data from the study on aggression in adolescence (Finkelstein et al., 1994) again. 114 adolescents who were 11 years of age at the first interview were asked to indicate the degree to which they feel they have aggressive impulses. Two and four years later, they were asked to indicate the amount of physical aggression they use against their peers. For the following analyses, each of these three variables was dichotomized at the median. The variables used for analysis are Aggressive Impulses (AI), and Physical Aggression against Peers, observed 2 and 4 years after AI was observed ($PAAP1$ and $PAAP2$). Each of the variables was scored as 1 = below median and 2 = above median. The log-linear base model for the prediction of the development of Physical Aggression against Peers based on Aggressive Impulses is

$$\log \hat{m} = \lambda + \lambda_i^{AI} + \lambda_j^{PAAP1} + \lambda_k^{PAAP2} + \lambda_{jk}^{PAAP1,PAAP2}.$$

This model can be contradicted only if one or more of the following interactions exist: $[AI, PAAP1]$, $[AI, PAAP2]$, $[AI, PAAP1, PAAP2]$. Types and antitypes will then indicate trajectories that occur more likely or less likely than chance, conditional on AI.

TABLE 5.15. Predicting the Developmental Trajectory of Physical Aggression against Peers ($PAAP1$ and $PAAP2$) from Aggressive Impulses (AI)

Configuration $AI\ PAAP1\ PAAP2$	m	$\hat{m}$	z	p	Type/Antitype
111	23	14.684	3.4902	.000241	Type
112	11	11.368	−.1688	.432990	
121	10	9.000	.5011	.308147	
122	10	18.947	−3.5012	.000232	Antitype
211	8	16.316	−3.4902	.000241	Antitype
212	13	12.632	.1688	.432990	
221	9	10.000	−.5011	.308147	
222	30	21.053	3.5012	.000232	Type

The base model of the cross-classification of these three variables is rejected ($LR - X^2 = 17.94$; $df = 3$; $p < 0.01$). Therefore, we anticipate that types and antitypes may emerge. For the following P-CFA, we use Lehmacher's (1981) z-test because it has more power than the standard z-test[2]. We protect α by using the Holland-Copenhaver procedure. Table 5.15 presents a summary of the P-CFA results. CFA of trajectories reveals two types and two antitypes. The first type, constituted by Configuration 1 1 1, suggests that adolescents who report below-average aggressive impulses at age 11 will also report low levels of physical aggression against peers over the following 4 years. This type is complemented by the first antitype (Configuration 1 2 2). This antitype suggests that adolescents who report below-average aggressive impulses at age 11 are very unlikely to report high levels of physical aggression against peers over the following 4 years. The second type, constituted by Configuration 2 2 2, suggests that adolescents who report above-average aggressive impulses at age 11 will also report high levels of physical aggression against peers over the following 4 years. Conversely, adolescents who report high levels of aggressive impulses at age 11 are very unlikely to report low levels of physical aggression against peers over the following 4 years (Antitype 2 1 1).

One log-linear model that describes these data well includes all main effects and the interactions $[AI, PAAP1], [AI, PAAP2]$ ($LR-X^2 = 5.33$; $df = 2$; $p = 0.07$). This model suggests that aggressive impulses at age 11 are associated with physical aggression against peers at both ages 13 and 15.

[2]Note that, for Lehmacher's test to be applicable, one must have a table spanned by variables with fixed probabilities at the margins (or in subtables). That is, sampling must be product-multinomial. If this is not the case, tests should be used that do not require product-multinomial sampling.

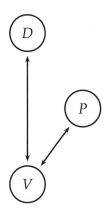

FIGURE 5.2. Maryland death penalty example.

The autoregression of *PAAP2* onto *PAAP1* is, therefore, not needed to explain the data in Table 5.15. Aggressive Impulses at age 11 predict Physical Aggression against Peers both 2 and 4 years later. The CFA results show where in the table these effects manifest.

5.4   Graphical Presentation of Results of P-CFA Models

In Figure 5.1, four P-CFA base models were depicted by way of relating variables to one another using bidirectional paths (double-headed arrows). These arrows indicate the associations that the base models take into account when estimating the expected cell frequencies. The results of logistic regression models can be depicted in analogous fashion. For example, the logistic regression results of the analysis of the Maryland death penalty data can be depicted as shown in Figure 5.2 (cf. Table 5.3). The figure depicts only the statistically significant associations from Table 5.3.

The results of P-CFA require a different graphical representation. The reason for this difference is that P-CFA, and CFA in general, do not relate variables to one another (except in the base models). Instead, these methods inspect individual configurations. Therefore, a graph will have to connect patterns of categories instead of variables. Consider the results of P-CFA of the Maryland death penalty data that are summarized in Table 5.6. This table shows that one type and one antitype were identified. In Figures 5.3 and 5.4 we present graphs for the type and for the antitype.

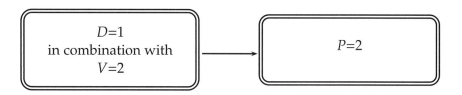

FIGURE 5.3. Graphical representation of prediction type 1 2 2 from Table 5.6.

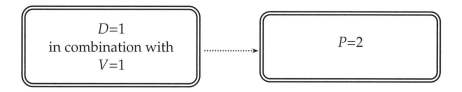

FIGURE 5.4. Graphical representation of prediction antitype 1 1 2 from Table 5.6.

Figures 5.3 and 5.4 show that P-CFA uses category patterns on the predictor side to predict category patterns on the criterion side. The expression "in combination with" indicates that both of the categories that it links were observed. Categories that constitute a P-CFA type are connected with a solid arrow. Categories that constitute a P-CFA antitype are connected with a dotted arrow. To give examples in which the criterion side also includes more than one variable, we depict the second type detailed in Table 5.13 in Figure 5.5 and the first antitype enumerated in Table 5.13 in Figure 5.6.

In general, graphs for CFA prediction models are created in the same

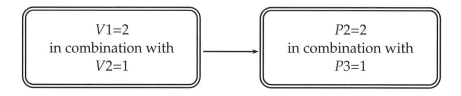

FIGURE 5.5. Type 2 1 2 1 from Table 5.13.

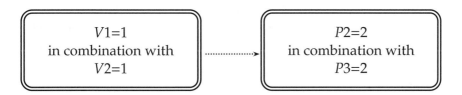

FIGURE 5.6. Antitype 1 1 2 2 from Table 5.13.

way as for variable-oriented prediction models, except that both on the sending and the receiving end, there are configurations instead of variables.

5.5   Chapter Summary

In contrast to linear regression, which yields a slope parameter that is assumed to be valid over the entire range of admissible scores both for the predictor and the criterion, Prediction CFA (P-CFA) allows one to predict particular criterion configurations from particular predictor configurations. This is in accordance with the general characteristic of CFA that researchers examine individual cells instead of variables in a cross-classification. P-CFA predictions can take two forms. The first is that, for a particular predictor configuration, a criterion configuration is predicted to occur with increased probability. The second is that, for a particular predictor configuration, a criterion configuration is predicted to occur with decreased probability. The former is particularly interesting, for instance, when intervention effects are studied. The latter is interesting when side effects are studied and researchers hope to be able to say that treatments are unlikely to result in configurations of undesired side effects.

The base model of P-CFA is saturated in the predictors, is saturated in the criteria, but proposes independence of predictors and criteria. Thus, types and antitypes can emerge only if particular predictor configurations are related to particular criterion configurations. The base models of logistic regression and P-CFA can be made parallel either by making the higher order interactions among predictors and criteria part of the logistic regression model or by including the higher order interactions that are not part of the logistic regression model in the P-CFA base model.

After a discussion of standard P-CFA, two special cases of P-CFA were introduced. The first allows one to predict an end point from a trajectory. The second allows one to predict a trajectory from a start point. As in all P-CFA models, the predictions operate at the level of configurations.

Graphical representations of P-CFA results proceed in a way similar to the graphical representation of regression models, in that paths are drawn that originate in the predictors and end in the criteria. However, in P-CFA, these paths do not connect variables. Instead, they originate in predictor configurations and end in criterion configurations.

6

Configural Mediator Models

Chapter 6 opens the doors to a new methodology in the search for CFA types and antitypes. Instead of conducting just one CFA run, we propose to conduct several CFA runs. The results of these runs are compared, providing the basis for particular interpretations of types and antitypes. In Chapter 6, it is shown how several CFA runs can be performed with the goal of determining whether, at the level of individual configurations, (1) processes of mediation can be identified at all, and (2) whether evidence exists in support of hypotheses of complete or partial mediation. Two approaches to configural mediation analysis are discussed. The first begins with logistic regression analysis. If results suggest that mediation exists, CFA is performed in a subsequent step, and those configurations are identified that carry the mediation at the level of individual cells. The second approach exclusively uses the tools of CFA. Starting from a standard CFA that uses the hypothesis of variable independence in its base model, four additional CFA runs are performed that use base models that reflect different hypotheses about the roles that potential predictors, mediators, and outcome variables may play. The comparison of the resulting patterns of types and antitypes is the basis for conclusions concerning the nature of mediation in individual cells. One of the most interesting characteristics of mediation CFA is that, in the same cross-classification, hypotheses involving partial mediation, complete mediation, or no mediation can find support.

Mediation is modeled mostly in the context of predictive, causal, or mechanistic concepts of the flow of effects. The underlying idea is that of a chain of effects (Kenny, 2005; von Eye & Brandtstädter, 1998). Consider a predictor variable (P), a mediating variable (M), and an outcome variable (Y). Using these three variables, mediation can be depicted as in Figure 6.1.

Not surprisingly, a number of methods has been proposed to model and test whether data support hypotheses about the existence of mediation effects (see MacKinnon, 2008; MacKinnon, Lockwood, Hoffman, West, & Sheets, 2002). The most frequently used method was proposed by Baron and Kenny (1986). This method involves four steps:

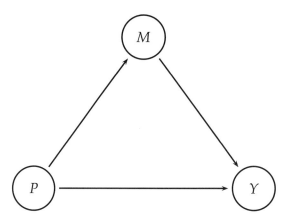

FIGURE 6.1. Variable M mediates the relationship between P and Y.

1. Establish the relationship between the predictor, P, and the criterion, Y. This can be achieved by simply regressing Y onto P. In continuous variable analysis, standard linear regression analysis is the routine method used for this purpose. In categorical variable analysis, logit models such as logistic regression can be used. In the context of configural analysis, the prediction models discussed in Section 5.1.2 can be used. It should be noted that some authors state that this relationship does not need to exist, because mediation can exist if only M is predicted from P and Y is predicted from M. Therefore, the results of this first step are not necessarily conclusive. In particular, a relationship between P and Y is not a necessary condition for the existence of a mediated relationship between P and Y.

2. Establish the relationship between the predictor, P, and the mediator, M. This relationship can be shown to exist by using the same methods as under Step 1, with M being regressed onto P. This relationship is a necessary condition for mediation to exist.

3. Establish the relationship between the mediator, M, and the criterion, Y. Here again, regression methods can be used to predict Y from M. However, in contrast to the first two steps, the third step requires that the effect of P be taken into account. Therefore, simple regression will not be sufficient. Partial regression models need to be estimated so that the effect of P is controlled when the effect of M on Y is estimated. This is needed because it is possible that both M and Y depend on P. The existence of a relationship between the mediator and the criterion is also a necessary condition for mediation.

4. Determine whether mediation is partial or complete. Mediation is partial if (1) the path from P to Y and (2) the paths from P to M and from M to Y exist. A relationship is completely (or fully) mediated if only the paths from P to M and from M to Y exist. If a relationship is fully mediated, the path from P to Y is statistically zero when the path from the mediator, M, to the criterion, Y, is taken into account. If the relationship between the predictor, P, and the criterion, Y, cannot be established in the first step of the procedure, mediation cannot be partial, only complete, if it exists at all. In a partially mediated relationship, this path may be less strong when M is taken into account than when M is not taken into account, but it still exists. In most cases, the decision as to whether mediation is full or partial is made based on the results of Step 3. That is, the regression model that contains the paths both from P to Y and from M to Y allows one to make the decision.

In the present context, we will not discuss the causal connotations of the concept of mediation. Instead, we discuss the idea that underlies the application of CFA in the context of mediation. The idea that carries CFA is that of local relationships (Hand & Viniciotti, 2003; Havránek & Lienert, 1984). At the aggregate level, variable-oriented data analysis, researchers implicitly assume that relationships apply over the entire range of admissible scores. If this is not the case, piecewise regression models are estimated (for examples, see von Eye & Schuster, 1998), or interaction terms are included in a model. In contrast, person-oriented (Bergman & Magnusson, 1997; Bergman, von Eye, & Magnusson, 2006; von Eye & Bergman, 2003), ideographic (Molenaar, 2004; von Eye, 2004b), and configural data analysis allow one to accommodate the assumption that a relationship exists only in a subset of variable categories. In the present context of mediation, CFA is applied if researchers assume that either complete or partial mediation relationships exist for some category patterns but not for others, and that the remaining configurations indicate variable (or configural) independence.

In the following sections, two approaches to Configural Mediation Analysis are introduced. The first approach has not been discussed in the literature before (we are grateful to Ryan Bowles for suggesting this approach). It proceeds in two steps. First, it establishes a mediation model by using methods of logistic regression. Second, using methods of CFA, it identifies the variable categories that carry the mediation. The second approach (von Eye, 2008a; von Eye, Mun, & Mair, 2009) performs mediation analysis by relying entirely on CFA methods. It first determines which variables are related to one another by searching for types and antitypes under various base models. Then, in a series of decisions in which the results of these analyses are compared, it is determined (1) whether mediation exists at all and, if it exists, (2) whether it is complete or partial. Mediation can be complete for some category patterns, partial for others, and may not exist for a third group of configurations. Both CFA approaches to mediation analysis are based on the sequence of steps proposed by Baron and Kenny (1986). However, these steps are modified for application in CFA.

6.1   Logistic Regression Plus Mediation

In this section, we describe the version of configural analysis of mediation that is based on logistic regression. This version proceeds in two phases. First, Baron and Kenny's (1986) four steps are performed that were described in the preceding section. These steps are performed by using methods of logistic regression, that is, logit models. In the second phase, the same variables are subjected to configural analysis. It is the goal of the second phase to determine which patterns of variable categories carry the relationships that are involved in the mediation process.

Consider the mediation example given in Figure 6.1. In this example, the paths from the predictor, P, to the criterion, Y, and the mediator, M, as well as the path from M to Y are depicted. In the first phase of analysis, the four steps proposed by Baron and Kenny (1986) are performed[1]:

1. *Establishing the relationship between the predictor, P, and the criterion, Y*: To establish the relationship between P and Y, the logit model

$$\log \frac{p(Y = 1)}{1 - p(Y = 1)} = \beta_0 + \beta_1 P$$

is estimated, which is equivalent to the log-linear model

$$\log \hat{m} = \lambda + \lambda^P + \lambda^Y.$$

These two models have the same degrees of freedom and yield the same overall goodness-of-fit scores. As was indicated before, some authors do not view this step as a necessary condition for the existence of a mediator relationship.

2. *Establishing the relationship between the predictor, P, and the mediator, M*: To establish the relationship between P and M, the logit model

$$\log \frac{p(M = 1)}{1 - p(M = 1)} = \beta_0 + \beta_1 P$$

[1]An alternative approach to mediation analysis with categorical variables was described by Vermunt (1997). An overview of this approach is given in the appendix to this section.

is estimated, which is equivalent to the log-linear model

$$\log \hat{m} = \lambda + \lambda^P + \lambda^M.$$

These two models are also equivalent (same degrees of freedom and same overall goodness-of-fit scores). If this model suggests that P is unrelated to M, mediation is impossible. In other words, this relationship is a necessary condition for mediation to exist. This applies to both partial and complete mediation.

3. *Establishing the relationship between the mediator, M, and the criterion, Y*: This relationship is also a necessary condition for mediation to exist. To establish the relationship between P and M, it is *not sufficient* to estimate the logit model

$$\log \frac{p(Y=1)}{1-p(Y=1)} = \beta_0 + \beta_1 M,$$

which would be equivalent to the log-linear model

$$\log \hat{m} = \lambda + \lambda^M + \lambda^Y.$$

These two models also have the same degrees of freedom and yield the same overall goodness-of-fit scores. The problem with this model is that it fails to take the effect of P into account. Therefore, partial logistic regression parameters must be estimated. That is, both predictors must be included in the equation. The equations thus become

$$\log \frac{p(Y=1)}{1-p(Y=1)} = \beta_0 + \beta_1 M + \beta_2 P$$

and

$$\log \hat{m} = \lambda + \lambda^P + \lambda^M + \lambda^Y + \lambda^{PM} + \lambda^{PY} + \lambda^{MY}.$$

Note again that the three-way interaction is not part of the model. It would render the model saturated. Thus, the three-way interaction is used as the residual against which the model is tested.

4. *Determining whether mediation is partial or complete*: Mediation is partial if all three paths exist: (1) the path from P to Y, (2) the path from P to M, and (3) the path from M to Y. In contrast, mediation is complete, if the path from P to Y is statistically zero when the path from M to Y is part of the model. Thus, the result of Step 3 allows one to make a decision concerning the type of mediation. If both λ^{PM} and λ^{MY} are significant but λ^{PY} is not, mediation is complete. If all three two-way interactions are significant, mediation is partial.

Data Example 1: For the following data example, we adapt an example from Vermunt (1997, Ch. 4, Example 4.1; Hagenaars, 1990, Table 2.1). We analyze the three variables Religion (R; 1 = member of a religious group, 2 = nonmember), Political Preference (P; 1 = left, 2 = right, 3 = Christian Democratic), and Voting Behavior (V; 1 = does vote, 2 = does not vote). The frequency distribution of the cross-tabulation of these three variables appears in Table 6.1. The question we ask is whether Political Preference mediates the relationship between Religion and Voting Behavior. In the first phase of the analysis, we perform a standard Baron and Kenny-type mediation analysis using logistic regression. We consider the three models

$$\log \hat{m} = \lambda + \lambda^R + \lambda^V,$$
$$\log \hat{m} = \lambda + \lambda^P + \lambda^R, \text{ and}$$
$$\log \hat{m} = \lambda + \lambda^P + \lambda^R + \lambda^V + \lambda^{PR} + \lambda^{PV} + \lambda^{RV}.$$

For a formulation of the mediator model in terms of conditional probabilities, see Vermunt (1997). A review of this approach is provided in the appendix to this section. For the reasons mentioned above, we keep using the log-linear notation. All models were estimated by using ℓEM^2. For the first model, we obtain the $LR - X^2 = 58.08$ ($df = 1$; $p < 0.01$). The model clearly does not fit. Still, we inspect the parameter for the Religion – Voting path from the model that included the interaction term $[RV]$. We find that $\lambda^{RV} = 0.30$ (se = 0.04; $z = -7.41$; $p < 0.01$). Because the model does not fit, this result can be interpreted only with caution. We only conclude that the path from Religion to Voting Behavior may exist, and we proceed to the next model in the sequence.

This model contains the path from the predictor, Religion, to the mediator, Political Preference. For this model, we obtain the $LR - X^2 = 56.28$ ($df = 2$; $p < 0.01$). The model clearly does not fit either. Still, in a way parallel to the result from the first step, we find that one of the two interaction parameters that were estimated for the path from Religion to Political Preference is significant ($\lambda^{RP1} = -0.30$; se = 0.06; $z = -5.21$; $p < 0.01$; and $\lambda^{RP2} = -0.06$; se = 0.06; $z = -1.10$; $p = 0.14$). Again, we tentatively conclude that this path may exist.

The final model to be estimated includes all three interactions. The frequency table for this model appears in Table 6.1.

The overall fit of this model is excellent. We obtain the $LR - X^2 = 2.69$ ($df = 2$; $p = 0.26$). The parameters thus can be interpreted. All of

---

[2]Results from SYSTAT, SPSS, or SAS should be equivalent to the ℓEM results. ℓEM uses effects coding whereas SPSS, SYSTAT, and SAS Proc Genmod use dummy coding. Therefore, the estimated parameters may differ in magnitude and interpretation. The estimates for the expected cell frequencies and the overall model fit are exactly the same.

TABLE 6.1. Logistic Regression Model with the Predictor, Religion (R), the Mediator, Political Preference (P), and the Criterion, Voting Behavior (V)

Configuration RPV	m	$\hat{m}$	Std. Res.
1 1 1	50	45.986	0.592
1 1 2	25	29.014	−0.745
1 2 1	88	90.068	−0.218
1 2 2	8	5.932	0.849
1 3 1	177	178.945	−0.145
1 3 2	47	45.055	0.290
2 1 1	39	43.014	−0.612
2 1 2	97	92.986	0.416
2 2 1	91	88.932	0.219
2 2 2	18	20.068	−0.462
2 3 1	61	59.055	0.253
2 3 2	49	50.945	−0.273

the interesting parameters are significant. Specifically, for the path from Religion to Political Preference, we obtain the two parameter estimates $\beta_1 = -0.16$ (se $= 0.06$; $z = -2.69$; $p < 0.01$) and $\beta_2 = -0.19$ (se $= 0.06$; $z = -3.16$; $p < 0.01$). For the path from Religion to Voting Behavior, we obtain the estimate $\beta = 0.31$ (se $= 0.05$; $z = 6.83$; $p < 0.01$). Finally, for the path from Political Preference to Voting Behavior, we obtain the two parameter estimates $\beta_1 = -0.53$ (se $= 0.06$; $z = -8.31$; $p < 0.01$) and $\beta_2 = 0.60$ (se $= 0.08$; $z = 7.58$; $p < 0.01$). These parameters can be interpreted as follows. First, looking at the individual parameters, we find, for $R \rightarrow P$, that

- members of a religious group are unlikely to identify their political preference as left;

- members of a religious group are also unlikely to identify their political preference as right.

For $R \rightarrow V$, we find that

- members of religious groups are more likely to vote.

For $P \rightarrow V$, we find that

- voters who identify with the political left are less likely to vote; and

- voters who identify with the political right are more likely to vote.

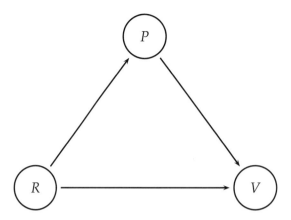

FIGURE 6.2. Partial mediation model for the variables Religion (R), Political Preference (P), and Voting Behavior (V).

Second, with respect to the path model, we note that, based on the three models that were estimated, all paths of the mediator model are significant. Mediation is thus partial, and the model can be retained. Figure 6.2 depicts the partial mediation model.

From the perspective of performing a configural mediation analysis, we now know that the paths exist that carry a partial mediation process. We also know how the variables are related to one another. What we do not know is whether the partial mediation process is carried by a specific selection of cells that stand out in the form of types and antitypes. To identify cells that possibly stand out, we perform a CFA. This analysis will be parallel to the most complete of the logistic regression models, that is, the model

$$\log \hat{m} = \lambda + \lambda^R + \lambda^P + \lambda^V + \lambda^{RP} + \lambda^{RV} + \lambda^{PV}.$$

The corresponding CFA base model depends on the type of mediation that was found by using the logistic regression models. If the hypothesis of full mediation is supported, the CFA base model is

$$\log \hat{m} = \lambda + \lambda^R + \lambda^P + \lambda^V + \lambda^{RV}.$$

If this model results in types and antitypes, the paths from Religion to Political Preference and/or from Political Preference to Voting Behavior exist. The types and antitypes show which configurations are responsible for the mediation. If, in contrast, the hypothesis of partial mediation is supported, the CFA base model becomes

$$\log \hat{m} = \lambda + \lambda^R + \lambda^P + \lambda^V.$$

Types and antitypes from this model indicate which configurations are responsible for the direct path from R to V and the indirect connection from R via P to V. The three-way interaction among the predictor, the mediator, and the criterion can be included in each of these base models, if the focus is on two-way interactions. To accomplish this, one formulates a nonhierarchical log-linear model. In the present example, the three-way interaction is $[R, P, V]$.

Readers will notice that these two base models are parallel to the logistic regression model only in part. Types and antitypes can be caused by the two-way interactions between the predictor, the mediator, and the criterion. These are the interactions $[R, V]$, $[R, P]$, and $[P, V]$. Up to this point, the logistic regression and the CFA models are equivalent. However, the CFA models leave the door open for the three-way interaction $[R, P, V]$ to have effects on the existence of types and antitypes. These effects may exist in addition to the two-way effects, but they can also be the only effects in the table (Meehl's paradox; Meehl, 1950; von Eye, 2002a). This interaction was not part of the logistic regression models.

In the present example, model fit was so good ($LR - X^2 = 2.69$) that it is impossible for the three-way interaction to improve the model-data correspondence. Therefore, omitting this interaction in the CFA base model is unlikely to affect the resulting pattern of mediation types and antitypes.

In the present example, the hypothesis of partial mediation was supported. Therefore, we use the second of the above CFA base models. This model coincides with a first order, global CFA base model. The overall goodness-of-fit of this model comes with a $LR - X^2 = 209.97$, which indicates that the model is not tenable ($df = 7$; $p < 0.01$). The rejection of the base model is a precondition for types and antitypes to emerge. Table 6.2 displays results of first order CFA. As with the earlier models, the z-test was used along with the Holland-Copenhaver procedure of α protection.

First order CFA of partial mediation shows that three types and five antitypes carry the mediation process. The first type, constituted by Configuration 1 3 1, suggests that more members of religious groups than expected who identify themselves as Christian Democratic can be predicted to vote. The second type is constituted by Configuration 2 1 2. It suggests that respondents who are not members of a religious group and identify with the political left are more likely than expected not to vote. The third type, constituted by Configuration 2 2 1, suggests that respondents who are not members of a religious group and identify with the political right are more likely than expected to vote.

The first antitype, constituted by Configuration 1 1 1, suggests that, for respondents who are members of a religious group and identify with

TABLE 6.2. Mediation CFA of the Cross-Tabulation of the Predictor, Religion (R), and the Mediator, Political Preference (P), with the Criterion, Voting Behavior (V)

Configuration RPV	m	$\hat{m}$	z	p	Type/Antitype
111	50	74.973	−2.8842	.001962	Antitype
112	25	36.153	−1.8549	.031803	
121	88	72.842	1.7761	.037859	
122	8	35.125	−4.5768	.000002	Antitype
131	177	118.678	5.3536	.000000	Type
132	47	57.228	−1.3521	.088177	
211	39	67.381	−3.4575	.000273	Antitype
212	97	32.492	11.3168	.000000	Type
221	91	65.465	3.1559	.000800	Type
222	18	31.568	−2.4149	.007870	Antitype
231	61	106.660	−4.4212	.000005	Antitype
232	49	51.433	−.3393	.367209	

the political left, it can be predicted that voting is unusually unlikely. The second antitype, constituted by Configuration 1 2 2, allows one to predict that it is unexpectedly unlikely that respondents who are members of a religious group and identify with the political right will not vote. The third antitype, constituted by Configuration 2 1 1, indicates that respondents who are not members of a religious group and politically on the left are less likely than expected to vote. The fourth antitype, constituted by Configuration 2 2 2, shows that respondents who are not members of a religious group and politically on the right are unlikely to refrain from voting. The fifth antitype, constituted by Configuration 2 3 1, suggests that respondents who are not members of religious groups and identify themselves as Christian Democratic are less likely than expected to vote.

These CFA results can be simplified by creating aggregate types or antitypes. Types can be aggregated with other types if they differ in just one characteristic (Quine-McCluskey algorithm; see Hoernes & Heilweil, 1964; von Eye & Brandtstädter, 1982). The same applies to antitypes. Types cannot be aggregated with antitypes (for a more detailed description of methods of aggregation, see von Eye, 2002a, sec. 10.8).

The three types were constituted by Configurations 1 3 1, 2 1 2, and 2 2 1. Each pair of types differs in two or more characteristics. Therefore, aggregation of types is not possible in the present example.

The five antitypes were constituted by Configurations 1 1 1, 1 2 2, 2 1 1, 2 2 2, and 2 3 1. Of these, two aggregate antitypes can be created: the first and the third and the second and the fourth antitypes can be aggregated. Specifically, when aggregating the first and the third antitypes, we obtain the composite antitype

$$1\ 1\ 1$$
$$\underline{2\ 1\ 1}$$
$$.\ 1\ 1$$

where the dot indicates the variable category aggregated across. This first aggregate antitype suggests that it is particularly unlikely that respondents who identify with the political left will vote, independent of religious orientation. From the perspective of testing a mediation hypothesis, this result indicates that the mediator, Political Preference, and the criterion, Voting Behavior, are related in a way independent of the predictor, Religion.

When aggregating the second and the fourth antitypes, we obtain the second composite antitype

$$1\ 2\ 2$$
$$\underline{2\ 2\ 2}$$
$$.\ 2\ 2$$

This aggregate antitype suggests that it can be predicted that it is very unlikely that respondents who identify with the political right will not vote. In other words, when a respondent is identified with the political right, religious group membership is irrelevant for the prediction that members are unlikely not to vote.

Note that the two antitypes 2 1 1 and 2 3 1 also differ in only one characteristic. However, the variable Political Preference has three categories, one of which is not involved in the definition of antitypes from members of religious groups and voters. Therefore, aggregating across the categories of this variable is not possible. This implies that the second variable, Political Preference, is needed for the prediction of voting of members of religious groups. Clearly, this pattern is a key element in the mediation process in the present example. In contrast, the aggregate antitypes show that, for the prediction of nonvoting of respondents who identify with the political left, religious group membership does not make a difference. This applies accordingly to predicting the voting behavior of respondents who identify with the political right. As was said above, these relationships support the notion that the mediator is related to the criterion. The fact, however, that the predictor does not play a role in these predictions shows that the current data also contain local relationships that are not constituent of the mediation process.

Creating Logistic Regression and CFA Models That Are Parallel: As was emphasized above, the CFA base model that was used to create the results in Table 6.2 is not exactly parallel to the logistic regression model used for the analysis of the same data. Specifically, whereas the logistic regression model focused on the two-way interactions between the predictors and the criteria, CFA also allowed the three-way interaction to play a role. In the following paragraphs, we make the models exactly parallel.

There are two options to create parallel models. The first option changes the logistic regression model so that it focuses on the same effects as the CFA model. The second option involves adapting the CFA model. In the present example, the first option would result in a saturated model. Therefore, we go with the second option.

When specifying alternative CFA base models for the present example, one can consider including the interactions $[R, P]$, $[P, V]$, and/or $[R, P, V]$ in the base model. Including one or both of the two-way interactions would change the meaning of the mediator model. Specifically, including either of the two-way interactions would interrupt the flow of information that originates in the predictor, R, goes through the mediator, P, and ends in the criterion variable, V. In contrast, including only $[R, P, V]$ would still result in a base model for full mediation. However, the focus would change from two- and/or three-way interactions as possible causes of types and antitypes to only two-way interactions as possible causes. In the present example, the hypothesis of partial mediation was supported. Therefore, and to illustrate a model that is parallel to the logistic regression model, we include the $[R, P, V]$ interaction in the CFA base model. The CFA base model thus becomes

$$\log \hat{m} = \lambda + \lambda^R + \lambda^P + \lambda^V + \lambda^{RPV}.$$

This model is nonhierarchical (Mair & von Eye, 2007), because it sets the parameters of the first order interactions between the predictors and the mediator, the mediator and the criterion, and the predictor and the criterion to zero. In hierarchical models, all lower order terms of higher order interactions are part of the model. The three two-way interaction terms set to zero here are lower order terms of the three-way interaction $[RPV]$. The design matrix for this base model appears in Table 6.3.

Using this design matrix, a CFA was performed on the voting data. It differs from the design matrix for the base model for Table 6.2 in that the last two vectors in Table 6.3 were included. To make results comparable with those reported in Table 6.2, the z-test was used again along with the Holland-Copenhaver procedure of α protection. Table 6.4 displays CFA results.

The overall $LR - X^2 = 184.27$ indicates that this base model is not tenable either $(df = 5; \ p < 0.01)$, although the model is significantly

TABLE 6.3. Design Matrix for CFA of a 2 × 3 × 2 Cross-Tabulation of the Variables Religion (R), Political Preference (P), and Voting Behavior (V); Nonhierarchical Base Model Includes Three-Way Interaction

	Main Effects			Three-Way Interaction	
R	$P1$	$P2$	V	$R \times P1 \times V$	$R \times P2 \times V$
1	1	0	1	1	0
1	1	0	−1	−1	0
1	0	1	1	0	1
1	0	1	−1	0	−1
1	−1	−1	1	−1	−1
1	−1	−1	−1	1	1
−1	1	0	1	−1	0
−1	1	0	−1	1	0
−1	0	1	1	0	−1
−1	0	1	−1	0	1
−1	−1	−1	1	1	1
−1	−1	−1	−1	−1	−1

TABLE 6.4. Mediation CFA of the Cross-Tabulation of the Two Predictors Religion (R) and Political Preference (P) with the Criterion Voting Behavior (V); Nonhierarchical Model; Three-Way Interaction Taken into Account

Configuration RPV	m	$\hat{m}$	z	p	Type/Antitype
111	50	81.694	−3.5066	.000227	Antitype
112	25	32.112	−1.2551	.104728	
121	88	53.293	4.7542	.000001	Type
122	8	44.189	−5.4440	.000000	Antitype
131	177	136.417	3.4746	.000256	Type
132	47	47.295	−.0428	.482919	
211	39	60.952	−2.8117	.002464	Antitype
212	97	36.242	10.0924	.000000	Type
221	91	83.875	.7780	.218282	
222	18	23.643	−1.1605	.122923	
231	61	89.769	−3.0364	.001197	Antitype
232	49	60.519	−1.4807	.069338	

better than the standard first order CFA base model ($\Delta LR - X^2 = 25.70$; $\Delta df = 2$; $p < 0.01$). We thus can expect a different pattern of types and antitypes to emerge. Indeed, Table 6.4 shows one new type, constituted by Configuration 1 2 1. In addition, one of the types and one of the antitypes that had emerged under the original first order CFA base model are no longer extreme enough to qualify as outstanding cells (Type-Configuration 2 2 1 and Antitype-Configuration 2 2 2). The remaining types and antitypes had been part of the results of the first analysis. We thus conclude that the mediation process that was confirmed, at the level of two-way interactions, by the sequence of logistic regression models is carried by the three types and four antitypes in Table 6.4. We conclude that, although the three-way interaction is not significant, it can, taken by itself, alter the resulting pattern of types and antitypes.

As before, the two Antitypes 1 1 1 and 2 1 1 can be aggregated to constitute the aggregate antitype . 1 1. The interpretation of the remaining types and antitypes requires all three variables. Figure 6.3 displays two of the mediation types as examples. Figure 6.4 displays two of the mediation antitypes as examples.

Interpretation of Mediation Types and Antitypes: The interpretation of mediation types and antitypes can be based on the predictive nature of the variables' relationships in the model. Given the right context, these relationships may even be causal. If a type suggests that (local) mediation is partial, one can formulate the interpretation as involving three predictive elements. The first is the one from the predictor to the criterion. One can say that a particular predictor category allows one to predict a particular criterion category. In addition, the same predictor category allows one to also predict a particular category of the mediator. This category, in turn, allows one to predict the same criterion category as the predictor itself, thus constituting a partially mediated relationship.

Consider, for example, the first type in Figure 6.3. This type is constituted by the category pattern $R = 1$, $P = 2$, and $V = 1$. In the context of a mediation model, a first element of this pattern can be interpreted such that, for more members of a religious group than expected, it can be predicted that they do vote in political elections. This describes the predictor-criterion relationship. In addition, the same members of religious groups are more likely than expected to have a preference for the political right. This describes the predictor-mediator relationship. Finally, the same individuals, all on the political right, have an increased probability of voting. This completes the mediated element of the relationship.

In a parallel way, one can interpret antitypes. Consider the second antitype in Figure 6.4. It is constituted by the category pattern $R = 2$,

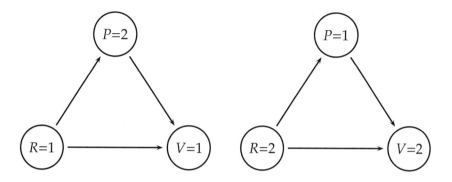

FIGURE 6.3. Mediation types in the voting behavior example (solid arrows indicate types).

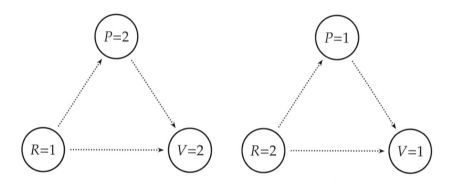

FIGURE 6.4. Mediation antitypes in the voting behavior example (dotted arrows indicate antitypes).

$P = 1$, and $V = 1$. This antitype indicates that, of those respondents who are not members of a religious group, fewer will vote than expected (predictor-criterion relationship). In addition, these individuals identify with the political left, fewer of them vote than expected (predictor-mediator and mediator-criterion).

Appendix to Section 6.1: An Alternative Method of Mediation Analysis (Vermunt, 1997)

An alternative, equivalent method of mediation analysis can be specified in terms of conditional probabilities, π (see Vermunt, 1997, p. 27). Specifically, the unrestricted model that is depicted in Figure 6.1 is

$$\pi_{RPV} = \pi_R \, \pi_{P|R} \, \pi_{V|RP}.$$

This model is saturated ($df = 0$). Still, the parameters indicate whether there is support for the mediational path model. Specifically, in the voting data example, we estimate, for the $P|R$ part of the model (main effect statistics are estimated in the analyzed models but not reported here or in later models), the following Wald statistics: for RP, 53.55 ($df = 2; p < 0.01$). For the $V|RP$ part of the model, we find, for RV, 33.56 ($df = 1; p < 0.01$); for PV, 61.30 ($df = 2; p < 0.01$); and for RPV, 2.70 ($df = 2; p = 0.259$). We, therefore, can conclude that each of the bivariate variable relationships that was proposed as part of the path model given in Figure 6.2 is significant, and the model as a whole is supported. In contrast, and as before, the three-way interaction among R, P, and V remains nonsignificant.

To obtain a more parsimonious (nonsaturated) model, we remove the three-way interaction. For the resulting model, we obtain a $LR - X^2 = 2.69$ ($df = 2; p = 0.26$), which indicates excellent model-data correspondence (note that this value is exactly the same as the one for the log-linear model that was estimated for Table 6.4). The Wald statistics for the individual parameters are, for the $P|R$ part of the model: for RP, 53.55 ($df = 2; p < 0.01$). For the $V|RP$ part of the model, we obtain: for RV, 46.67 ($df = 1; p < 0.01$); and for PV, 77.60 ($df = 2; p < 0.01$). At this level, we can conclude that mediation exists, and it is, at the least, partial.

To test whether a fully mediated model can be defended, we set the parameter for the direct path from R to V to zero. The resulting model has 3 degrees of freedom, and comes with a $LR - X^2 = 51.39$ ($df = 1; p < 0.01$). This model is rejected. In addition, it is significantly worse than the less parsimonious model of partial mediation. We thus retain the model of partial mediation.

6.2 CFA-Based Mediation Analysis

The method of probing potential mediation described in the last chapter is a hybrid. It combines two different approaches into one method: variable-oriented logistic regression is combined with methods of person-oriented CFA. The latter is used only if logistic regression yields a mediation model that can be retained. In this chapter, we describe an alternative approach to configural mediation analysis. This approach is based entirely on CFA. In many instances, these two approaches will yield the same results. However, the regression and the configural approaches to mediation analysis can differ in two important aspects. First, types and antitypes can exist even if logistic regression does not support mediation hypotheses. In these instances, and when researchers wish to stay within the domain of person-oriented methods of analysis, the method described in this chapter is the method of choice (von Eye, 2008a; von Eye, Mun, & Mair, 2009). Second, patterns of types and antitypes can emerge that suggest that, whereas some type- or antitype configurations reflect mediation, others, in the same table, may reflect simple bivariate relationships that are unrelated to the mediation process. The aggregate antitypes in the preceding section are examples of such a situation.

The method that is described in the following paragraphs was designed to be parallel to Baron and Kenny's (1986) method that was used already in the preceding section. Steps are performed that examine the same relationships as proposed for the Baron and Kenny procedure. After performing these steps, results are compared and a decision is made about the nature of the mediation process. However, results are not expressed in terms of variable relationships. Instead, results are expressed solely in terms of types and antitypes, that is, in terms of the patterns of variable categories that carry the mediation relationship.

Definition: A configural mediation model is defined by three elements:

1. the types and antitypes that link predictors, mediators, and criteria;

2. rules that allow one to make a decision about the existence of mediation; and

3. rules that allow one to make a decision about the nature of mediation as either partial or complete.

In the following paragraphs, we describe a two-stage procedure that leads to statements about a mediation process. This procedure involves (1) performing a series of four configural analyses that allow one to make conclusions parallel to the ones based on Baron and Kenny's (1986) sequence of steps; and (2) comparing the results of these analyses with one another. In the following paragraphs, we first describe the series of the four configural analyses. We name the predictor P, the mediator M, and the criterion Y.

Step 1. First Order CFA: This step involves performing a standard first order CFA, as explained in the first chapter of this book (cf. Lienert, 1968; von Eye, 2002a; von Eye & Gutiérrez Peña, 2004). This is the main effect model $[P][M][Y]$. This step allows one to determine whether variable relationships exist at all in the form of types and antitypes. If no types or antitypes emerge from this first step, configural mediation cannot exist and configural mediation analysis can stop here. If, however, types or antitypes do emerge, they may constitute evidence of configural mediation, and the following steps are needed to determine (1) which patterns of variable categories carry the mediation, and (2) the type of mediation.

Types and antitypes that result from the first step can reflect any (local) variable relationship. Therefore, the following steps aim at determining whether the types and antitypes support the notion that relationships exist that are compatible with full or partial mediation. In the following three steps, we use the configural regression and prediction models that were discussed in Sections 5.1 and 5.2 (cf. von Eye & Bogat, 2005; von Eye et al., 2005). The order in which the following three steps are performed has no implication for the final results.

Step 2. Predicting the criterion from predictor and mediator: This step corresponds to the second step in Baron and Kenny's (1986) procedure. It involves a CFA base model in which the predictor and the mediator are allowed to be associated with each other. That is, we use the base model $[PM][Y]$, a configural multiple regression model. If no types and no antitypes result from this model, neither the predictor nor the mediator is related to the criterion, and the analysis can stop with the conclusion that the types and antitypes that were found in Step 1 are solely due to the $[PM]$ interaction (and, possibly, the three-way interaction $[PMY]$). If, however, types or antitypes result, there must be a relationship between the predictor and the mediator on one side, and the criterion on the other. The nature of this relationship is, at this point, unknown. Therefore, the following steps are necessary.

Step 3. Predicting the criterion from the mediator: In the third step, a CFA is performed, using a base model in which the predictor is allowed to be associated with the mediator and also with the criterion (see Steps 2 and 3 in Baron and Kenny's procedure). That is, we use the base model $[PM][PY]$. If types and antitypes result from this model, the mediator must be related to the criterion, and one of Kenny's (2005) conditions for mediation is fulfilled.

Step 4. Predicting the criterion from the predictor: In the base model for the fourth configural model, the mediator is allowed to be associated with the predictor as well as with the criterion (see Step 4 in Baron and Kenny's procedure). That is, we perform a CFA, using the base model $[PM][MY]$. Resulting types and antitypes indicate a relationship between the predictor and the criterion, thus fulfilling the first of Kenny's (2005) conditions.

These four steps tell us whether (1) the variables P, M, and Y are related at all (Step 1); (2) both, the predictor and mediator, are related to the criterion (Step 2); (3) the mediator is related to the criterion (Step 3); and (4) the predictor is related to the criterion (Step 4). Table 6.5 summarizes the

TABLE 6.5. Models for Configural Mediation Analysis of Variables P, M, and Y

Step	CFA Base Model	Types and Antitypes Can Be Due to
1	$[P], [M], [Y]$	$[P, M], [P, Y], [M, Y], [P, M, Y]$
2	$[P, M], [Y]$	$[M, Y], [P, Y], [P, M, Y]$
3	$[P, M], [P, Y]$	$[M, Y], [P, M, Y]$
4	$[P, M], [M, Y]$	$[P, Y], [P, M, Y]$

results from the four steps. Remember that the associations of interest are the ones not included in the CFA base models.

If the results from these steps point to the existence of mediation — that is, if types and antitypes emerge — we need to make a decision concerning the nature of the mediation as either partial or complete. To come to this decision, we compare the results from these four steps. Three comparisons are needed before a decision can be made.

Comparison 1: We first compare the results from Steps 2 and 3. If the types and antitypes found by these models are the same, P is unrelated to Y, but M is in a relationship with Y. The reason for this conclusion is that the relationship between P and Y is taken into account in Step 3, but not in Step 2. So, if the type and antitype patterns from Steps 2 and 3 are the same (and different from the type and antitype patterns found in Steps 1 and 4), they can only be due to the relationship between M and Y. This relationship (and the three-way interaction $[P, M, Y]$; see below) can be the cause for types and antitypes in both Step 2 and Step 3 (see the right column of Table 6.5). If, however, Steps 2 and 3 yield different results of types and antitypes, we compare the two patterns. Two of the possible patterns are of particular importance:

1. Types or antitypes result in Step 2, but not in Step 3. This pattern reflects the effect of the relationship between P and Y, that is, the predictor and the criterion. In addition, M is unrelated to Y. This indicates that the mediator is unrelated to the criterion. If this is the case, the three variables are not in a mediated relationship, and the analysis can be terminated at this point.

2. Types and antitypes result in both steps, but in different patterns. This difference is due to the fact that the relationship between P and Y (predictor and criterion) is included in Step 3, but not in Step 2. This pattern suggests that both P, the predictor, and M, the mediator, are related to the criterion.

Because the model in Step 2 is nested in the models in Steps 3 and 4, it will not occur that types or antitypes result in Step 3 or 4 but not in Step 2.

After the first comparison of the patterns of types and antitypes (Steps 2 and 3), we know whether the predictor, P, the mediator, M, or both are related to the criterion, Y. We now need to determine whether the predictor and the mediator are related to each other. To prepare this decision, we perform the next comparison.

Comparison 2: The second comparison involves the results from all four analytic steps. The main effect base model used in Step 1 is the only one that leaves the door open for the predictor and the mediator to be unrelated to each other. In addition, this model proposes that none of the other relationships exists that are part of the mediation process. These relationships are part of Models 2, 3, and 4. In other words, the model used in Step 1 differs from all others in that it does not contain the $[P, M]$ association. Therefore, if, after Comparison 1, the pattern of types and antitypes found in Step 1 differs from any of the patterns of types and antitypes found in the subsequent steps, the association between P and M exists.

After the second comparison, we know the role played by the $[P, M]$ relationship. Finally, we need to know about the relationship among all three variables, that is, $[P, M, Y]$. This is the relationship that rendered the logit models in the last section saturated. The third comparison allows us to come to a decision about this relationship.

Comparison 3: The three-way interaction $[P, M, Y]$ can show its effects in three forms. First, it is possible that types and antitypes exist only because the three-way relationship $[P, M, Y]$ exists (this can be determined by performing a second order CFA; see von Eye & Lienert, 1984). If this is the case, all steps will yield the same types and antitypes. Therefore, a comparison of the results from all models listed in Table 6.5 will allow one to decide whether this three-way interaction is the sole reason for the existence of types and antitypes. Second, if a subset of types and antitypes consistently emerges in all steps, these are most likely caused by the three-way interaction. Third, types and antitypes can disappear, and new types and antitypes can surface when the three-way interaction is taken into account.

As is obvious from Table 6.5 and the third comparison, the three-way interaction, $[P, M, Y]$, plays a special role in configural mediation analysis. It can be the cause for types and antitypes to emerge (or to disappear) in any of the four models that are estimated. In addition, in standard P-CFA as well as in its extensions in the context of mediation analysis, higher order interactions are often among the reasons for a particular pattern of types and antitypes. In variable-oriented mediation analysis of three variables, taking the three-way interaction into account implies a saturated model (unless the model is nonhierarchical). Therefore, researchers typically focus on two-way interactions. Accordingly, when more than three variables

TABLE 6.6. Models for Configural Mediation Analysis of Variables P, M, and Y; Highest Order Interaction Included in the Base Model

Step	CFA Base Model	Types and Antitypes Can Be Due to
1	$[P], [M], [Y], [P, M, Y]$	$[P, M], [P, Y], [M, Y]$
2	$[P, M], [Y], [P, M, Y]$	$[M, Y], [P, Y]$
3	$[P, M], [P, Y], [P, M, Y]$	$[M, Y]$
4	$[P, M], [M, Y], [P, M, Y]$	$[P, Y]$

are involved in a mediation process, taking the highest order interaction among predictor, mediator, and criterion variables into account also implies a saturated model. In these cases, constraining lower order interaction parameters helps "create" degrees of freedom.

In contrast, the base models of P-CFA and mediation CFA do not take any of the effects into account that are of interest. Therefore, none of the higher order interactions among predictors, mediators, and criterion variables that can be suspected to be a cause of types and antitypes is part of the base model. Thus, we are in a situation that is similar to the one encountered when we compared logistic regression with P-CFA. Models are not fully comparable because they differ in the reasons for a possibly mediated relationship. Standard, variable-oriented mediation modeling that uses logistic regression rarely includes the highest order interaction. In contrast, mediation CFA does include this interaction as a possible cause of types and antitypes by way of not including the contrast vectors for this interaction in the base model.

In a way parallel to making logistic regression and P-CFA comparable, logit model mediation analysis and configural mediation analysis can be made comparable. The general rule is that, in order to create comparable models, either

1. the base model of mediation CFA includes all effects in the base model that are not included in the logit model, specifically, the $[P, M, Y]$ interaction; or

2. the logit model includes all effects that are not included in the base model of mediation CFA.

The second approach usually results in a saturated model. Therefore, to illustrate the first approach, consider again the models in Table 6.5. If the corresponding logit models focus on the lower order interactions, the base model of mediation CFA has to include the three-way interaction in the base model. The models in Table 6.5 thus become as shown in Table 6.6.

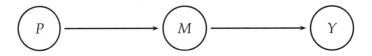

FIGURE 6.5. Full mediation in the model of the variables P, M, and Y.

It should be emphasized again that including the highest order interaction in the base model of mediation CFA does not imply that the base model becomes saturated. Instead, including this interaction implies that the model becomes nonhierarchical (Mair & von Eye, 2007). The higher order interaction no longer implies that all lower order terms are part of the model. For example, adding the highest order interaction to the first model in the series of models (Step 1; see Table 6.6), does not imply that all three two-way interactions are part of the base model. These interactions are considered possible causes of types nd antitypes. Similarly, adding the highest order interaction to the fourth model in the series of models (Step 4; see Table 6.6), does not imply that the remaining two-way interaction, $[P, Y]$, is part of the base model.

We have now developed all elements that are needed for a complete mediation CFA. Thus, we are ready for a data example. Before we present a complete example, however, we summarize the conclusions from the comparisons of the results obtained with the four mediation CFA base models.

Conclusions: From the four steps shown in Table 6.5 and the comparisons of results, five possible outcomes are of interest:

1. If Model 1 (standard, first order CFA) yields no types and no antitypes, there is no mediation because the variables P, M, and Y are, locally, unrelated to each other (note that types and antitypes may not emerge even if variables are associated with each other). Configural mediation analysis can, therefore, stop here.

2. If Model 1 yields types and antitypes, Model 2 yields the same types and antitypes as Model 3, and Comparison 3 leads to the conclusion that at least some of the types and antitypes are due to sources other than the three-way interaction, and the model of *full configural mediation* is supported, that is, the path model in Figure 6.5 holds[3].

---

[3]Note that the models in Figures 6.1 and 6.2 are presented at the level of variable relationships. The particular patterns that carry a configural mediation relationship, emerge from the specific analyses proposed in this text, and are best depicted using the methods introduced in Section 5.4.

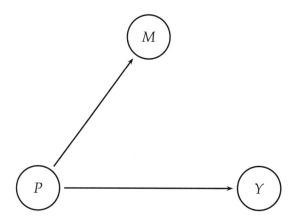

FIGURE 6.6. Model of a direct effect only of P on Y.

3. If Model 1 yields types and antitypes and Model 2 yields the same types and antitypes as Model 4, the model presented in Figure 6.6 is supported. This is the *direct effects-only* model. There is no mediation.

4. If Model 1 yields types and antitypes, if Models 2 and 3 or Models 2 and 4 yield different types and antitypes (compared to each other and to Model 1), and if Models 3 and 4 yield different types and antitypes (also compared to each other and to Model 1), all pairwise variable relationships exist, and the model of *partial mediation* is supported that was depicted in Figure 6.1.

5. If Model 2 yields types and antitypes, but Model 3 fails to do so, the mediator is unrelated to the criterion, and there is no mediation (see Figure 6.6).

It should be noted that other outcomes are possible. For example, it is possible that there is only a relationship between the mediator, M, and the criterion, Y, and that P is not related to either M or Y. Just as with Conclusion 1, this result would contradict the hypothesis of mediation.

Finally, we ask which of the models listed in Tables 6.5 and 6.6 the researcher should interpret. The only model that leaves all variable relationships open is Model 1. Therefore, Model 1 can always be interpreted. The results from Models 2 through 4 need to be known, however, before an interpretation in the context of mediation hypotheses is attempted. Models 2 through 4 cover only aspects of the mediation relationship. The only model that covers the entire set of relationships is Model 1.

If mediation is not supported, or if mediation is not considered or, in

TABLE 6.7. Design Matrix for the Saturated Model for the Cross-Tabulation of the Three Variables Religion (R), Political Preference (P), and Voting Behavior (V) (Constant Vector Implied)

Main Effects				1st Order Interactions					2nd Order Interaction	
R	$P1$	$P2$	V	$RP1$	$RP2$	RV	$P1\,V$	$P2\,V$	$RP1\,V$	$RP2\,V$
1	1	0	1	1	0	1	1	0	1	0
1	1	0	−1	1	0	−1	−1	0	−1	0
1	0	1	1	0	1	1	0	1	0	1
1	0	1	−1	0	1	−1	0	−1	0	−1
1	−1	−1	1	−1	−1	1	−1	−1	−1	−1
1	−1	−1	−1	−1	−1	−1	1	1	1	1
−1	1	0	1	−1	0	−1	1	0	−1	0
−1	1	0	−1	−1	0	1	−1	0	1	0
−1	0	1	1	0	−1	−1	0	1	0	−1
−1	0	1	−1	0	−1	1	0	−1	0	1
−1	−1	−1	1	1	1	−1	−1	−1	1	1
−1	−1	−1	−1	1	1	1	1	1	−1	−1

a particular context, meaningless, Model 1 can always be interpreted as a standard first order CFA. That is, types and antitypes from Model 1 indicate local relationships among variables. If, however, mediation assumptions are supported, results from the same model can be interpreted in the context of a predictive (or, given the right context, causal) mediated process.

Data Example 2: Partial Mediation: In the following paragraphs we present a reanalysis of the voting behavior data (see Vermunt, 1997) that were analyzed in the preceding section by using the logit model plus CFA approach. We ask again whether there are patterns of types and antitypes that support the assumption that Religion predicts Voting Behavior directly or via Political Preference. Two analyses will be presented. The first is a mediation CFA for which none of the four base models includes the three-way interaction, $[R, P, V]$. For the second analysis, this interaction will be part of each of the four base models. The cross-tabulation of the three variables, R, P, and V, has $2 \times 3 \times 2$ cells. The design matrix for the saturated model for this cross-tabulation appears in Table 6.7.

Analysis 1: Three-way interaction $[R, P, V]$ is not part of the Mediation CFA Base Model:

The following four models are estimated for the first CFA-based configural mediation analysis (see Table 6.5):

1. CFA Base Model 1:

$$\log \hat{m} = \lambda + \lambda^R + \lambda^P + \lambda^V.$$

This model uses the first four column vectors of the design matrix given in Table 6.7. These are the vectors for the main effects of the variables.

2. CFA Base Model 2:

$$\log \hat{m} = \lambda + \lambda^R + \lambda^P + \lambda^V + \lambda^{RP}.$$

This model uses the first four vectors of the design matrix and, for the $R \times P$ interaction, the first two vectors of the center panel of the matrix in Table 6.7.

3. CFA Base Model 3:

$$\log \hat{m} = \lambda + \lambda^R + \lambda^P + \lambda^V + \lambda^{RP} + \lambda^{RV}.$$

This model uses the first four vectors of the design matrix. In addition, for the $R \times P$ interaction, it uses the first two vectors of the center panel of the matrix. For the $R \times V$ interaction, it uses the third vector of the center panel of the matrix in Table 6.7.

4. CFA Base Model 4:

$$\log \hat{m} = \lambda + \lambda^R + \lambda^P + \lambda^V + \lambda^{RP} + \lambda^{PV}.$$

This model uses all main effect vectors, and the first two and the last two vectors of the center panel of the design matrix in Table 6.7.

In each of the four following CFAs, we use the z-test and protected the significance level using the same, Bonferroni-adjusted $\alpha^* = 0.00417$. This protection is stricter than the Holland-Copenhaver procedure. We selected it because of the large number of tests that are performed using the same data. Now, instead of interpreting each CFA result in detail, we present an overview table that allows one to easily perform the comparisons that lead to a decision about the nature of the mediation in these data. Table 6.8 displays this overview. The detailed results for Model 1 were shown already in Table 6.1.

Based on the results in Table 6.8, we now (1) summarize the results from the four models with respect to the assumption of mediation, and (2) perform the model comparisons:

Model 1. The main effect, first order CFA base model yields three types and four antitypes[4]. If the mediation assumption can be retained, we

---

[4]Note that this is the same base model as the one used for the analysis for Table 6.2. The fact that Cell 2 2 2, in Table 6.8, does not constitute an antitype is due to the stricter level of α protection used for the present analyses.

TABLE 6.8. CFA-Based Configural Mediation Analysis of the Variables Religion (R), Political Preference (P), and Voting Behavior (V)

Configuration RPV	m	CFA Base Model Model 1 [R][P][V]	Model 2 [R][P][V][RP]	Model 3 [R][P][V] [RP][RV]	Model 4 [R][P][V] [RP][PV]
111	50	Antitype			Type
112	25				Antitype
121	88		Type		
122	8	Antitype	Antitype		
131	177	Type			
132	47		Antitype		
211	39	Antitype	Antitype	Antitype	
212	97	Type	Type	Type	
221	91	Type		Type	
222	18		Antitype	Antitype	
231	61	Antitype			
232	49				Type
$LR - X^2(df)$		209.97 (7)	153.69 (5)	95.60 (4)	51.39 (3)

interpret this result. At this point, all we know is that the three variables are associated and that mediation may exist. The following steps are performed to identify the type of mediation (if any).

Model 2. This model yields two types and four antitypes. We conclude that a mediation process may exist because the predictor, Religion, the mediator, Political Preference, or both are related to the criterion, Voting Behavior. The details of the mediation process are still unknown. To identify these, we need the following models (see Table 6.8).

Model 3. This model results in two types and two antitypes. We conclude that the mediator, Political Preference, and the criterion, Voting Behavior, are associated.

Model 4. This model yields two types and one antitype. We conclude that the predictor, Religion, and the criterion, Voting Behavior, are associated.

Now, these results need to be compared. The result of the comparisons will be a decision about the nature of the mediation process. We proceed in the sequence of steps outlined for the four models, above.

Comparison 1: The comparison of Models 2 and 3 shows that different types and antitypes emerged. From this comparison, we conclude that Religion, Political Preference, or both are related to Voting Behavior. We now need to determine whether Religion and Political Preference are related to each other.

Comparison 2: Table 6.8 shows that the pattern of types and antitypes found for Model 1 differs from the patterns found for each of the Models 2, 3, and 4. Therefore, we conclude that the association between Religion and Political Preference exists.

Comparison 3: The third comparison concerns the effects of the three-way interaction. Table 6.8 shows that the overlap between the type and antitype patterns from the four models is zero, that is, not one type or antitype appears under *all four* CFA base models. We, therefore, conclude that the types and antitypes found by the four models are not solely due to the three-way interaction. It is important to note that this conclusion does not imply that the three-way interaction plays no role. For example, the results in Table 6.2 show a pattern of types and antitypes that is different from the results of Model 2 in Table 6.8. The differences are due to the fact that, for the results in Table 6.2, the three-way interaction was included in the CFA base model.

At this point, in the present example, we are in a position in which we can make a decision about the nature of configural mediation in the cross-classification of the variables Religion, Political Preference, and Voting Behavior. Specifically, we found, that

- Each model resulted in types and/or antitypes;

- the patterns of types and antitypes are unique for each model; and

- the types and antitypes are not solely due to the three-way interaction [*RPV*].

We conclude that the hypothesis of *local partial mediation* is supported. This is the same hypothesis that was already supported at both the variable and the configural levels in the last section. However, the types and antitypes found here differ from the ones interpreted in the last section, because, here, we did not make an effort to produce a base model that was parallel to the standard logit models that we had specified for mediation analysis.

The types and antitypes found here can be interpreted in a fashion parallel to the last section. Therefore, we will not repeat the interpretation. Instead, we ask whether aggregation of types and antitypes is possible that leads to a picture that distinguishes configural mediation analysis from variable-oriented mediation analysis even more. The three types that resulted for Model 1 are 1 3 1, 2 1 2, and 2 2 1. The pairwise comparisons of these type patterns show that each type differs in more than one category from each other type. Aggregation that uses the Quine-McCluskey method, therefore, cannot be performed.

The four antitypes that resulted for Model 1 are 1 1 1, 1 2 2, 2 1 1, and 2 3 1. As in the last section, the first and the third of these differ in only one category. By way of aggregation, we obtain

$$1\ 1\ 1$$
$$\underline{2\ 1\ 1}$$
$$.\ 1\ 1$$

where the dot indicates the variable categories aggregated across. The aggregated antitype, denoted by . 1 1, indicates that it is less likely than expected that respondents who identify with the political left will vote. This result is independent of the religious orientation of the respondents.

In the context of mediation configural analysis, this result is important. It shows that the data contain one element of the mediator-criterion relationship that does not originate in the predictor (cf. the interpretation of the P-CFA results in Table 5.15).

Analysis 2: Three-way interaction [R, P, V] is part of the CFA base model:

In the following section, we reanalyze the Voting data using CFA-based Configural Mediation Analysis again. However, in contrast to the models in the last section, we now include the three-way interaction among Religion, Political Preference, and Voting Behavior in each of the base models. Two goals are pursued in this section. First, the CFA base models that are being used in this section will be closer or, in some instances, identical to the ones used for the logistic regression analysis of the same data. Second, these models illustrate that a change in the base model can lead to a change in results, even if the effect that is included in the base model is not significant.

We proceed in the same sequence of steps as in the first analysis, that is, the analysis without the three-way interaction in the base model. The following four base models are nonhierarchical because some (or all, as in Step 1) of the terms that are of lower order with respect to the three-way interaction that now is included as part of the base models are set to zero (see Mair & von Eye, 2007). These steps are (see Table 6.6):

1. CFA Base Model 1:

$$\log \hat{m} = \lambda + \lambda^R + \lambda^P + \lambda^V + \lambda^{RPV}.$$

This model uses the first four and the last two column vectors of the design matrix given in Table 6.7. These are the vectors for the main effects of the variables and the three-way interaction (second order interaction term), respectively. The detailed results of this step are shown in Table 6.4.

2. CFA Base Model 2:

$$\log \hat{m} = \lambda + \lambda^R + \lambda^P + \lambda^V + \lambda^{RP} + \lambda^{RPV}.$$

This model uses the first four and the last two vectors of the design matrix and, for the $R \times P$ interaction, the first two vectors of the center panel of the matrix in Table 6.7. As with the first model, this and the following base models use the last two vectors in the design matrix in Table 6.7 to include the three-way interaction.

3. CFA Base Model 3:

$$\log \hat{m} = \lambda + \lambda^R + \lambda^P + \lambda^V + \lambda^{RP} + \lambda^{RV} + \lambda^{RPV}.$$

This model uses the first four and the last two vectors of the design matrix. For the $R \times P$ interaction, it uses the first two vectors of the center panel of the matrix. For the $R \times V$ interaction, it uses the third vector of the center panel of the matrix in Table 6.7.

4. CFA Base Model 4:

$$\log \hat{m} = \lambda + \lambda^R + \lambda^P + \lambda^V + \lambda^{RP} + \lambda^{PV} + \lambda^{RPV}.$$

This model uses all main effect vectors, the two vectors for the three-way interaction, and the first two and the last two vectors of the center panel of the design matrix in Table 6.7.

In each of the four following CFAs, we used the z-test and protected the significance level using the Bonferroni-adjusted $\alpha^* = 0.00417$ again, because this protection is stricter than the Holland-Copenhhaver procedure. We selected this more conservative protection procedure because of the large number of tests that are performed using the same data. As in Analysis 1, instead of interpreting each result in detail, we present an overview table that allows one to easily perform the comparisons that lead to a decision about the nature of the mediation in these data. Table 6.9 displays this overview. The detailed results for Model 1 were shown already in Table 6.4.

The interpretation and comparison of the results from the four steps, when the three-way interaction [RPV] is taken into account (i.e., Analysis 2), lead to the same conclusion as when this interaction is not taken into account (i.e., Analysis 1). Partial mediation is supported again. However, the results are not exactly the same. For example, consider CFA Base Model 1: In comparison with the results from the main effects-only base model in Table 6.8, the present result shows one new type (constituted by Cell 1 2 1).

TABLE 6.9. CFA-Based Configural Mediation Analysis (Three-Way Interactions Included) of the Variables Religion (R), Political Preference (P), and Voting Behavior (V)

Configuration $R\ P\ V$	m	Model1 $[R][P][V]$ $[RPV]$	Model2 $[R][P][V]$ $[RP]$ $[RPV]$	Model3 $[R][P][V]$ $[RP][RV]$ $[RPV]$	Model4 $[R][P][V]$ $[RP][PV]$ $[RPV]$
			CFA Base Model		
111	50	Antitype			
112	25			Type	
121	88	Type	Type		
122	8	Antitype	Antitype	Antitype	
131	177	Type			
132	47				
211	39	Antitype	Antitype		
212	97	Type	Type		
221	91				
222	18			Antitype	Type
231	61	Antitype			
232	49				
$LR-X^2(df)$		184.27 (5)	128.66 (3)	71.39 (2)	35.89 (1)

In addition, one type (Cell 2 2 1) does not surface any longer. However, also as before, whereas the types cannot be aggregated, the antitypes can. The same antitype results. It is constituted by pattern . 1 1.

We thus conclude again that the data are structured such that they contain (1) elements that support the hypothesis of partial mediation and (2) other elements that just describe the relationship between the mediator and the criterion variable. This form of result is unique to analysis with CFA.

Data Example 3: Full Mediation: In the following paragraphs, we present an example of full mediation. Figure 6.5 depicts full mediation in three variables. To illustrate a process that is fully mediated, we now present a data example using data from the longitudinal project on intimate partner violence (Bogat et al., 2006). A sample of 204 women filled out, in 1-year intervals, a questionnaire that was administered to assess the degree to which they showed symptoms of posttraumatic stress disorder (PTSD scale for battered women; Saunders, 1994). For the following analyses, we use the information that was provided on perpetration of severe violence by their intimate partners in the 12-month periods before the third, fourth, and fifth interviews. The observed variable, Severe Violence (S), was coded as 1 = did not occur, and 2 = did occur. The three observations will be labeled as $S1$, $S2$, and $S3$.

The question we ask here is whether S2 is the mediator that links S1 and S3. If the relationship between S1 and S3 is fully mediated by S2, the direct link between S1 and S3 is not needed to explain types and antitypes from Model 1. The resulting model would be comparable to a first order autoregressive Markov model.

As in the last section, we analyze the data by using two approaches to configural mediation analysis. First, we apply the logistic regression plus CFA method (Section 6.1). Second, we apply the CFA-only method (Section 6.2). Crossed, the three observations of severe partner violence span the 2 × 2 × 2 table given in Table 6.10.

Analysis 1: Logistic regression plus CFA:

In a first step, we run a reference model. This model is used for comparison purposes. In this example, we use the model of variable independence, that is, the first order CFA base model, as the reference model:

$$\log \hat{m} = \lambda + \lambda_i^{S1} + \lambda_j^{S2} + \lambda_k^{S3}.$$

This model was estimated by using ℓ_{EM} (Vermunt, 1997). All other programs, such as the CFA program discussed in Chapter 13, SYSTAT, and R, yielded the same results (see Chapter 13 for sample scripts and results from the different programs). The same applies to the models discussed later in this section. The reference model describes the data poorly ($LR - X^2 = 37.19$; $df = 4$; $p < 0.01$). We, therefore, reject it and anticipate that types and antitypes will emerge.

Table 6.10 displays the observed and the estimated expected cell frequencies for the reference model, along with the results for the base model of first order CFA. For analysis, we use the binomial test and the Holland-Copenhaver procedure of α protection. The binomial test was used because the estimated expected frequency for Cell 2 2 2 was rather small. If an expected frequency is small, the exact binomial test can be trusted more than any of the asymptotic tests. Still, results from small expected values have to be viewed and interpreted with caution.

From the rejection of the reference model, we conclude that interactions must exist. If the full mediation hypothesis prevails, the interactions between time-adjacent observations of severe partner violence explain these data. To test this hypothesis, we estimate the model

$$\log \hat{m} = \lambda + \lambda_i^{S1} + \lambda_j^{S2} + \lambda_k^{S3} + \lambda_{ij}^{S1,S2} + \lambda_{jk}^{S2,S3}.$$

This model describes the data very well ($LR - X^2 = 3.95$; $df = 2$; $p = 0.139$). In addition, this model is significantly better than the reference model of first order CFA ($\Delta LR - X^2 = 33.24$; $df = 2$; $p < 0.01$). In addition, each

TABLE 6.10. First Order CFA of the Cross-Tabulation of Severe Violence, Observed at Three Occasions ($S1$, $S2$, and $S3$); Three-Way Interaction Not Taken into Account

Configuration $S1$ $S2$ $S3$	m	$\hat{m}$	p	Type/Antitype
111	157	143.2134	.01915750	
112	2	5.8454	.06650423	
121	8	18.1984	.00469242	Antitype
122	1	.7428	.52486050	
211	20	30.6886	.01886143	
212	2	1.2526	.35657128	
221	11	3.8997	.00208993	Type
222	3	.1592	.00058901	Type

of the critical parameters is significant. Specifically, the parameter for the $[S1, S2]$ interaction is estimated to be $\lambda^{S1,S2} = 0.61$ ($z = 4.999$; $p < 0.01$), and the parameter for the $[S2, S3]$ interaction is estimated to be $\lambda^{S2,S3} = 0.56$ ($z = 2.986$; $p < 0.01$). We thus conclude that the hypothesis of full mediation is confirmed. Severe partner violence predicts itself from one observation point to the next. Only knowledge from the period before an interview is needed for prediction of the current observation period. Model fit is so good that significant improvement is almost impossible.

In the second step (of two) of this analysis, we ask which configurations carry the relationships between $S1$ and $S2$, and between $S2$ and $S3$. This question is answered by using CFA. The base model for this CFA includes

1. All main effects;

2. The interaction between $S1$ and $S3$; and

3. The three-way interaction among $S1$, $S2$, and $S3$.

If this model is rejected, only the interactions between time-adjacent responses, that is, the interactions $[S1, S2]$ and $[S2, S3]$, can cause types and antitypes. The base model is thus

$$\log \hat{m} = \lambda + \lambda_i^{S1} + \lambda_j^{S2} + \lambda_k^{S3} + \lambda_{ik}^{S1,S3} + \lambda_{ijk}^{S1,S2,S3}.$$

Note that this model is nonhierarchical because the two-way interactions $[S1, S2]$ and $[S2, S3]$ are set to zero. The design matrix for this model appears in Table 6.11.

TABLE 6.11. Design Matrix for CFA of Full Mediation Hypothesis after Logit Model Fit

Main Effects			Interactions	
$S1$	$S2$	$S3$	$S1 \times S3$	$S1 \times S2 \times S3$
1	1	1	1	1
1	1	−1	−1	−1
1	−1	1	1	−1
1	−1	−1	−1	1
−1	1	1	−1	−1
−1	1	−1	1	1
−1	−1	1	−1	1
−1	−1	−1	1	−1

TABLE 6.12. CFA of Full Mediation Hypothesis Concerning Severe Violence, Observed at Three Occasions ($S1$, $S2$, and $S3$); Three-Way Interaction Taken into Account

Configuration $S1\ S2\ S3$	m	$\hat{m}$	p	Type/Antitype
111	157	154.3235	.36593879	
112	2	1.9412	.57909197	
121	8	10.6765	.25502512	
122	1	1.0588	.71407553	
211	20	20.0588	.55366868	
212	2	4.6765	.15153541	
221	11	10.9412	.53619432	
222	3	.3235	.00438656	Type

The results of the CFA of the full mediation hypothesis appears in Table 6.12. This base model represents the data poorly ($LR - X^2 = 10.75$; $df = 2$; $p < 0.01$). We, therefore, reject it and anticipate that types and antitypes will emerge. We see one type.

Substantively, the CFA results in Table 6.12 suggest that the hypothesis of full mediation is carried by those three women who are victims of severe partner violence during the entire observation period (Configuration 2 2 2). None of the other configurations contradicts the base model, according to which time-adjacent pairs of responses are independent of each other. The resulting process can thus be depicted as in Figure 6.7.

The results shown in Table 6.12 illustrate two characteristics of CFA results (cf. the discussion of CFA results in Section 1.3). First, only one configuration (cell) emerged as "outlandish". This is as rare as the result that all cells constitute types and antitypes. However, it shows that it is possible to have just one extreme cell in a table. In the present example,

FIGURE 6.7. Full mediation type of severe partner violence.

TABLE 6.13. First Order CFA of Severe Violence, Observed at Three Occasions ($S1$, $S2$, and $S3$); Three-Way Interaction Taken into Account

Configuration S1 S2 S3	m	$\hat{m}$	p	Type/Antitype
111	157	154.2109	.35907685	
112	2	2.7647	.47666270	
121	8	9.4440	.39447973	
122	1	1.5804	.53054999	
211	20	20.5804	.50496449	
212	2	3.4440	.32899789	
221	11	11.7647	.48611043	
222	3	.2109	.00131946	Type

this cell is extreme because its estimated expected cell frequency is so small. Therefore, as was emphasized previously, this type must be interpreted with caution.

Second, it is not the case that the largest cells always constitute types and the smallest always constitute antitypes. This pattern would be a characteristic of *zero order CFA* (von Eye, 2002a). In all other models of CFA, a rare result such as the one in Table 6.12, in which one of the smallest cells constitutes a type, is conceivable and, evidently, can occur.

Analysis 2: Full Mediation CFA:

In this section, we illustrate the analysis of a cross-classification under a full mediation hypothesis. We use the same data as in the last section, in which we performed a logistic regression plus CFA, also under a full mediation hypothesis. Here, we use the CFA-based method of analysis. To come to a decision about the nature of mediation, we take the steps that were described earlier in this section. Specifically, we estimate four CFA base models, following the four steps shown in Table 6.6. Because the three-way interaction is not necessarily part of the hypothesis of full mediation, we include the three-way interaction [$S1, S2, S3$] in each of the base models.

1. *CFA Base Model 1: First Order CFA, including* [$S1, S2, S3$]: The base model

for first order CFA of the severe partner violence data is

$$\log \hat{m} = \lambda + \lambda_i^{S1} + \lambda_j^{S2} + \lambda_k^{S3} + \lambda_{ijk}^{S1,S2,S3}.$$

If types and antitypes emerge from this model, full mediation may exist. If there are no types or antitypes, the analysis can stop here. As in Analysis 1, we use the binomial test and protect α by using the Holland-Copenhaver procedure. The first order CFA base model does not describe the data well ($LR - X^2 = 11.89$; $df = 3$; $p = 0.008$). It is, thus, rejected, and we anticipate types or antitypes to emerge. The CFA results from this base model are summarized in Table 6.13. The results in Table 6.13 are very similar to those in Table 6.12. With only one exception, all expected cell frequencies are close to the corresponding observed frequencies, thus suggesting that, in large parts of the table, the three severe violence responses are independent of one another. The only exception is, as in the prior analysis, Cell 2 2 2. This cell constitutes a type. From this result alone, we conclude that, if the hypothesis of full mediation is supported at all, it is represented by this configuration. This result would confirm the one obtained from logistic regression plus CFA. Still, to make sure the hypothesis of full mediation can be retained, we need to perform the remaining three steps of analysis.

2. *CFA Base Model 2: Predicting S3 from S1 and S2*: The base model for this step is

$$\log \hat{m} = \lambda + \lambda_i^{S1} + \lambda_j^{S2} + \lambda_k^{S3} + \lambda_{ij}^{S1,S2} + \lambda_{ijk}^{S1,S2,S3}.$$

This model again fails to describe the data well ($LR - X^2 = 9.29$; $df = 2$; $p = 0.010$). The only type that results from this model is constituted by Configuration 2 2 2. We thus know that the interaction $[S1, S2]$ makes only a small, nonsignificant contribution to explaining the data ($\Delta LR - X^2 = 2.6$; $\Delta df = 1$; $p = 0.107$). In addition, we know that there must be a relationship between $S1$ and $S3$ and/or between $S2$ and $S3$. The following steps and comparisons will provide more detail.

3. *CFA Base Model 3: Predicting S3 from S2*: The base model for this step is

$$\log \hat{m} = \lambda + \lambda_i^{S1} + \lambda_j^{S2} + \lambda_k^{S3} + \lambda_{ij}^{S1,S2} + \lambda_{ik}^{S1,S3} + \lambda_{ijk}^{S1,S2,S3}.$$

This model describes the data very well ($LR - X^2 = 3.36$; $df = 1$; $p = 0.067$). No type or antitype emerges. This model was estimated to determine whether there is a relationship between the mediator and the criterion that results in types or antitypes. Clearly, this is not the case, and we can stop here. The fourth CFA base model that tests the link between $S1$ and $S3$ would also have failed to result in types or antitypes. This result would have indicated that there is no predictor-criterion relationship at the level of types and antitypes and, thus, would have supported the hypothesis of full mediation. The result from Step 3, however, brings the hypothesis of mediation down, and there is no need to examine the fourth CFA base model.

Based on the results in the first and the second sets of analyses, we conclude that logistic regression plus CFA and CFA-based analysis of the same data can yield different results. The reason for this difference is that the results of logistic regression are based on different models than CFA-based analysis would include. One asks which of the two methods is the one to prefer. The answer to this question depends on the research strategy under which data are analyzed.

If researchers ask whether types and antitypes exist that represent relationships that were found in the context of *variable-oriented research*, logistic regression plus CFA is the right approach to mediation analysis. If, however, researchers proceed in the context of *person-oriented research* (Bergman & Magnusson, 1997; von Eye & Bergman, 2003), and ask whether patterns of types and antitypes exist that support mediation hypotheses solely at the level of configurations, CFA-based mediation analysis is the method of choice. The present results illustrate that selecting one of these two approaches to mediation analysis is not trivial, and can lead to different conclusions.

6.3   Configural Chain Models

There exist many more prediction models that are conceptually related to mediation analysis. One prominent example is the model of a prediction chain. To define a chain, consider the three variables A, B, and C. According to the definition given by von Eye and Brandtstädter (1998), these three variables constitute a chain if A predicts (or causes) B, and B predicts (or causes) C. Direct-path models assume that A and C are directly connected with each other. In contrast, indirect-path models assume that the effect of A on C goes through B. It is also conceivable that both the direct and the indirect connections between A and C exist. Figure 6.8 displays the indirect-path-only chain model for the three variables A, B, and C.

Naturally, longer chains are conceivable. It is doubtful whether the link between two variables can meaningfully be labeled a chain. Clearly, the concepts of Mediation and Chain are conceptually related to each other. The indirect-path-only chain corresponds to a fully mediated process. The chain that also contains the direct connection between A and C corresponds to a partially mediated process. When more than three variables are studied

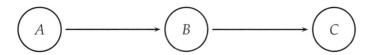

FIGURE 6.8. Illustration of a chain with three variables.

as a chain, one can describe this relationship as a fully mediated process with multiple mediators. Mediation processes with multiple mediation steps are also conceivable. To analyze chain hypotheses, the same methods can be used as described in Sections 6.1 and 6.2, on mediation models. Therefore, chains will not be elaborated in detail in this context.

6.4 Chapter Summary

Mediation processes link predictor, mediator, and response variables such that the path from the predictor reaches the criterion either only through the mediator indirectly (full mediation) or through the mediator both indirectly and directly. To evaluate mediator models, most researchers use regression models or structural models. These models establish the existence of the proposed paths in a sequence of simple and partial regression models. When CFA is used to analyze mediation hypotheses, mediation is assumed to manifest in patterns of configurations instead of variables.

For CFA of mediation hypotheses, two approaches are proposed. The first involves establishing type of mediation using logit models. If mediation exists, CFA is performed to identify those patterns of configurations that carry the mediation process. This approach uses methods from both variable- and person-oriented research.

The second approach uses exclusively CFA methods. A series of CFA base models is specified with the goal of establishing links between the predictor, mediator, and response variables, at the level of configurations. The comparison of the results from these models allows one to make decisions concerning the type of mediation that may exist for each pattern of configurations. One possible outcome of the approach that uses only CFA methods is that, in the same table, patterns of configurations may exist that support hypotheses of full mediation while other patterns of configurations may support hypotheses of partial mediation, and the remaining patterns of configurations support the null hypotheses.

7

Auto-Association CFA

In contrast to mediation CFA, which can be performed using cross-sectional but also longitudinal data, Auto-Association CFA (A-CFA) is a method for the analysis of repeated observations. A-CFA allows one to analyze two or more repeatedly observed variables, that is, two or more series of scores. The question A-CFA allows one to answer concerns the relationships among these series that go above and beyond autocorrelations. To that effect, A-CFA uses a base model that takes autocorrelations of all possible orders into account. As a result, A-CFA will identify types and antitypes that are indicative of relationships among the observed series of scores, at the level of individual configurations. The role that covariates play in the identification of types and antitypes in A-CFA is discussed. Alternative approaches to specifying base models when covariates are part of the analysis are proposed and applied in data examples.

In Section 7.1, we present auto-association CFA (A-CFA; von Eye, Mun, & Bogat, 2008, 2009) without covariates, and, in Section 7.2, A-CFA with covariates.

7.1 A-CFA without Covariates

A standard result of repeated measures analysis is that associations among repeated, time-adjacent measures, that is, *auto-associations*, are strong. In many studies, these associations are stronger than those between different variables. However, researchers are often interested in the relationships among two or more behavior trajectories. A-CFA allows one to examine the relationships among two or more behavior trajectories. Specifically, A-CFA

- identifies types and antitypes that exist beyond auto-associations; these types and antitypes reflect relationships among different series of measures instead of relationships within individual series of measures;

- operates at the manifest variable level; no assumptions concerning latent variables are needed; and

- creates results in the form of local associations, that is, types and antitypes, instead of associations at the variable level.

Reflecting these characteristics, the *A-CFA base model* is specified as follows:

1. it includes the main effects of all variables;

2. it includes interactions of any order within each series of measures; the A-CFA base model is thus saturated within each series of measures; and

3. it proposes independence between the series of measures.

A-CFA types and antitypes, therefore, can result only if the series of measures are related to each other. In the simplest case, there is only one series of measures and one additional variable that is observed only once. In this case, temporal patterns of the series would be related to categories of the variable that was observed once. Let this variable be X, and let the second variable, observed twice, be $Y1$ and $Y2$. The A-CFA base model for these three scores is

$$\log \hat{m} = \lambda + \lambda^X + \lambda^{Y1} + \lambda^{Y2} + \lambda^{Y1,Y2}.$$

There are only three terms that can be included before this model becomes completely saturated. These are the terms $[X, Y1]$, $[X, Y2]$, and $[X, Y1, Y2]$. Each of these terms links the once-observed variable, X, with the repeatedly observed variable, Y. The auto-association of Y is part of the base model. Therefore, types and antitypes will reflect associations between X and Y above and beyond the auto-association in the series of Y measures.

At this point, the base models of A-CFA and CFA of end points (Section 5.2) or trajectories (Section 5.3) are indistinguishable. Now, however, suppose X was observed twice also. We obtain the scores $X1$ and $X2$. Then the A-CFA base model becomes

$$\log \hat{m} = \lambda + \lambda^{X1} + \lambda^{X2} + \lambda^{X1,X2} + \lambda^{Y1} + \lambda^{Y2} + \lambda^{Y1,Y2}.$$

This model is saturated in both series of measures. Only those interactions that relate X-measures to Y-measures are not part of the base model. These are the interactions $[X1, Y1]$, $[X1, Y2]$, $[X2, Y1]$, $[X2, Y2]$,

$[X1, X2, Y1]$, $[X1, X2, Y2]$, $[X1, Y1, Y2]$, $[X2, Y1, Y2]$, and $[X1, X2, Y1, Y2]$. If any of these interactions exists, they can manifest in types and antitypes.

Readers will notice that this model has the same form as some of the P-CFA models in Chapter 5. The difference is that P-CFA can also be used when (1) all measures stem from different variables, and (2) the data are cross-sectional. The interactions among predictors and criteria, therefore, will not reflect auto-associations. Extensions of the A-CFA model can include

- longer series of measures,

- more than two series of measures, and

- continuous or categorical covariates.

The last of these extensions is discussed later, in Section 7.2. Before introducing the extension, we present a data example.

Data Example 1: The following example uses the same data as Data Example 3 in Chapter 1. In a study on the development of aggression in adolescence (Finkelstein et al., 1994), 114 adolescents (67 females) indicated at the ages of 11 and 15, whether they were, subjectively, above or below average in aggressive impulses ($A83$ and $A87$) and in physical aggression against peers ($P83$ and $P87$). The variables A and P were scored as 1 = below their respective mean and 2 = above mean. Dichotomization was performed at the grand mean of each variable, so that development toward higher or lower than average could be reflected in the dichotomous scores.

In a first step, the cross-classification $A83 \times A87 \times P83 \times P87$ was analyzed under the main effect base model of standard, first order CFA, that is, the log-frequency model

$$\log \hat{m} = \lambda + \lambda^{A83} + \lambda^{A87} + \lambda^{P83} + \lambda^{P87}.$$

Any association in this group of four variables can result in types and antitypes. This includes the auto-associations. Therefore, in a second step, we reanalyze these data, using A-CFA. The base model for this analysis is

$$\log \hat{m} = \lambda + \lambda^{A83} + \lambda^{A87} + \lambda^{A83,A87} + \lambda^{P83} + \lambda^{P87} + \lambda^{P83,P87},$$

where, as before, single superscripts indicate main effects and double superscripts indicate two-way interactions. Each of the interactions that was not included in this model relates variables from the two series to each other. Specifically, these are the interactions $[A83, P83]$, $[A83, P87]$, $[A87, P83]$, $[A87, P87]$, $[A83, A87, P83]$, $[A83, A87, P87]$, $[A83, P83, P87]$, $[A87, P83, P87]$, and $[A83, A87, P83, P87]$.

TABLE 7.1. First Order CFA of the Developmental Trajectories of Physical Aggression against Peers (P83 and P87) and Aggressive Impulses (A83 and A87)

Configuration A83 A87 P83 P87	m	$\hat{m}$	z	p	Type/Antitype
1111	24	10.288	4.2748	.000010	Type
1112	1	3.843	−1.4501	.073513	
1121	9	11.037	−.6130	.269933	
1122	4	4.122	−.0601	.476028	
1211	5	8.329	−1.1534	.124375	
1212	4	3.111	.5042	.307050	
1221	3	8.934	−1.9854	.023552	
1222	3	3.337	−.1844	.426835	
2111	10	11.841	−.5351	.296302	
2112	1	4.423	−1.6275	.051816	
2121	12	12.702	−.1971	.421882	
2122	2	4.744	−1.2599	.103850	
2211	9	9.586	−.1892	.424971	
2212	1	3.580	−1.3636	.086339	
2221	11	10.283	.2236	.411524	
2222	15	3.841	5.6943	.000000	Type

For both analyses, we use the z-test and the Holland-Copenhaver procedure of α-protection. Table 7.1 shows the results from first order CFA, and Table 7.2 shows the results from A-CFA.

The $LR - X^2$ for the first order CFA base model is 51.27 ($df = 11; p < 0.01$), indicating significant model-data discrepancies. This applies accordingly to the $LR - X^2$ for the A-CFA base model ($LR - X^2 = 28.46; df = 9; p = 0.001$). This base model is significantly better than the base model of first order CFA ($\Delta LR - X^2 = 22.81; \Delta df = 2; p < 0.01$). However, it still does not describe the data well. Therefore, we expect types and antitypes to emerge from both runs.

Table 7.1 shows that consistently below average aggressive impulses go hand-in-hand with consistently below average physical aggression against peers (Configuration 1 1 1 1). Accordingly, consistently above average aggressive impulses go hand-in-hand with consistently above average physical aggression against peers (Configuration 2 2 2 2). None of the patterns that show change in one or both of the repeatedly observed variables is particularly unlikely.

As was indicated above, auto-associations are often the strongest effects in repeated-measures designs. Therefore, we now ask whether these two types are the results of auto-associations or indicate cross-variable relationships. If auto-associations are the sole reasons for the emergence of

TABLE 7.2. A-CFA of the Developmental Trajectories of Physical Aggression against Peers ($P83$ and $P87$) and Aggressive Impulses ($A83$ and $A87$)

Configuration A83 A87 P83 P87	m	$\hat{m}$	z	p	Type/Antitype
1111	24	16.000	2.000	.022750	
1112	1	2.333	−.873	.191332	
1121	9	11.667	−.781	.217401	
1122	4	8.000	−1.414	.078681	
1211	5	6.316	−.542	.293909	
1212	4	0.921	3.208	.000668	Type
1221	3	4.605	−.748	.227230	
1222	3	3.158	−.089	.464541	
2111	10	10.526	−.162	.435653	
2112	1	1.535	−.432	.332871	
2121	12	7.675	1.561	.059262	
2122	2	5.263	−1.582	.056825	
2211	9	15.158	−.814	.207822	
2212	1	2.211	−.016	.493617	
2221	11	11.053	−.089	.464541	
2222	15	7.579	2.696	.003509	

the two types, they will disappear if the corresponding interaction terms are included in the base model. Table 7.2 shows the results of A-CFA.

Table 7.2 shows that none of the types that emerged from first order CFA (Table 7.1) also emerged from A-CFA. We thus conclude that one of the reasons for the existence of these types is that the auto-associations are strong. One new type surfaced from A-CFA. This type, however, suggesting that a shift from below to above average aggressive impulses goes hand-in-hand with a synchronous and parallel shift in physical aggression against peers, can be interpreted only with caution, for two reasons. First, the expected frequency is rather small. Therefore, the approximation of the normal distribution by the test statistic may not be optimal. Second, the observed frequency is rather small also. Therefore, a replication of this study with a larger sample may be needed to confirm this result.

We now ask which log-linear model can be used to explain the joint distribution of the four variables used in Tables 7.1 and 7.2. One model that describes the data well includes, in addition to all main effects, the auto-associations that are carried by the interactions $[A83, A87]$ and $[P83, P87]$, and the synchronous interactions $[A83, P83]$ and $[A87, P87]$ $(LR - X^2 = 5.05; df = 7; p = 0.65)$. Table 7.3 displays the corresponding parameters and test statistics, estimated by using ℓ_{EM}.

TABLE 7.3. Parameters and Test Statistics for the Data in Tables 7.1 and 7.2, Using the A-CFA Base Model plus the Two Synchronous Interactions [$A83, P83$] and [$A87, P87$]

Effect	Parameter	se	z
$P83$	−0.197	0.124	−1.587
$P87$	0.606	0.131	4.636
$A83$	−0.106	0.104	−1.027
$A87$	−0.052	0.123	−0.421
$P87, A87$	0.407	0.119	3.435
$P83, A83$	0.278	0.099	2.802
$A83, A87$	0.296	0.101	2.930
$P83, P87$	0.357	0.122	2.933
Intercept	1.582		

Table 7.3 shows that each of the interaction parameters is significant. We conclude that aggressive impulses and physical aggression against peers predict each other when they are observed in the same year. Across a span of 4 years, however, only the auto-associations remain. CFA shows that these effects are carried by a very small number of configurations.

7.2 A-CFA with Covariates

A covariate is defined as a variable that is not under control of the experimenter, but may be a predictor of the outcome variable(s). In person-oriented research, typical covariates are stratification variables. For example, the effects of alcohol may be gender-specific, the timing of pubertal development is gender-specific, the incidence rates of such diseases as cancer or Parkinson's disease are age-specific, intimate partner violence varies across income brackets, car insurance rates vary across age brackets and location of residence, or the selection of movies to watch depends on who will be around to watch the movie with.

In the present context, we focus on categorical covariates. In addition, we cross-tabulate the four covariates with all other variables in the table. However, continuous covariates or categorical covariates that are not crossed with all other variables can be taken into account also (Glück & von Eye, 2000; von Eye, 2002a; von Eye & Mun, 2005, see also Chapter 4). Two extended A-CFA submodels will be considered. In the first, types and antitypes reflect any of the possible predictor-criterion relationships, and the covariate plays the role of just another variable used to span the table. The second extended A-CFA submodel will be specified such that types and antitypes reflect predictor-criterion relationships that are specific to the categories of the covariate. Examples of such categories are the strata of a stratification variable. Each of the models discussed here can be specified in a parallel way for standard P-CFA (von Eye, Mun, & Bogat, 2009), mediation CFA, moderation CFA, and most of the other CFA base models discussed in this text.

7.2.1 A-CFA with Covariates I: Types and Antitypes Reflect Any of the Possible Relationships Among Two or More Series of Measures

For the following introduction of A-CFA with covariates, consider the four variables $X1$, $X2$, $Y1$, and $Y2$. Let $X1$ and $X2$ be the measures of a first time series and $Y1$ and $Y2$ the measures of a second time series. Let G be the categorical covariate. New to the present case is the addition of the covariate to the base model. The base model for A-CFA can be set up such that types and antitypes necessarily reflect relationships between the two series of measures. Specifically, this base model includes

1. the main effect of all variables, including the covariate;

2. all possible interactions within each of the series of measures;

3. all two-way interactions of the covariate with each of the measures of the first series;

4. all two-way interactions of the covariate with each of the measures of the second series;

5. all three-way interactions that include two measures from just one of the series and the covariate; and

6. all higher order interactions that include solely measures from one series of scores and the covariate (if the time series contains more than two observation points).

This model specification has the effect that relationships between the two series can be specific to categories of the covariate. The reason for this is that the relationships among the measures of just one series and the covariate are part of the base model and, therefore, can be no causes for the emergence of types and antitypes. Types and antitypes that possibly emerge from this A-CFA base model reflect relationships among the two series of any kind. This applies accordingly when more than two series of measures span a table. The A-CFA base model that results for the four variables and the sole covariate in the current example is

$$
\begin{aligned}
\log \hat{m} = \lambda \quad &+ \quad \lambda_i^G + \lambda_j^{X1} + \lambda_k^{X2} + \lambda_l^{Y1} + \lambda_m^{Y2} \\
&+ \quad \lambda_{jk}^{X1,X2} + \lambda_{lm}^{Y1,Y2} + \lambda_{ij}^{G,X1} + \lambda_{ik}^{G,X2} + \lambda_{il}^{G,Y1} + \lambda_{im}^{G,Y2} \\
&+ \quad \lambda_{ijk}^{G,X1,X2} + \lambda_{ilm}^{G,Y1,Y2}.
\end{aligned}
$$

If any of the associations that were omitted in this base model exist, types and antitypes can emerge. Specifically, the following interactions can result in types and antitypes:

• *Two-way interactions*: six of the possible $\binom{5}{2} = 10$ two-way interactions are already included in the base model. Each of the remaining four interactions reflects relationships between the two series that were not taken into account in the base model. Each of these interactions reflects relationships between the two series of measures that can result in types and antitypes. These interactions are $[X1, Y1]$, $[X1, Y2]$, $[X2, Y1]$, and $[X2, Y2]$.

• *Three-way interactions*: two of the possible $\binom{5}{3} = 10$ three-way interactions are already included in the base model. Each of the omitted interactions also relates the series to each other. These interactions are $[G, X1, Y1]$, $[G, X1, Y2]$, $[G, X2, Y1]$, $[G, X2, Y2]$, $[X1, X2, Y1]$, $[X1, X2, Y2]$, $[X1, Y1, Y2]$, and $[X2, Y1, Y2]$. The last four of these interactions do not include the covariate.

• *Four-way interactions*: none of the possible $\binom{5}{4} = 5$ four-way interactions is already included in the base model. Each of these omitted interactions also relates the series to each other. These interactions are $[G, X1, X2, Y1]$, $[G, X1, X2, Y2]$, $[G, X1, Y1, Y2]$, $[G, X2, Y1, Y2]$, and $[X1, X2, Y1, Y2]$. The last of these interactions does not include the covariate.

• *Five-way interaction*: the sole five-way interaction is not included in the base model. Therefore, it can be the cause for types and antitypes to emerge. This is the interaction $[G, X1, X2, Y1, Y2]$.

A data example of this model of A-CFA — we call it A-CFA Model 1 — will be presented later, in tandem with A-CFA Model 2, which will be introduced in the next section.

7.2.2 A-CFA with Covariates II: Types and Antitypes Reflect Only Relationships between the Series of Measures and the Covariate

A-CFA Model 1 was specified such that types and antitypes reflect any relationships between the two (or more) series of measures. The covariate was included in a subset of these interactions. However, researchers may wish to focus on relationships between the series of measures that are specific to categories of the covariate(s). To examine this kind of covariate-specific associations, Model 2 also includes those interactions that relate the two series of measures to each other without inclusion of the covariate. For the same variables as used for A-CFA Model 1, the base model for A-CFA Model 2 (von Eye, Mun, & Bogat, 2009) is

$$
\begin{aligned}
\log \hat{m} = \lambda \quad &+ \quad \lambda_i^G + \lambda_j^{X1} + \lambda_k^{X2} + \lambda_l^{Y1} + \lambda_m^{Y2} \\
&+ \quad \lambda_{jk}^{X1,X2} + \lambda_{lm}^{Y1,Y2} + \lambda_{ij}^{G,X1} + \lambda_{ik}^{G,X2} + \lambda_{il}^{G,Y1} + \lambda_{im}^{G,Y2} \\
&+ \quad \lambda_{ijk}^{G,X1,X2} + \lambda_{ilm}^{G,Y1,Y2} \\
&+ \quad \lambda_{jl}^{X1,Y1} + \lambda_{jm}^{X1,Y2} + \lambda_{kl}^{X2,Y1} + \lambda_{km}^{X2,Y2} \\
&+ \quad \lambda_{jkl}^{X1,X2,Y1} + \lambda_{jkm}^{X1,X2,Y2} + \lambda_{jlm}^{X1,Y1,Y2} + \lambda_{klm}^{X2,Y1,Y2} \\
&+ \quad \lambda_{jklm}^{X1,X2,Y1,Y2}.
\end{aligned}
$$

The first three lines of this equation reproduce the base model of A-CFA Model 1. The next three lines display all two-way, three-way, and four-way interactions that need to be included when the focus is on relationships between the two series of measures that are specific to categories of the covariate.

The interactions that are not part of this base model include (1) the covariate, (2) at least one measure from the first (time) series, and (3) at least one measure from the second (time) series of scores. Specifically, the following interactions can result in types and antitypes:

• Three-way interactions: the remaining four of the possible $\binom{5}{3}$ = 10 three-way interactions are $[G, X1, Y1]$, $[G, X1, Y2]$, $[G, X2, Y1]$, and $[G, X2, Y2]$.

• Four-way interactions: the remaining four of the possible $\binom{5}{4}$ = 5 four-way interactions are $[G, X1, X2, Y1]$, $[G, X1, X2, Y2]$, $[G, X1, Y1, Y2]$, and $[G, X2, Y1, Y2]$.

• Five-way interaction: the sole five-way interaction is not included in the base model. It can be the cause for types and antitypes to emerge. This is the interaction $[G, X1, X2, Y1, Y2]$.

The types and antitypes that result from A-CFA Model 2 have a different meaning than some of those that result from A-CFA Model 1. Types and antitypes from Model 1 reflect any interaction between the two series of measures. Only a selection of these interactions includes the covariate (see Section 7.2.1). In contrast, types and antitypes from Model 2 reflect interactions between the two series of measures that are specific to particular categories of the covariate.

Data Example 2: For the following example, we use data from the study on intimate partner violence again that was used already in Chapter 5 (Bogat et al., 2006). We use data from the first and the third years of observation. For these observations, a total of 193 respondents was available. The following question is asked. Are the relationships between the series of violence and psychopathological symptoms that can be found for women with various patterns of intimate partner violence specific to child gender? We use the following five variables:

1. gender (G), coded as 1 = boy and 2 = girl;

2. dichotomized violence at Time 1 ($V1$), coded as 1 = respondent did experience violence and 2 = respondent did not experience violence;

3. dichotomized violence at Time 3 ($V3$), coded in the same way;

4. dichotomized symptom measure at Time 1 ($DX1$; coded as 1 = above clinical cutoff and 2 = below clinical cutoff; and

5. dichotomized symptom measure at Time 3 ($DX3$), coded in the same way as $DX1$.

The dichotomization of V and DX was performed at their respective grand means so that development can be described both ipsatively and comparatively. The cross-tabulation of these five variables will be analyzed by using three CFA base models. The first is the model of standard first order CFA that includes the main effects of all variables. This is the model

$$\log \hat{m} = \lambda + \lambda^G + \lambda^{V1} + \lambda^{V3} + \lambda^{DX1} + \lambda^{DX3}.$$

If types and antitypes emerge from this model, we will know that local relationships among these five variables exist. What we will not know is whether these types and antitypes reflect strong auto-associations or cross-variable relationships, and whether the types and antitypes are specific to child gender. To be able to make decisions about these two issues, we perform an A-CFA Model 1 with gender as covariate. The base model for this analysis is

$$
\begin{aligned}
\log \hat{m} = \lambda \quad &+ \quad \lambda_i^G + \lambda_j^{V1} + \lambda_k^{V3} + \lambda_l^{DX1} + \lambda_m^{DX3} \\
&+ \quad \lambda_{jk}^{V1,V3} + \lambda_{lm}^{DX1,DX3} + \lambda_{ij}^{G,V1} + \lambda_{ik}^{G,V2} + \lambda_{il}^{G,DX1} + \lambda_{im}^{G,DX3} \\
&+ \quad \lambda_{ijk}^{G,V1,V3} + \lambda_{ilm}^{G,DX1,DX3}.
\end{aligned}
$$

In the third analysis, we focus on types and antitypes that solely reflect interactions of the two series of measures that are child gender-specific. The base model for this analysis is

$$
\begin{aligned}
\log \hat{m} = \lambda \quad &+ \quad \lambda_i^G + \lambda_j^{V1} + \lambda_k^{V3} + \lambda_l^{DX1} + \lambda_m^{DX3} \\
&+ \quad \lambda_{jk}^{V1,V3} + \lambda_{lm}^{DX1,DX3} + \lambda_{ij}^{G,V1} + \lambda_{ik}^{G,V3} + \lambda_{il}^{G,DX1} + \lambda_{im}^{G,DX3} \\
&+ \quad \lambda_{ijk}^{G,V1,V3} + \lambda_{ilm}^{G,DX1,DX3} \\
&+ \quad \lambda_{jl}^{V1,DX1} + \lambda_{jm}^{V1,DX3} + \lambda_{kl}^{V3,DX1} + \lambda_{km}^{V3,DX3} \\
&+ \quad \lambda_{jkl}^{V1,V3,DX1} + \lambda_{jkm}^{V1,V3,DX3} + \lambda_{jlm}^{V1,DX1,DX3} + \lambda_{klm}^{V3,DX1,DX3} \\
&+ \quad \lambda_{jklm}^{V1,V3,DX1,DX3} .
\end{aligned}
$$

The complete design matrix for this A-CFA base model is given in Section 13.1.2, on sample applications. The $LR - X^2$ for the base model of first order CFA is 126.28 ($df = 26$; $p < 0.01$). The $LR - X^2$ for the base model of A-CFA Model 1 is 50.17 ($df = 18$; $p < 0.01$). The difference between these two nested models is significant ($\Delta LR - X^2 = 76.11$; $\Delta df = 8$; $p < 0.01$). We thus can conclude that the auto-associations, the associations of the individual variables with gender, and the associations of the two series with gender make a substantial contribution to the explanation of this table. Specifically, two of the parameters of this model are significant. These are the parameters for the auto-associations ($\lambda^{V1,V3} = 0.56$; se = 0.10; $p < 0.01$; and $\lambda^{DX1,DX3} = 0.55$; se = 0.13; $p = 0.01$). Because of the significant reduction of the overall goodness-of-fit X^2, we anticipate that some (or all) of the types and antitypes that emerged from first order CFA may have disappeared.

The log-linear base model for A-CFA Model 2 is improved even more. It describes the data well. We calculate $LR - X^2 = 13.46$ ($df = 9$; $p = 0.14$). This model is significantly better than the base model of first order CFA ($\Delta LR - X^2 = 112.82$; $\Delta df = 16$; $p < 0.01$) and also than A-CFA Model 1 ($\Delta LR - X^2 = 36.71$; $\Delta df = 9$; $p < 0.01$). We thus anticipate that no types and antitypes emerge. The results of the three configural analyses are displayed in Table 7.4. For each CFA, we used the z-test and protected the significance threshold by using the Holland-Copenhaver procedure.

First order CFA revealed four types and no antitype. The first type, constituted by Configuration 1 1 1 1 1, indicates that mothers of boys who experienced intimate partner violence at both Time 1 and Time 3 are more likely than expected to display above-cutoff symptoms, also at both observation points. The third type, constituted by Configuration 2 1 1 1 1, indicates that the same holds true for mothers of girls. We, therefore,

TABLE 7.4. Standard CFA and Two Extended A-CFA Analyses of Victim Status and Symptom Status with Child Gender as Covariate (* Indicates Estimated Zeros, Not Structural Zeros)

Configuration G V1 V3 DX1 DX3	m	$\hat{m}$	z	$\hat{m}$	z	$\hat{m}$	z
	First Order CFA (Independence Model)			A-CFA Model 1 (Interactions with Gender)		A-CFA Model 2 (Child Gender-Specific Interactions)	
11111	28	10.567	5.3631[a]	17.515	2.505	25.989	0.394
11112	0	2.260	−1.5032	0.687	−0.829	0.399	−0.632
11121	5	8.316	−1.1500	10.646	−1.731	5.458	−0.196
11122	1	1.778	−.5837	5.152	−1.829	2.153	−0.786
11211	3	7.642	−1.6792	2.576	0.264	3.667	−0.348
11212	1	1.634	−.4961	0.101	2.829	0.351	1.096
11221	1	6.014	−2.0447	1.566	−0.452	0.495	0.718
11222	0	1.286	−1.1341	0.758	−0.870	0.487	−0.698
12111	10	15.919	−1.4834	15.455	−1.387	10.112	−0.035
12112	0	3.404	−1.8450	0.606	−0.778	0.000*	0.000
12121	11	12.528	−.4318	9.394	0.524	13.303	−0.631
12122	9	2.679	3.8618[a]	4.545	2.089	6.584	0.941
12211	10	11.513	−.4458	15.455	−1.387	11.231	−0.367
12212	1	2.462	−.9317	0.606	0.506	1.250	−0.224
12221	14	9.061	1.6409	9.394	1.503	11.744	0.658
12222	5	1.938	2.2001	4.545	0.213	5.775	−0.323
21111	23	10.033	4.0938[a]	17.362	1.353	25.011	−0.402
21112	1	2.145	−.7820	1.362	−0.310	0.601	0.514
21121	5	7.896	−1.0307	8.851	−1.294	4.542	0.215
21122	3	1.689	1.0093	4.426	−0.678	1.847	0.849
21211	5	7.256	−.8375	3.255	0.967	4.333	0.321
21212	0	1.552	−1.2456	0.255	−0.505	0.649	−0.806
21221	0	5.711	−2.3897	1.660	−1.288	0.505	−0.711
21222	1	1.221	−.2001	0.830	0.187	0.513	0.680
22111	6	15.115	−2.3444	8.681	−0.910	5.888	0.046
22112	0	3.232	−1.7978	0.681	−0.825	0.000*	0.000
22121	9	11.896	−.8396	4.426	2.174	6.697	0.890
22122	1	2.544	−.9679	2.213	−0.815	3.416	−1.307
22211	17	10.931	1.8356	21.702	−1.009	15.769	0.310
22212	3	2.337	.4334	1.702	0.995	2.750	0.157
22221	12	8.603	1.1581	11.064	0.281	14.256	−0.598
22222	8	1.840	4.5419[a]	5.532	1.049	7.225	0.288

[a]Types.

can aggregate these two types to form the composite type . 1 1 1 1, where the period indicates that the variable gender does not play a role in the constitution of this type.

In contrast to the first and third types, the second type is gender-specific. It is constituted by Configuration 1 2 1 2 2 and suggests that mothers of boys who experienced intimate partner violence only at Time 3 — that is, after the child was born — are more likely than expected to display below-cutoff symptoms, also at both observation points. This type does not come with a companion type in the sample of mothers with girls (see Cell 2 2 1 2 2).

The fourth type is also gender-specific. Constituted by Configuration 2 2 2 2 2, it indicates that mothers of girls who did not experience intimate partner violence at either point in time are more likely than expected to remain below the clinical cutoff for psychopathological symptoms, at both points in time. The corresponding configuration for mothers of boys (Configuration 1 2 2 2 2) does not constitute a type.

As expected, based on the significant difference between the two base models, A-CFA Model 1 yields a type pattern that is different from the one produced by first order CFA. Not a single type was reproduced. Without α protection, the first and the third types would have surfaced again. However, because of the possible dependence of tests and because of the risk of capitalizing on chance, we refrain from interpreting these configurations as constituting A-CFA Model 1 types. A-CFA Model 2 also yields no types or antitypes, because the model describes the data well.

The present example illustrates which effects are the causes for the types in the first two panels of Table 7.4. Including these effects makes the types disappear. It also shows clearly that different base models can yield different patterns of types and antitypes (Mellenbergh, 1996). Therefore, we emphasize again that the selection of the appropriate base model is of utmost importance for the interpretability of CFA results.

7.3   Chapter Summary

In repeated observation studies, auto-associations (the categorical data equivalent to autocorrelations) are usually the strongest effects. Auto-associations link observations from different points in time. Therefore, researchers interested in types and antitypes that reflect cross-variable associations need to look beyond auto-associations. The base model of Auto-association CFA (A-CFA) takes all possible auto-associations into account for each of the repeatedly observed variables. Types and antitypes, therefore, can result only if cross-variable associations exist. These associations can reflect links between variables that are specific to one or more points in time. However, they can also reflect associations across time and associations between entire series of measures.

Two models are described. The first is A-CFA without covariates, the second does allow one to include covariates. For the A-CFA model with covariates, two submodels are introduced. In Submodel A-CFA 1, types and antitypes can result from any of the interactions beyond the ones considered in the base model. In Submodel A-CFA 2, types and antitypes emerge only if they are the results of interactions that involve the covariate.

8

Configural Moderator Models

Variables that change the parameter estimates in models when they are taken into account are called moderators. In CFA, however, we are not interested in model parameters because we hope to reject the base model. Instead, we are interested in patterns of types and antitypes. Therefore, in CFA, moderators are those variables that change the pattern of resulting types and antitypes when they are made part of a model. Chapter 8 introduces configural moderator analysis, also new to the arsenal of CFA methods, and illustrates it by using data examples. Four variants of configural moderator analysis are introduced. The first compares patterns of types and antitypes from models that do versus do not include the moderator variable. The second is an extension of A-CFA (Chapter 7). It considers moderator effects on the relationships between series of scores. The third is moderated mediation, an extension of mediator CFA (Chapter 6). This variant of moderator CFA allows one to answer questions concerning moderator effects on mediation types and antitypes. The fourth approach concerns moderated mediation. The chapter concludes with a section on the graphical representation of results of moderator CFA.

A *moderator effect* exists if the parameters that describe the relationship between a predictor variable and a criterion variable depend on the values (or categories) of a *moderator variable*. In CFA, a moderator effect exists if type and antitype patterns vary across the categories of a variable not included in a configural analysis. Taking into account Prediction CFA (Chapter 5), Mediator CFA (Chapter 6), and, now, Moderator CFA, we thus distinguish among regression-type relations (Figure 8.1), mediated relations (Figure 8.2), and moderated relations (Figure 8.3).

Moderated relations are of particular interest in person-oriented research. As Beaubien (2005) notes, moderation processes address "the issues of 'when?', 'for whom?', or 'under what conditions?'." One could enrich this list by adding all kinds of conditionals that can be addressed by modeling moderated relations.

FIGURE 8.1. Regression-type relation.

FIGURE 8.2. Fully mediated relation.

Unlike mediation processes, moderated processes can, in continuous variable analysis, be expressed by using single, nonadditive linear functions. In moderated processes, the dependent variable, Y, is a function of both the independent variable, X, and the moderator variable, Z (see Baron & Kenny, 1986; Beaubien, 2005; James & Brett, 1984), or, algebraically, $Y = f(X, Z)$. In standard regression contexts, that is, when at least X and Y are continuous, moderated processes are typically analyzed by including interaction terms in regression models. An example of such an equation is

$$Y = \beta_0 + \beta_1 X + \beta_2 Z + \beta_3 XZ + \varepsilon.$$

This equation shows that standard analysis of moderation takes the main effects of X and Z into account as well as their interaction.

There are many ways to analyze moderated relations. Often,

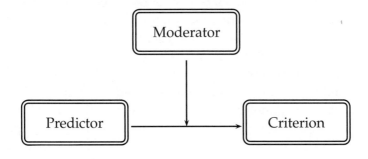

FIGURE 8.3. Moderated relation.

descriptions of methods of analysis are grouped, based on the scale level of the variables X, Y, and Z. If one classifies variables as either categorical or metrical, the three variables X, Y, and Z can be combined to form eight patterns of scale levels, from all metrical, to X and Y metrical, and Z categorical, ..., to all three variables categorical. In the present context, naturally, we focus on the analysis of moderator processes (1) in the context of variables that are all categorical, and (2) at the level of types and antitypes.

In the following four sections, we introduce four approaches to exploring possible moderator effects using CFA. The first involves running consecutive analyses that do versus do not include possible moderator variables. The second discusses moderator hypotheses in the context of Auto-Association CFA, and the third approach involves using CFA models of group comparison, specifically, n-sample analysis. The fourth approach concerns moderated mediation.

8.1   Configural Moderator Analysis: Base Models with and without Moderator

As was exemplified by Beaubien's (2005) sample questions, moderator analysis yields conditional statements. For example, a relationship between variables can be found in one population but not in some other, a treatment effect varies with the conditions under which it is administered, or certain actions will be taken only if particular reasons are given.

In CFA application, we do not ask whether relationships among variables incrementally change over the range of values of possible moderator variables. Specifically, we ask whether types and antitypes emerge or disappear for specific categories of moderator variables. Therefore, a two-step strategy of analysis can be considered.

Step 1: Performing CFA without the moderator: Expressed differently, one can perform CFA on a table that is collapsed over the categories of a variable that can, possibly, have the effects of a moderator. *Collapsibility* is a widely discussed issue in the realm of categorical variable analysis (e.g., Agresti, 2002; Bishop et al., 1975; Christensen, 1997; Clogg & Shihadeh, 1994).

Based on Bishop et al. (1975, p. 47), we define collapsibility as follows: The variables that are summed over are said to be *collapsible* with respect to particular λ parameters if the parameters in the model before collapsing are identical to those from the corresponding log-linear model after collapsing. This definition has a number of implications that are of interest for configural moderator analysis (and in general):

1. Collapsibility is defined with respect to parameters. Therefore, a table may be collapsible with respect to some categories of possible moderator

variables, but not with respect to others. We, therefore, distinguish between *collapsing* and *condensing*. Collapsing means that a table is summed over all categories of a particular variable. Condensing means that a selection of categories is combined.

2. If the λ-parameters that are removed by collapsing exist, that is, are different from zero, other λ-parameters will change in response to collapsing (or condensing).

3. If a variable is independent of all other variables, at all levels of association, this variable can be removed by summing over all its categories, that is, by collapsing, without any change in the remaining λ-parameters.

In log-linear analysis, collapsing is of interest when it comes to reducing the dimensionality of a table and, thus, the complexity of models. In configural analysis, collapsing is of interest (1) for the same reason (i.e., reducing the size of the cross-classification), and (2), in particular, in the context of considering moderator hypotheses. In the context of moderator analysis, *cross-classifications cannot be collapsed over moderator variables.* Stated the other way around, variables that can be collapsed across cannot be moderator variables. However, in configural frequency analysis, we do not ask whether parameters change when tables are collapsed. Instead, we ask whether patterns of types or antitypes change when possible moderator variables are included in a base model or removed from it. Note, however, that changes in parameter values and changes in patterns of types and antitypes are generally linked.

Step 2: Performing CFA with the moderator included: If the pattern of types and antitypes changes from Step 1 when the potential moderator variable is included, this variable can be considered a moderator variable. Resulting changes in the pattern of types and antitypes are the effects of moderation. More specifically, if the pattern of types and antitypes found in Step 1 differs across the categories of an additional variable, this variable can be considered a moderator.

To illustrate these two steps, consider the outcome variable, Y, the predictor, X, and Variable M, a potential mediator. Standard, first order CFA uses, in Step 1, the base model

$$\log \hat{m} = \lambda + \lambda^Y + \lambda^X.$$

This model can also be used as a P-CFA base model. In Step 2, this model becomes

$$\log \hat{m} = \lambda + \lambda^Y + \lambda^X + \lambda^M$$

TABLE 8.1. Longitudinal CFA of Aggressive Impulses

Configuration AI83 AI85 AI87	m	$\hat{m}$	z	p	Type/Antitype
111	31	12.589	5.1888	.000000	Type
112	5	10.191	−1.6262	.051957	
121	7	16.700	−2.3737	.008806	
122	10	13.519	−.9571	.169255	
211	8	14.490	−1.7049	.044110	
212	5	11.730	−1.9650	.024710	
221	17	19.221	−.5066	.306226	
222	31	15.560	3.9143	.000045	Type

when first order CFA is performed, and

$$\log \hat{m} = \lambda + \lambda^Y + \lambda^X + \lambda^M + \lambda^{YX} + \lambda^{YM} + \lambda^{XM}$$

when P-CFA is performed.

Data Example 1: For the following example, we use the aggression development data used before, that is, Finkelstein et al. (1994) aggression data. 114 adolescents (67 girls) indicated their level of aggressive impulses (*AI*) in 1983, 1985, and 1987. At these points in time, they were, on average, 11, 13, and 15 years of age. Here, we first ask whether typical and atypical pathways of aggressive impulses (AI) exist that emerge in the form of types and antitypes. Then, we ask whether gender is a moderator of these developmental patterns. The answer to this question is affirmative if (1) particular developmental pathways that emerged as types or antitypes in the first analysis are gender-specific, (2) types or antitypes from the first step disappear, or (3) new types or antitypes emerge.

For the following analyses, we use the dichotomized *AI* scores. Dichotomization was done at the grand mean, so that developmental shifts from below to above average (or the other way around) can be ascertained at the level of the individual.

For the first step of moderator analysis, we cross the three observations of *AI*. Gender is not included in the analysis. In terms of collapsing, one can say that the main effect of gender and all two- and higher-way associations of the *AI* observations with gender are assumed to be zero. We perform a first order CFA. The base model for this analysis is, thus,

$$\log \hat{m} = \lambda + \lambda^{AI83} + \lambda^{AI85} + \lambda^{AI87}.$$

Table 8.1 displays CFA results. For this and the following CFAs in this chapter, we use the z-test and protect α by using the Holland-Copenhaver procedure.

TABLE 8.2. Longitudinal CFA of Aggressive Impulses, with Gender as Possible Moderator

Configuration G AI83 AI85 AI87	m	$\hat{m}$	z	p	Type/Antitype
1111	20	7.399	4.6325	.000002	Type
1112	4	5.990	−.8130	.208116	
1121	5	9.815	−1.5369	.062157	
1122	3	7.945	−1.7545	.039674	
1211	6	8.516	−.8621	.194311	
1212	5	6.894	−.7213	.235372	
1221	9	11.297	−.6833	.247217	
1222	15	9.145	1.9362	.026420	
2111	11	5.190	2.5501	.005385	
2112	1	4.202	−1.5620	.059149	
2121	2	6.885	−1.8617	.031319	
2122	7	5.574	.6041	.272873	
2211	2	5.974	−1.6258	.051991	
2212	0	4.836	−2.1991	.013936	
2221	8	7.924	.0269	.489289	
2222	16	6.415	3.7844	.000077	Type

Table 8.1 shows that two stability types of aggressive impulses exist, and no antitype. The stability types suggest that adolescents rate themselves either as consistently below average in aggressive impulses (Configuration 1 1 1) or consistently above average (Configuration 2 2 2). None of the other configurations deviates significantly from expectation.

We now ask whether these statements hold equally for both gender groups. To answer this question, we create a new table by including the Gender variable. The base model for the new, first order CFA is

$$\log \hat{m} = \lambda + \lambda^{Gender} + \lambda^{AI83} + \lambda^{AI85} + \lambda^{AI87}.$$

Types and antitypes can result from this model if the auto-associations among the AI observations are strong, but also if there is some interaction with gender. Table 8.2 displays the results from this analysis.

Table 8.2 shows a pattern that seems to be very similar to the one shown by Table 8.1. There are only two types, both indicating stability. However, considering that configurations are now listed by Gender, we see that both of these new types are gender-specific. Type 1 1 1 1 suggests that consistently below average aggressive impulses occur more often than expected only in the female population. Type 2 2 2 2 suggests that consistently above average aggressive impulses occur more often than expected only in the male population. We thus conclude that Gender is a moderator of the development of aggressive impulses.

One important issue of log-linear as well as configural moderator analysis is that adding a moderator variable to a model implies that the number of cells of the table under study increases by a factor of two (if the moderator is dichotomous) or more (if the moderator has more than two categories). As a consequence, power for cell-specific tests is bound to decrease. Therefore, moderator analysis that proceeds along the two steps discussed here tends to suggest nonconservative decisions about the possible existence of moderation and, thus, conservative decisions about the existence of types and antitypes in the table that was extended by the moderator variable.

Consider, for example, the results in Table 8.2. Configuration 1 1 1 1 suggests that consistently below average aggressive impulses are female-specific. This statement implies that the corresponding type for males, 2 1 1 1, does not exist. Table 8.2, however, suggests that Configuration 2 1 1 1 comes with a tail probability of 0.0054. Clearly, this tail probability is not smaller than the critical one for this cell, which is $\alpha_3^* = 0.0037$. However, in a larger sample, this configuration might have constituted a type also. For Type 2 2 2 2, the corresponding configuration, 1 2 2 2, is less suspicious. Therefore, we retain our conclusion that Gender has the effect of a moderator on the development of aggressive impulses in adolescence. This applies in particular to above average aggressive impulses.

8.2 Longitudinal Configural Moderator Analysis under Consideration of Auto-Associations

In a way parallel to the version of A-CFA that restricts the base model such that only interactions between the series of measures and the covariate can be the causes for the emergence of types and antitypes, we can specify a base model for Moderator CFA such that only interactions among the moderator and the remaining variables, but not the interactions among the remaining variables alone, can cause types and antitypes to emerge. The base model that thus results for Moderator CFA is parallel in form and function to the extended base model that can be formulated for A-CFA. Specifically, the base model for this version of Moderator CFA takes into account

1. the main effects of all variables in the analysis;

2. interactions of any order among the variables that are not considered moderators; the base model thus is saturated in these repeated observations;

3. if more than one moderator is included in the analysis, interactions of any order among the moderators; the base model thus is saturated in the moderators.

The only effects that are not included in the base model are the interactions that link moderators with the other variables. If any of these effects exist, moderation may take place and affect the resulting pattern of types and antitypes. Consider, for example, the three variables X, Y, and Z, and the moderator M. The base model for these four variables is

$$\log \hat{m} = \lambda + \lambda^M + \lambda^X + \lambda^Y + \lambda^Z + \lambda^{XY} + \lambda^{XZ} + \lambda^{YZ} + \lambda^{XYZ}.$$

Each of the interactions not included in this model links the moderator to one or more of the other variables. Specifically, these are the interactions $[M, X]$, $[M, Y]$, $[M, Z]$, $[M, X, Y]$, $[M, X, Z]$, $[M, Y, Z]$, and $[M, X, Y, Z]$. In the following example, we apply this base model in the context of longitudinal and Auto-Association Moderator CFA.

Data Example 2: For the following example, we use data from the Overcoming The Odds (OTO) study (Lerner, Taylor, & von Eye, 2002; Taylor et al., 2002). The OTO is a longitudinal study of the nature of positive functioning, and the role that individual and ecological assets play in this functioning, in African American male youth. The youth who participated in this study were either gang members ($n = 45$; average age at the beginning of the study = 15.82 y) or members of community-based organizations (CBO; $n = 50$; average age at the beginning of the study = 16.31 y). The participants indicated in interviews how many from a list of individual and ecological assets were available to them. For the following analyses, we use the total number of assets from two interviews, conducted 1 year apart. These scores were dichotomized at the grand mean. Thus, for the following analyses, three variables are used: Assets in Year 1 ($A1$) and Year 2 ($A2$) as the dichotomized asset scores (1 = below grand mean; 2 = above grand mean), and Group Membership (G; 1 = gang member; 2 = CBO member).

In the following paragraphs, we analyze the responses, using three CFA base models. For each analysis, we used the normal approximation of the binomial test and the Holland-Copenhaver procedure of α protection. The first base model is that of first order CFA of the $A1 \times A2$ cross-classification,

$$\log \hat{m} = \lambda + \lambda^{A1} + \lambda^{A2}.$$

Types and antitypes from this analysis indicate stability and change in the availability of assets over a span of 1 year. The $LR - X^2$ for this model is a large 97.78 ($df = 1$; $p < 0.01$), thus indicating a strong auto-association

TABLE 8.3. First Order CFA of Repeatedly Observed Asset Scores ($A1$ and $A2$) in Male African American Adolescents

Configuration $A1$ $A2$	m	$\hat{m}$	z	p	Type/Antitype
11	39	17.684	5.6187	.000000	Type
12	1	22.316	−5.1587	.000000	Antitype
21	3	24.316	−5.0114	.000000	Antitype
22	52	30.684	4.6768	.000001	Type

between the two observations of total assets. We thus expect types and antitypes to emerge. Table 8.3 presents the results from first order CFA.

Clearly, this table shows a strong association such that respondents with many assets in Year 1 will also report many assets in Year 2. Similarly, low asset counts remain stable. The total number of individuals with changes in the number of assets is only 4, that is, about 4%.

Considering that the 2×2 table under study has, under the first order CFA base model, only one df, the CFA tests are more dependent than in any other table, and the CFA results will not make a major contribution above and beyond the statement that the two variables are strongly associated with each other. In fact, based on von Weber et al. (2003a), we can state that a first order CFA of a 2×2 table almost never presents interesting results. We therefore refrain from interpreting each type and antitype from this analysis and instead move to analyzing the moderator hypothesis. We ask whether the strong association between the two observations of total assets is the same for gang members and for CBO members. In other words, we ask whether group membership moderates the auto-association between the two asset counts. Two base models are considered. The first of these takes group membership into account, and searches for types and antitypes using a first order CFA. This model is

$$\log \hat{m} = \lambda + \lambda^G + \lambda^{A1} + \lambda^{A2}.$$

Types and antitypes from this model indicate whether there are group-specific local associations. The $LR - X^2$ for this model is 122.2 ($df = 4$; $p < 0.01$), thus indicating that strong variable associations exist. Again, we expect types and antitypes to emerge. Table 8.4 displays the results from the first order CFA base model that takes group membership into account.

The results in Table 8.4 suggest that one of the types is specific to members of gangs, the other is specific to CBO members. Specifically, having consistently below average numbers of assets describes a type in gang members (Configuration 1 1 1), but not in CBO members

TABLE 8.4. First Order CFA of Repeatedly Observed Asset Scores (*A*1 and *A*2) in Male African American Adolescents in Gangs and Community-Based Organizations (*G*)

Configuration A1 A2 G	m	$\hat{m}$	z	p	Type/Antitype
111	28	8.377	7.1003	.000000	Type
112	11	9.307	.5841	.279567	
121	0	10.571	−3.4488	.000282	Antitype
122	1	11.745	−3.3492	.000405	Antitype
211	3	11.518	−2.6774	.003710	Antitype
212	0	12.798	−3.8458	.000060	Antitype
221	14	14.535	−.1524	.439447	
222	38	16.150	5.9681	.000000	Type

(Configuration 1 1 2). Mirroring this pattern, consistently above average numbers of assets constitutes a type in CBO members (Configuration 2 2 2), but not in gang members (Configuration 2 2 1). None of the antitypes is group-specific.

The downside of the base model used for Table 8.4 (as well as the one used for Table 8.2) is that one cannot see whether possible types and antitypes result from the auto-association of the asset scores, or whether group membership is associated with the availability of assets. Therefore, a third analysis is performed, with group membership as moderator variable. The base model for this analysis takes the auto-association between the two asset observations into account. If types and antitypes result from this analysis, they must reflect the association of group membership with asset availability. The base model for this analysis is

$$\log \hat{m} = \lambda + \lambda^G + \lambda^{A1} + \lambda^{A2} + \lambda^{A1,A2}.$$

Each of the interactions not included in this model links asset scores with the group membership variable. Specifically, these are the interactions [*A*1, *G*], [*A*2, *G*], and [*A*1, *A*2, *G*]. The base model used for the results in Table 8.4 had not taken the interaction [*A*1, *A*2] into account. Therefore, at least some of the types and antitypes could be the effect of the auto-association between *A*1 and *A*2. Table 8.3 had shown that this auto-association is strong. Table 8.5 shows the results of this version of Moderator CFA of the cross-classification of *A*1, *A*2, and *G*.

The results in Table 8.5 suggest that (1) Group Membership indeed is a moderator of the auto-association between numbers of assets, observed at two occasions, 1 year apart, (2) each of the antitypes in Table 8.4 is solely due to the [*A*1, *A*2] auto-association, and (3) the moderator effect caused a new antitype to emerge. In all, two types and one antitype emerge.

TABLE 8.5. Moderator CFA of Repeatedly Observed Asset Scores (*A*1 and *A*2) in Male African American Adolescents in Gangs and Community-Based Organizations (*G*), with Group Membership as Moderator

Configuration A1 A2 G	m	$\hat{m}$	z	p	Type/Antitype
111	28	18.474	2.4695	.006766	Type
112	11	20.526	−2.3748	.008779	Antitype
121	0	.474	−.6900	.245107	
122	1	.526	.6547	.256316	
211	3	1.421	1.3346	.091012	
212	0	1.579	−1.2671	.102553	
221	14	24.632	−2.4890	.006405	
222	38	27.368	2.4086	.008007	Type

The first type, constituted by Configuration 1 1 1, suggests that below average counts of assets at both observation points are more often found in gang members than expected. The antitype, constituted by Configuration 1 1 2, suggests that consistently below average assets are particularly unlikely in CBO members. The second type, constituted by Configuration 2 2 2, indicates that CBO members report consistently above average counts of assets.

8.3 Configural Moderator Analysis as *n*-Group Comparison

It is an interesting fact about CFA that types or antitypes that emerge in only one comparison group but not in others do not necessarily result in discrimination types when examined in an *n*-group CFA. The reason for this is that the differences between the observed and the expected cell frequencies may go in the same direction in all groups, but may not be strong enough to establish types and antitypes in each of the groups. We encountered an example of such a situation in Table 8.2, where Configuration 1 1 1 constituted a type for girls but not for boys, although almost twice as many females as expected showed this pattern. Using *n*-group CFA (see also the data example in Section 1.3; von Eye, 2002a), one can determine not only whether a moderator variable caused group-specific types or antitypes to emerge but also whether discrimination types can be found.

Interestingly, the base model for *n*-group CFA is, in the context of moderator analysis, identical to the base model for Moderator CFA.

TABLE 8.6. Two-Group Analysis of the $A1 \times A2$ Cross-Classification

Configuration A1 A2 G	m	Statistic	p	Type/Antitype
111	28			
112	11	3.979	.000035	Discrimination Type
121	0			
122	1	−.954	.170114	
211	3			
212	0	1.855	.031779	
221	14			
222	38	−4.389	.000006	Discrimination Type

Consider, for example, the base model that was used for Table 8.5. If variables X and Z are used to discriminate between the groups labeled, using variable G, the base model is

$$\log \hat{m} = \lambda + \lambda^G + \lambda^X + \lambda^Z + \lambda^{X,Z}.$$

This model is identical in form to the one for the example in Table 8.5. However, the cell-wise significance tests that are usually performed in CFA are replaced by the tests described in Section 1.3 (see Tables 1.5 and 1.6). These tests compare the n groups in each of the configurations of categories of X and Y. This procedure is illustrated in the following data example.

Data Example 3: In the following example, we complete the analysis of the OTO data used in Sections 8.1 and 8.2. We now ask not only whether group membership causes the development of availability of assets to be specific to gang versus CBO members, but also whether it causes discrimination types to emerge. Table 8.6 displays the results of two-group analysis for the $A1 \times A2 \times G$ cross-classification. The normal approximation of the binomial test was used along with the Holland-Copenhaver procedure of α protection.

The results in Table 8.6 show that Moderator CFA resulted in two discrimination types. The antitype in Table 8.5 is part of the first discrimination type. The following interpretation can thus be retained:

1. Consistently below average assets, that is, Asset pattern 1 1 . , is typical for gang members and cannot be found at the same rate among CBO members.

2. Consistently above average assets, that is, Asset pattern 2 2 . , is typical for CBO members and cannot be found at the same rate in gang members.

8.4   Moderated Mediation

The processes of mediation and moderation can be combined in various ways. Consider the three variables X, the predictor (or explanatory or independent variable), Y, the dependent (or outcome) variable, and Me, the mediator. These three variables can be in a fully or partially mediated relationship, as depicted in Figure 6.2. According to Muller, Judd, and Yzerbyt (2005), mediation can be moderated by a fourth variable, Mo, a moderator. *Moderated mediation* exists if strength or type of mediation depends on a moderator variable. Conversely, a moderated relationship that involves X, Y, and Mo, can be mediated. *Mediated moderation* would first imply that moderation occurs, that is, the strength of the relationship between X and Y depends on Mo. This moderator effect can be mediated by a mediating variable.

In the following section, we focus on moderated mediation. We ask whether the pattern of types and antitypes that reflects mediation varies across the categories of a moderator variable. This question can be asked for any of the five moderated mediation path models that can be distinguished, based on Preacher, Rucker, and Hayes (2007). The panels of Figure 8.4 depict these moderated mediation path models.

Additional scenarios are conceivable. For example, one can consider models with multiple mediators, multiple predictors, or multiple outcomes. One of the characteristics of the current approach is that each of these models allows one to take variable associations into account. Thus, unrealistic assumptions do not need to be made. An example of such unrealistic assumptions is that, in survey data, independent variables are uncorrelated with one another.

Base Models and Outcome Patterns of Moderated Mediation: In the context of configural moderator analysis, we do not ask whether parameters change in the presence of other parameters in the model. Instead, we ask whether a pattern of types and antitypes that emerged when the table was collapsed over the categories of a covariate (moderator) remains the same or changes over the categories of this covariate when the table is unfolded. The base model for moderated mediation, therefore, has the same characteristics as the base model for moderation, except that the moderated model is that of a mediated process. We consider two sets of base models for moderated mediation. The first compares the resulting type/antitype patterns from a model that does not include the moderator variable(s) with the patterns from a model that does. Specifically, the first set of moderated mediation base models has the following characteristics:

1. The first base model that is used for the examination of possible

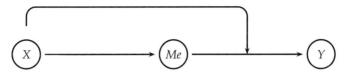

(a) Value of Predictor Determines Mediation Effect

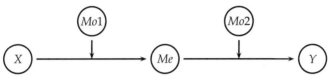

(b) Moderator Determines Relationship between Predictor and Mediator or/and between Mediator and Outcome Variable

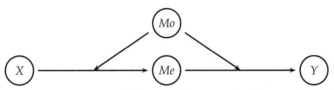

(c) One Moderator Determines Relationship between Predictor and Mediator as well as between Mediator and Outcome

FIGURE 8.4. Moderated mediation path models.

moderator effects is that of a mediation process (see Chapter 6 for two approaches to configural analysis of mediation). This is the model that is collapsed over some or all categories of a potential moderator variable. It is important to note that this model does not necessarily have to suggest that mediation exists. It may be the case that mediation exists in subgroups only and that, overall, mediation effects cancel each other out such that no types or antitypes hint at the existence of mediation. The first base model corresponds to the model used in Step 1 in Section 8.1 (this model does not include a moderator).

2. The second base model takes potential moderator variable(s) into account. Corresponding to the model used in Step 2 in Section 8.1 (this model does include a moderator), this model includes the main effect(s) of and the interactions among potential moderator variables. One possible result from this model is that the type and antitype patterns indicate that mediation varies over the categories of a moderator (the covariate). This

variation can assume a number of forms. First, it is possible that mediation exists for some categories of the moderator but not for others. Second, it is possible that mediation exists for categories of the moderator but not in the collapsed table. Third, it is possible that the type of mediation varies across the categories of a moderator (to obtain this result, separate mediation analyses may need to be performed for the categories of the moderator).

To give an example, consider the variables X, Y, Me, and Mo, defined as independent variable, outcome variable, Mediator, and Moderator, respectively. As was discussed in Chapter 2, one possible base model for the mediation between X and Y is the main effect model (more complex models are conceivable, for example, mediation in a Prediction CFA context). This is the model:

$$\log \hat{m} = \lambda + \lambda^X + \lambda^Y + \lambda^{Me}.$$

The comparison model that takes the moderator into account is then

$$\log \hat{m} = \lambda + \lambda^X + \lambda^Y + \lambda^{Me} + \lambda^{Mo}.$$

Types and antitypes can result from this model when any combination of the following interactions exist: $[X, Y]$, $[X, Me]$, $[X, Mo]$, $[Y, Me]$, $[Y, Mo]$, $[Me, Mo]$, $[X, Y, Me]$, $[X, Y, Mo]$, $[X, Me, Mo]$, $[Y, Me, Mo]$ and $[X, Y, Me, Mo]$. This model yields easily interpreted results. It is the interpretation of a mediation model that takes into account the main effect of a potential moderator variable. However, 4 of these 11 interactions do not contain the moderator variable. Therefore, a second set of models may be considered, with the following characteristics:

1. The first base model that is used for the examination of possible moderator effects is, as before, that of a mediation process. As in the first set of models, this model corresponds to the model used in Step 1 in Sections 8.1 and 8.2.

2. The second base model takes the moderator variable(s) into account. Corresponding to the model used in Section 8.2, this model includes not only the main effect(s) of potential moderator variables but also all interactions that do not involve the moderator. Types and antitypes that result from this model necessarily indicate that the moderator interacts with X, Y, Me, or any combination of these. If moderation exists, it can assume the same forms as for the first model, but the causes of this moderator category-specific variation are restricted to interactions that involve the moderator.

Consider, for example, the same variables as above and the same first base model. The base model that is used to explore moderated mediation under the present constraints is

$$\log \hat{m} = \lambda + \lambda^X + \lambda^Y + \lambda^{Me} + \lambda^{Mo} + \lambda^{X,Y} + \lambda^{X,Me} + \lambda^{Y,Me} + \lambda^{X,Y,Me}.$$

The interactions in this equation does not include the Moderator. Therefore, only those interactions that do include the moderator are possible causes for types and antitypes.

Data Example 4: For the following data example, we use data from a study on the recipients of social welfare in Mexico (Lobato, Martínez, Miranda, Rivera, & Serrato, 2007). A sample of 250 recipients was asked whether they perceived the services rendered as low versus high in quality (*QUA*: predictor), whether they were satisfied with the services (*SAT*: mediator), and whether they would use the services again (*USE*: criterion variable). In addition, they were asked about their expectations concerning these services (*EXP*: high vs. low: moderator). Each of the questions was asked on a 10-point scale. Each of the response distributions was heavily skewed toward positive evaluation. Therefore, dichotomization was not done at the median or the scale midpoint, but at the item score 8.1 for *QUA*, and at the item score 9.1 for the other items. In the following analyses, each of the four variables is scored as 1 = below the cutoff and 2 = above the cutoff, and will be interpreted as "low" and "high", respectively.

In the following analyses, we first ask whether the intention to use the services again can be predicted from perceived quality and is mediated by satisfaction with the services. Second, we ask whether this mediation process, if it exists, is moderated by the respondents' expectations.

To answer the first question, we have to establish whether mediation exists. To do this, we perform Mediation CFA, using the following four base models (see Table 6.5 in Chapter 6):

1. First Order CFA-Main effect model:

$$\log \hat{m} = \lambda + \lambda_i^{QUA} + \lambda_j^{SAT} + \lambda_k^{USE};$$

2. Predicting the criterion from the predictor and the mediator:

$$\log \hat{m} = \lambda + \lambda_i^{QUA} + \lambda_j^{SAT} + \lambda_k^{USE} + \lambda_{ij}^{QUA,SAT};$$

3. Predicting the criterion from the mediator:

$$\log \hat{m} = \lambda + \lambda_i^{QUA} + \lambda_j^{SAT} + \lambda_k^{USE} + \lambda_{ij}^{QUA,SAT} + \lambda_{ik}^{QUA,USE};$$

TABLE 8.7. First Order CFA of the Cross-Classification of Perceived Quality of Services (*QUA*), Satisfaction with Services (*SAT*), and Intention to Use Services Again (*USE*)

Configuration QUA SAT USE	m	$\hat{m}$	z	p	Type/Antitype
111	65	27.216	7.2425	.000000	Type
112	38	41.512	−.5450	.292861	
121	8	20.700	−2.7913	.002625	Antitype
122	10	31.572	−3.8392	.000062	Antitype
211	16	29.016	−2.4163	.007840	Antitype
212	23	44.256	−3.1952	.000699	Antitype
221	10	22.068	−2.5690	.005100	Antitype
222	80	33.660	7.9874	.000000	Type

4. Predicting the criterion from the predictor:

$$\log \hat{m} = \lambda + \lambda_i^{QUA} + \lambda_j^{SAT} + \lambda_k^{USE} + \lambda_{ij}^{QUA,SAT} + \lambda_{jk}^{SAT,USE}.$$

Table 8.7 shows the results of the first step, that is, first order, main effect CFA. These are the results that will be interpreted if mediation exists. The $LR - X^2$ for this model is 141.78 ($df = 4$; $p < 0.01$). The model is, therefore, rejected, and we expect types and antitypes to emerge.

Table 8.7 shows that, with the exception of Configuration 1 1 2, every configuration constitutes a type or an antitype. Now, instead of interpreting each of these in detail, we ask whether hypotheses concerning the existence of complete or partial mediation can be supported. We perform a CFA-based mediation analysis (see Section 6.2). Table 8.8 displays the summary table of the results of the four models listed above.

To determine whether mediation exists, we now perform the steps outlined in Section 6.2, on CFA-based mediation analysis.

Comparison 1: The comparison of the results from Steps 2 and 3 shows that the main effect base model and the one that takes the interaction between Quality and Satisfaction into account result in different patterns of types and antitypes. We conclude that Quality, Satisfaction, or both are related to the outcome, Intention to Use Services Again.

Comparison 2: The pattern of types and antitypes from Step 1 differs from the patterns of types and antitypes from all other steps. We conclude that the path from the predictor, Quality, to the mediator, Satisfaction, exists.

Comparison 3: To determine the role played by the three-way interaction [*QUA, SAT, USE*], we add this interaction to the fourth model in Table 8.8. The $LR - X^2$ for this model is 15.23 ($df = 1$; $p < 0.01$). This model is not significantly better than Model 4 ($\Delta LR - X^2 = 0.17$; $\Delta df = 1$; $p = 0.68$), and

TABLE 8.8. CFA-Based Configural Mediation Analysis of the Variables Perceived Quality of Services (QUA), Satisfaction with Services (SAT), and Intention to Use Services Again (USE)

Configuration QUA SAT USE	m	Model 1 [QUA][SAT] [USE]	Model 2 [QUA][SAT] [USE] [QUA, SAT]	Model 3 [QUA][SAT] [USE] [QUA, SAT] [QUA, USE]	Model 4 [QUA][SAT] [USE] [QUA, SAT] [SAT, USE]
			CFA Base Model		
111	65	Type	Type		
112	38		Antitype		
121	8	Antitype			Type
122	10	Antitype			
211	16	Antitype		Type	
212	23	Antitype			
221	10	Antitype	Antitype		
222	80	Type	Type		
$LR - X^2(df)$		141.78 (4)	59.73 (3)	16.25 (2)	15.40 (2)

the same type as indicated in Table 8.8. We, therefore, conclude that the three-way interaction explains no additional aspects of the data.

Based on the results of these comparisons, we can come to the following conclusions about the mediation process that was hypothesized to relate the variables Quality, Satisfaction, and Intention of Use to one another.

Conclusion: Model 1 yields types and antitypes, and because Models 2-4 yield patterns of types and antitypes that differ from the pattern for Model 1 and from each other, the model of partial mediation is supported.

We now ask whether this mediation process is moderated by expectations. Specifically, we ask whether the resulting pattern of mediator types and antitypes is different for respondents with high expectations than for respondents with low expectations. To answer this question, two CFA models need to be estimated. The first is the one that is interpreted as possibly supporting mediation hypotheses. The results for this model are displayed in Table 8.8. The second model contains the moderator variable, *EXP*. Table 8.9 shows the results of a first order, main effect CFA of the *EXP* $\times QUA \times SAT \times USE$ cross-tabulation. The $LR - X^2$ for this model is 180.75 ($df = 11$; $p < 0.01$). We, therefore, expect types and antitypes to emerge.

Table 8.9 shows that two types and three antitypes from Table 8.7 remain when the moderator variable, Expectations (*EXP*), is included. There are two reasons why this reduction in the number of types and antitypes can happen. The first is that, in the presence of the moderator, types and antitypes disappear, or additional types and antitypes emerge. The second

TABLE 8.9. First Order, Main Effect CFA of the Cross-Classification of Variables *EXP*, *QUA*, *SAT*, and *USE*

Configuration EXP QUA SAT USE	m	$\hat{m}$	z	p	Type/Antitype
1111	40	11.431	8.4500	.000000	Type
1112	18	17.435	.1353	.446175	
1121	7	8.694	−.5745	.282821	
1122	6	13.260	−1.9938	.023087	
1211	5	12.187	−2.0586	.019764	
1212	6	18.588	−2.9197	.001752	Antitype
1221	6	9.269	−1.0737	.141489	
1222	17	14.137	.7614	.223200	
2111	25	15.785	2.3192	.010191	
2112	20	24.077	−.8308	.203031	
2121	1	12.006	−3.1763	.000746	Antitype
2122	4	18.312	−3.3445	.000412	Antitype
2211	11	16.829	−1.4209	.077669	
2212	17	25.669	−1.7110	.043541	
2221	4	12.800	−2.4596	.006955	
2222	63	19.523	9.8400	.000000	Type

reason is that the more restrictive significance threshold of the larger table that includes the moderator, in tandem with the smaller cell frequencies, can have the effect that the discrepancies between observed and expected cell frequencies become so small that types and antitypes no longer emerge.

For the present data, Configurations 1 1 1 1 and 2 1 1 1 in Table 8.9 correspond with Configuration 1 1 1 in Table 8.7. Here, we find that only Configuration 1 1 1 1 constitutes a type. We conclude that Moderation Type . 1 1 1 exists only for those who approach their receiving of welfare with low expectations. Specifically, if expectations are low, satisfaction is low also, and one can predict that the quality of services is perceived as low and that the intention to use the services again is weak also. This pattern occurs more often than expected.

Configurations 1 1 2 1 and 2 1 2 1 in Table 8.9 correspond with Configuration 1 2 1 in Table 8.7. Of these, only Configuration 2 1 2 1 constitutes an antitype. For Configuration 1 1 2 1, the model-data discrepancy is so small that one is tempted to conclude that this antitype exists only for those who have high expectations. Specifically, we find that it is highly unlikely that those with high expectations perceive the quality of services as low but are highly satisfied and still do not intend to use the services any more.

This applies accordingly to Antitype 2 1 2 2. High expectations, perceiving the quality of services as low, but high satisfaction and the intention of using the services in the future are unlikely to be observed together.

The third antitype in Table 8.9, constituted by Configuration 1 2 1 2, corresponds with Antitype 2 1 2 in Table 8.7. This antitype is moderated also because Configuration 2 2 1 2 does not constitute an antitype. This pattern suggests that, for respondents with low expectations, the inconsistent pattern 2 1 2 is highly unlikely to be observed. For respondents with high expectations, this pattern tends to be unlikely also. However, the discrepancy is not strong enough for the configuration to constitute an antitype.

Configurations 1 2 2 2 and 2 2 2 2 in Table 8.9 correspond with Configuration 2 2 2 in Table 8.7. Only Configuration 2 2 2 2 constitutes a type again. The observed and the expected frequencies in Cell 1 2 2 2 do not differ enough to constitute a type. We conclude that the consistent pattern . 2 2 2 indicates that, for respondents with high expectations, perceiving quality as high allows one to predict that satisfaction is also high and the intention is strong that the services will be used in the future.

As was indicated above, the interactions among the variables in the mediator model may be among the reasons for types and antitypes to (not) emerge in the cross-tabulation that includes the moderator. Therefore, the model that includes these interactions may be of interest. For the present example, this is the model

$$\log \hat{m} = \lambda + \lambda_i^{QUA} + \lambda_j^{SAT} + \lambda_k^{USE} + \lambda_{ij}^{QUA,SAT} + \lambda_{ik}^{QUA,USE} + \lambda_{jk}^{SAT,USE} + \lambda_{ijk}^{QUA,SAT,USE}.$$

The $LR - X^2$ for this model is 38.97 ($df = 7$; $p < 0.01$). This base model does not describe the data well either. However, only one type remains. It is constituted by Configuration 1 2 2 2. No other type or antitype emerges under this model. We conclude that, if the moderator is taken into account, the interactions among the variables in the mediation model explain more variability than when the moderator is not taken into account. Mediation still exists, but only for one of the configurations in the table.

8.5 Graphical Representation of Configural Moderator Results

The graphical representation of configural moderator models can be developed in a way parallel to the graphical representation of configural prediction or mediator models. The basic idea is that the relationships identified in the form of types and antitypes do not involve variables but

FIGURE 8.5. Prediction type $X1$ $Y2$.

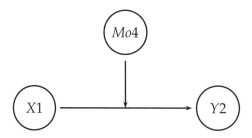

FIGURE 8.6. Moderated prediction relationship: $X1$ $Y2$ is found only for $Mo4$.

configurations, that is, patterns of categories of categorical variables. In Figure 8.4, moderator models were depicted at the level of variables.

In this section, we describe and illustrate how graphical representations of configural moderation can be created. The graphs consist of two elements. The first element is that of a configural regression relation, depicted as in Figure 6.3, for mediation types, and in Figure 6.4, for mediation antitypes. From these figures, we take the part that relates two configurations to each other. For example, let $X1$ be the first category of the predictor, X, and $Y2$ the second category of the criterion, Y. Let $X1$ $Y2$ constitute a prediction type. Then, the graphical representation of this relationship can be depicted as in Figure 8.5.

The moderation element comes into play when the graph indicates that a configural relationship is found for a particular category of a moderator variable only. Consider the moderator variable Mo. Let the prediction type be found only for category $Mo4$. Then, the graph in Figure 8.5 becomes as shown in Figure 8.6.

Data Example 5: In the following example, we depict the first moderator type and the moderator antitype that were found in Table 8.5. The type indicates that below average number of assets over a period of 2 years, denoted by $A1 = 1$ and $A2 = 1$, are found only in youth who are members of gangs, $G = 1$. Figure 8.7 depicts this relationship.

The antitype in Table 8.5 (Cell Configuration 1 1 2) indicates that below average number of assets over a period of 2 years, denoted by $A1 =$

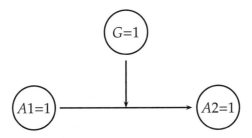

FIGURE 8.7. Moderated type-prediction relationship of asset number and group membership.

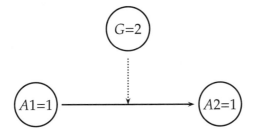

FIGURE 8.8. Moderated antitype-prediction relationship of asset number and group membership.

1 and $A2 = 1$, are unlikely to be found in youth who are members of community-based organizations, $G = 2$. Figure 8.8 depicts this relationship. In this figure, the antitype relationship is depicted with dotted lines.

8.6 Chapter Summary

Moderator effects are said to exist if the relationship between two (or more) variables changes across the categories of another variable. In configural analysis, moderator effects exist if patterns of types and antitypes vary across the categories of the moderator variable. CFA of moderator effects proceeds in a series of major steps. These two steps first involve performing CFA runs sequentially in which the moderator variable is, versus is not, taken into account. Second, the resulting patterns of types and antitypes are compared with one another. If a type/antitype pattern changes when the moderator is taken into account, that is, if a resulting type/antitype pattern is group-specific, a moderation effect is said to exist at the level of individual configurations.

A variant of moderation CFA is introduced that allows one to test whether mediation processes are moderated by grouping variables. This variant allows one to perform moderated mediation analysis at the level of individual configurations. This variant performs mediation CFA first without a moderator, followed by mediation CFA that does take the moderator into account. If mediation effects are group-specific, they can be said to be moderated.

The graphical representation of configural moderator effects follows the lines of graphing variable-oriented moderator models. However, it proceeds at the level of configuration patterns. This is necessary because, parallel to mediation CFA, the same table can contain configurations that reflect moderator effects, and other configurations that do not. In addition, graphical representation at the level of configurations is necessary to be able to distinguish between moderator types and antitypes.

9

The Validity of CFA Types and Antitypes

> Distinctions between individuals do not need to be made if they
> carry no implications. In CFA, tables are analyzed with the goal of
> identifying types, antitypes, and those configurations that are observed
> as often as expected. One way of determining the validity of types
> and antitypes involves asking whether these configurations can also
> be distinguished in the space of variables that had not been used for
> CFA. The methods that can be applied to answer this question include,
> for example, MANOVA, discriminant analysis, and logit models. In
> Chapter 9, repeated measures ANOVA is applied to determine whether
> configurations of physical aggression against peers can be distinguished
> based on physical pubertal development.

9.1 Validity in CFA

An important question that has been asked in the context of classification methods is whether the groups that are being discussed are "for real". In taxometric research, several methods have been proposed to establish the existence of clusters (Blashfield & Aldenderfer, 1984; Everitt, Landau, & Leese, 2001; von Eye, Mun, & Indurkhya, 2004). One of these methods involves repeating an analysis by using a different clustering algorithm. The hypothesis is that different algorithms will yield similar solutions if the clusters exist. A second method involves split-sample, jackknifing, or bootstrapping methods. Using these methods, clustering is repeated based on repeatedly drawn subsamples (with replacement). Robust solutions will emerge more often than solutions that are specific to subsamples. A third method involves using significance tests against null hypotheses according to which a particular data generation process will not lead to groupings (see, e.g., von Eye, 2010; von Eye & Gardiner, 2004; Wood, 2004). A fourth method involves establishing the *external validity of groupings* by using variables that were not included when groups or clusters were established. When this method is applied, researchers ask whether groupings are also different in the space of other variables than those used for clustering (see also von Eye & Bergman, 2003).

When it comes to establishing types and antitypes from CFA, the second, third, and fourth of these methods have been discussed. The second method is part of a CFA software package (for a sample application, see Lautsch & von Weber, 1995, Table 8). The third method is an established routine in CFA applications. Types and antitypes are interpreted only if cell-wise null hypotheses can be rejected. The fourth method has not found many applications yet. Therefore, we discuss it in this text.

Establishing the external validity[1] of CFA solutions is straightforward. Two sets of variables are used. The first is the basis for CFA. The second set of variables is selected such that it is conceptually related but not identical to the first. This selection proceeds in the same way as the selection of variables when the external validity of psychometric instruments is established. For example, to establish the external validity of intelligence tests, one can use existing tests, grades in college, job performance, and, as a matter of course, wins in the lottery (maybe not).

Once types, antitypes, and those configurations have been identified that do not deviate from expectation, one can use analysis of variance, discriminant analysis, or logit models to answer the question whether these groups of cases (or subsets of these groups) also differ in the space of those variables that were not used for CFA. When ANOVA is used, one asks whether types, antitypes, and those cells that reflect the base model (these are the cells that constitute neither types nor antitypes) differ in their means in the second set of variables. When discriminant analysis or logit models are used, one asks whether membership in the groups of types, antitypes, and nonsuspicious cells (again, these are the cells that constitute neither types nor antitypes) can be predicted from the second set of variables.

Data Example 1: For the following example, we use the Finkelstein et al. (1994) aggression data again. 114 adolescents indicated their level of physical aggression against peers (*PAAP*) in 1983, 1985, and 1987. At these points in time, they were, on average, 11, 13, and 15 years of age. In addition, progress in physical pubertal development was determined for each student by a nurse. Tanner scores were used to indicate progress in stages. Here, we first ask whether typical and atypical pathways of PAAP

[1]Note that, in the present context, the term *external validity* has a different meaning than usual. Here, it means that types, antitypes, and other configurations are established by using different variables, not different samples.

TABLE 9.1. First Order CFA of the Development of Physical Aggression against Peers over Three Observation Points

Configuration P83 P85 P87	m	$\hat{m}$	z	p	Type/Antitype
111	42	24.237	3.6081	.000154	Type
112	2	9.052	−2.3440	.009539	Antitype
121	6	15.807	−2.4666	.006819	Antitype
122	5	5.904	−.3719	.354967	
211	18	26.000	−1.5689	.058337	
212	7	9.711	−.8699	.192180	
221	17	16.956	.0106	.495773	
222	17	6.333	4.2387	.000011	Type

exist that emerge in the form of types and antitypes. Then, we ask whether these pathways correspond to specific developmental curves in physical pubertal development. The first question will be answered by using CFA. The second question will be answered by using repeated measures ANOVA with polynomial decomposition.

For CFA, we use the three variables *P83*, *P85*, and *P87*. These are the dichotomized scores of the *PAAP* variable, measured at three different points in time. Dichotomization was performed at the grand mean so that development can be described both ipsatively and comparatively. A score of 1 indicates below average aggression, and a score of 2 indicates above average aggression. A first order CFA was performed which assumes, in its base model, that the three repeated observations are independent of one another. Types and antitypes then reflect various forms of auto-associations. The *z*-test was used, and α was protected by using the Holland-Copenhaver procedure. Table 9.1 displays the results of this first order CFA.

The $LR - X^2$ for the base model of first order CFA is 42.70 ($df = 4$; $p < 0.01$). The base model is thus rejected, and we expect types and antitypes to emerge.

Table 9.1 shows that two types and two antitypes exist. The types reflect stability over time. Configuration 1 1 1 describes those adolescents who rate themselves as below average in physical aggression against peers over the entire observation period. Parallel to the first type, the second describes those adolescents who rate themselves as above average over the entire observation period (Configuration 2 2 2). The two antitypes show that an increase from below to above average aggression against peers for just the second or the third observation period is particularly unlikely (Configurations 1 1 2 and 1 2 1).

TABLE 9.2. Between-Subjects Effects: Results of Repeated Measures ANOVA

Source	SS	df	MS	F	p
Configuration	101.97	7	14.57	1.207	.305
Error	1279.19	106	12.07		

TABLE 9.3. Within-Subjects Effects: Results of the Repeated Measures ANOVA

Source	SS	df	MS	F	p
Time	1789.14	2	894.57	414.49	< .01
Time × Configuration	71.49	14	5.11	2.37	.005
Error	457.55	212			

Now, to establish external validity for these types, antitypes, and non-suspicious cells, we perform a repeated measures ANOVA. This analysis uses time (1983, 1985, and 1987) as the repeated measures factor and the eight configurations as the between-groups factor. The Tanner scores of physical pubertal development are used as dependent measures. A decomposition into orthogonal polynomials of up to second order will be performed to determine whether curvature is configuration group-specific. Table 9.2 shows the results for the between-subjects part of the repeated measures ANOVA.

The results in Table 9.2 suggest that the eight groups (configurations) do not differ significantly in their means in physical pubertal development. Accordingly, the multiple $R^2 = 0.057$ is rather small. The within-subjects part of the ANOVA will tell us whether the eight configurations differ in curvature over time. Table 9.3 displays the overview of the within-subjects part of the repeated measures ANOVA. The Huynh-Feldt ε was used to adjust the tail probabilities to the serial dependence in the data.

The results for the main effect of Time in Table 9.3 show that the configurations, overall, differ in their pubertal development scores over time. This is as expected. The Tanner score means are 4.48, 8.19, and 12.35, for 1983, 1985, and 1987, respectively. Wilks' Lambda for this effect is $\Lambda = 0.12$. This value indicates that 88% of the variation of the dependent measure that can be explained based on time was explained. This effect is, thus, strong. The interaction of Configuration with Time suggests that the developmental curves are specific to configurations rather than common to all configurations. Wilks' Lambda for this interaction is $\Lambda = 0.76$. This value indicates that this interaction explains 24% of the variation of the dependent measure. This effect is, thus, weak to medium in magnitude.

TABLE 9.4. Orthogonal Decomposition of the Main Effect of Time

Source	SS	df	MS	F	p
Linear Trend	1785.76	1	1785.76	757.80	< .01
Error	249.79	106			
QuadraticTrend	3.38	1	3.38	1.73	.19
Error	207.75	106	1.96		

TABLE 9.5. Polynomial Decomposition of the Time × Configuration Group Interaction

Source	SS	df	MS	F	p
Linear Trend	22.80	7	3.26	1.38	.220
Error	249.79	106			
Quadratic Trend	48.69	7	6.96	3.55	.002
Error	207.75	106	1.96		

Table 9.4 displays the results for the decomposition of the effect of Time into orthogonal polynomials. Linear and quadratic polynomials are considered.

Table 9.4 shows that, overall, the increase in physical pubertal development is linear. The quadratic component is nonsignificant. We conclude that, over the observation period of 4 years (the respondents were 11-15 years of age), there is, overall, no significant acceleration or deceleration in this development. Table 9.5 shows whether this result varies with the eight groups under study.

Table 9.5 shows that the linear trend is not group-specific. In other words, the straight-line increase is about the same for each of the eight groups. In contrast, the groups differ significantly in their quadratic trends. Figure 9.1 displays the developmental curves of physical pubertal development, by group.

The curves in Figure 9.1 indicate that those adolescents who indicate that they are below average in physical aggression against peers (Configuration 1: 1 1 1) show a negatively accelerated curve of physical pubertal development. Those adolescents who see themselves as above average in physical aggression against peers (Configuration 8: 2 2 2) show a positively accelerated curve of physical pubertal development. Members of the second antitype (Configuration 3: 1 2 1) show a curve with no acceleration.

We note that the members of the two types and the two antitypes differ from each other in the quadratic component of their developmental curves, but not in the means or linear trends. The curvatures of the nonsuspicious respondents seem to show less pronounced acceleration or deceleration.

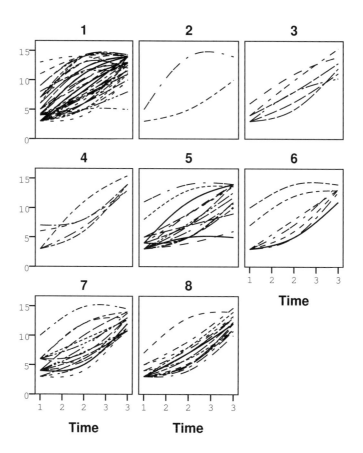

FIGURE 9.1. Developmental curves of physical pubertal development, by configuration.

With respect to the quest for external validity, we conclude that these results support the classification of cells into types, antitypes, and nonsuspicious cells. This classification also holds in the space of physical pubertal development, which had not been used for the definition of the table that had been subjected to the CFA.

9.2   Chapter Summary

The interpretation of types and antitypes is based on two key elements of information. The first is given by the meaning of the categories in a configuration. The second is given by the base model. Types and antitypes are considered externally valid if they can also be discriminated in the space of variables that were not used for the configural analysis that resulted in the types and antitypes. Methods of discriminant analysis, MANOVA, or logit models can be used to establish this form of external validity. In these analyses, each type, antitype, and configuration that does not stand out as a type or antitype constitutes a factor level (or group in discriminant analysis). The variables not used for configural analysis are used as dependent variables, and one asks whether members in one of the configurations of CFA also differ in these dependent variables.

10
Functional CFA

Chapter 10 presents two methods of Functional CFA (F-CFA). One of the characteristics of CFA is that the tests that are performed to identify types and antitypes are, to a certain degree (that depends, among other things, on the base model and the size of a table), dependent. Therefore, there exists the risk that types and antitypes may emerge because other types and antitypes emerge. These types and antitypes are called *phantom types* and *phantom antitypes*. The first version of F-CFA presented in Chapter 10 involves strategies to identify phantom types and antitypes. Two strategies for this first version of F-CFA are discussed. The first focuses on optimizing overall goodness-of-fit. The second focuses on the largest model-data discrepancies. The second version of F-CFA presented in Chapter 10 aims at identifying those effects in a table that cause types and antitypes to emerge. The *ascending strategy* of this version of F-CFA systematically adds, beginning from the base model that resulted in types and antitypes, effects to the base model until the following two conditions are fulfilled. First, all types and antitypes disappear. Second, no new types or antitypes emerge. The most parsimonious model that has these characteristics contains the effects that are called *type- and antitype-constituting*. In contrast to the ascending strategy of F-CFA, the *descending strategy* starts from the saturated model. It systematically removes effects, beginning with the most complex. The iteration ends when a model is found that (1) fits the data and (2) results in no types or antitypes. The effects not included in this model are called *type- and antitype-constituting*. The choice between these two strategies is guided by the importance of higher order terms. If higher order terms are not significant, the ascending strategy is preferred. If, however, higher order terms explain significant portions of the variability in a table, the descending strategy is preferable over the ascending strategy.

In this chapter, we present two versions of *Functional CFA* (F-CFA; von Eye & Mair, 2008a, 2008b, 2009). Both of these versions of CFA are called *functional* because they allow one to make statements about the role that elements of configural frequency analysis play in the resulting pattern of types and antitypes. The first version of F-CFA to be discussed here, in Section 10.1, leads to statements about the role played by individual cells of a table. The second version, discussed in Sections 10.3.1 and 10.3.2, leads to statements about the role played by individual effects as they are modeled in the design matrix. These effects are used to explain the emerging types and antitypes.

10.1 F-CFA I: An Alternative Approach to Exploratory CFA

One interesting consequence of the mutual dependence of types and antitype tests is that so-called phantom types and phantom antitypes can emerge. This was shown by Victor (1983) and Kieser and Victor (1991, 1999, 2000), using an example like the following one. Consider a 3×3 contingency table, spanned by the variables X and Y, such as the one given in Table 10.1. The frequencies in this table were determined for the purpose of this example. Specifically, the observed frequencies, m, in Table 10.1 were determined so that they reflect the following characteristics:

1. each cell of the table contains 100 cases;

2. the frequency of Cell 1 1 was reduced by 90 cases; therefore, Cell 1 1 is a candidate for a CFA antitype;

3. the frequency of Cell 3 3 was increased by 90 cases; therefore, Cell 3 3 is a candidate for a CFA type;

4. Cells 1 2 through 3 2 reflect a uniform distribution and independence of X and Y; therefore, they are candidates for configurations that do not deviate from the first order CFA base model.

The analysis performed is a first order CFA of variable independence. The z-test was used along with the Holland-Copenhaver procedure of α protection.

The results of first order CFA in Table 10.1 show that the type/antitype pattern that was unearthed by first order CFA fails to reflect the structure of the data. Whereas Cell 1 1 does constitute an antitype, Cell 3 3 does not constitute a type. In addition, Cells 1 2 and 2 1 constitute types and Cells 2 3 and 3 2 constitute antitypes. None of these cells deviates from the data structure.

In addition to the dependence of CFA tests, a second problem is lurking. When CFA base models are used to estimate expected cell frequencies, the fact that types or antitypes may exist is not taken into account. To

TABLE 10.1. Illustration of Phantom Types and Antitypes; Artificial Data

Configuration X Y	m	$\hat{m}$	z	p	Type/Antitype
11	10	49	−5.5714	.000000	Antitype
12	100	70	3.5857	.000168	Type
13	100	91	.9435	.172724	
21	100	70	3.5857	.000168	Type
22	100	100	.0000	.500000	
23	100	130	−2.6312	.004255	Antitype
31	100	91	.9435	.172724	
32	100	130	−2.6312	.004255	Antitype
33	190	169	1.6154	.053114	

the contrary, the estimation proceeds under the assumption that types or antitypes do not exist. One effect of this procedure is that marginal frequencies can be distorted by existing types and antitypes, and cells that, otherwise, would conform with the assumptions put forth in the base model, emerge as phantom types or phantom antitypes. In computer science, phantom types are defined as data types "with type constraints associated with different cases" (Cheney & Hinze, 2003). In other words, phantom types exist only if certain conditions are met. In CFA, phantom types and phantom antitypes exist only because other types and antitypes in a table exist. Without those, they would not emerge (Kieser & Victor, 2000). In the example in Table 10.1, two phantom types and two phantom antitypes emerge, and the type that is part of the data structure looks non-suspicious.

In the following sections, we discuss two approaches to dealing with the problems of phantom types or antitypes. The first approach was proposed by Kieser and Victor (1999, 2000). It involves sequential identification of types and antitypes with the goal of minimizing overall deviations from the base model. The second approach was proposed by von Eye and Mair (2008a, 2008b, 2009). This approach also involves sequential identification of types and antitypes. However, in contrast to Kieser and Victor's approach, the goal is to identify, at each step of the sequence, the cell with the largest discrepancy from the base model. Both approaches conclude their iterations when either no types or antitypes remain in the table or the base model fits.

10.1.1 Kieser and Victor's Alternative, Sequential CFA: Focus on Model Fit

Kieser and Victor (1999) proposed both a confirmatory and an exploratory version of their alternative CFA. In the present context, we focus on the exploratory version. To explain this model, consider the log-linear CFA base model

$$M_\emptyset : \log \hat{m} = X\lambda,$$

where, as before, X is the design matrix and λ is the parameter vector. Now, let τ be a parameter vector that characterizes the deviations of the cells that constitute types and antitypes. Taking into account τ, the base model becomes the type/antitype base model

$$M_{T/A} : \log \hat{m} = X\begin{pmatrix}\lambda \\ \tau\end{pmatrix}.$$

In the first base model, the design matrix has r rows and c columns with $r > c$. In the type/antitype base model, the design matrix still has r rows, but now it has $c + t$ columns, where t indicates the number of type/antitype cells, and $(c + t) < r$. For identification, we assume that X is of full rank. The type/antitype model allows one to model any type structure and any number of type/antitype cells (as long as there is a sufficient number of degrees of freedom). In addition, any base model can be modeled.

The confirmatory procedure proposed by Kieser and Victor (1999) involves estimating the parameters in τ for a priori specified type- and antitype-constituting cells. The exploratory procedure proceeds in the following steps:

1. Estimate the first base model and calculate the $LR - X^2$ for this model. If the model fits, stop, and no type or antitype resulted (this is no different than in standard CFA).

2. If the model does not fit, blank out each single cell, one after the other, (that is, declare each individual cell a structural zero; see Chapter 3) and calculate the $\Delta LR - X^2$ with respect to the first base model. If this $\Delta LR - X^2$ is significant, the cell that was blanked out for this step is a candidate to constitute a type or antitype. If not, the procedure terminates here.

3. Add the vector for the cell with the largest $\Delta LR - X^2$, or, equivalently, the smallest overall $LR - X^2$, to the design matrix for the base model, and iterate Step 2 until the model fits.

The result of this procedure is, typically, (1) an extended base model that fits and (2) a pattern of types and antitypes. In addition, the results of

TABLE 10.2. $LR-X^2$ Values That Result When Individual Cells of the Cross-Classification in Table 10.1 Are Blanked Out

Blanked-Out Cell	1 1	1 2	1 3	2 1	2 2	2 3	3 1	3 2	3 3
$LR - X^2$	21.48	63.88	86.13	63.88	88.17	69.57	86.13	69.57	80.05

Kieser and Victor's CFA are usually more parsimonious than the results of standard CFA because blanking out cells reduces the probability of phantom types/antitypes emerging.

To illustrate this procedure, consider again the example in Table 10.1. The base model for this 3×3 table comes with the design matrix

$$X = \begin{pmatrix} 1 & 0 & 1 & 0 \\ 1 & 0 & 0 & 1 \\ 1 & 0 & -1 & -1 \\ 0 & 1 & 1 & 0 \\ 0 & 1 & 0 & 1 \\ 0 & 1 & -1 & -1 \\ -1 & -1 & 1 & 0 \\ -1 & -1 & 0 & 1 \\ -1 & -1 & -1 & -1 \end{pmatrix}.$$

The $LR-X^2$ for the base model is 88.17 ($df = 4$). Blanking out one individual cell after the other, we obtain the $LR - X^2$ values given in Table 10.2.

Clearly, the largest effect is observed when Cell 1 1 is blanked out ($LR - X^2$ is smallest). The $\Delta LR - X^2$ for the base model and the model after blanking out Cell 1 1 is 66.69 ($\Delta df = 1$; $p < 0.01$). We, therefore, add the vector that blanks out Cell 1 1 to the design matrix of the original base model and obtain the following new design matrix:

$$X = \left(\begin{array}{cccc|c} 1 & 0 & 1 & 0 & 1 \\ 1 & 0 & 0 & 1 & 0 \\ 1 & 0 & -1 & -1 & 0 \\ 0 & 1 & 1 & 0 & 0 \\ 0 & 1 & 0 & 1 & 0 \\ 0 & 1 & -1 & -1 & 0 \\ -1 & -1 & 1 & 0 & 0 \\ -1 & -1 & 0 & 1 & 0 \\ -1 & -1 & -1 & -1 & 0 \end{array} \right).$$

The additional vector has the effect that Cell 1 1 is blanked out. We now proceed as in the last step and calculate the $LR - X^2$ values for the model

TABLE 10.3. $LR-X^2$ Values That Result When Individual Cells of the Cross-Classification in Table 10.1 Are Blanked Out (Cell 1 1 Already Blanked out)

Blanked-Out Cell	1 1	1 2	1 3	2 1	2 2	2 3	3 1	3 2	3 3
$LR - X^2$	—	16.63	16.63	16.63	20.22	12.56	16.63	12.56	0.00

after blanking each of the remaining cells out. The result of this step is summarized in Table 10.3.

The results in Table 10.3 are clear. Each of the new base models improves model fit. One of them stands out. If Cell 3 3 is blanked out, the remaining cell frequencies are perfectly reproduced, the $LR-X^2$ becomes zero ($df = 2$), and the search for types and antitypes can be concluded. Cell 1 1 constitutes an antitype and Cell 3 3 constitutes a type. The design matrix for this model is

$$X = \begin{pmatrix} 1 & 0 & 1 & 0 & 1 & 0 \\ 1 & 0 & 0 & 1 & 0 & 0 \\ 1 & 0 & -1 & -1 & 0 & 0 \\ 0 & 1 & 1 & 0 & 0 & 0 \\ 0 & 1 & 0 & 1 & 0 & 0 \\ 0 & 1 & -1 & -1 & 0 & 0 \\ -1 & -1 & 1 & 0 & 0 & 0 \\ -1 & -1 & 0 & 1 & 0 & 0 \\ -1 & -1 & -1 & -1 & 0 & 1 \end{pmatrix}.$$

The result of this analysis has four important characteristics:

- The type/antitype structure perfectly depicts the structure of the frequency table (Table 10.1).

- The resulting pattern of types and antitypes is more parsimonious than that of standard CFA, which needed three types and two antitypes to describe deviations from the base model.

- The model used to describe the data structure does not consider the cells that deviate from the data structure.

- The extended base model fits. This characteristic greatly facilitates the interpretation of types and antitypes. They now reflect deviations from a fitting base model. In contrast, in standard CFA, the base model does not necessarily fit after types and antitypes were identified. Thus, the data structure that types and antitypes deviate from can be unclear.

10.1.2   von Eye and Mair's Sequential CFA: Focus on Residuals

Kieser and Victor's approach to sequential CFA has three characteristics that make it attractive in the context of configural frequency analysis. First, the probability of falling for phantom types or antitypes is greatly reduced. Therefore, second, the role that each individual cell plays in the description of a table and in the identification of types and antitypes becomes clear: Types and antitypes clearly suggest deviations from an otherwise fitting model instead of possibly reflecting dependence of CFA tests. Third, the solutions obtained from Kieser and Victor's method usually are more parsimonious than the solutions from standard CFA.

However, there are two downsides to Kieser and Victor's CFA. The first is that it can be numerically intensive. After the first step (fitting a base model), c log-linear models have to be estimated; after this step, $c - 1$ models have to be estimated, and so forth. Second, the focus of Kieser and Victor's method is the fit of the base model. Types and antitypes are a mere by-product.

Therefore, von Eye and Mair (2008a, 2008b, 2009) proposed an alternative to Kieser and Victor's method. This alternative also proceeds iteratively by blanking out cells one by one until some criteria are fulfilled. However, the focus of this method is on the magnitude of individual cell residuals instead of global goodness-of-fit statistics. This method proceeds in the following steps:

1. Estimate the base model and calculate the $LR - X^2$ for this model. If the model fits, stop, and no type or antitype resulted (this is no different than in standard CFA or in Kieser and Victor's sequential CFA).

2. Select the cell with the largest absolute residual, blank it out, and reestimate the thus extended base model.

3. One after the other, blank out the cell with the largest residual (that is, declare each individual cell a structural zero), until either the base model fits or there is no residual left to blank out.

In contrast to Kieser and Victor's CFA, the overall goodness-of-fit plays no role in this procedure until the base model fits, that is, until the overall goodness-of-fit statistic indicates no significant overall model-data discrepancies any more.

To illustrate this procedure, we use the data example in Table 10.1 again. In this table, the largest residual was calculated for Cell 1 1 ($z = -5.57$; see Table 10.1). In the second step of von Eye and Mair's procedure, this cell will be blanked out and the CFA will be reestimated. The results of this run appear in Table 10.4.

TABLE 10.4. CFA of the Data in Table 10.1 after Blanking Out Cell 1 1

Configuration X Y	m	$\hat{m}$	z	p	Type/Antitype
11	10	—	—	—	
12	100	86.957	1.3988	.080943	
13	100	113.043	−1.2268	.109951	
21	100	86.957	1.3988	.080943	
22	100	92.628	.7660	.221833	
23	100	120.416	−1.8605	.031408	
31	100	113.043	−1.2268	.109951	
32	100	120.416	−1.8605	.031408	
33	190	156.541	2.6743	.003745	Type

TABLE 10.5. CFA of the Data in Table 10.1 after Blanking Out Cells 1 1 and 3 3

Configuration X Y	m	$\hat{m}$	z	p	Type/Antitype
11	10	—	—	—	
12	100	100	.0000	.500000	
13	100	100	.0000	.500000	
21	100	100	.0000	.500000	
22	100	100	.0000	.500000	
23	100	100	.0000	.500000	
31	100	100	.0000	.500000	
32	100	100	.0000	.500000	
33	190	—	—	—	

The design matrix for this model is the same as the one for the second step in Victor and Kieser's model. The overall goodness-of-fit is also the same. Most important for the present purposes is that the number of types and antitypes now is dramatically reduced. Only one residual is significant, from a CFA perspective. This is the residual for Cell 3 3. Blanking out this cell results in the second of the above design matrices. The results of the CFA that uses this design matrix as its extended base model are given in Table 10.5.

The results in this table replicate the results in Section 10.1.1. The fit of the extended base model is perfect, Cell 1 1 constitutes an antitype, and Cell 3 3 constitutes a type. It should be noted, however, that when empirical data are analyzed and the data structure is not known before analysis (as is the case in the present example), the methods presented in Sections 10.1.1 and 10.1.2 will rarely yield the same type/antitype pattern. The data examples provided by von Eye and Mair (2008a) illustrate this difference.

The method presented in this section is straightforward and more economical than the method proposed by Kieser and Victor (1999). Specifically, at each step, only one CFA needs to be performed. The maximum number of CFA runs is, therefore, $df - 1$, which is much smaller than the number of log-linear models that need to be estimated for Kieser and Victor's procedure.

When focusing on residuals in a CFA context, researchers make decisions concerning the protection of the significance threshold, α. Usually, the total number of tests is used as the basis for determining α. In the present context, this number is unknown. It can maximally be $(df - 1)c$ and minimally c. If a researcher uses $(df - 1)c$ as the reference number, the resulting α-level can be prohibitively small, with the effect that (1) no types or antitypes are identified and (2) the base model does not fit. Alternatively, if c is used as reference number, α may not be properly protected, and researchers may capitalize on chance. A third option discussed by von Eye and Mair is even more liberal. It involves always selecting the largest residual, regardless of significance level, until either the extended base model fits or there is no cell left to be blanked out.

Another decision to be made by the researchers concerns the residual measure to be used. In the present and the following examples, we used the standard normal z statistic. Alternatively, Pearson's X^2 can be used, Lehmacher's z, the adjusted residual, the Freeman-Tukey deviate (the software package SYSTAT uses this statistic to identify outlandish cells that have an interpretation similar to types and antitypes in Kieser and Victor's CFA), even the tail probability of the binomial test. Depending on the distributions and the power of these and other statistics, different patterns of types and antitypes may result (Indurkhya & von Eye, 2000; von Eye & Mun, 2003; von Weber et al., 2004). This issue, however, is well known from many statistical applications. The selection of test statistics can influence the results of statistical testing.

In sum, the main characteristics of von Eye and Mair's F-CFA include that

1. types and antitypes can be interpreted as deviations from a model that fits the structure of the remaining cells in the table (Victor and Kieser's version of F-CFA shares this characteristic); in contrast, the interpretation of types and antitypes from standard CFA can be unclear when the base model does not fit after types and antitypes are taken into account;

2. the probability of falling for phantom types and antitypes is very small (Victor and Kieser's version of F-CFA shares this characteristic); and

3. it retains the focus on local deviations from a base model that otherwise

TABLE 10.6. First Order CFA of Glück's Spatial Strategy Data

Configuration R P V	m	$\hat{m}$	z	p	Type/Antitype
111	30	164.480	−13.8295	.000000	Antitype
112	59	28.132	6.1967	.000000	Type
121	304	236.873	6.5911	.000006	Type
122	77	40.515	6.2593	.000000	Type
211	1215	1069.467	11.0785	.000000	Type
212	141	182.921	−4.1341	.000018	Antitype
221	1462	1540.180	−5.7994	.000000	Antitype
222	238	263.432	−2.4032	.008126	Antitype

fits; this focus is shared with standard CFA but not with Kieser and Victor's CFA.

Data Example 1: The following example uses data from a study on strategies employed when solving spatial ability tasks (Glück, 1999; Glück & von Eye, 2000). 181 high school students processed the 24 items of a cube comparison task. After completing this task, the students indicated the strategies they had used to solve the task. Three strategies were used: Mental Rotation (R), Pattern Comparison (P), and Change of Viewpoint (V). Each of these strategies was coded as either not used (= 1) or used (= 2). In the following analyses, we ask whether patterns of strategy use versus nonuse stand out. We use von Eye and Mair's alternative, sequential CFA. The first step of this method involves performing a standard CFA. Here, we apply first order CFA, using the standardized Pearson residual (see Section 1.3) and the Holland-Copenhaver procedure. The results of this analysis are given in Table 10.6.

The overall goodness-of-fit $LR - X^2 = 271.86$ ($df = 4$; $p < 0.01$) suggests poor model-data correspondence. We, therefore, expect types and antitypes to emerge.

The result in Table 10.6 is extreme in the sense that, with no exception, each cell constitutes a type or an antitype. Instead of interpreting these many configurations, we ask whether the sequential CFA discussed in this section can suggest a more parsimonious solution. Note that the focus of the following reanalysis is on the parsimony of a CFA solution. It is hard to discuss the possible existence of phantom types or antitypes when there are no a priori hypotheses concerning the data structure. The design matrix for the base model of the CFA in Table 10.6 was (constant implied)

TABLE 10.7. First Order CFA of Glück's Spatial Strategy Data; Cell 1 1 1 Blanked Out

Configuration $R\,P\,V$	m	$\hat{m}$	z	p	Type/Antitype
111	30	—	—	—	Antitype[a]
112	59	43.970	2.5340	.011707	
121	304	341.992	−4.8299	.000000	Antitype
122	77	54.038	3.4910	.000241	Type
211	1215	1183.953	3.0025	.001339	Type
212	141	187.077	−4.4866	.000004	Antitype
221	1462	1455.056	.5995	.274420	
222	238	229.914	.7910	.214471	

[a]This antitype is the result of the first in the sequence of steps in F-CFA.

$$X = \begin{pmatrix} 1 & 1 & 1 \\ 1 & 1 & -1 \\ 1 & -1 & 1 \\ 1 & -1 & -1 \\ -1 & 1 & 1 \\ -1 & 1 & -1 \\ -1 & -1 & 1 \\ -1 & -1 & -1 \end{pmatrix}.$$

The largest residual in Table 10.6 was calculated for Cell 1 1 1 ($z = -13.83$). In the next step, we blank this cell out and reestimate the CFA. The design matrix for this run is

$$X = \left(\begin{array}{ccc|c} 1 & 1 & 1 & 1 \\ 1 & 1 & -1 & 0 \\ 1 & -1 & 1 & 0 \\ 1 & -1 & -1 & 0 \\ -1 & 1 & 1 & 0 \\ -1 & 1 & -1 & 0 \\ -1 & -1 & 1 & 0 \\ -1 & -1 & -1 & 0 \end{array} \right),$$

where the last column has the effect that Cell 1 1 1 is blanked out.

The results from this run are displayed in Table 10.7. The overall goodness-of-fit for this run is dramatically and significantly reduced, from $LR - X^2 = 271.86$ ($df = 4$; $p < 0.01$) to $LR - X^2 = 31.17$ ($df = 3$; $p < 0.01$). Still, this result indicates that significant model-data discrepancies remain. We, therefore, expect types and antitypes to emerge again.

Table 10.7 shows that two types and two antitypes remain. The procedure, therefore, continues its iterations. The next cell to be blanked out is 1 2 1 (see Table 10.7). After blanking out Cell 1 2 1, the overall goodness-of-fit is significantly reduced again, to $LR - X^2 = 9.17$ ($df = 2$; $p = 0.01$). This reduction in $LR - X^2$, however, is still not enough to result in a fitting base model. The CFA table after blanking out Cells 1 1 1 and 1 2 1 (not shown here) suggests that there is no cell left that, under protection of α, would constitute a type or an antitype. Considering, however, that this base model does not fit either and that Cell 2 1 2 comes with a z score that would be significant without α protection, we proceed and blank this cell out also. The design matrix for the extended base model for this run is

$$X = \begin{pmatrix} 1 & 1 & 1 & 1 & 0 & 0 \\ 1 & 1 & -1 & 0 & 0 & 0 \\ 1 & -1 & 1 & 0 & 0 & 0 \\ 1 & -1 & -1 & 0 & 1 & 0 \\ -1 & 1 & 1 & 0 & 0 & 0 \\ -1 & 1 & -1 & 0 & 0 & 1 \\ -1 & -1 & 1 & 0 & 0 & 0 \\ -1 & -1 & -1 & 0 & 0 & 0 \end{pmatrix}.$$

The results from this run appear in Table 10.8. Table 10.8 shows that no cell is left that could be considered constituting a type or an antitype. The overall goodness-of-fit is significantly reduced once more, to $LR - X^2 = 0.21$ ($df = 1$; $p = 0.646$). This result suggests that model fit is close to perfect.

Table 10.8 also shows that, in the third step, two configurations were blanked out instead of only one. The decision to blank out two cells if certain conditions are met is discussed in the next section, 10.2.

The result of this analysis is that the alternative sequential CFA yielded two types and three antitypes. The first type is constituted by Configuration 1 2 2. It indicates that the two strategies of Pattern Comparison (P) and Change of Viewpoint (V) were used more often in tandem than expected. The second type, constituted by Configuration 2 2 2, shows that all three strategies are used together more often than expected. The first antitype, constituted by Configuration 1 1 1, suggests that using no strategy at all was reported less often than expected. The second antitype, constituted by Configuration 1 2 1, suggests that Pattern Comparison is rarely used as the sole strategy. The third antitype, constituted by Configuration 2 1 2, shows that the two strategies Mental Rotation (R) and Change of Viewpoint (V) were less often used together than expected. For a more detailed analysis of these data, see Glück and von Eye (2000).

When compared with the results of standard CFA (Table 10.6), the results of von Eye and Mair's functional sequential CFA are more

TABLE 10.8. First Order CFA of Glück's Spatial Strategy Data; Cells 1 1 1, 2 1 2, and 1 2 2 Blanked Out

Configuration R P V	m	$\hat{m}$	z	p	Type/Antitype
111	30	—	—	—	Antitype[a]
112	59	61.59	−.4581	.323440	
121	304	—	—	—	Antitype[a]
122	77	74.41	.4581	.323440	
211	1215	1212.41	.4581	.323440	
212	141	—	—	—	Antitype[a]
221	1462	1464.59	−.4581	.323440	
222	238	—	—	—	

[a]These antitypes is the result of earlier steps in the sequence of steps in F-CFA.

parsimonious. Two types instead of four, and three antitypes instead of four, resulted. In other words, 37.5% of the cells that standard CFA marked as types and antitypes may not be needed for the description of the configural characteristics of Glück's spatial strategy data, under the base model of first order CFA.

To compare Kieser and Victor's approach with von Eye and and Mair's approach, we also analyzed Glück's (1999) spatial strategy data, using Kieser and Victor's sequential CFA. The results of this analysis are the same as the results from von Eye and Mair's analysis. Therefore, they are not reported here in any detail. However, it should be emphasized that, in many data sets, the two alternative strategies can yield different appraisals of the type-antitype structure in a table (for examples, see von Eye & Mair, 2008b).

In general, it is not only possible but likely that the two methods yield different outcomes. The choice between the two methods is clear. If researchers focus on fitting a base model, Kieser and Victor's method is selected. If, however, the focus is, at each step, on the largest model-data discrepancy, that is, on types and antitypes, von Eye and Mair's method is selected. Both methods prevent researchers from interpreting phantom types and antitypes.

10.2   Special Case: One Dichotomous Variable

An interesting case that can have effects on the selection of cells to be blanked out in F-CFA was discussed by von Eye and Mair (2008b) and is

TABLE 10.9. First Order CFA of Wurzer's Waiting Data

Configuration W P	m	$\hat{m}$	z	p	Type/Antitype
11	173	142.102	5.2366	.0000	Type
12	76	106.898	−5.2366	.0000	Antitype
21	50	54.216	−.9555	.3393	
22	45	40.784	.9555	.3393	
31	15	15.409	−.1627	.8707	
32	12	11.591	.1627	.8707	
41	51	61.064	−2.1765	.0295	
42	56	45.936	2.1765	.0295	
51	27	39.948	−3.3343	.0009	Antitype
52	43	30.052	3.3343	.0009	Type
61	15	18.262	−1.1985	.2307	
62	17	13.738	1.1985	.2307	

given in Table 10.8 in Section 10.1.2. Consider the situation in which one of the variables used to span a table is dichotomous. For this table, standard CFA can be performed.

So far, the decision as to which cell to blank out next was based on the largest absolute value of a residual. If two scores are exactly the same, this rule is no longer applicable. When the standardized Pearson residual is used, as was the case in the data example in the last chapter (see Table 9.1), or Lehmacher's asymptotic hypergeometric test, the residual scores for corresponding categories of the dichotomous variable will be the same (see Table 10.8), and a single largest absolute value of residual scores is not defined any more. Therefore, von Eye and Mair propose that, in these cases, the cells with exactly the same absolute residual be blanked out simultaneously. An illustration is given in the following data example.

Data Example 2: Consider the following data example (from Wurzer, 2005). The variable Weather is crossed with the variable Waiting at a Public Internet Terminal (self-reported). Weather (W) has the six categories 1 = dry and warm, 2 = dry and cold, 3 = raining and warm, 4 = raining and cold, 5 = snowing and warm, and 6 = snowing and cold. Waiting at a Public Internet Terminal (P) had categories 1 = yes, and 2 = no. Table 10.9 displays the results of first order CFA of Wurzer's waiting data. The standardized Pearson residual was used. The $LR - X^2$ for this model is 31.82 ($df = 5$; $p < 0.01$).

Clearly, when, for dichotomous data, the standardized Pearson residual (or Lehmacher's test) is used, identical r_i scores (in absolute values) result for corresponding cells. When F-CFA is used, the corresponding type- and antitype-constituting cells have to be blanked out simultaneously. In the analysis of Wurzer's data, the first iteration step would involve blanking out both Cells 1 1 and 1 2.

10.3   F-CFA II: Explaining Types and Antitypes

In Section 10.1, we presented two approaches to F-CFA that lend a new meaning to CFA types and antitypes. In contrast to standard CFA where the base model may not fit, types and antitypes in functional CFA indicate deviations from an otherwise fitting base model. In the present section, we present a second approach to F-CFA. We ask which effects in a log-linear model explain the types and antitypes in a table, given a particular base model. The term *explain* is used when the effects are identified that have the following characteristics: They

1. are not included in the base model;

2. make types and antitypes completely disappear;

3. do not result in new types and antitypes; and

4. are most parsimonious in the sense that the effects used for explanation are as small in number as possible and of the lowest possible order.

Effects that have these characteristics will be termed *type-constituting* or *antitype-constituting*. Both hierarchical and nonhierarchical models are considered. Two strategies are discussed. The first is called *ascending, inclusive*. The second is called *descending, exclusive*[1]. Both methods examine all models that fulfill specified conditions. Both methods can result in nonhierarchical models. They can also result in nonstandard models (for the distinction between non-hierarchical and nonstandard models, see Mair & von Eye, 2007) when covariates are part of the base model, cells need to be blanked out for reasons other than configural analysis, or if the table contains structural zeros. In the remainder of this chapter, we focus on log-linear base models. However, other types of base models can be used in the context of functional CFA also.

---

[1]Note that, for the descending, exclusive strategy, the concept of *explaining* a type/antitype pattern is slightly changed from the present definition (see Section 10.3.2).

10.3.1 Explaining Types and Antitypes: The Ascending, Inclusive Strategy

The CFA base model serves two purposes (von Eye, 2004a). First, it provides the basis for the estimation of expected cell frequencies that are used when testing cell-wise CFA null hypotheses. Second, it represents the variable relationships that describe the population that types and antitypes deviate from. Using CFA, these types and antitypes are identified.

Log-linear modeling is usually employed to pursue different goals. Under the assumption that all respondents belong to the same population, the method is used to model the variable relationships present in a population (Goodman, 1984). If this goal can be reached, deviations from the estimated expected cell frequencies will be random, and types and antitypes will not emerge.

The variant of F-CFA to be introduced in this chapter combines these two goals. This variant is used to find those variable relationships that explain types and antitypes. The ascending, inclusive strategy involves systematically adding/removing terms and effects to/from a base model until a model is found that fits and the four characteristics listed above are fulfilled.

To describe the method, consider a cross-classification that is spanned by d variables. Then, the ascending, inclusive strategy to F-CFA involves the following steps:

1. Estimate the CFA base model of interest. This can be any base model (except, naturally, the saturated model).

2. Proceed to add the lowest hierarchical-level effect to the base model. If the base model is a *global base model*, proceed to the next higher hierarchical level. If, however, there are terms at this hierarchical level that are not part of the base model, select any of these terms and perform a CFA that includes this extra term. For this model, ask (1) whether all types and antitypes have disappeared, (2) whether no new types or antitypes have emerged, and (3) whether the model fits. If all three conditions are fulfilled, continue the model-fitting-plus-CFA at this hierarchical level, until all possible models at this hierarchical level have been tested. Completing these hierarchical steps one hierarchical level at a time is necessary to determine whether alternative models exist that are equally parsimonious and also explain all types and antitypes. These models differ from one another because they contain, in addition to the base model that they share, individual terms that are unique to a model. Consider, for example, the base model of a first order CFA of the three variables A, B, and C. This model contains all main effects of these three variables. The next higher hierarchical model

includes two-way interactions. So, the first model to be considered would include the three main effects and, say, the interaction $[A, B]$. The next model to be considered would include the three main effects and, say, the interaction $[A, C]$. Suppose this model explains the types and antitypes that had emerged under the base model. Then, the search would continue with the last possible model at this hierarchical level. This is the model that includes the interaction $[B, C]$. After estimation of this model, the search can stop. Models with more than one interaction do not need to be considered, because they are less parsimonious, even if they also explain types and antitypes[2].

3. If the individual terms that are examined in the second step do not allow one to explain the types and antitypes, proceed and create all pairs of interaction terms. Include each of them in the base model. For each model, ask the questions listed above, under Step 2. For the three variables A, B, and C, in the example under Step 2, this step involves estimating the models that include the three pairs of two-way interactions $[A, B]$ and $[A, C]$, $[A, B]$ and $[B, C]$, and $[B, C]$ and $[A, C]$.

4. Proceed, if needed, by creating all possible triplets, quadruplets, etc. of two-way interactions. For the three variables A, B, and C, there is only one triplet of two-way interactions that can be formed, the triplet $[A, B][A, C][B, C]$.

5. If needed, proceed to the next higher hierarchical level.

6. Combine the effects from the lower levels with those from the higher levels of the hierarchy of effects. Note that this can lead to nonhierarchical models when higher order effects are used without the corresponding lower order effects. Focusing on hierarchical models may reduce the number of models to be estimated. However, the risk that comes with this decision is that more parsimonious models may be overlooked.

7. Move up in hierarchical level as long as needed for an explanation of all types and antitypes.

Data Example 3: For the following example, we use data from a study on the satisfaction of welfare recipients in Mexico with the services provided by the

[2]Note that, in the present context, the term *parsimonious* is defined as using terms at a hierarchical level as low as possible. Other definitions also include degrees of freedom. Under these alternative definitions, nonhierarchical models that include terms from higher hierarchical levels can be more parsimonious than models at lower hierarchical levels if they use fewer degrees of freedom. In addition, nonstandard models can be more parsimonious than standard hierarchical models.

TABLE 10.10. First Order CFA of the Cross-Classification of Desire to Use Services Again (A), Recommendation (R), and Satisfaction (S)

Configuration $A\,R\,S$	m	$\hat{m}$	z	p	Type/Antitype
111	63	11.505	15.1819	.000000	Type
112	10	7.755	.8063	.210029	
113	1	6.166	−2.0803	.018748	
121	8	14.457	−1.6983	.044727	
122	6	9.745	−1.1996	.115147	
123	0	7.748	−2.7835	.002689	Antitype
131	2	14.763	−3.3217	.000447	Antitype
132	0	9.951	−3.1545	.000804	Antitype
133	0	7.912	−2.8127	.002456	Antitype
211	18	15.468	.6439	.259817	
212	8	10.426	−.7512	.226254	
213	0	8.289	−2.8791	.001994	Antitype
221	42	19.437	5.1177	.000000	Type
222	31	13.101	4.9450	.000000	Type
223	9	10.417	−.4389	.330362	
231	2	19.848	−4.0062	.000031	Antitype
232	6	13.378	−2.0172	.021838	
233	5	10.637	−1.7283	.041967	
311	7	24.160	−3.4912	.000241	Antitype
312	3	16.285	−3.2920	.000497	Antitype
313	3	12.948	−2.7646	.002850	Antitype
321	19	30.360	−2.0618	.019614	
322	18	20.464	−.5447	.292987	
323	9	16.271	−1.8025	.035736	
331	20	31.002	−1.9759	.024081	
332	40	20.896	4.1791	.000015	Type
333	70	16.614	13.0974	.000000	Type

state again (Lobato et al., 2007). 400 respondents indicated on three-point scales whether they found the variety of services satisfactory (S), whether they would use the services again (A), and whether they would recommend the services they received (R). The Satisfaction scale was coded as 1 = little or no satisfaction, 2 = average satisfaction, and 3 = high satisfaction. The other two scales were coded in a parallel fashion. In the first step of analysis, we perform a first order CFA of variable independence on the 3 × 3 × 3 cross-classification of these three variables. We use the z-test and the Holland-Copenhaver procedure of α protection. Results of this analysis appear in Table 10.10. The $LR - X^2$ for the model is large and significant, 449.18 ($df = 20$; $p < 0.01$). Types and antitypes are, therefore, bound to emerge.

As expected based on the large $LR - X^2$, the table contains many types and antitypes. Three of the five types describe respondents who give the same score to each of the three questions. For example, the first type is constituted by Configuration 1 1 1. These are respondents who express negative attitudes throughout. Configuration 2 2 2 describes respondents who express medium levels of satisfaction, and Configuration 3 3 3 describes respondents who express high levels of satisfaction. The two remaining types, constituted by configurations 2 2 1 and 3 3 2, show deviations from uniform responses by only one scale point.

In contrast, each of the nine antitypes shows at least one deviation among responses by two scale points. For example, it is very unlikely that a respondent indicates that he/she will probably not use the services again, that he/she is ambivalent about recommending the services provided by the state to someone else, but that he/she is highly satisfied with the services (Antitype 1 2 3). Similarly, it is also very unlikely that a respondent indicates that he/she will most likely use the services again, that he/she will not recommend the services provided by the state, and that he/she is highly dissatisfied with the services (Antitype 3 1 1).

We now ask, which combination of the four possible interactions causes these many types and antitypes to emerge. The four possible interactions are $[A, R]$, $[A, S]$, $[R, S]$, and $[A, R, S]$. If the three-way interaction is used alone or in combination with some of the three two-way interactions, the model that explains the types and antitypes in Table 10.10 will be non-hierarchical. None of the main effects can be omitted because they are part of the base model that resulted in this type/antitype pattern shown in Table 10.10.

Proceeding as indicated above, we first add each of the two-way interactions to the base model separately. The entry order of terms in this process is of no importance. This results in three models. If none of the three two-way interactions singly explains all 14 types and antitypes in Table 10.11, we create all possible pairs of two-way interactions. This results in three more models. If this is still not enough, we consider all three two-way interactions simultaneously, which requires one more model. Taken together, we need to perform seven CFAs before we even consider the three-way interaction (this number includes the original CFA).

Table 10.11 summarizes the results from the search for a model that explains all five types and nine antitypes in Table 10.10. The table shows the $LR - X^2$ for each model, the degrees of freedom; it indicates whether all types and antitypes disappeared and whether new types or antitypes emerged.

Table 10.11 shows an interesting result. Two models, with different degrees of freedom but located at the same hierarchical level, fulfill the

TABLE 10.11. Ascending, Inclusive Search for and Explanation of the Five Types and Nine Antitypes in Table 10.10

New Terms in Model	$LR - X^2$	df	p	Types/Antitypes Disappeared?	New Types/Antitypes?
[A, R]	170.07	16	0.00	No	Yes
[A, S]	329.62	16	0.00	No	Yes
[R, S]	308.09	16	0.00	No	Yes
[A, R][R, S]	28.98	12	0.00	No	Yes
[A, S][R, S]	188.53	12	0.00	No	No
[A, R][A, S]	50.51	12	0.00	Yes	No
[A, R][A, S][R, S]	10.08	8	0.26	Yes	No

TABLE 10.12. Second Order CFA of the Cross-Classification of Desire to Use Services Again (A), Recommendation (R), and Satisfaction (S)

Configuration A R S	m	$\hat{m}$	z	p
111	63	62.200	.1015	.459592
112	10	11.178	−.3523	.362308
113	1	.622	.4787	.316072
121	8	9.797	−.5742	.282921
122	6	3.980	1.0126	.155615
123	0	.223	−.4722	.318402
131	2	1.003	.9956	.159733
132	0	.842	−.9178	.179366
133	0	.155	−.3933	.347040
211	18	17.976	.0056	.497751
212	8	6.457	.6074	.271789
213	0	1.567	−1.2519	.105298
221	42	40.792	.1891	.425004
222	31	33.119	−.3682	.356366
223	9	8.089	.3203	.374355
231	2	3.232	−.6852	.246622
232	6	5.425	.2471	.402423
233	5	4.344	.3149	.376431
311	7	7.824	−.2946	.384142
312	3	3.366	−.1993	.421025
313	3	1.810	.8842	.188295
321	19	18.411	.1374	.445369
322	18	17.901	.0233	.490693
323	9	9.688	−.2211	.412514
331	20	19.765	.0528	.478952
332	40	39.733	.0423	.483116
333	70	70.502	−.0597	.476185

conditions that (1) all types and antitypes disappeared and (2) no new types or antitypes emerged. The first of these models adds the interactions $[A, R]$ and $[A, S]$ to the base model (second row from bottom in Table 10.11). The largest z-score for this model is 2.85 for Cell 2 3 3. The tail probability for this score is 0.007, a value that is larger than the protected $\alpha^* = 0.002$. Therefore, Cell 2 3 3 does not constitute a type. From a pure CFA perspective, this model does not yield any types or antitypes. However, overall, the model does not fit. The overall goodness-of-fit $LR - X^2$ for this model is 50.51. This value indicates that significant model-data discrepancies exist. For this reason, we decide that all three pairs of two-way interactions are needed to explain the data (this is the model shown in the last row of Table 10.11). This model does not result in any types or antitypes at all. The largest z-score is -1.252, for Cell 2 1 3. The tail probability for this score is 0.895. In addition, there is no significant model-data discrepancy, as is indicated by the $LR - X^2$ in Table 10.11. This model, therefore, fulfills all three conditions, and we retain it as the one that explains the five types and nine antitypes in Table 10.10.

The CFA results that are based on this model appear in Table 10.12. Because it includes all possible two-way interactions, this model is equivalent to the base model of second order CFA. The z-test and the Holland-Copenhaver procedure were used again. No types or antitypes emerged.

In the following paragraphs, we show how the design matrix for the first order CFA base model that was used for Table 10.10 changed for the model that was used for Table 10.12. This is done for two reasons. First, it illustrates the models that are used in F-CFA. These models are not always the same as the ones used in standard CFA. Second, these design matrices are used to briefly describe an alternative strategy to explaining types and antitypes by using F-CFA. The first design matrix shown here is that of the first order CFA model.

$$X = \begin{pmatrix}
0 & 1 & 1 & 0 & 1 & 0 \\
0 & 1 & 0 & 0 & 1 & 1 \\
0 & 1 & -1 & 0 & 1 & -1 \\
0 & 0 & 1 & 1 & 1 & 0 \\
0 & 0 & 0 & 1 & 1 & 1 \\
0 & 0 & -1 & 1 & 1 & -1 \\
0 & -1 & 1 & -1 & 1 & 0 \\
0 & -1 & 0 & -1 & 1 & 1 \\
0 & -1 & -1 & -1 & 1 & -1 \\
1 & 1 & 1 & 0 & 0 & 0 \\
1 & 1 & 0 & 0 & 0 & 1 \\
1 & 1 & -1 & 0 & 0 & -1 \\
1 & 0 & 1 & 1 & 0 & 0 \\
1 & 0 & 0 & 1 & 0 & 1 \\
1 & 0 & -1 & 1 & 0 & -1 \\
1 & -1 & 1 & -1 & 0 & 0 \\
1 & -1 & 0 & -1 & 0 & 1 \\
1 & -1 & -1 & -1 & 0 & -1 \\
-1 & 1 & 1 & 0 & -1 & 0 \\
-1 & 1 & 0 & 0 & -1 & 1 \\
-1 & 1 & -1 & 0 & -1 & -1 \\
-1 & 0 & 1 & 1 & -1 & 0 \\
-1 & 0 & 0 & 1 & -1 & 1 \\
-1 & 0 & -1 & 1 & -1 & -1 \\
-1 & -1 & 1 & -1 & -1 & 0 \\
-1 & -1 & 0 & -1 & -1 & 1 \\
-1 & -1 & -1 & -1 & -1 & -1
\end{pmatrix}$$

The order of effects in this design matrix is: main effects of A_2 (Categories 2 vs. 3), R_1 (Categories 1 vs. 3), S_1 (Categories 1 vs. 3), R_2 (Categories 2 vs. 3), A_1 (Categories 1 vs. 3), and S_2 (Categories 2 vs. 3). For main effects, two vectors in the design matrix are needed when a variable has three categories. The order of the columns in the design matrix has no consequences for the estimates of parameters or expected cell frequencies. Therefore, we reproduce the design matrices here as they are printed by the CFA program discussed in Chapter 13.

The design matrix for the final model, results for which are printed in in Table 10.12, appears next. This is the model that includes, in addition to the three main effects, all three two-way interactions.

$$X = \begin{pmatrix}
0 & 1 & 1 & 0 & 1 & 0 & 0 & 1 & 0 & 0 & 0 & 1 & 0 & 1 & 0 & 0 & 0 & 0 \\
0 & 1 & 0 & 0 & 1 & 1 & 0 & 0 & 1 & 0 & 0 & 0 & 1 & 1 & 0 & 0 & 0 & 0 \\
0 & 1 & -1 & 0 & 1 & -1 & 0 & -1 & -1 & 0 & 0 & -1 & -1 & 1 & 0 & 0 & 0 & 0 \\
0 & 0 & 1 & 1 & 1 & 0 & 0 & 0 & 0 & 1 & 0 & 1 & 0 & 0 & 1 & 0 & 0 & 0 \\
0 & 0 & 0 & 1 & 1 & 1 & 0 & 0 & 0 & 0 & 1 & 0 & 1 & 0 & 1 & 0 & 0 & 0 \\
0 & 0 & -1 & 1 & 1 & -1 & 0 & 0 & 0 & -1 & -1 & -1 & -1 & 0 & 1 & 0 & 0 & 0 \\
0 & -1 & 1 & -1 & 1 & 0 & 0 & -1 & 0 & -1 & 0 & 1 & 0 & -1 & -1 & 0 & 0 & 0 \\
0 & -1 & 0 & -1 & 1 & 1 & 0 & 0 & -1 & 0 & -1 & 0 & 1 & -1 & -1 & 0 & 0 & 0 \\
0 & -1 & -1 & -1 & 1 & -1 & 0 & 1 & 1 & 1 & 1 & -1 & -1 & -1 & -1 & 0 & 0 & 0 \\
1 & 1 & 1 & 0 & 0 & 0 & 0 & 1 & 0 & 0 & 0 & 0 & 0 & 0 & 0 & 1 & 0 & 1 \\
1 & 1 & 0 & 0 & 0 & 1 & 0 & 0 & 1 & 0 & 0 & 0 & 0 & 0 & 0 & 0 & 1 & 1 \\
1 & 1 & -1 & 0 & 0 & -1 & 0 & -1 & -1 & 0 & 0 & 0 & 0 & 0 & 0 & -1 & -1 & 1 \\
1 & 0 & 1 & 1 & 0 & 0 & 1 & 0 & 0 & 1 & 0 & 0 & 0 & 0 & 0 & 1 & 0 & 0 \\
1 & 0 & 0 & 1 & 0 & 1 & 1 & 0 & 0 & 0 & 1 & 0 & 0 & 0 & 0 & 0 & 1 & 0 \\
1 & 0 & -1 & 1 & 0 & -1 & 1 & 0 & 0 & -1 & -1 & 0 & 0 & 0 & 0 & -1 & -1 & 0 \\
1 & -1 & 1 & -1 & 0 & 0 & -1 & -1 & 0 & -1 & 0 & 0 & 0 & 0 & 0 & 1 & 0 & -1 \\
1 & -1 & 0 & -1 & 0 & 1 & -1 & 0 & -1 & 0 & -1 & 0 & 0 & 0 & 0 & 0 & 1 & -1 \\
1 & -1 & -1 & -1 & 0 & -1 & 1 & 1 & 1 & 1 & 1 & 0 & 0 & 0 & 0 & -1 & -1 & -1 \\
-1 & 1 & 1 & 0 & -1 & 0 & 0 & 1 & 0 & 0 & 0 & -1 & 0 & -1 & 0 & -1 & 0 & -1 \\
-1 & 1 & 0 & 0 & -1 & 1 & 0 & 0 & 1 & 0 & 0 & 0 & -1 & -1 & 0 & 0 & -1 & -1 \\
-1 & 1 & -1 & 0 & -1 & -1 & 0 & -1 & -1 & 0 & 0 & 1 & 1 & -1 & 0 & 1 & 1 & -1 \\
-1 & 0 & 1 & 1 & -1 & 0 & -1 & 0 & 0 & 1 & 0 & -1 & 0 & 0 & -1 & -1 & 0 & 0 \\
-1 & 0 & 0 & 1 & -1 & 1 & -1 & 0 & 0 & 0 & 1 & 0 & -1 & 0 & -1 & 0 & -1 & 0 \\
-1 & 0 & -1 & 1 & -1 & -1 & -1 & 0 & 0 & -1 & -1 & 1 & 1 & 0 & -1 & 1 & 1 & 0 \\
-1 & -1 & 1 & -1 & -1 & 0 & 1 & -1 & 0 & -1 & 0 & -1 & 0 & 1 & 1 & -1 & 0 & 1 \\
-1 & -1 & 0 & -1 & -1 & 1 & 1 & 0 & -1 & 0 & -1 & 0 & -1 & 1 & 1 & 0 & -1 & 1 \\
-1 & -1 & -1 & -1 & -1 & -1 & 1 & 1 & 1 & 1 & 1 & 1 & 1 & 1 & 1 & 1 & 1 & 1
\end{pmatrix}$$

This design matrix contains 18 column vectors. The first 6 of these are for the main effects. These are the same vectors as in the first design matrix shown in this section. The remaining 12 are for the three two-way interactions among A, R, S. The order of these 12 vectors is A_2R_2, R_1S_1, R_1S_2, R_2S_1, R_2S_2, A_1S_1, A_1S_2, A_1R_1, A_1R_2, A_2S_1, A_2S_2, and A_2R_1. Again, the order of vectors is of no importance for the results of computation.

F-CFA, as it is described in the present chapter, operates at the level of main effects and interactions. By implication, as soon as variables have more $k_i > 2$ categories, $k_i - 1 > 1$ vectors are added for the main effect of variable i, $(k_i - 1)(k_j - 1)$ vectors are added for each two-way interaction ($i \neq j$), $(k_i - 1)(k_j - 1)(k_l - 1)$ vectors are added for each three-way interaction ($i \neq j \neq l$), and so on. Now, using design matrices, F-CFA can be reformulated so that individual vectors are added to the design matrix instead of all vectors for a particular effect. This procedure would increase the number of steps to perform by F-CFA. However, each step would be simple, and the final solution has the potential of being more parsimonious. Consider the model used for Table 10.12. This model, for which the parameter estimates are given in Table 10.13, was estimated by using SYSTAT 12.

As can be seen, not all parameters of the model are significant. For example, the parameter for the $A_2 \times S_2$ part of the $A \times S$ interaction (sixth row from bottom of Table 10.13) comes with a z-score of -0.108 ($p = 0.46$). Similarly, the parameter for the $R_1 \times S_2$ part of the $R \times S$ interaction (fourth row from bottom of Table 10.13) comes with a z-score of -0.699 ($p = 0.24$). Based on these results, one can attempt to make the final model more parsimonious by eliminating nonsignificant parameters as long as possible,

TABLE 10.13. Parameter Estimates for the Model in Table 10.12

Effect	Parameter	se	z-value
$S1$	0.686	0.136	5.054
$S2$	0.278	0.140	1.978
$R1$	−0.092	0.159	−0.577
$R2$	0.396	0.136	2.912
$A1$	−1.085	0.277	−3.917
$A2$	0.319	0.165	1.932
$[A1, R1]$	1.426	0.200	7.138
$[A1, R2]$	−0.364	0.212	−1.717
$[A2, R1]$	−0.267	0.160	−1.672
$[A2, R2]$	0.610	0.143	4.274
$[A1, S1]$	0.763	0.262	2.918
$[A1, S2]$	0.242	0.279	0.868
$[A2, S1]$	−0.189	0.164	−1.153
$[A2, S2]$	−0.018	0.170	−0.108
$[R1, S1]$	0.657	0.167	3.944
$[R1, S2]$	−0.129	0.184	−0.699
$[R2, S1]$	0.111	0.126	0.885
$[R2, S2]$	0.141	0.129	1.091
$CONSTANT$	1.774	—	—

that is, as long as (1) the model still fits, (2) all types and antitypes disappear, and (3) no new types or antitypes emerge.

10.3.2 Explaining Types and Antitypes: The Descending, Exclusive Strategy

The ascending, inclusive strategy described in the last section guarantees that one or more models will be found that explain all types and antitypes. These models can be hierarchical, nonhierarchical, or nonstandard. The main characteristic of these models is that they are built by adding terms to a base model, and this inclusive strategy makes the model increasingly complex. Based on the *sparsity of effects principle* that is discussed in the context of design (e.g., Wu & Hamada, 2000), it can be expected that most systems are driven largely by a limited number of main effects and interactions of a low order. This topic is taken up in more detail in Chapter 12. Higher order interactions are, therefore, relatively unimportant, in many circumstances. Therefore, the most complex terms that could possibly be included, interactions of high order, will rarely be needed to explain the data or a type/antitype pattern. This implies that, in log-linear modeling, the contributions made by the corresponding effects are not considered because they are set to zero. These contributions are typically small and nonsignificant. However, the contribution to model fit made by the individual effect can still change if the higher order effects are made part of the model. Similarly, patterns of types and antitypes can change even if nonsignificant terms are included in the base model. Therefore, as an alternative to the ascending, inclusive strategy described in the last section, the *descending, exclusive strategy* can be considered for the exploratory explanation of CFA types and antitypes.

In contrast to the ascending, inclusive strategy, which starts from the CFA base model, the descending, exclusive strategy starts from the saturated model. It is also the goal of the descending, exclusive search procedure to explain types and antitypes. However, the term *explanation* now has a different meaning. The term now means that types and antitypes are explained when all those effects are identified without which (1) types or antitypes disappear, or (2) new types and antitypes emerge. The resulting model will not fit the data. However, it will contain all effects that are unrelated to the types and antitypes. The types and antitypes found with the original base model will still be in the table. By implication, the effects that were excluded from the model caused the types and antitypes. These effects will be termed *type- and antitype-constituting*.

The descending, exclusive strategy excludes, step by step, terms from the saturated model, that is, effects are set to zero. This is achieved in an iteration that proceeds as follows (von Eye & Mair, 2008b):

1. Starting with effects that are located at the same hierarchical level as the base model (or one above, if the base model is global), exclude one effect, at this hierarchical level, after the other from the saturated model, with replacement. All higher order terms are still part of the model. Determine, for each model, whether (1) the observed pattern of types and antitypes is still present, and (2) no new types and antitypes have emerged. If both conditions are fulfilled, complete the examination of models at this level of the hierarchy. Completion is necessary to see whether there are competing models that are equally parsimonious. This concludes the search. Alternatively, if either or both of the two conditions are not fulfilled, proceed to the next iteration step.

2. If needed for the complete explanation of all types and antitypes, combine terms.

3. Proceed to the next higher level of the hierarchy. Select out only the terms of this level of the hierarchy.

4. Combine these terms with the terms from the lower levels of the hierarchy and with one another.

5. Proceed until the model is found that yields only the types and the antitypes of the original base model.

Here, as with the ascending, inclusive strategy, the search can fail in the sense that no model can be found that is more parsimonious than the saturated model.

The total number of models that can be examined is the same as for the ascending, inclusive strategy. However, different models are considered. With the exception of the model that requires that all effects be considered as constituting types and antitypes, the models for the descending, exclusive strategy are always nonhierarchical, and many are nonstandard. When structural zeros, covariates, or special effects are part of the model, the models for both search strategies will always be nonstandard.

To illustrate, we now compare models that are used under the two search strategies, considering the $2 \times 2 \times 2$ cross-classification of the variables A, B, and C. This table is, in a first step, analyzed under the first order base model of Lienert's classical CFA, that is, the main effect model $[A], [B], [C]$. The design matrix for this model is

$$X = \begin{pmatrix} 1 & 1 & 1 \\ 1 & 1 & -1 \\ 1 & -1 & 1 \\ 1 & -1 & -1 \\ -1 & 1 & 1 \\ -1 & 1 & -1 \\ -1 & -1 & 1 \\ -1 & -1 & -1 \end{pmatrix}.$$

In the first step of the search, the ascending, inclusive search strategy adds the effect of the interaction between the first two variables. The design matrix becomes

$$X = \left(\begin{array}{ccc|c} 1 & 1 & 1 & 1 \\ 1 & 1 & -1 & 1 \\ 1 & -1 & 1 & -1 \\ 1 & -1 & -1 & -1 \\ -1 & 1 & 1 & -1 \\ -1 & 1 & -1 & -1 \\ -1 & -1 & 1 & 1 \\ -1 & -1 & -1 & 1 \end{array} \right),$$

where the last column represents the $[A, B]$ interaction. In contrast, the design matrix for the descending, exclusive strategy becomes, in its next step, the saturated model minus the vector for the interaction parameter between variables A and B. This matrix is

$$
X = \left(
\begin{array}{rrr|rrr}
1 & 1 & 1 & 1 & 1 & 1 \\
1 & 1 & -1 & -1 & -1 & -1 \\
1 & -1 & 1 & 1 & -1 & -1 \\
1 & -1 & -1 & -1 & 1 & 1 \\
-1 & 1 & 1 & -1 & 1 & -1 \\
-1 & 1 & -1 & 1 & -1 & 1 \\
-1 & -1 & 1 & -1 & -1 & 1 \\
-1 & -1 & -1 & 1 & 1 & -1
\end{array}
\right),
$$

where the last column represents the three-way interaction $[A, B, C]$ and the two columns before the last column represent the two-way interactions $[A, C]$ and $[B, C]$. The design matrices from the two search strategies differ in two respects, highlighting the differences between the two strategies. First, the interaction between the first and the second variables is the only column vector that the ascending, inclusive strategy adds, in this step, to the design matrix of the base model. In contrast, the very same vector is the only one not included in the design matrix under the exclusive, descending search strategy. The goal of both strategies is the same. With both strategies, researchers attempt to determine the role that this interaction (and the following ones, in the sequence of steps) plays in the explanation of types and antitypes. The second difference is that the descending, exclusive strategy includes the effects for all higher order terms in the design matrix. Thus, the unique role is examined that individual effects play. The number of degrees of freedom for the design matrix under the ascending, inclusive strategy is 3. For the design matrix under the descending, exclusive strategy, we obtain $df = 1$.

Regarding model identification, it should be noted that, under the search routines discussed in this chapter, models may be overspecified. That is, models can come with negative degrees of freedom. For example, consider the base model for a $2 \times 2 \times 2 \times 2$ cross-classification in which four cells are structural zeros. If this model is analyzed using a first order CFA, there are 7 residual degrees of freedom (1 degree of freedom had been invested in the constant, 4 in the main effect terms, and 4 in the blanked-out zeros) and nine estimated parameters. The ascending, inclusive search strategy adds, in the first step of the search, one vector for an interaction to the design matrix. The residual degrees of freedom for this model are now 6 (if the model can be estimated). In contrast, for the following model for the descending, exclusive search strategy, -3 residual degrees of freedom result. The reason for this negative number is that the model starts from the saturated model, with 0 degrees of freedom. From this model, one interaction term is removed, which results in $df = 1$.

TABLE 10.14. First Order CFA of Three Consecutive Observations of Aggressive Impulses

Configuration A1 A2 A3	m	$\hat{m}$	z	p	Type/Antitype
111	31	12.589	5.1888	.000000	Type
112	5	10.191	−1.6262	.051957	
121	7	16.700	−2.3737	.008806	
122	10	13.519	−.9571	.169255	
211	8	14.490	−1.7049	.044110	
212	5	11.730	−1.9650	.024710	
221	17	19.221	−.5066	.306226	
222	31	15.560	3.9143	.000045	Type

However, 4 degrees of freedom are still invested in blanking out four cells. Therefore, the resulting degrees of freedom are negative, and the model cannot be estimated. Similarly, when covariates are included or more cells are blanked out, more complex models may not be estimable even under the ascending, inclusive strategy. It is also important to note that the number of parameters, including the intercept, is only a necessary but not sufficient condition for identifiability. In particular, when nonstandard models are considered, it is important to make sure that the columns of the design matrix be linearly independent.

Data Example 4: In the following example, we use data from the study on aggression in adolescence (Finkelstein et al., 1994) again. 114 adolescents who were 11 years of age at the first interview were asked to indicate the degree to which they feel they have aggressive impulses. For the following analyses, we use the variable Aggressive Impulses, observed on three consecutive occasions ($A1$, $A2$, and $A3$). The scores were dichotomized at the grand mean. We first ask whether particular longitudinal patterns stand out. To answer this question, we perform a first order CFA, using the z-test and the Holland-Copenhaver procedure. The base model of variable independence fails to describe the data well ($LR - X^2 = 51.08$; $df = 4$; $p < 0.01$). We thus anticipate types and antitypes to emerge. Table 10.14 displays the CFA results.

The table shows that, surprisingly, aggressive impulses show stability during adolescence. Two types emerge. The first is constituted by Configuration 1 1 1. It describes those adolescents who report consistently below average aggressive impulses. The second type, constituted by Configuration 2 2 2, describes the adolescents at the other end of the spectrum. These respondents indicate consistently above average aggressive impulses.

TABLE 10.15. Descending, Exclusive Search for an Explanation of the Two Types in Table 10.14

Effects Removed	$LR - X^2$	df	p	Type/Antitype Disappeared?	New Types/Antitypes?
$[A1, A2]$	12.65	1	< .01	Yes	No
$[A1, A3]$	2.84	1	.09	Yes	No
$[A2, A3]$	12.64	1	< .01	Yes	No
$[A1, A2][A1, A3]$	27.03	2	< .01	No	Yes
$[A1, A3][A2, A3]$	24.55	2	< .01	Yes	Yes
$[A1, A2][A2, A3]$	37.22	2	< .01	No	Yes
$[A1, A2][A1, A3][A2, A3]$	49.84	3	< .01	No	No
$[A1, A2, A3]$	1.39	1	.24	Yes	No

We now ask which interactions explain these two types. To answer this question, we employ the descending, exclusive search strategy of F-CFA. We perform the following steps. Please note that, with the exception of the very last model (Step 3), each of the models discussed here is non-hierarchical.

1. We proceed to the hierarchy level right above the one used for the base model of first order CFA. This is the level of two-way interactions. From the saturated model, we remove systematically each of the three two-way interactions (with replacement) and ask, for each of the resulting models, (1) whether the two types still exist, and (2) whether no new types and antitypes emerged. In the present example, three models are estimated at this step. These are the models that include (1) $[A1]$, $[A2]$, $[A3]$, $[A1, A3]$, $[A2, A3]$, $[A1, A2, A3]$; (2) $[A1]$, $[A2]$, $[A3]$, $[A1, A2]$, $[A2, A3]$, $[A1, A2, A3]$; and (3) $[A1]$, $[A2]$, $[A3]$, $[A1, A2]$, $[A1, A3]$, $[A1, A2, A3]$. If none of these three models leads to affirmative answers to both of the two questions, we proceed to Step 2 of the search.

2. At this step, we remove pairs of two-way interactions from the three two-way interactions in the saturated model. In the present example, the following three models result: (1) $[A1]$, $[A2]$, $[A3]$, $[A2, A3]$, $[A1, A2, A3]$; (2) $[A1]$, $[A2]$, $[A3]$, $[A1, A2]$, $[A1, A2, A3]$; and (3) $[A1]$, $[A2]$, $[A3]$, $[A1, A3]$, $[A1, A2, A3]$. If none of these three models leads to affirmative answers to the both of two questions, we have only two more options.

3. At this step, we remove all three two-way interactions. The resulting model is $[A1]$, $[A2]$, $[A3]$, $[A1, A2, A3]$.

4. If the model at Step 3 also fails to explain the two types, we specify the last possible model of the search, that is, the one in which we remove the

TABLE 10.16. First Order CFA of Three Consecutive Observations of Aggressive Impulses; Base Model Includes the Three-Way Interaction $[A1, A2, A3]$

Configuration A1 A2 A3	m	$\hat{m}$	z	p	Type/Antitype
111	31	13.923	4.5768	.000002	Type
112	5	9.160	−1.3746	.084625	
121	7	14.958	−2.0577	.019808	
122	10	14.958	−1.2820	.099913	
211	8	12.958	−1.3774	.084189	
212	5	12.958	−2.2108	.013524	
221	17	21.160	−.9044	.182882	
222	31	13.923	4.5768	.000002	Type

three-way interaction from the saturated model, which gives a base model that includes the terms $[A1]$, $[A2]$, $[A3]$, $[A1, A2]$, $[A1, A3]$, $[A2, A3]$.

Table 10.15 summarizes the results from this search. The results in Table 10.15 show that

• when just one of the three two-way interactions is removed from the saturated model, the two types disappear in all three models and, in one instance, the resulting model fit is acceptable (second model in Table 10.15: $[A1]$, $[A2]$, $[A3]$, $[A1, A2]$, $[A2, A3]$, $[A1, A2, A3]$);

• when two of the three two-way interactions are removed, the two types disappear in one model and remain in the two other models, but new types/antitypes emerge in all three instances;

• when all three pairs of two-way interactions are removed from the saturated model, the model does not fit, the types remain, and no new types or antitypes emerge; this model is a candidate for the solution;

• when only the three-way interaction is removed from the saturated model, the resulting model fits, the two types disappear, and no new types/antitypes emerge; this is the model that includes all three two-way interactions.

In sum, there is only one model that fulfills the two conditions that (1) the original types and antitypes remain, and (2) no new types or antitypes emerge. This is the model that excludes all three two-way interactions but retains the three-way interaction. From this result, we conclude that the three two-way interactions $[A1, A2]$, $[A1, A3]$, and $[A2, A3]$ are type-constituting.

A CFA that uses this model as its base model yields the same types (and antitypes) as the original CFA, although the estimated expected cell frequencies can differ. This is exemplified in Table 10.16 in which the result of a CFA are presented that includes, in addition to the main effects, the three-way interaction $[A1, A2, A3]$. The original CFA results were given in Table 10.14.

The design matrix for this model is

$$X = \begin{pmatrix} 1 & 1 & 1 & 1 \\ 1 & 1 & -1 & -1 \\ 1 & -1 & 1 & -1 \\ 1 & -1 & -1 & 1 \\ -1 & 1 & 1 & -1 \\ -1 & 1 & -1 & 1 \\ -1 & -1 & 1 & 1 \\ -1 & -1 & -1 & -1 \end{pmatrix}.$$

In this design matrix, the first three columns represent the main effects, and the last column represents the three-way interaction.

10.4   Chapter Summary

Models of *functional CFA* (F-CFA) focus on the role that specific elements of a configural analysis play in the identification of types and antitypes. Two elements are considered. The first is the test performed for an individual cell (configuration) in a cross-classification. It is well known that the cell-wise tests in CFA are never completely independent. Because of this (partial) dependence, there is a risk that standard one-step CFA identifies *phantom types/antitypes*. These are types or antitypes that exist only because other types and antitypes exist. Sequential examination of cells in a table alleviates this problem, to a degree.

Two procedures of sequential examination of cells are discussed and compared. The first is Kieser and Victor's procedure, which aims at minimizing the overall lack-of-fit statistic. At each step, those configurations are selected as types and antitypes that have the potential of minimizing the overall goodness-of-fit statistic. The second is von Eye and Mair's procedure, which aims at identifying, at each step of the sequence, the most extreme residual. Because of these differences in the goal function, the two procedures do not always yield the same results, and types and antitypes have to be interpreted with these differences in mind. However, the two procedures share the characteristics that they (1) result in more parsimonious solutions than a standard base model, in most applications, and (2) prevent one from falling for phantom types and antitypes. That is, the number of types and antitypes from the sequential methods is typically smaller than the number of types and antitypes from standard, one-step CFA.

The second element that is evaluated with respect to the role it plays for the identification of types and antitypes is the individual effect in a model. In general, CFA types and antitypes result because, at the level of variables, one or more of those effects exist that are not included in the CFA base model. Two strategies are discussed for the identification of those effects that explain the existence of types and antitypes.

The first of these two strategies is ascending and inclusive. Beginning with the base model, effects are added to the model until a pattern of effects is identified for which (1) no type or antitype remains (2) without new types or antitypes emerging. The effects that have these two characteristics are called *type- or antitype-constituting*. The second strategy starts from the saturated model. It systematically removes effects from this model. The goal of this strategy is to remove as many effect terms as needed without affecting the original type/antitype pattern. The result of this procedure is the model that lacks only those effects that are needed for the types and antitypes to emerge. In the second strategy, it is called the *descending strategy*, and these effects are also termed *type- or antitype-constituting*.

The difference between these two strategies lies in the treatment of higher order interactions. The ascending strategy begins with adding effects of the lowest possible order. Higher order effects are set to zero. They will be included in the base model only when lower order effects cannot explain all types and antitypes. In contrast, the descending strategy removes higher order effects only when the removal does not affect the resulting type/antitype pattern. The ascending strategy is more parsimonious only when higher order effects play either no role or a very limited role. On the plus side of the descending strategy is that all possible effects are considered, including all higher order effects.

11

CFA of Intensive Categorical Longitudinal Data

Another new step in the development of CFA methods is taken in Chapter 11. This chapter presents two approaches to analyzing intensive data, that is, data that involve more than the usual number of variables or repetitions. Using the sample case of number of repetitions, a first method is proposed that uses the concept of *runs* to describe the data. Runs identify series of scores that exhibit a particular characteristic. For example, they are all the same, they are ascending, etc. Information that describes runs can then be categorized and analyzed by using standard methods of CFA. A second method of configural analysis of intensive data involves the examination of lags. A lag is defined as an interval in a series of scores. A lag of 1 is used to relate, for example, information from one day to information from the next. By performing CFA of lags, one can find types and antitypes that indicate whether configurations are more (or less) likely to be observed than expected over a predefined number of lags.

Until 2006, when Walls and Schafer published their book *Models for Intensive Longitudinal Data*, an interesting gap existed in the arsenal of methods for the analysis of longitudinal data. There were no methods of analysis available for series of medium length. Consider, for example, a comparative study on the effects of various forms of psychotherapy with 30 repeated observations. Data from this design are hard to analyze. Unless the sample is very large (or the model conceptualizes change in behavior in rather broad strokes), 30 observation points are too many for structural modeling. For repeated measures ANOVA with polynomial decomposition, polynomials of up to the 29th order would have to be estimated (which is the easy part) and interpreted (which is the hard part). This applies accordingly to hierarchical linear models of this design. So, whereas for some methods of analysis the 30 observation points are too many, for others, these 30 are not enough. Consider, for example, longitudinal, P-technique factor analysis. For this method, at least 100 observations are needed. Methods of time series analysis also require large numbers of (equidistant) observation points.

Intensive longitudinal data can be defined as data that come from more than the usual three or four observation points in time, yet from fewer than the 100 or more assessments required, for example, for longitudinal factor analysis. In brief, data that are intensive in the sense that more observations are made over time than usual pose specific analytic problems.

This situation gets even worse when categorical data are analyzed. Crossing the data from 30 observation points is out of the question. When only one dichotomous variable is analyzed, the number of cells of this cross-classification will be $2^{30} = 1,073,741,824$, that is, over a billion cells. When multiple categorical variables are analyzed, the situation becomes even more complex. Poisson regression models and marginal models are among the few options available for analysis (for overviews, see, e.g., Agresti, 2002; Lawal, 2003). However, these options constrain the types of questions that can be asked.

In this chapter, we present two new variants of CFA that allow one to analyze intensive categorical longitudinal data. The first new variant uses concepts that have first been discussed in the context of the well-known *runs tests* (Stevens, 1939; Swed & Eisenhart, 1943; Wald & Wolfowitz, 1940).

To introduce runs tests, consider a series of K scores. For this series, a *run* is defined as the uninterrupted sequence of $k \leq K$ scores that fulfill specified conditions. Sample conditions are introduced in Section 11.1. Runs tests are used to detect nonrandomness in a series of scores that can be observed, for instance, in the form of serial correlation. The classical runs test is a permutation test or a randomization test (Lunneborg, 2005). Under the null hypothesis, the observed number of runs does not differ from the number expected based on a reference distribution.

To detect nonrandomness of runs, univariate and multivariate as well as one-sample and two-sample tests have been proposed. These tests are reviewed in textbooks of nonparametric statistics (e.g., Bortz, Lienert, & Boehnke, 1990; Siegel, 1956), or encyclopedias (e.g., Lunneborg, 2005), and will not be described here. For the present purposes, we are not concerned with the runs tests themselves. Instead, we discuss the type of information created for runs tests and the use of this information for the analysis of intensive categorical longitudinal data.

The method presented here allows one to pursue both variable-oriented analysis, for example, log-linear modeling, and person-oriented analysis (Bergman & Magnusson, 1997; von Eye & Bergman, 2003). In the present context, the reader will not be surprised if we focus on the application of the runs concept in CFA (von Eye & Bogat, 2009). The second new variant is Configural Lag Analysis. It allows one to identify types and antitypes of predictability of behavior over lags, that is, intervals of time.

11.1   CFA of Runs

In this section, we begin with sample definitions of runs. We then apply these definitions in the CFA of intensive longitudinal data. We present five definitions of runs. More definitions are easily conceived.

1. A run can be defined as the *length, k, of an uninterrupted series of scores of the same value*. Consider the series 1111335222. This series contains 4 runs, including a run of $k = 4$ (value 1), a run of $k = 2$ (value 3), a run of $k = 1$ (value 5), and a run of $k = 3$ (value 2). To establish this sequence of 4 runs, the scale level of the scores is of no importance. All that is asked is whether adjacent scores are equal or different. Therefore, runs of scores of the same value use no more than nominal scale information.

2. A run can be defined as the *length of an uninterrupted series of scores of increasing value*. The series 1234533234 contains 2 runs. The first contains the first five scores, and the second contains the last three scores. To describe the runs of increasing series of scores, ordinal information is needed.

3. A run can be defined as the *length of an uninterrupted series of scores of decreasing value*. The series 1234533234, used already under (2), contains 2 runs using this defintion. The first contains the scores 5 and 3, and the second contains the scores 3 and 2. To describe the runs of decreasing series of scores, ordinal information is needed.

4. A run can be defined as the length of an uninterrupted series of scores with values that go up-and-down or down-and-up (runs up-and-down test, Wallis & Moore, 1941). The series 1234533234 contains two runs, under the current definition. It is constituted by the series 4, 5, and 3 and by the series 323. To describe the runs of up-and-down series of scores, ordinal information is needed.

5. A run can be defined as the length of an uninterrupted series of scores within a prespecified range. Consider, for example, a machine tool that is supposed to produce parts for mechanical watches that do not deviate from a prespecified size by more than 2μ. Suppose this machine has produced parts with the following deviations in μ: 0 1 2 1 2 6 6 2 2. This series contains two runs of tools within specification. The first run involves the first five parts, and the second involves the last two parts. These two runs

are separated by a run of two parts that are outside the admissible range. To describe these runs, ratio scale information is used. In general, however, the type of information used for this definition of runs depends on the scale level used to specify the range.

Taking an algorithmic perspective, the following sample variables describe runs in series of K scores:

1. Number of runs of any sort, k_r, with $k_r \leq K$;

2. Length of jth run of equal scores, k^e_j, with ranges $1 \leq k^e_j \leq K$ and $1 \leq j \leq K$;

3. Length of jth run of increasing scores, k^a_j, with range $2 \leq k^a_j \leq K - 1$;

4. Length of jth run of decreasing scores, k^d_j, with range $2 \leq k^d_j \leq K - 1$;

5. Length of jth run of up-and-down scores (or down-and-up), k^u_j, with range $3 \leq k^u_j \leq K - 3$;

6. Length of jth run of scores within a prespecified interval, k^w_j, with $0 \leq k^w_j \leq K$.

Of these six variables, the second is the one used in standard runs tests. These tests ask whether the number of runs, k^e_j, is smaller or larger than expected based on a null distribution. When k^e_j is smaller than expected, there may be a process that prevents scores from changing. When k^e_j is larger than expected, there may be a process that causes overly frequent change. This applies accordingly to all types of runs.

Length of run information is partially dependent on the number of runs. This number sets limits to both the maximum and the minimum run length. Still, the length of runs is of importance. Consider, for example, a study on the effects of psychotherapy on compulsive behavior. After establishing a baseline run pattern, the beginning of therapy can be expected to cause a run pattern that suggests improvement. This can be indicated by a pattern of decreases in the frequency of compulsive behavior occurrences over time. Other indicators of improvement include interrupted series (= shorter runs) of compulsive acts and longer periods with no compulsive acts. Therapy success can be measured by using, among other indicators, length of run information. The number of runs, in this example, has an upper limit that is determined by the number of therapy sessions.

Now, let x_j be the score obtained at time j, and $1 \leq j \leq K$. Then, the *number of runs of equal scores*, r_e, can be calculated in the following two steps (von Eye & Bogat, 2009):

$$\delta_j = \begin{cases} 1 & \text{if } x_j = x_{j+1} \\ 0 & \text{else} \end{cases} ,$$

where δ_j compares the scores x_j and x_{j+1}, for $j = 1, \ldots, K-1$, and $r_e = \sum_j \delta_j$.

Accordingly, the *number of runs of increasing scores*, r_a, can also be calculated in the two steps

$$\delta_j = \begin{cases} 1 & \text{if } x_j < x_{j+1} \\ 0 & \text{else} \end{cases}$$

and $r_a = \sum_j \delta_j$.

The *number of runs of decreasing scores*, r_d, can be calculated in the two steps

$$\delta_j = \begin{cases} 1 & \text{if } x_j > x_{j+1} \\ 0 & \text{else} \end{cases}$$

and $r_d = \sum_j \delta_j$.

The *number of runs of up-and-down scores*, r_u, can be calculated in the two steps

$$\delta_j = \begin{cases} 1 & \text{if } x_j < x_{j+1} \text{ and } x_{j+1} > x_{j+2} \\ 0 & \text{else} \end{cases}$$

and $r_u = \sum_j \delta_j$.

Finally, the *number of runs of scores within a prespecified interval*, r_w, can be calculated in the two steps

$$\delta_j = \begin{cases} 1 & \text{if } |x_j - x| < \varepsilon \\ 0 & \text{else} \end{cases} ,$$

where x is the prespecified target score and ε indicates the prespecified threshold, for $j = 1, \ldots, K$, and $r_w = \sum_j \delta_j$.

Each of these steps can be performed by using the appropriate commands in general purpose statistical software packages, for example, the TRANSFORM command in SYSTAT. Similar operations are easily implemented in spreadsheet programs such as Lotus 1-2-3, Quattro Pro, or Excel. The result of these calculations is one value that indicates the number of runs per case per series of scores.

Runs scores can be directly compared only if the number of observation points is the same for each case. If this number varies, as is natural in training or therapy studies, the observed number of runs can be related to the maximum number of runs, $r_{max} = R$, where R can vary by the definition of runs used. For example, $R = K$ for runs of equal, increasing, or decreasing scores and for series of scores within a prespecified interval. The resulting *relative number of runs*, $r_r = r/r_{max}$, can be directly compared with other r_r scores, both intra- and inter-individually. In the following section, we illustrate the use of number of runs, r, in the context of configural data analysis.

Data Example 1: The following example uses data from the longitudinal project on intimate partner violence again (Bogat et al., 2006) that was used in Chapter 5, on prediction models of CFA. For the example, we use data from the first five observation points (during pregnancy and when the children were at ages 1, 2, 3, and 4), and analyze the variables Posttraumatic Stress Disorder symptoms (PTSD; P) and Violence Status (V). PTSD was coded as 1 = respondent exceeds cutoff for clinical-level PTSD symptoms, and 0 = else. The following analyses could have been performed using the raw scores also. Here, however, we focus on runs of clinical-level PTSD ($P = 1$ vs. $P = 0$). Violence Status was coded as 1 = respondent reports one or more incidents of intimate partner violence that equal or exceed threats of moderate violence in the preceding year, and 0 = no violence or violence below cutoff.

For each of these two variables, each woman was assigned a score for runs of equal numbers. The maximum score per variable and respondent was 5 (5 time-adjacent scores were created for each variable; thus, the maximum number of runs of scores of equal value is 5; a comparison of these numbers allows one to describe the change in score from every point in time to the next). The number of cases with 5 runs in either variable was so small that these cases were subsumed under the rubric of "4 or more" runs. The resulting four scores per respondent were crossed to form a 4 × 4 contingency table with 16 cells. This table was first analyzed by using standard first order CFA. No cell was blanked out, and no covariate was included. For the CFA, we used the z-test and the Holland-Copenhaver procedure to protect α. For the base model, we obtain a $LR - X^2 = 126.85$ ($df = 9$; $p < 0.01$) and, therefore, expect types and antitypes to emerge. Table 11.1 displays the CFA results.

The results in Table 11.1 suggest that runs in violence and PTSD covary in an interesting way. Four types emerge, each indicating that the number of runs is more often the same in these two variables than expected. The three antitypes suggest that particular patterns of discrepant numbers of runs occur less often than expected.

One characteristic of the runs variable is that it can be considered ordinal. Therefore, one can improve the model by taking into account

TABLE 11.1. CFA of Runs of PTSD (P) and Intimate Partner Violence (V), over Five Observation Points

Configuration $P\,V$	m	$\hat{m}$	z	p	Type/Antitype
11	64	36.235	4.6124	.000002	Type
12	19	27.294	−1.5876	.056191	
13	7	17.882	−2.5734	.005035	Antitype
14	6	14.588	−2.2486	.012271	
21	6	18.873	−2.9631	.001523	Antitype
22	31	14.216	4.4516	.000004	Type
23	10	9.314	.2249	.411039	
24	3	7.598	−1.6681	.047648	
31	2	13.588	−3.1437	.000834	Antitype
32	7	10.235	−1.0113	.155946	
33	19	6.706	4.7475	.000001	Type
34	8	5.471	1.0814	.139751	
41	5	8.304	−1.1465	.125787	
42	1	6.255	−2.1011	.017814	
43	2	4.098	−1.0364	.150009	
44	14	3.343	5.8284	.000000	Type

the ordinal nature of this variable in the base model. For the present data, both variables that span the cross-classification in Table 11.1 are ordinal. Therefore, we decide to use Goodman's (1979) linear by linear interaction model as the CFA base model. For the present case with two ordinal runs variables, labeled as V and P, this model can be specified as

$$\log \hat{m} = \lambda + \lambda_i^V + \lambda_j^P + \gamma x_i w_j,$$

where the x_i and the w_j are the quantitative levels of the variables V and P, respectively, and γ is the parameter that is estimated for the linear by linear interaction term. If, as is the case in the present example, the quantitative levels are evenly spaced, this model is equivalent to

$$\log \hat{m} = \lambda + \lambda_i^V + \lambda_j^P + \gamma(i)(j).$$

The parameters γ in these two equations are identical if $x_i = i$ and $w_j = j$.

Using the linear by linear interaction model as the CFA base model implies including a covariate with entries that result from calculating the outer product of the two vectors that contain the quantitative levels. In the present example, both of these vectors have entries {1, 2, 3, 4}. The outer product of the two vectors yields a vector with the entries {1, 2, 3, 4, 2, 4, 6, 8, 3, 6, 9, 12, 4, 8, 12, 16}. The design matrix for the new, nonstandard base model thus becomes

$$
X = \begin{pmatrix}
1 & 0 & 0 & 1 & 0 & 0 & 1 \\
1 & 0 & 0 & 0 & 1 & 0 & 2 \\
1 & 0 & 0 & 0 & 0 & 1 & 3 \\
1 & 0 & 0 & -1 & -1 & -1 & 4 \\
0 & 1 & 0 & 1 & 0 & 0 & 2 \\
0 & 1 & 0 & 0 & 1 & 0 & 4 \\
0 & 1 & 0 & 0 & 0 & 1 & 6 \\
0 & 1 & 0 & -1 & -1 & -1 & 8 \\
0 & 0 & 1 & 1 & 0 & 0 & 3 \\
0 & 0 & 1 & 0 & 1 & 0 & 6 \\
0 & 0 & 1 & 0 & 0 & 1 & 9 \\
0 & 0 & 1 & -1 & -1 & -1 & 12 \\
1 & -1 & -1 & 1 & 0 & 0 & 4 \\
1 & -1 & -1 & 0 & 1 & 0 & 8 \\
1 & -1 & -1 & 0 & 0 & 1 & 12 \\
1 & -1 & -1 & -1 & -1 & -1 & 16
\end{pmatrix}.
$$

The first six columns of this design matrix are standard for effects coding of two 4-category variables. Each variable has 4 categories. Therefore, for each variable, three contrast vectors are needed. The last column contains the vector for the linear by linear interaction. The log-linear model that uses this design matrix yields a $LR - X^2 = 53.92$ ($df = 8$; $p < 0.01$). Clearly, the part of the interaction between the runs from violence and PTSD that can be explained based on the ordinal nature of the two runs variables covers a considerable portion of the variability in the $P \times V$ cross-classification. Still, the $LR - X^2$ suggests significant model-data discrepancies. Therefore, we expect types and antitypes to emerge. The results of the CFA that uses this extended base model, the z-test, and the Holland-Copenhaver procedure are summarized in Table 11.2.

The results in Table 11.2 suggest that none of the antitypes from Table 11.1 and only one of the types (Configuration 2 2) remain. In addition, there is a new type, constituted by Configuration 4 1. This type indicates that more women were found than expected who exhibit the maximum number of runs in PTSD but only one run in violence. The estimated expected frequency for this type is small. Therefore, we consider it with the recommendation of conducting a replication study to make sure this type is not sample-specific.

TABLE 11.2. CFA of Runs of PTSD and Intimate Partner Violence, over Five Observation Points; with Linear by Linear Interaction

Configuration $P\ V$	m	$\hat{m}$	z	p	Type/Antitype
11	64	54.806	1.2419	.107143	
12	19	29.041	−1.8633	.031213	
13	7	9.603	−.8400	.200455	
14	6	2.550	2.1609	.015353	
21	6	16.734	−2.6239	.004346	
22	31	17.001	3.3952	.000343	Type
23	10	10.779	−.2372	.406265	
24	3	5.487	−1.0617	.144188	
31	2	4.720	−1.2520	.105285	
32	7	9.194	−.7237	.234628	
33	19	11.177	2.3401	.009640	
34	8	10.909	−.8807	.189240	
41	5	.740	4.9522	.000000	Type
42	1	2.764	−1.0609	.144357	
43	2	6.442	−1.7500	.040058	
44	14	12.055	.5603	.287635	

11.2   Configural Lag Analysis[1]

The method of CFA for intensive, longitudinal, categorical data to be presented in this section allows one to answer questions that, so far, had been inaccessible to configural analysis. The same applies to configural lag analysis, to be discussed here. Consider the concept of a *lag*. Let temporal observations take place at T points in time. Then, with reference to an observation that is made at time t, an observation that takes place at point in time $t + k$ is said to occur with a k time units lag (for $k > 0$). Accordingly, negative lags can be defined, with $k < 0$. An observation that takes place at point in time $t − k$ is said to occur with a negative lag of k time units, or k time units before the observation at time t.

Lag analysis has been discussed extensively in the context of methods for the analysis of longitudinal data (e.g., Finkel, 2008; Greenberg, 2008; Sanders & Ward, 2008), including the context of intensive longitudinal data (Ho, Shumway, & Ombao, 2006; Rovine & Walls, 2006). The application of the concept of lags is new in the context of CFA.

To describe lag analysis of intensive, categorical longitudinal data,

---

[1]The idea for the method presented in this section was proposed by Peter Molenaar and Mike Rovine in June 2007. We are grateful for this idea, apologize for possibly having distorted it, and confer on both of them the title of "Co-Conspirator".

TABLE 11.3. Strings with Lag 1, Lag 2, and Lag 3

Time	Original Observations	Observations with Lag 1	Observations with Lag 2	Observations with Lag 3
1	x_1	—	—	—
2	x_2	x_1	—	—
3	x_3	x_2	x_1	—
4	x_4	x_3	x_2	x_1
5	x_5	x_4	x_3	x_2
⋮	⋮	⋮	⋮	⋮
$n-1$	x_{n-1}	x_{n-2}	x_{n-3}	x_{n-4}
n	x_n	x_{n-1}	x_{n-2}	x_{n-3}

TABLE 11.4. Cross-Classification of One Variable with Itself, for a Lag of 1

Original Observations	Lag 1 Observations		
	$I = 1$	$I = 2$	$I = 3$
$I = 1$	m_{11}	m_{12}	m_{13}
$I = 2$	m_{21}	m_{22}	m_{23}
$I = 3$	m_{31}	m_{32}	m_{33}

consider a string of observations of the same variable, X, with the scores $x_1, \ldots, x_n$. Let the subscripts denote observation points in time, and let the observations describe just one individual. For this string of observations, a corresponding one can be created, with a lag of 1. This string will contain the same scores, just shifted down by one point in time so that x_i of the original string of observations is now positioned next to x_{i+1} of the second string, with $i \geq 1$. The number of scores in the second string is $n - 1$. A second corresponding string can be created, with a lag of 2. It contains the scores $x_1, \ldots, x_{n-2}$, and so forth. Obviously, the second string contains one fewer score than the first, the third string contains one fewer than the second or, in general, a string with a lag of k contains k fewer scores than the original string. This is illustrated in Table 11.3.

Now, suppose we cross two of these strings, say the original string of scores with the second string, that is, the one with lag 1. The result will be a contingency table with $I \times I$ cells, where I is the number of categories of the observed variable. A sample cross-classification is given in Table 11.4, for the case of $I = 3$.

Entry ij (for $i, j = 1, \ldots, I$) in this table indicates the frequency with which an observation of Category i at Time t was preceded by an observation of Category j, at Time $t - 1$. The cross-classifications in Table 11.4 can be

- extended to any number of lags (number of observations permitting);

- created for one or more variables;

- crossed with variables that were observed only once, e.g., covariates or stratification variables; and

- analyzed by using standard methods of categorical variables analysis such as log-linear modeling, logistic regression, and CFA.

In the following sections, we present two applications of CFA of lagged data.

Data Examples 2 and 3: For the following two examples, we use data from a project on the development of alcoholism (Perrine, Mundt, Searles, & Lester, 1995). A sample of alcoholic adult males provided information every morning about their drinking the day before, their subjective ratings of mood, health, or quality of the day. Here, we ask, whether the mood of Respondent 49 can be predicted from one day to the next. The interesting aspect of lagged configural analysis is that the days are required to be consecutive. They do not need to be equidistant, but for comparability the distance pattern should be the same for each participant. In the CFA of the lagged mood data, we do not ask whether mood is predictable from one particular day to another. Instead, we ask whether mood is predictable for any 2 consecutive days. The respondent had provided information for an uninterrupted series of 792 days, that is, 2 years and 3 months. The sample size of mood self-ratings thus is, for the following analysis, 791 days.

Mood was rated on a 10-point Likert scale, with 1 indicating terrible mood and 10 indicating "just wonderful". Respondent 49 tended to not use the lower end points on this scale. Therefore, scores 5 and below were condensed into a single category. Similarly, this respondent practically never used scores 9 or 10. Therefore, scores 8-10 were condensed into a single category also. The resulting scale thus ranged from 1 to 4, with 1 indicating average mood or below and 4 indicating good or better mood. For the analysis of the resulting 4×4 table, we use the z-test and the Holland-Copenhaver procedure. For the base model of first order CFA, we obtain a $LR - X^2 = 109.37$ ($df = 9$; $p < 0.01$). Therefore, we anticipate that types and antitypes emerge. Table 11.5 summarizes the CFA results.

The type-antitype pattern in Table 11.5 is clear. The four types, constituted by Configurations 1 1, 1 2, 2 2, and 4 4, suggest that, more often than expected based on chance, the mood on any given day is the same as the mood on the day before (Configurations 1 1, 2 2, 4 4), or slightly better (Configuration 1 2). The three antitypes, constituted by Configurations 2 4,

TABLE 11.5. First Order CFA of Lag-1 Analysis of Mood Data for Respondent 49 for a Period of 791 Days

Configuration Mood Lag-1-Mood	m	$\hat{m}$	z	p	Type/Antitype
11	12	2.338	6.3199	.000000	Type
12	11	4.186	3.3306	.000433	Type
13	8	15.710	−1.9453	.025869	
14	12	20.766	−1.9237	.027198	
21	9	4.186	2.3530	.009310	
22	21	7.496	4.9326	.000000	Type
23	30	28.133	.3520	.362402	
24	17	37.186	−3.3102	.000466	Antitype
31	14	15.765	−.4445	.328343	
32	32	28.230	.7095	.238996	
33	110	105.954	.3930	.347153	
34	134	140.051	−.5113	.304580	
41	8	20.712	−2.7932	.002610	Antitype
42	13	37.088	−3.9554	.000038	Antitype
43	141	139.202	.1524	.439448	
44	219	183.997	2.5804	.004934	Type

4 1, and 4 2, suggest that mood swings by two or more scale points are rather unlikely, in particular swings toward worse mood.

Considering that this respondent was an alcoholic (as per his own, self-reported diagnosis), we ask whether this pattern of types and antitypes remains the same if we take into account the amount of alcohol consumed on the day before the first mood rating was given. In different words, we ask whether alcohol consumption corresponds with the mood rating on the next day and the following one.

Alcohol consumption was, for this particular respondent, measured in units of 12-ounce beer bottles or cans consumed per day (amount of consumption refers to the day before mood was observed). The number of beers consumed by Respondent 49 ranged between the extremes of 0 and 18 (included). However, the respondent rarely had fewer than 4 beers a day. Therefore, 0-4 beers were condensed into a single category. Similarly, the respondent rarely had more than 9 beers a day. Therefore, 9 and more beers were condensed into a single category also. The resulting scale had six categories, with 1 indicating 4 beers or fewer, and 6 indicating 9 beers or more.

For the following CFA, the beer consumption variable was crossed with the two mood variables. The resulting 6 × 4 × 4 cross-classification was analyzed under the first order CFA base model by using the z-test and

TABLE 11.6. First Order CFA of Alcohol Consumption and Mood on the Following 2 Days

Configuration *Beer Mood Lag-1-Mood*	m	$\hat{m}$	z	p	Type/Antitype
111	4	1.001	2.9966	.001365	
112	4	1.793	1.6480	.049676	
⋮	⋮	⋮	⋮	⋮	
143	68	59.633	1.0835	.139289	
144	116	78.616	4.2162	.000012	Type
211	0	.264	−.5135	.303802	
⋮	⋮	⋮	⋮	⋮	
344	16	16.281	−.0698	.472193	
411	2	.210	3.9021	.000048	Type
412	0	.377	−.6137	.269695	
⋮	⋮	⋮	⋮	⋮	
544	25	20.933	.8888	.187046	
611	5	.391	7.3701	.000000	Type
612	3	.700	2.7481	.002997	
⋮	⋮	⋮	⋮	⋮	
621	1	.700	.3581	.360117	
622	5	1.254	3.3452	.000411	Type
623	6	4.707	.5962	.275529	
⋮	⋮	⋮	⋮	⋮	
643	16	23.289	−1.5103	.065480	
644	29	30.702	−.3072	.379343	

the Holland-Copenhaver procedure. For this base model, we obtain a $LR - X^2 = 228.27$ ($df = 84$; $p < 0.01$). Therefore, we are reasonably certain that types and antitypes will emerge. Table 11.6 presents a selection of the CFA results.

Table 11.6 shows four types and no antitype. These types are constituted by Configurations 1 4 4, 4 1 1, 6 1 1, and 6 2 2. The estimated expected cell frequencies for Types 4 1 1 and 6 1 1 are rather small. Therefore, we refrain from interpreting these configurations as type-constituting. The first of the two remaining types, 1 4 4, suggests that, if Respondent 49 consumed 4 beers or fewer on any given day, his mood was more often than expected good or better during the following two consecutive days. In contrast, Type 6 2 2 also suggests that when the respondent had 9 beers or more on any given day, his mood on the following 2 days was more often than expected average (that is, rated as a 2 on a scale from 1 to 4 where 1 indicates average mood or below). This may be described as a "hangover type".

Table 11.6 shows again that CFA focuses on model-data discrepancies instead of the magnitude of cell frequencies. Consider Configuration 6 2 2, which constitutes a type. In clearly more instances than observed for this configuration, 9 or more beers correspond with good or very good mood on the following 2 days (e.g., Configurations 6 3 4 and 6 4 4). However, these instances do not deviate significantly from expectation and, therefore, do not constitute a type under the current base model of variable independence.

11.3 Chapter Summary

Intensive longitudinal data are characterized by a number of observation points that lies between what can easily be processed by using methods of ANOVA, on one end, and what is required for longitudinal factor analysis and methods of time series analysis, on the other. When categorical variables are analyzed, crossing all variables is out of the question because the resulting table would have a colossal number of cells.

For analysis with CFA or log-linear modeling, two strategies are proposed for the analysis of intensive longitudinal data. The first is based on the concept of runs. A run is defined as an uninterrupted string of scores that fulfill a particular condition. For example, a run can be a string of equal numbers, a string of increasing numbers, a string of odd numbers, etc. Using CFA, one can then analyze numbers of strings and length of strings.

The second strategy focuses on the structure of series of scores. One characteristic of a structure can be captured by using lags. A lag of 1 allows one to predict, from each day, the scores observed on the following day. A lag of 2 allows one to predict the scores observed 2 days later, a lag of 7 allows one to predict the scores observed 1 week later, etc. For analysis with CFA, one can cross a series of scores and the lagged series. Results emerge in the form of types and antitypes that indicate which score can be expected with beyond chance probability one, two, ..., seven, or a larger number of observation points later.

12

Reduced CFA Designs

Chapter 12 addresses an issue that is rarely discussed in social science categorical data analysis. It concerns the completeness of a cross-classification. In particular, when higher order effects are not considered interesting, interpretable, or important, so-called fractional factorial designs can be considered. These designs result in incomplete tables that, depending on the fraction of a complete design that is realized, allow one to interpret effects up to a specific order. The application of fractional factorial designs in CFA can be interesting when higher order interactions are considered unimportant as causes for types and antitypes. The advantage of such designs is that, given the sample size, far more variables can be analyzed than in complete designs. In Chapter 12, base models are derived, and patterns of types and antitypes are compared for complete and fractional factorial designs by using data examples.

There is an interesting principle that seems to be at work when higher order interactions among factors of experimental designs or categorical variables that span a cross-classification are examined, the *Sparsity of Effects Principle*. According to this principle, which is discussed in the contexts of linear models and design (e.g., Hamada & Wu, 1992; Kutner, Neter, Nachtsheim, & Li, 2004; Wu & Hamada, 2000), responses in most systems are driven largely by a limited number of main effects and lower order interactions. Higher order interactions are, therefore, usually relatively unimportant. In the context of CFA, the sparsity of effects principle would have the effect that patterns of types and antitypes result from main effects or lower order interactions, and higher order interactions rarely affect these patterns (von Eye, 2008b). Exceptions include distributions in which higher order interactions define the variable relationships, for example, distributions that reflect Meehl's (1950) paradox (see von Eye, 2002a) or the well-known Simpson paradox.

In addition to this principle, three other issues are of concern when planning study designs in which factors are completely crossed. The first issue involves cost and effort. Creating large numbers of treatment combinations is complex and cost-intensive. The second issue concerns interpretation. Interactions of very high order are hard to interpret. Third, theories in the social and behavioral sciences rarely imply hypotheses that require the testing of high order interactions.

Because of these issues and the sparsity of effects principle, full factorial designs, that is, designs that fully cross all factors, are often not only cost-intensive when many factors are taken into account. They can also be wasteful and may yield little information above and beyond designs that allow one to consider only the main effects and lower order interactions that are sufficient to explain what is going on in a table[1]. Consider, for example, the cross-classification of six dichotomous variables. The analysis of this design comes with 1 df for the intercept, 6 df for the main effects, 15 df for the two-way interactions, 20 df for the three-way interactions, 15 df for the four-way interactions, 6 df for the five-way interactions, and 1 df for the six-way interaction. Now, suppose that only the intercept, the main effects, and the first order interactions are needed to explain the frequency distribution in the table. In this case, two-thirds of the degrees of freedom in this design are used to estimate parameters that are not of interest and will not be interpreted.

Fractional factorial designs use only a subset of the treatment combinations, or cells, of a completely crossed design. This subset can be chosen based on the sparsity of effects principle. Specifically, fractional designs allow the data analyst to estimate the effects of interest. Based on the sparsity of effects principle, these effects are assumed to be of low order. In fractional factorial designs, higher order effects are either not estimable or confounded. More details follow below.

In this chapter, we discuss the use of fractional factorial designs in the context of CFA. We treat the categorical variables that span a cross-classification as if they were factors of an experimental design. We focus on Box-Hunter designs (Box, Hunter, & Hunter, 2005; Wu & Hamada, 2000) because they allow one to specify designs based on the order of interactions that are of importance in a study. We discuss these designs from the perspective of the order of effects that cause types and antitypes to emerge. We then show that fractional factorial designs can fruitfully be applied when the outcome variables are categorical, in particular in applications of CFA (for fractional factorial designs in log-linear modeling, see von Eye, 2008b).

In the following sections, we introduce specific fractional factorial

---

[1]It is important to note that higher order interaction effects can still be used for a better error estimate. So, they can still be useful.

designs, give examples, and discuss the application of such designs in CFA.

12.1 Fractional Factorial Designs

Optimal designs are specified with the goal of obtaining efficient parameter estimates and maximum power of statistical tests while minimizing cost and effort (Berger, 2005; Dodge, Fedorov, & Wynn, 1988; Liski, Mandal, Shah, & Sinha, 2002; Pukelsheim, 2006). For example, optimal designs have been devised to estimate kinetic model parameters in pharmacological research (e.g., Reverte, Dirion, & Cabassud, 2006), to improve the accuracy of parameter estimates in research on the physiology of rats (e.g., Verotta, Petrillo, La Regina, Rocchetti, & Tavani, 1988), to maximize the information content of measured data while observing safety and operability constraints in process control research (e.g., Bruwer & MacGregor, 2005), to discriminate between two or more rival regression models in applied statistics (e.g., Atkinson & Fedorov, 1975), or to compare the probabilities from binomial data with misclassifications (Zelen & Haitovsku, 1991).

Often, additional, mostly statistical, criteria are set for optimality as well as the criterion of parsimony (Pukelsheim, 2006; Stigler, 1971). Using these criteria, researchers attempt to maximize the information content of data and the precision of parameter estimates while minimizing the necessary effort or pecuniary cost of an experiment. These criteria are optimized when the number of treatment combinations (cells) of a design (in the context of fractional factorial designs, this number is called the number of runs) is minimized without compromising the interpretability of the parameters of interest or, in the context of CFA, distorting the resulting pattern of types and antitypes. Clearly, here the sparsity of effects principle comes into play again. If higher order effects are unimportant, omitting these effects in the model or design does not pose much risk of biased results. Similarly, if less important effects are confounded, the damage that is caused by the confounds is unimportant also.

Fractional factorial designs are sample cases of optimal designs. They include only a fraction of the cells of a completely crossed design. That is, they contain only one-half, one-quarter, or an even smaller portion of the cells of a completely crossed factorial design. The earliest fractional factorial design discussed in the literature is the well-known *Latin square* (Euler, 1782). This design allows one to estimate only the main effects of the factors. Therefore, Latin squares are only of importance in the application of zero order CFA, which uses the null model as its base model. Because of the limited utility of zero order CFA, Latin squares will not be discussed in more detail in this volume.

The theory of fractional designs was developed originally by Finney (1945, 1946) and Kempthorne (1947). Recent treatments include the text by Mukerjee and Wu (2006). Statistical software packages such as Minitab, Statistica, and SYSTAT contain modules that allow one to create fractional factorial designs (Kessels, Goos, & Vandebroek, 2006).

A key characteristic of a fractional factorial design is its *resolution*, that is, the degree to which main effects and interactions can be independently estimated and interpreted. Expressed differently, the resolution of a design indicates the order of effects that can be estimated without their being confounded with one another. Box et al. (2005) describe the hierarchy of resolution of designs for metric outcome variables as follows. For designs with *Resolution I*, no effect is independently estimable. Therefore, designs with *Resolution I* are not interesting. Similarly, *Resolution II* is largely useless. Main effects would be confounded with other main effects. In the analysis of metric outcome variables, the most useful fractional factorial designs have *Resolution III*, *IV*, and *V*. At *Resolution III*, main effects can be estimated, but they are confounded with two-way interactions.

More interesting to researchers is often *Resolution IV*. At this level, main effects can be uniquely estimated, and they are not confounded with any of the two-way interactions. Two-way interactions, however, are confounded with one another.

Resolution IV designs are of interest in particular when researchers seek to determine whether two-way interactions are important at all without specifying which interaction in particular. Designs at Resolution level IV will leave some of the two-factor interactions unconfounded. If the researchers are interested in these interactions in particular, *Resolution IV* can be viable.

Moving up the resolution ladder, designs with *Resolution V* allow one to estimate main effects and two-way interactions independently, and neither will be confounded with each other, but possibly with higher-order interactions. Three-way interactions can be estimated also. However, they are confounded. Designs with *Resolution V* are needed to guarantee that two-way interactions are not confounded. Accordingly, designs with *Resolution VI* allow one to estimate three-way interactions such that they are not confounded with one another, but four-way interactions are confounded with one another.

When categorical dependent variables are analyzed, one has to take into account that, in order to estimate the same effect, interactions of one order higher need to be included in the design than is necessary for metric outcome variables (this issue is explained in more detail below). Thus, when the outcome variables are categorical, designs with

- Resolutions I, II, and III are largely uninteresting and of little or no use (see the discussion of Data Example 1, in Section 12.2);

- Resolution level IV allows one to estimate main effects (in the form of two-way interactions) that are confounded with three-way associations;

- Resolution level V allows one to uniquely estimate main effects and two-way interactions such that interactions are not confounded with one another.

In general, in the analysis of categorical outcome variables, beginning with Resolution level V, interactions of an increasingly higher order can be estimated without confounds. Therefore, designs with resolution levels V or higher are needed for the analysis of fractional factorial designs with categorical dependent variables when predictor-criterion relationships are of interest. Application examples of such designs are given in the following sections.

Clearly, as the resolution level increases, a design becomes more complex and requires more runs (= cells in a table). Designs with higher resolution levels carry more information. Fractional factorial designs allow researchers to balance the need for parsimony and the desire for information by making decisions concerning the point from which higher order interactions carry no additional useful, important, variance-explaining information.

Types of Fractional Factorial Designs: As one can imagine, the number of fractional factorial design types is large. Here, we review just a selection of design types (for more types, see, e.g., Box et al., 2005; Wu & Hamada, 2000). Practically all of the following design types can be generated by using numerical algorithms. Therefore, they are also called *computer-aided designs*.

The first type listed here includes homogeneous *fractional factorial designs*. In these designs, all factors have the same number of levels. *Mixed-level fractional factorial designs* include factors that differ in number of levels.

A subtype of homogeneous fractional factorial designs is known as *Box-Hunter designs* (Box et al., 2005). As was indicated above, these designs use only a fraction of the completely crossed design, for example, one-half, one-quarter, or an even smaller fraction of the total number of runs. For each factor, the number of factor levels in Box-Hunter designs is two, and the number of runs is a power of two. If each factor has three levels, *Box-Behnken designs* (Box & Behnken, 1960) can be considered. These designs do not use those treatment combinations for which all factors assume extreme values (e.g., treatment combinations 3-3-3 or 1-1-1). Whereas Box-Hunter designs can be considered for nominal-level factors, Box-Behnken designs require factors that are assessed at least at the ordinal scale level. The number of runs in Box-Behnken designs is a multiple of three.

Plackett-Burman designs (Plackett & Burman, 1946; Ledolter & Swersey, 2007), also called screening designs, operate at Resolution level III. They are very economical in that the number of runs can be very small, when the dependent variable is metrical. For example, up to 11 dichotomous factors can be studied by using only 12 runs; up to 19 factors can be studied by using 20 runs, and up to 23 factors can be studied by using 24 runs. These designs are used to explore whether main effects exist in metric variables. However, one has to assume that two-way interactions are absent. These designs are also called *saturated main effect designs*, because all available degrees of freedom go into the estimation of main effects. These designs are used to determine the factors that may have (main) effects on the outcome variable.

Plackett-Burman designs will simplify to fractional factorial designs with binary factors if the number of runs is 2^k. For example, for 8, 16, or 32 runs, they are the same as fractional factorial designs with binary factors. However, they are unique for 12, 20, 24, etc. runs.

To increase the resolution of Plackett-Burman designs, the use of *foldover designs* has been proposed. These designs result from reversing the signs of all scores in the design matrix, and appending the thus mirrored design matrix to the original one. The resulting design allows one to estimate all main effects such that they are no longer confounded with two-way interactions, at the expense of doubling the number of runs.

As was noted above, a main effect in the context of the General Linear Model relates a predictor to a criterion. In contrast, in the General Log-linear Model, a main effect allows statements about the univariate marginal distribution of a variable. To describe the relationship between a predictor and a criterion variable in a log-linear model or in CFA, a two-way interaction is needed. Therefore, standard Plackett-Burman designs are of lesser importance in the context of categorical variable analysis. To create a screening design for categorical outcome variables, Resolution at level IV is needed.

Generating Fractional Designs: Many general purpose software packages contain modules that allow one to create a wide variety of fractional and optimal designs. In this section, we present an algorithmic description of how fractional factorial designs can be generated. We focus on Box-Hunter designs (see Box et al., 2005). Consider the number of dichotomous variables, p, and the number of runs, 2^{p-k}, where $p - k$ is the number of factors whose main effects can be coded as usual, in a completely crossed design ($k < p$). The main effects of the remaining k factors have to be coded differently, because, in fractional factorial designs, the number of rows in the design matrix can be reduced by at least 50% when compared to a completely crossed design. Then, a Box-Hunter design and the corresponding design matrix can be generated as follows (note that all factors have two levels):

1. For the first $p-k$ factors, create a design matrix with main effects specified just as in a completely crossed design with 2^{p-k} cells (= rows in the design matrix).

2. For the remaining factor $p - k + i$, create the main effect as if it were the interaction among the factors in the first of the $\binom{p-k}{p-k-1} = \binom{p-k}{1}$ combinations of the first $p - k$ factors. In other words, the remaining k main effects are expressed in terms of the $(p - k)$-way interactions of those factors that can be coded as in a $(p - k)$-factorial design. Thus, confounds will exist at least at the level of the $(p - k)$-way interactions.

3. Repeat Step 2 a total of k times, until all main effects are created for the p factors.

4. Generate two-way interactions as in a standard ANOVA design, that is, by element-wise multiplication of vector elements from two different factors.

5. Generate three-way interactions also as in a standard ANOVA design, that is, by element-wise multiplication of vector elements from three different factors.

6. Repeat generating interactions until either the design is saturated or all unconfounded and important interactions are included in the design matrix.

It is important to realize that the number of designs that can be created this way is $p!/(p - k)!$. This number results from selecting different factors that are coded as in a completely crossed design with $p - k$ cells, and changing their order. This process is also called randomizing the runs. Expressed differently, for fractional designs, alternatives often exist at the same level of resolution.

TABLE 12.1. Box-Hunter Design with 8 Runs from 4 Factors; Resolution = III; All Interactions Included

Int.	Main Effects				2-Way Interactions						3-Way Interactions				4-Way
1	−1	−1	−1	−1	1	1	1	1	1	1	−1	−1	−1	−1	1
1	1	−1	−1	1	−1	−1	1	1	−1	−1	1	−1	−1	1	1
1	−1	1	−1	1	−1	1	−1	−1	1	−1	1	−1	1	−1	1
1	1	1	−1	−1	1	−1	−1	−1	−1	1	−1	−1	1	1	1
1	−1	−1	1	1	1	−1	−1	−1	−1	1	1	1	−1	−1	1
1	1	−1	1	−1	−1	1	−1	−1	1	−1	−1	1	−1	1	1
1	−1	1	1	−1	−1	−1	1	1	−1	−1	−1	1	1	−1	1
1	1	1	1	1	1	1	1	1	1	1	1	1	1	1	1

12.2   Examples of Fractional Factorial Designs

In this section, we present sample fractional factorial designs, with an emphasis on Box-Hunter designs, that is, designs for dichotomous variables. For each of the designs, we discuss the savings in the number of necessary runs, in comparison to the corresponding completely crossed design, the resolution, and the interpretation of parameters. Typically, parameters are not tested in CFA. Parameter interpretability, however, is of importance. If parameters cannot be interpreted, types and antitypes cannot be traced back to particular effects in a clear-cut way. Therefore, the interpretation of a selection of parameters is presented.

Two perspectives will be taken. In the first, we seek to create parsimonious designs, mostly based on resolution levels (Data Examples 1 and 3). In the second, we seek to create parsimonious designs with a specific method of analysis (P-CFA and logistic regression) in mind (Data Example 4). We also show an example in which Box-Hunter and Plackett-Burman designs coincide (Data Example 2).

Data Example 1: Box-Hunter Design with 8 Runs from 4 Factors; Resolution Level III. We begin with a Box-Hunter design in which we study the four dichotomous variables A, B, C, and D. The complete cross-classification of these variables has 24 = 16 cells (runs). We decide to create a design that has 50% fewer cells, that is, 8 runs. The matrix with all main effects and interactions for this design appears in Table 12.1.

The matrix in Table 12.1 has eight rows (runs) and 16 columns. Thus, it is bound to be nonorthogonal. The main effect vectors are pairwise orthogonal. However, the following confounds are in the matrix:

- Interaction AD is confounded with Interaction BC: $AD = BC$

- Interaction AC is confounded with Interaction BD: $AC = BD$

- Interaction AB is confounded with Interaction CD: $AB = CD$

- Main effect D is confounded with Interaction ABC: $D = ABC$

- Main effect C is confounded with Interaction ABD: $C = ABD$

- Main effect B is confounded with Interaction ACD: $B = ACD$

- Main effect A is confounded with Interaction BCD: $A = BCD$; and

- The Intercept I is confounded with Interaction $ABCD$: $I = ABCD$.

Because of these confounds, the application of this design requires the assumption that all three- and four-way interactions are zero. In addition, the model cannot be fitted when all two-way interactions are included, because X would not be orthogonal, and $X'X$ would have no inverse. There would be more unknowns (parameters) than equations (rows in X). This design has a Resolution of III, that is, two-way interactions are confounded with one another. When estimating parameters, only up to three of the six two-way interactions can be uniquely estimated. When the outcome variable is categorical, this design is saturated.

From the perspective of interpreting types and antitypes, it is important to remember that main effects in metric variables correspond to two-way interactions in categorical variables. Therefore, a design such as the one in Table 12.1 is of interest in CFA only if a zero order base model (that is, a null model) is considered. The fact that some of the two-way interactions are confounded places constraints on the interpretability of types and antitypes. The foregoing list of confounds shows which of the two-way interactions (main effects in categorical variables) can be estimated, but they are confounded. If any of these two-way interactions turns out to be significant, all one can conclude is that either this or the corresponding confounded interaction, or both, are important. Which of the two-way interactions actually exist, remains unknown until a design with higher resolution is used. Thus, if types and antitypes emerge from this design, one can conclude that they are caused by, for instance, the interaction between variables A and D, B and C, or both; A and C, B and D, or both; or A and B, C and D, or both. If researchers wish to specify which of these interactions are the main causes for the emergence of types and antitypes, a design with Resolution level IV or higher needs to be implemented.

Data Example 2: Plackett-Burman Design with 4 Runs from 3 Factors; Resolution Level III. When the number of runs is small and the resolution level is the same, it can occur that designs that were created by using different models are the same. Consider the Plackett-Burman design with

TABLE 12.2. Plackett-Burman Design with 4 Runs from 3 Factors; Resolution Level III; All Interactions Included

Int.	Main Effects			2-Way Interactions			3-Way Interaction
I	A	B	C	AB	AC	BC	ABC
1	1	1	−1	1	−1	−1	−1
1	1	−1	1	−1	1	−1	−1
1	−1	1	1	−1	−1	1	−1
1	−1	−1	−1	1	1	1	−1

3 variables and 4 runs (Resolution Level = III) in the Intercept and Main Effect panels of Table 12.2. This design is identical to a Box-Hunter design with 3 variables and 4 runs.

Here again, the savings, measured in the number of runs, over the completely crossed design is 50%. The main effect vectors are mutually orthogonal. However, there are confounds with the two- and the three-way interactions. Specifically,

- $A = -BC$
- $B = -AC$
- $C = -AB$, and
- Intercept $I = -ABC$.

The design matrix for this design appears in Table 12.2.

Parameters for this model cannot be estimated unless confounded vectors are eliminated from the design matrix. Typically, the vectors for the interactions are taken out, reflecting the assumption that only the main effects are of interest (which is rarely the case in CFA). One has to make the assumption that none of the interactions explains important aspects of the data.

Data Example 3: Box-Hunter Design with 16 Runs from 5 Factors; Resolution Level V. Naturally, higher levels of resolution can be achieved only with more factors. The following example presents a Box-Hunter design in which 16 runs are realized for five factors. This design has a Resolution level of V. Table 12.3 displays the design matrix for the main effects.

The confounds in this design are as follows:

- $A = BCDE$
- $C = ABDE$
- $D = ABCE$
- $E = ABCD$
- $AB = CDE$
- $AC = BDE$

TABLE 12.3. Main Effects in Box-Hunter Design with 16 Runs from 5 Factors; Resolution Level V; Intercept Omitted

		Factor		
A	B	C	D	E
−1	−1	−1	−1	1
−1	−1	−1	1	−1
−1	−1	1	−1	−1
−1	−1	1	1	1
−1	1	−1	−1	−1
−1	1	−1	1	1
−1	1	1	−1	1
−1	1	1	1	−1
1	−1	−1	−1	−1
1	−1	−1	1	1
1	−1	1	−1	1
1	−1	1	1	−1
1	1	−1	−1	1
1	1	−1	1	−1
1	1	1	−1	−1
1	1	1	1	1

- $AD = BCE$
- $AE = BCD$
- $BC = ADE$
- $BD = ACE$
- $BE = ACD$
- $CD = ABE$
- $CE = ABD$
- $DE = ABC$, and
- Intercept $I = ABCDE$.

This confound pattern shows again how the sparsity of effects principle can be translated into a parsimonious design. If indeed three- and four-way effects are unimportant, then this design allows one to estimate main effects and two-way interactions that are mutually independent. In addition to the vector for the intercept, the design matrix will then include only the 5 vectors for the main effects and the 10 vectors for the two-way interactions. When the outcome variable is categorical, this model is saturated. Only if interactions are either set equal or taken out of the model, will a nonsaturated model result.

Models with a Resolution level of V are of interest when the relationships in pairs of variables are targeted. Methods of factor analysis, latent variables analysis, multidimensional scaling, cluster analysis, or correspondence analysis often start from similarity matrices (e.g., a correlation matrix) that only reflect the relationships in pairs of variables. Models with a Resolution level of V can also be of interest in P-CFA and logistic regression. This is illustrated in Data Example 4, below.

To illustrate the confounds, consider the researcher who first estimates the model for the current design that includes all 10 two-way interactions. This model can be estimated, and the parameters can be interpreted as indicated in the design matrix. For example, the parameter for the interaction effect between variables D and E is estimated using the vector $\{-1, -1, 1, 1, 1, 1, -1, -1, 1, 1, -1, -1, -1, -1, 1, 1\}$. The resulting parameter has the interpretation

$$\begin{aligned}
\lambda^{DE} = 1/16(&- \log m_{22221} - \log m_{22221} + \log m_{22122} + \log m_{22111} \\
&+ \log m_{21222} + \log m_{21211} - \log m_{21121} - \log m_{21112} \\
&+ \log m_{12222} + \log m_{12211} - \log m_{12121} - \log m_{12112} \\
&- \log m_{11221} - \log m_{11212} + \log m_{11122} + \log m_{11111}).
\end{aligned}$$

In this equation, a subscript of 1 corresponds to a score of 1 in the design matrix given in Table 12.3. A subscript of 2 corresponds to a score of -1. Now, in a follow-up step, the same researcher decides to estimate the hierarchical model that only includes the two-way interactions AB, AC, AD, AE, BC, BD, and BE. The interactions CD, CE, and DE are replaced by the three-way interactions ABE, ABD, and ABC. This model can also be estimated. However, because of $DE = ABC$, the three-way interaction, ABC, comes with exactly the same interpretation as the substituted two-way interaction DE, and $\lambda^{ABC} = \lambda^{DE}$. This applies accordingly to λ^{CD} and λ^{DE} because $\lambda^{DE} = \lambda^{ABC}$ and $\lambda^{CD} = \lambda^{ABE}$. Thus, because of these confounds, no new information is gained by replacing the three two-way interactions with the corresponding three-way interactions. In other words, substituting, in this type of design, a two-way interaction with its confounded three-way interaction makes sense only if the assumption is entertained that the two-way interaction is zero.

Designs with Resolution level V are positioned, in the analysis of categorical outcome variables, one resolution level above Plackett-Burman designs in the analysis of metric variables. Therefore, interactions of higher order that are untestable with screening designs can be examined using designs at Resolution level V. Specifically, at Resolution level V, one is able to examine all pairwise relationships between predictor and criterion variables. Interestingly, when the categorical variables in such a design are grouped into predictors and criteria, the model is not necessarily saturated. If one assumes that the p predictors are independent of one another and the q criterion variables are also independent of one another, the number of interactions that need to be part of the model is pq. This number is always less than or equal to the number $\binom{p+q}{2}$ of interactions for the model in which the distinction between predictors and criteria is not made and all pairwise interactions are estimated. The remaining degrees of freedom can be used to make statements about model fit or to include covariates.

Data Example 4: Box-Hunter Designs for P-CFA or Logistic Regression. Instead of creating designs based on resolution, we now create a design based on the analytic goals of a study that aims at the analysis of predictor-criterion relationships. Here, the analytic goals determine the required resolution. Consider P-CFA or a logistic regression model (Agresti, 2002; von Eye et al., 2005). Standard logistic regression models make no assumptions about interactions among predictors. Therefore, these models are often saturated in the predictors by default, and the standard design is completely crossed (if all predictors are categorical). The models typically focus on bivariate predictor-criterion relationships. To examine these relationships, two-way interactions are estimated. Higher order interactions are often deemed unimportant. In these cases, a fractional factorial design like the one shown in Data Example 3, that is, a design with Resolution level V, will do the job, at a savings of 50% of the cells.

To illustrate, suppose that variable A in Table 12.3 (Data Example 3) is the criterion variable in a logistic regression model, and variables B, C, D, and E are the predictors. If only the predictive power of individual predictors is of interest, the logistic regression model can be cast in the form of the following standard hierarchical log-linear model,

$$\log \hat{m} = \lambda + \lambda^{AB} + \lambda^{AC} + \lambda^{AD} + \lambda^{AE} + \lambda^{BCDE},$$

where $\hat{m}$ is the array of model frequencies, the λ are the model parameters, and the superscripts indicate the interacting variables. All lower order terms are implied. If the three-way interactions among pairs of predictors and the criterion are also of interest, the model becomes

$$\log \hat{m} = \lambda + \lambda^{ABC} + \lambda^{ABD} + \lambda^{ABE} + \lambda^{ACE} + \lambda^{ADE} + \lambda^{BCDE},$$

and if the four-way interactions among predictors and the criterion are of interest, the model becomes

$$\log \hat{m} = \lambda + \lambda^{ABCD} + \lambda^{ABCE} + \lambda^{ABDE} + \lambda^{ACDE} + \lambda^{BCDE}.$$

If the five-way interaction is included, the model becomes saturated. Based on the sparsity of effects principle, interactions become less and less interesting as their hierarchical order increases. If this applies to the interactions among the predictors also, the first of these logistic regression models can be made more parsimonious by setting the four- and three-way interactions among the predictors to zero. If (1) only the two-way interactions between predictors and the criterion are considered, and (2) the three- and four-way interactions among predictors are set to zero, we obtain the following hierarchical model:

$$\log \hat{m} = \lambda + \lambda^{AB} + \lambda^{AC} + \lambda^{AD} + \lambda^{AE} + \lambda^{BC} + \lambda^{BD} + \lambda^{BE} + \lambda^{CD} + \lambda^{CE} + \lambda^{CD}.$$

If (1) only the two-way interactions among predictors and the criterion are considered, and (2) only the four-way interaction is set to zero, we obtain the hierarchical model

$$\log \hat{m} = \lambda + \lambda^{AB} + \lambda^{AC} + \lambda^{AD} + \lambda^{AE} + \lambda^{BCD} + \lambda^{BCE} + \lambda^{BDE} + \lambda^{CDE}.$$

Other models can be specified in which both the order of interactions that involve predictors and criteria and the interactions among predictors are varied.

From the perspective of creating parsimonious designs, we now ask whether logistic regression parameters can be estimated, using fractional factorial designs. The model in Table 12.3 operates at Resolution level V. It thus allows one to estimate main effects and all two-way interactions such that they are not confounded with one another. Thus, if we set all three-, four-, and five-way interactions to zero, the second last of the above logistic regression models — that is, the one with only two-way interactions — can be estimated by using the Box-Hunter design in Table 12.3. To estimate the logistic regression model that includes three-way interactions, a Resolution level of VI is needed. A Box-Hunter design that allows one to estimate such a model requires six variables and 32 runs. The completely crossed factorial design for six variables would require 64 runs. For 64 runs, a Box-Hunter design for seven variables with a Resolution level of VII can be created, or a screening design with 11 variables with a Resolution level of IV. This last design would represent a savings of 96.88% over the completely crossed design, which has 2,028 cells.

12.3   Extended Data Example

In this section, we present a data example in which we explore the cross-time association structure of social welfare reception, and ask whether social welfare reception is related to depression (see von Eye & Bogat, 2006). In addition, we compare results from fractional and from completely crossed designs.

FIGURE 12.1. Social welfare (Medicaid) and depression.

In a study on the effects of social welfare on mental health in battered women, von Eye and Bogat (2006) asked (cf. Levendosky, Bogat, Davidson, & von Eye, 2000), whether depression is linked to receiving social welfare in the form of food stamps and Medicaid. Longitudinal data from six observation points are available, each collected at 1-year intervals. The first observation occurred during the last trimester of the women's pregnancy, and the second was 3 months after birth. The second observation was performed to collect information about the child. In the following analyses, we focus on the data from the third and the following three observation points. For the following illustration of the application of fractional factorial designs in the analysis of categorical outcome variables, we use the following measures:

- Social welfare (Medicaid) received at observation points 3, 4, 5, and 6 (*M3*, *M4*, *M5*, and *M6*; all scored as 1 = did not receive and 2 = did receive); and

- Depression at observation point 6 (*D6*; scored as 1 = below the cutoff for clinical-level depression and 2 = above cutoff; depression was measured by using the BDI; Beck, Ward, & Mendelson, 1961).

Completely crossed, these five variables span a contingency table with $2^5 = 32$ cells. For the following analyses, we hypothesize that

1. Social welfare (Medicaid) reception predicts itself over time; and

2. At Time 6, social welfare reception predicts concurrent depression.

This model is depicted in Figure 12.1.

The model in Figure 12.1 shows that only two-way interactions are needed to test the hypothesized relationships. From a modeling perspective, the hierarchical log-linear model that corresponds to this graphical model is

$$\log \hat{m} = \lambda + \lambda^{M3,M4} + \lambda^{M4,M5} + \lambda^{M5,M6} + \lambda^{M6,D6}.$$

This model can be enriched by also testing whether social welfare reception at observation points 3, 4, and 5 is also predictive of depression at Time 6, above and beyond their auto-regressive chain effect via $M6$. The enriched model is

$$\log \hat{m} = \lambda + \lambda^{M3,M4} + \lambda^{M4,M5} + \lambda^{M5,M6} + \lambda^{M6,D6} + \lambda^{M3,D6} + \lambda^{M4,D6} + \lambda^{M5,D6},$$

where the new interactions appear in the last three terms of the equation. The interactions tested in the enriched model are also two-way interactions. An analysis of this model based on all 32 cells of the complete cross-classification comes with a maximum of 32 degrees of freedom. Of these, 16, that is, 50%, are needed for the three-, four-, and five-way interactions that are not of interest, as they are not included in the model depicted in Figure 12.1 or in the enriched model. Therefore, there is no need to screen women in all 32 cells of the design. Instead, a more parsimonious design will allow one to make a decision concerning the parameters in these models as well as about overall model fit.

A fractional factorial design that, in categorical variable analysis, allows one to estimate all two-way interactions so that they are not confounded with main effects or one another requires Resolution level V. The Box-Hunter design given in Table 12.3 has these characteristics. Therefore, we employ, for the following analyses, this design. Table 12.4 shows the design matrix with all two-way interactions that are part of the model in Figure 12.1 and the enriched model. The design has 16 runs. This represents a savings of 50% over the completely crossed design, which has 32 cells. A complete cross-classification table is shown in Table 12.7.

In the following paragraphs, we present four applications of CFA to the social welfare data. These include the first applications of CFA to fractional factorial designs reported in the literature:

1. First order CFA of the social welfare data created for the fractional factorial design application in Table 12.4. Only main effects are included in the base model. If types and antitypes emerge, they must be caused by two-way interactions. The model is

$$\log \hat{m} = \lambda + \lambda^{M3} + \lambda^{M4} + \lambda^{M5} + \lambda^{M6} + \lambda^{D6}.$$

2. First order CFA of the social welfare data created for the completely crossed design in Table 12.7. Again, only main effects are included in the model (first order CFA). However, because higher order effects can, in principle, exist, types and antitypes can be caused by interactions of any order. Based on the enriched log-linear model discussed above, we conclude, based on the completely crossed design, that there are no higher order interactions needed to explain this data set ($LR - X^2 = 29.96; df = 19; p = 0.052$). Therefore, the type-antitype patterns are expected to be very

TABLE 12.4. Box-Hunter Design with 16 Runs from Five Factors; Resolution = V; Intercept Omitted; Interactions Included for the Model in Figure 12.1 and the Enriched Model; Cell Frequencies in Last Column

Main Effects[a]					Two-Way Interactions							m
−1	−1	−1	−1	1	1	1	1	−1	−1	−1	−1	45
−1	−1	−1	1	−1	1	1	−1	−1	1	1	1	0
−1	−1	1	−1	−1	1	−1	−1	1	1	1	−1	0
−1	−1	1	1	1	1	−1	1	1	−1	−1	1	2
−1	1	−1	−1	−1	−1	−1	1	1	1	−1	1	0
−1	1	−1	1	1	−1	−1	−1	1	−1	1	−1	0
−1	1	1	−1	1	−1	1	−1	−1	−1	1	1	1
−1	1	1	1	−1	−1	1	1	−1	1	−1	−1	1
1	−1	−1	−1	−1	−1	1	1	1	−1	1	1	0
1	−1	−1	1	1	−1	1	−1	1	1	−1	−1	1
1	−1	1	−1	1	−1	−1	−1	−1	1	−1	1	2
1	−1	1	1	−1	−1	−1	1	−1	−1	1	−1	1
1	1	−1	−1	1	1	−1	1	−1	1	1	−1	7
1	1	−1	1	−1	1	−1	−1	−1	−1	−1	1	0
1	1	1	−1	−1	1	1	−1	1	−1	−1	−1	1
1	1	1	1	1	1	1	1	1	1	1	1	55

[a]Note that the codes −1 and 1 represent 1 (= did receive social welfare) and 2 (= did not receive social welfare), respectively, based on the original codes (see also the Appendix to this chapter). The codes for $D6$ indicate 1 = low depression (originally 1) and −1 = high depression (originally 2).

similar in the analyses for the completely crossed and the fractional factorial designs. The base model for this analysis is the same as the base model for the first analysis.

3. The first two applications use straight main effect base models. None of the interactions is included. Therefore, in principle, types and antitypes can emerge from those two-way interactions that link earlier social welfare reception with depression at Time 6, that is, from those two-way interactions among the social welfare scores that were not included in the model. Specifically, these are the interactions $[M3, M5]$, $[M3, M6]$, $[M4, M6]$, $[M3, D6]$, $[M4, D6]$, and $[M5, D6]$. The good fit of the enriched model (not reported in detail here) suggests that none of these terms is needed to explain the social welfare data in the fractional design. Here, we focus on the long-term prediction of depression, and we ask whether including the interactions $[M3, D6]$, $[M4, D6]$, and $[M5, D6]$ in the base model alters the pattern of types and antitypes from the first CFA. Therefore, we now include these interactions in the base model. If types and antitypes still emerge, they indicate the relationships among the variables that are depicted in Figure 12.1, and, possibly, additional cross-time relationships among the social welfare scores. The model for CFA thus becomes

$$\log \hat{m} = \lambda + \lambda^{M3} + \lambda^{M4} + \lambda^{M5} + \lambda^{M6} + \lambda^{D6} + \lambda^{M3,D6} + \lambda^{M4,D6} + \lambda^{M5,D6}.$$

4. Same as CFA 3, just from the completely crossed design.

CFA 1: First-Order CFA from Fractional Factorial Design: For the base model in this application, we use the design matrix that is displayed in the main effects panel of Table 12.4. To perform the cell-wise tests, we use the z-test, and we protect α by using the Holland-Copenhaver procedure. Table 12.5 displays results of this CFA.

The base model does not fit, $LR - X^2 = 218.16$, $df = 10$, $p < .01$. Correspondingly, the results in Table 12.5 show that CFA identified two types and five antitypes. The first type, constituted by Configuration 1 1 1 1 1, indicates that more women than expected with reference to the base model exhibit low depression when they never received Medicaid or food stamps over the entire observation period. The second type, constituted by Configuration 2 2 2 2 1, shows that more women than expected who did receive social welfare over the entire observation period show also below-threshold depression. These two types seem to suggest that having received Medicaid or food stamps is unrelated to later depression (see von Eye & Bogat, 2006).

However, the five antitypes show that a relationship between social welfare and depression does exist. The first antitype, constituted by

TABLE 12.5. First Order CFA of Fractional Factorial Design for Social Welfare Data

Configuration[a] M3 M4 M5 M6 D6	m	$\hat{m}$	z	p	Type/Antitype
11111	45	9.285	11.7205	.000000	Type
11122	0	.263	−.5132	.303913	
11212	0	.293	−.5410	.294242	
11221	2	11.776	−2.8489	.002194	Antitype
12112	0	.314	−.5603	.287631	
12121	0	12.631	−3.5540	.000190	Antitype
12211	1	14.039	−3.4800	.000251	Antitype
12222	1	.398	.9537	.170110	
21112	0	.337	−.5804	.280815	
21121	1	13.553	−3.4099	.000325	Antitype
21211	2	15.065	−3.3660	.000381	Antitype
21222	1	.427	.8762	.190459	
22111	7	16.158	−2.2782	.011356	
22122	0	.458	−.6770	.249217	
22212	1	.509	.6875	.245899	
22221	55	20.492	7.6229	.000000	Type

[a]Configuration labels indicate, for M3-M6: 1 = Did not receive social welfare; 2 = did receive social welfare; D6: 1 = low depression; 2 = high depression. (See the footnote under the design matrix in Table 12.4.)

Configuration 1 1 2 2 1, suggests that fewer women than expected show below-threshold, subclinical-level depression when they were placed on social welfare reception between Time 4 and Time 5. Similarly, fewer women than expected show subclinical-level depression when they received social welfare only at Times 4 and 6 (Antitype 1 2 1 2 1). The same applies when social welfare was received only at Times 4 and 5 (Antitype 1 2 2 1 1). The remaining antitypes (2 1 1 2 1 and 2 1 2 1 1) also show that fewer than expected women who experience an unstable pattern of social welfare reception are able to remain at below-threshold depression. We thus conclude that stability in social welfare reception over time seems to be linked to subclinical levels of depression. In contrast, unstable patterns of social welfare reception make it less likely than expected to maintain low levels of depression.

CFA 2: First-Order CFA from Completely Crossed Design: First-order CFA of the table from the completely crossed factors of the social welfare data also used the z-test and the Holland-Copenhaver procedure. In addition, the log-linear base model was the same as before. However, the design matrix was that of a completely crossed design instead of a fractional factorial design. If the fractional design does not lead to a distortion of the relationships in the table, results of the two analyses should be largely the same, even at the level of individual cells. Indeed, the results (not shown here) show strong overlap with the results from the fractional design. Specifically, the overall model for the completely crossed design did not fit, $LR - X^2 = 292.16$, $df = 26$, $p < 0.01$. In addition, the same types, 1 1 1 1 1 and 2 2 2 2 1, surfaced again.

However, the results from the fully crossed design differ from the ones for the fractional design in a few interesting ways. Specifically, none of the configurations that previously constituted antitypes differed from expectation strongly enough to constitute antitypes again, under the stricter levels of α protection that result for the larger table. Therefore, we asked whether they constitute a composite antitype (see von Eye, 2002a). The Stouffer $Z = -5.78$ ($p < 0.01$) suggests that this is the case. We, therefore, conclude that this difference between the two analyses may be due to the stricter α levels that result from α protection in larger tables. Equally important is that a new type emerged. It is constituted by Configuration 2 2 2 2 2, indicating that those women who received social welfare annually throughout the 4-year period are more likely than expected to show clinical-level depression. Types 2 2 2 2 2 and 2 2 2 2 1 differ only in the last digit. Therefore, they can be aggregated. The five antitypes were constituted by Configurations 1 1 1, 1 2 2, 2 1 1, 2 2 2, and 2 3 1. Of these, two aggregate antitypes can be created: the first and third and the second and fourth antitypes can be aggregated. Specifically, when aggregating the first and third antitypes, we obtain the composite antitype

$$\begin{array}{c} 1\ 1\ 1 \\ \underline{2\ 1\ 1} \\ .\ 1\ 1 \end{array}$$

From aggregating the second and fourth antitypes, we obtain

$$\begin{array}{c} 1\ 2\ 2 \\ \underline{2\ 2\ 2} \\ .\ 2\ 2 \end{array}$$

From aggregating the types 2 2 2 2 1 and 2 2 2 2 2, we obtain

$$\begin{array}{c} 2\ 2\ 2\ 2\ 1 \\ \underline{2\ 2\ 2\ 2\ 2} \\ 2\ 2\ 2\ 2\ . \end{array}$$

to form the aggregated type 2 2 2 2 ., where the . indicates the variable aggregated over. The aggregated type suggests that more women than

TABLE 12.6. CFA of Fractional Factorial Design for Social Welfare Data; Design Matrix Given in the First and Third Panels of Table 12.4

Configuration M3 M4 M5 M6 D6	m	$\hat{m}$	z	p	Type/Antitype
11111	45	9.610	11.416	.000000	Type
11122	0	0	−.000	.499996	
11212	0	.312	−.559	.282716	
11221	2	11.690	−2.834	.002298	Antitype
12112	0	0.001	−.028	.499995	
12121	0	13.017	−3.608	.000154	Antitype
12211	1	13.682	−3.429	.000303	Antitype
12222	1	.688	.376	.343199	
21112	0	0.001	−.028	.499995	
21121	1	13.992	−3.473	.000257	Antitype
21211	2	14.707	−3.313	.000416	Antitype
21222	1	.688	.376	.439396	
22111	7	16.377	−2.317	.010251	
22122	0	0.002	−.042	.499994	
22212	1	1.311	−.272	.447382	
22221	55	19.922	7.859	.000000	Type

expected under the assumption of variable independence received social welfare in all 4 years, and that receiving social welfare for 4 years in a row, in and of itself, does not increase one's risk for clinical-level depression. Clearly, this result is an example that shows that CFA can lead to a more detailed and differing description of the relationships in data than log-linear modeling.

CFA 3: Long-Term Prediction of Depression: CFA from Fractional Factorial Design: In the following sample application, we ask whether those of the six interactions that would suggest long-term predictability of depression from social welfare reception indeed play no role in the detection of types and antitypes in the social welfare data. These are the interactions $[M3, D6]$, $[M4, D6]$, and $[M5, D6]$. None of these is among the interactions that were needed to explain the data. Another way of presenting this analysis is that we ask which types and antitypes emerge when we no longer consider the associations among the social welfare scores $M3$, $M4$, and $M5$ and depression at Time 6. The log-linear base model for this CFA is

$$\log \hat{m} = \lambda + \lambda^{M3} + \lambda^{M4} + \lambda^{M5} + \lambda^{M6} + \lambda^{D6} + \lambda^{M3,D6} + \lambda^{M4,D6} + \lambda^{M5,D6}.$$

Considering that (1) the design for this analysis is fractional factorial with Resolution at level V (three- and higher-way interactions either cannot be estimated or are confounded), and (2), the two-way interactions [M3, M4], [M4, M5], [M5, M6], and [M6, D6] are not part of the base model, types and antitypes from this CFA base model reflect, by necessity, the cross time associations among the social welfare reception variables, and the association between social welfare reception and depression, at Time 6. If the three interactions [M3, D6], [M4, D6], and [M5, D6] indeed play no role in the detection of types and antitypes in the social welfare data, the same types and antitypes will emerge from this analysis, as in the first data example (first order CFA base model). The design matrix for this design appears in the first and the third panels of Table 12.4. For the CFA that uses this design matrix in its base model, we again employ the z-test and the Holland-Copenhaver procedure. The overall goodness-of-fit $LR - X^2$ for the model that uses the fractional factorial design is 214.15 ($df = 7$; $p < 0.01$). This indicates major discrepancies between model and data, and also provides evidence that predicting depression from social welfare over a span of more than 2 years does not add unique information above and beyond the effects on depression of receiving social welfare concurrently. We thus can expect types and antitypes to emerge. Table 12.6 displays the results of this CFA.

The CFA types and antitypes in Table 12.6 are, with no exception, identical to the ones in Table 12.5. We thus conclude that the long-term associations between social welfare reception and depression have no effect on the pattern of types and antitypes. In other words, there are no lagged effects of social welfare on depression. Therefore, the types and antitypes in Tables 12.5 and 12.6 result solely from the cross-time associations among the social welfare scores and the concurrent association of social welfare reception and depression at Time 6.

Note that alternative base models are conceivable. For example, instead of asking which effects do not cause the types and antitypes in Table 12.5, one can ask which effects do cause these types and antitypes. To answer this question, a base model is needed that includes the cross-time associations among the social welfare scores and the association between social welfare and depression at T6. This is the base model

$$\log \hat{m} = \lambda + \lambda^{M3} + \lambda^{M4} + \lambda^{M5} + \lambda^{M6} + \lambda^{D6} + \lambda^{M3,M4} + \lambda^{M4,M5} + \lambda^{M5,M6} + \lambda^{M5,D6}.$$

If the interactions in this model are the causes for the types and antitypes in Table 12.5, they all will disappear under this base model (they do).

CFA 4: Long-Term Prediction of Depression: CFA from Completely Crossed Design: Using the table from the completely crossed variables and the hierarchical log-linear base model that includes the three interactions [M3, D6], [M4, D6], and [M5, D6], we obtain CFA results that mirror the ones from the second CFA, above (details not shown here). Configurations 1 1 1 1 1 and 2 2 2 2 1 constitute types. Also as before, each of the configurations that constituted antitypes in the first analysis was observed less frequently than expected, and the composite antitype exists. The additional type was not observed again. Thus, these results are even closer to the ones from Data Example 3 than the results from Data Example 2 were to the ones from Data Example 1.

We conclude that using the fractional factorial design can lead to appraisals of data structures that differ only minimally from those found by using the complete design.

12.4   Chapter Summary

The *Sparsity of Effects Principle* proposes that most systems (1) are carried by a small number of effects, and (2) these effects are of low order. If this principle applies, designs may be wasteful that allow one to model those higher order effects that (1) may not exist in the first place, (2) may be hard to interpret when they exist, and (3) may explain only minuscule portions of variability, when they exist.

Therefore, it is proposed to adopt fractional factorial designs into the canon of methods for the analysis of categorical data. Fractional designs are discussed that are orthogonal and contain only a fraction of the cells of a complete design. Because the number of cells is smaller, these designs allow one to estimate only lower order effects. Depending on the number of cells, higher order effects may be estimable without confound. The highest order effects can be estimated only when a design is complete.

For analysis with CFA, this chapter focuses on Box-Hunter designs. These are fractional factorial designs for binary variables. It is shown that, to be able to estimate effects of a particular order, one needs a design with a higher resolution (more cells) than one would need for an analysis in the context of the General Linear Model. As in standard CFA of completely crossed designs, CFA focuses on configurations instead of relationships among variables. Resulting types and antitypes are interpreted as usual, based on (1) the meaning of the categories that define a configuration and (2) the base model. The only difference to a standard, completely crossed design is that the choice of base models is limited by the level of effect that a design allows one to estimate.

To be able to employ a fractional factorial design in categorical data analysis, standard observational methods of data collection can no longer be applied. Screening of respondents is needed. Only those respondents who display the profile needed for a fractional design are included in a

TABLE 12.7. Complete Cross-Classification for the Social Welfare Data Example

M3	M4	M5	M6	T6 Depression [D6][a] 1	2
1	1	1	1	**45**	2
1	1	1	2	5	**0**
1	1	2	1	4	**0**
1	1	2	2	**2**	0
1	2	1	1	2	**0**
1	2	1	2	**0**	0
1	2	2	1	**1**	0
1	2	2	2	5	**1**
2	1	1	1	7	**0**
2	1	1	2	**1**	0
2	1	2	1	**2**	1
2	1	2	2	4	**1**
2	2	1	1	7	0
2	2	1	2	4	**0**
2	2	2	1	9	**1**
2	2	2	2	**55**	9

[a]Bold-faced numbers in the last two columns indicate observed frequencies shown in Tables 12.4, 12.5, and 12.6 with Box-Hunter design with 16 runs.

study. In an empirical example, the same data are analyzed using the fractional part of the design as well as the complete part. It is illustrated that fractional designs can yield the same results as complete designs. This applies in particular when the sparsity of effects principle applies.

13

Computational Issues

Chapter 13 presents computer applications of programs that can be obtained free of charge. The application of three programs is demonstrated. The first of these is a stand-alone, specialized CFA program. The second program is a package in the R environment for statistical computing. The third program is ℓEM, a general program for the analysis of categorical data. The first two programs provide output that is specific to CFA. ℓEM does not allow one to directly test CFA hypotheses. However, as is shown, the output of ℓEM contains information that can be used for CFA. The detailed applications are described in Chapter 13 and are presented step by step on the book's companion website, which can be accessed from www.guilford.com/p/voneye.

In this chapter, we present sample commands for a selection of the CFA models proposed in this book, using several programs. Our focus is on base models that are log-linear. CFA can be performed by using most of the log-linear modules in specialized or general-purpose statistical software packages or using specialized CFA programs. In this chapter, we illustrate the application of three program packages, all of which can be obtained free of charge. The first package is a specialized CFA package (von Eye, 2007). It can be requested by sending an e-mail to voneye@msu.edu. The second program is a new CFA package within the R environment (Funke, Mair, & von Eye, 2008). This program can be downloaded from the website of the R Development Core Team (2007), http://www.R-project.org, also free of charge. It requires that the R kernel be available, which can be downloaded from the same web site. The third program is ℓEM, a general program for the analysis of categorical data (Vermunt, 1997). It can be downloaded from http://www.uvt.nl/faculteiten/fsw/organisatie/departementen/mto/software2.html, also free of charge.

13.1   A CFA Program

In the following sections, we first describe a specialized CFA program. Then, we present application examples.

13.1.1   Description of CFA Program

The CFA program was written in FORTRAN 90 and compiled by using the MS PowerStation. It contains two subroutines from *Numerical Recipes* (Press, Flannery, Teukolsky, & Vetterling, 1989). These subroutines, used for the z- and the χ^2-tests, are part of the PowerStation. The program was compiled and tested under the 32-bit Windows operating systems XP Professional, Vista Business, and Windows 7 Professional.

The CFA program is interactive and keyboard-oriented. Data are either read from ASCII files (raw data or frequency tables) or interactively typed in via the keyboard when prompted (frequency tables). Output is written into ASCII files that can be read by using virtually any word processor. The current version of the CFA program (the most recent change was implemented in 2009) has the following characteristics:

- Size of executable program file: 410 KB
- Operating systems: Windows XP, Windows Vista, Windows 7
- Number of subroutines: 37
- Input options:

     Raw data: from ASCII files

     Frequency tables: from ASCII files or keyboard
- Output: written into ASCII file; parts of output appear on screen
- Number of variables that can be simultaneously analyzed: up to 10
- Number of categories per variable: up to 9
- Memory allocation: dynamic
- Variants of CFA: This CFA program can, in principle, perform any model that can be expressed as a log-linear model. A selection of frequently used models is preprogrammed. These are (1) all global base models, that is, zero order, first order, second order, and any higher order base models, and (2) two-group models. Any other models as well as the search algorithms described in Chapters 6 (mediation), 8 (moderation), and 10 (functional CFA) can be applied also, but some of the design matrices for these models need to be typed in vector-by-vector. For models with covariates, the covariates need to be typed in, cell-wise. The same applies to models with special effects.

- Statistical tests for global base models:

   Exact binomial test (CFA Option 1)

   Binomial test that uses Stirling's approximation of factorials (CFA Option 2)

   Pearson's X^2 test (CFA Option 3)

   z-test (CFA Option 4)

   Normal approximation of the binomial test (CFA Option 5)

   Lehmacher's asymptotic hypergeometric test (CFA Option 6)

   Lehmacher's test with Küchenhoff's continuity correction (CFA Option 7)

   Anscombe's z approximation (CFA Option 8)

   The Freeman-Tukey test (CFA Option 9)

- Statistical tests for two-group CFA:

   X^2 test for 2×2 tables

   X^2 test with continuity correction

   Normal approximation of the binomial test

   z-test

   λ, the log-linear interaction with a significance test that is based on jackknife procedures

   $\tilde{\lambda}$ the marginal-dependent version of λ (Goodman, 1991) with a jackknife significance test

   ρ, the correlation in 2×2 tables with a significance test that is based on jackknife procedures

   δ, the absolute value of ρ with a significance test that is based on jackknife procedures;

   θ, the marginal-free log-odds ratio plus asymptotic significance test.

- Descriptive measures for global CFA:

   Relative risk ratio, RR (see DuMouchel, 1999)

   $\log P$, the Poisson probability of the observed cell frequency, given the estimated expected cell frequency.

   Rank of RR

   Rank of $\log P$

- Descriptive measure for two-group CFA: coefficient π, which describes the goodness-of-fit in cross-classifications (Rudas, Clogg, & Lindsay, 1994); here, the variant for 2×2 tables is used (Gonzáles-Debén & Méndez-Ramírez, 2000).
- Additional significance test: Stouffer's Z to test hypotheses about composite types or composite antitypes
- Protection of α: Three procedures are currently available:

  Bonferroni (Option 1)

  Holm (Option 2)

  Holland-Copenhaver (Option 3)

13.1.2   Sample Applications

In this section, we present sample applications of the CFA program. The applications exemplify models discussed in this text. For additional examples, see von Eye (2002a). For readers to replicate the sample runs presented in this section, they need the executable program file CFA.EXE. When an ASCII data file is read, this file needs to be in the same directory as the program file. If this is not the case, the complete path to the data file needs to be typed in.

Data Example 1: Multiple, Multivariate Prediction CFA with Multiple Predictors: For this illustration, we use the example from Table 5.13. Violence at Time 1 ($V1$) and Time 2 ($V2$) is used to predict PTSD at Time 2 ($P2$) and Time 3 ($P3$). As was indicated in Section 5.1.2, the cross-classification $V1 \times V2 \times P2 \times P3$ is analyzed by using the P-CFA base model

$$\log \hat{m} = \lambda + \lambda^{V1} + \lambda^{V2} + \lambda^{V1,V2} + \lambda^{P2} + \lambda^{P3} + \lambda^{P2,P3},$$

where the double-superscripted terms indicate two-way interactions. From this base model, types and antitypes can emerge only if there is a relationship between violence and PTSD. For this example of P-CFA, we use the z-test and the Holland-Copenhaver procedure. The following steps result in a P-CFA of the violence data. The table is typed in via the keyboard.

- Click shortcut to CFA program: Starts CFA program; black program window appears on screen; the program asks the user whether data will be input via file (= 1) or interactively (= 2). For this example, we select interactive data input and type "2".

- The program responds by asking for the number of variables. For our example, type "2". This number indicates that we use both the two predictors and the two criterion variables as two composite variables. The composites result from crossing the variables that constitute the composite. For example, the variable Violence has two categories. Crossed with each other, the two observations of violence constitute four combinations. These combinations are the categories of the new composite violence variable. This applies accordingly for the composite PTSD variable. Note that, alternatively, we could tell the program that there are four variables. If we do this, the interaction vector for the violence variables and the interaction vector for the PTSD variables need to be typed in as two covariates. The results from these two approaches will be identical, in overall goodness-of-fit, degrees of freedom, and the emerging type and antitype pattern.

• The program now asks for the number of categories of the first (composite) variable. We type "4".

• To indicate the number of categories of the second (composite) variable, we type "4".

• The program now presents the number of cells of the table, and it prompts the individual cell frequencies. For the first cell, 1 1, we type "82" as the cell frequency (see Table 5.13). For Cell 1 2, we type "7". This is done until all 16 cell frequencies are typed in, one-by-one. The program responds by presenting the sample size ($N = 204$) and by asking whether we wish to save the frequency table. We indicate that "yes" by typing "1".

• The name of the data file is then given by typing "V1V2P2P3.dat" (the maximum length of the name plus path is 80 characters).

• The program follows up by asking about the base model for this analysis. We type "1" to request that a first order CFA be performed. By forming the composite variables, all main effects and the associations between the two violence observations and between the two PTSD observations are taken into account.

• The program now needs to know whether the Delta option of adding a constant to each cell is invoked. We type "2" to indicate that no constant is added to each cell. The program responds by presenting the marginal frequencies. In the present example, these are the cell frequencies of the 4 × 4 cross-classifications of the violence and the PTSD variables.

• The program now asks whether covariates will be typed in. To indicate that this is not the case, we type "2".

• In response, the program presents the currently available nine options for type/antitype tests. We select the z-test and type "4". To set the significance threshold to 0.05, we type ".05", and to select the Holland-Copenhaver procedure of α protection, we type "3".

• The program now requests the name of the output file. We type "V1V2P2P3.out".

• The program then responds by asking whether we wish to test hypotheses about composite types or composite antitypes. In the present example, we do not entertain such hypotheses and type "2".

• Finally, by typing "1" we indicate that we would like the design matrix included in the output file. The program window now disappears, and the output file is complete. The output file V1V2P2P3.out can be accessed in the same directory as the program file, CFA.EXE.

The above series of commands resulted in the following (slightly edited) output file, V1V2P2P3.out:

```
              Configural Frequency Analysis
              ---------- --------- --------
       author of program: Alexander von Eye, 2002
                    last revision: March 2007
     Marginal Frequencies
     --------------------

     Variable Frequencies
     -------- -----------
        1      149.   17.   19.   19.
        2       85.   10.   61.   48.


   sample size N =        204
   the normal z-test was used
              with Holland-Copenhaver protection
   a CFA of order   1  was performed


                            Table of results
                            ----- -- -------
   Configuration    fo      fe   statistic      p
   -------------   ----  --------  --------   -------
           11     82.00  62.083    2.5277    .005740
           12      7.00   7.304    -.1125    .455231
           13     47.00  44.554     .3665    .357011
           14     13.00  35.059   -3.7255    .000097    Antitype
           21      3.00   7.083   -1.5342    .062484
           22      3.00    .833    2.3735    .008811
           23       .00   5.083   -2.2546    .012078
           24     11.00   4.000    3.5000    .000233    Type
```

31	.00	7.917	-2.8137	.002449	Antitype
32	.00	.931	-.9651	.167253	
33	12.00	5.681	2.6509	.004014	Type
34	7.00	4.471	1.1963	.115791	
41	.00	7.917	-2.8137	.002449	Antitype
42	.00	.931	-.9651	.167253	
43	2.00	5.681	-1.5445	.061236	
44	17.00	4.471	5.9258	.000000	Type

```
        chi2 for CFA model = 109.4
            df =    9     p =  .00000000
     LR-chi2 for CFA model =  114.5
            df =    9     p =  .00000000
```

Descriptive indicators of types and antitypes
----

cell	Rel. Risk	Rank	logP	Rank
11	1.321	6	2.18342	4
12	.958	8	.325107	10
13	1.055	7	.717484	8
14	.371	10	3.59177	2
21	.424	9	.387703	9
22	3.600	2	1.28143	6
23	.000	12	.000000	16
24	2.750	3	2.54978	3
31	.000	16	.000000	14
32	.000	13	.000000	15
33	2.112	4	1.86858	5
34	1.566	5	.799061	7
41	.000	14	.000000	13
42	.000	15	.000000	12
43	.352	11	.322998	11
44	3.803	1	5.31589	1

Design Matrix
------ ------

```
  .0    .0    .0   1.0    .0   1.0
  .0   1.0    .0   1.0    .0    .0
  .0    .0   1.0   1.0    .0    .0
  .0  -1.0  -1.0   1.0    .0  -1.0
  .0    .0    .0    .0   1.0   1.0
  .0   1.0    .0    .0   1.0    .0
  .0    .0   1.0    .0   1.0    .0
  .0  -1.0  -1.0    .0   1.0  -1.0
 1.0    .0    .0    .0    .0   1.0
 1.0   1.0    .0    .0    .0    .0
 1.0    .0   1.0    .0    .0    .0
 1.0  -1.0  -1.0    .0    .0  -1.0
-1.0    .0    .0  -1.0  -1.0   1.0
```

```
-1.0    1.0     .0  -1.0  -1.0     .0
-1.0     .0    1.0  -1.0  -1.0     .0
-1.0  -1.0   -1.0  -1.0  -1.0  -1.0
```

CARPE DIEM

Reading from the top, this output can be interpreted as follows. After information about the version of the program, the first numerical information contains the marginal frequencies of the two four-category composite variables that we created for the current run. Note that this part of the output is different from the one reproduced in Table 5.13, where we had used the four individual variables plus the interactions between $V1$ and $V2$ and between $P2$ and $P3$. The design matrix for the run in Table 5.13 is shown below (constant vector is implied).

$$X = \begin{pmatrix}
1 & 1 & 1 & 1 & 1 & 1 \\
1 & 1 & 1 & -1 & 1 & -1 \\
1 & 1 & -1 & 1 & 1 & -1 \\
1 & 1 & -1 & -1 & 1 & 1 \\
1 & -1 & 1 & 1 & -1 & 1 \\
1 & -1 & 1 & -1 & -1 & -1 \\
1 & -1 & -1 & 1 & -1 & -1 \\
1 & -1 & -1 & -1 & -1 & 1 \\
-1 & 1 & 1 & 1 & -1 & 1 \\
-1 & 1 & 1 & -1 & -1 & -1 \\
-1 & 1 & -1 & 1 & -1 & -1 \\
-1 & 1 & -1 & -1 & -1 & 1 \\
-1 & -1 & 1 & 1 & 1 & 1 \\
-1 & -1 & 1 & -1 & 1 & -1 \\
-1 & -1 & -1 & 1 & 1 & -1 \\
-1 & -1 & -1 & -1 & 1 & 1
\end{pmatrix}$$

The design matrix for the current run (4 × 4 table) is

$$X = \begin{pmatrix} 1 & 0 & 0 & 1 & 0 & 0 \\ 1 & 0 & 0 & 0 & 1 & 0 \\ 1 & 0 & 0 & 0 & 0 & 1 \\ 1 & 0 & 0 & -1 & -1 & -1 \\ 0 & 1 & 0 & 1 & 0 & 0 \\ 0 & 1 & 0 & 0 & 1 & 0 \\ 0 & 1 & 0 & 0 & 0 & 1 \\ 0 & 1 & 0 & -1 & -1 & -1 \\ 0 & 0 & 1 & 1 & 0 & 0 \\ 0 & 0 & 1 & 0 & 1 & 0 \\ 0 & 0 & 1 & 0 & 0 & 1 \\ 0 & 0 & 1 & -1 & -1 & -1 \\ -1 & -1 & -1 & 1 & 0 & 0 \\ -1 & -1 & -1 & 0 & 1 & 0 \\ -1 & -1 & -1 & 0 & 0 & 1 \\ -1 & -1 & -1 & -1 & -1 & -1 \end{pmatrix}.$$

These two design matrices differ in the sense that, whereas the first allows one to estimate the main effect parameters of all four variables and the parameters for the $[V1, V2]$ and the $[P2, P3]$ interactions, the second treats the same frequencies as if they had been created for two variables with four categories each. However, the estimated expected cell frequencies and the overall model fit are exactly the same for both design matrices. The first design matrix can be created in the CFA program by indicating that four dichotomous variables are being used and then typing the last two vectors, that is, the interaction vectors, as covariates.

After the marginal frequencies, the program indicates the size of the sample and confirms the selections of significance test, the procedure for the protection of α, and the base model. The Table of results contains the observed and the estimated expected frequencies for each of the 16 cells, the test statistic, its one-sided tail probability, and the type/antitype decision.

The next block of output information contains the Pearson and the $LR - X^2$ tests for the base model. If these tests indicate that the base model describes the data well, types and antitypes are extremely unlikely to emerge. In the present example, the base model was rejected, and types and antitypes did emerge.

The next block of information contains the descriptive information specified above. It is interesting to see that the rank orders of the relative risk measure and $\log P$ are strongly correlated ($r_s = 0.81$). Only Configuration 1 4 shows a larger discrepancy in rank.

The last block of output information presents the design matrix used for this run. It is identical to the one shown above (only the order of vectors is arranged differently, but this has no effect on results). CARPE DIEM means SEIZE THE DAY.

Data Example 2: Predicting a Trajectory: In the following example, we illustrate how the data example in Section 5.3 can be calculated. We reproduce Table 5.15 (the only difference between the present solution and the one in Table 5.15 is that here we use the Freeman-Tukey instead of the z-test; see below). In this example, we predict the development of physical aggression against peers (*PAAP*1 and *PAAP*2) from aggressive impulses (*AI*). The base model for predicting the *PAAP*1-*PAAP*2 trajectory from *AI* is

$$\log \hat{m} = \lambda + \lambda_i^{AI} + \lambda_j^{PAAP1} + \lambda_k^{PAAP2} + \lambda_{jk}^{PAAP1,PAAP2}.$$

As was discussed in Section 5.3, this model can be contradicted only if one or more of the following interactions exist: $[AI, PAAP1]$, $[AI, PAAP2]$, and $[AI, PAAP1, PAAP2]$. If types and antitypes emerge, they indicate trajectories that occur more likely or less likely than chance, conditional on *AI*.

As in the last example, the base model used here is not global. That is, not all possible two-way interactions are included. We have two options to incorporate the $[PAAP1, PAAP2]$ interaction into the base model. The first involves creating a composite variable by crossing *PAAP*1 with *PAAP*2. This option was illustrated in the first application example. The second option involves typing in the interaction vector in the form of a covariate. This option is illustrated in the present example. The following commands are issued:

• Click shortcut to CFA program: Starts CFA program; black program window appears on screen; the program asks whether data will be input via file (= 1) or interactively (= 2). For this example, we select interactive data input and type "2".

• The program responds by asking for the number of variables. We type "3".

• This is the real number of variables, as we do not use composite variables. The program now prompts, for each variable, the number of categories. In this example, all variables are dichotomous. Therefore, we answer each question by typing "2".

• The program now prompts the frequencies for each cell. We type "23" for Cell 1 1 1, "11" for Cell 1 1 2, and so forth, until the frequency table is completed (for the frequencies, see Table 5.15).

- We now type "1" to indicate that we wish to save the table, and we give the name of the file as "AIP1P2.dat".

- We now select the first order CFA base model by typing "1".

- We opt against invoking the Delta option by typing "2".

- The program now offers for covariates to be included. In this example, we need to type in the vector for the $[PAAP1, PAAP2]$ interaction. We type "1" to indicate that a covariate will be typed in.

- The program now prompts the cell-wise covariate scores. The vector that we include in the design matrix is $[1, -1, -1, 1, 1, -1, -1, 1]$. We type "1" for the first score, -1 for the second, and so forth until the entire vector is typed in.

- The program now asks whether we wish to include a second covariate, and it indicates that only two more covariates can be included before the model becomes saturated. Because we have no more covariates to include, we type "2".

- We then type "9" to select the Freeman-Tukey test, and ".05" to set the significance threshold to 0.05. We also type "3" which selects the Holland-Copenhaver procedure of α protection.

- We specify the name of the output file to be "AIP1P2.out" and by typing "2" we indicate that we do not wish to test hypotheses about composite types or antitypes.

- Finally, we type "1" which makes the program print the design matrix into the output file. This is the last question the program asks. The program window closes, and the output file can be opened.

The above commands result in the following, slightly edited output file, AIP1P2.out:

```
                    Configural Frequency Analysis
                    ---------- --------- --------
            author of program: Alexander von Eye, 2002
                         last revision: March 2007

        Marginal Frequencies
        --------------------
        Variable Frequencies
        -------- -----------
            1       54.      60.
            2       55.      59.
```

```
      3     50.   64.
   sample size N =        114
```

the Freeman-Tukey test was used
                with Holland-Copenhaver protection
a CFA of order   1 was performed

Table of results
----- -- -------

Configuration	fo	fe	statistic	p
111	23.00	14.684	1.9658	.024658
112	11.00	11.368	-.0364	.485468
121	10.00	9.000	.3961	.346001
122	10.00	18.947	-2.2841	.011184
211	8.00	16.316	-2.3118	.010395
212	13.00	12.632	.1690	.432888
221	9.00	10.000	-.2408	.404837
222	30.00	21.053	1.8140	.034836

```
             chi2 for CFA model = 17.21
             df =     3     p =  .00064005
          LR-chi2 for CFA model =  17.94
             df =     3     p =  .00045251
```

Descriptive indicators of types and antitypes
----

cell	Rel. Risk	Rank	logP	Rank
111	1.566	1	1.61491	1
112	.968	5	.388057	7
121	1.111	3	.470132	5
122	.528	7	1.03960	3
211	.490	8	.983709	4
212	1.029	4	.447687	6
221	.900	6	.338436	8
222	1.425	2	1.48532	2

Design Matrix
------ ------

```
  1.0   1.0   1.0   1.0
  1.0   1.0  -1.0  -1.0
  1.0  -1.0   1.0  -1.0
  1.0  -1.0  -1.0   1.0
 -1.0   1.0   1.0   1.0
 -1.0   1.0  -1.0  -1.0
 -1.0  -1.0   1.0  -1.0
 -1.0  -1.0  -1.0   1.0
```

                        CARPE DIEM

This output differs from the one in the first example in two important respects. First, the marginal frequencies are those of the original variables instead of composite variables. Second, the design matrix at the end of the output displays effects coding vectors for the main effects of the original variables and the interaction between the two PAAP observations instead of the main effects of composite variables. Thus, this output may be easier to interpret than the first. However, the price that must be paid for this ease of interpretation is that the effects coding vector for the $[PAAP1, PAAP2]$ interaction must be determined and typed into the program. As was said before, it does not matter whether composite variables are used or the original variables plus interactions. The estimated expected cell frequencies, the CFA test results, and the overall goodness-of-fit will be exactly the same.

The CFA tests in this output differ from the ones in Table 5.15 in that, here, we used the Freeman-Tukey test instead of the z-test. This was done to illustrate that the z-test typically has more power than the Freeman-Tukey test. In fact, with only one exception (Configuration 2 1 2), each of the tail probabilities here are larger than those in Table 5.15. The Freeman-Tukey test can be expected to suggest more conservative decisions than the z-test, under most conditions.

Data Example 3: Auto-Association CFA with Covariate: For the following illustration, we use the example from the third panel of Table 7.4. The five variables child gender (G), Violence at Time 1 ($V1$), Violence at Time 3 ($V3$), Diagnosis at Time 1 ($DX1$), and Diagnosis at Time 3 ($DX3$) were crossed. For the analysis of this cross-classification, we use

$$
\begin{aligned}
\log \hat{m} = \lambda \quad &+ \quad \lambda_i^G + \lambda_j^{V1} + \lambda_k^{V3} + \lambda_l^{DX1} + \lambda_m^{DX3} \\
&+ \quad \lambda_{jk}^{V1,V3} + \lambda_{lm}^{DX1,DX3} + \lambda_{ij}^{G,V1} + \lambda_{ik}^{G,V3} + \lambda_{il}^{G,DX1} + \lambda_{im}^{G,DX3} \\
&+ \quad \lambda_{ijk}^{G,V1,V3} + \lambda_{ilm}^{G,DX1,DX3} \\
&+ \quad \lambda_{jl}^{V1,DX1} + \lambda_{jm}^{V1,DX3} + \lambda_{kl}^{V3,DX1} + \lambda_{km}^{V3,DX3} \\
&+ \quad \lambda_{jkl}^{V1,V3,DX1} + \lambda_{jkm}^{V1,V3,DX3} + \lambda_{jlm}^{V1,DX1,DX3} + \lambda_{klm}^{V3,DX1,DX3} \\
&+ \quad \lambda_{jklm}^{V1,V3,DX1,DX3} .
\end{aligned}
$$

There are 17 interactions in this base model. One can be tempted to use composite variables, as in the first application example. However, the equation contains first, second, and third order interactions among individual variables such that composite variables cannot be used. Instead, the interactions of the base model have to be typed in individually (in Section 13.2, we show how interactions can be specified more easily by using the program ℓEM). The design matrix for this base model is

```
 1  1  1  1  1  1  1  1  1  1  1  1  1  1  1  1  1  1  1  1  1  1
 1  1  1  1 -1  1 -1  1  1  1 -1  1 -1  1 -1  1 -1  1 -1 -1 -1 -1
 1  1  1 -1  1  1 -1  1  1 -1  1  1 -1 -1  1 -1  1 -1  1 -1 -1 -1
 1  1  1 -1 -1  1  1  1  1 -1 -1  1  1 -1 -1 -1 -1 -1 -1  1  1  1
 1  1 -1  1  1 -1  1  1 -1  1  1 -1  1  1  1  1 -1 -1 -1  1 -1 -1
 1  1 -1  1 -1 -1 -1  1 -1  1 -1 -1 -1  1 -1  1  1 -1  1 -1  1  1
 1  1 -1 -1  1 -1 -1  1 -1 -1  1 -1 -1  1 -1 -1  1 -1  1 -1  1  1
 1  1 -1 -1 -1 -1  1  1 -1 -1 -1 -1  1 -1 -1 -1  1  1  1  1 -1 -1
 1 -1  1  1  1 -1  1  1  1  1 -1  1 -1  1  1  1 -1 -1 -1  1 -1 -1
 1 -1  1  1 -1 -1 -1  1  1 -1 -1 -1 -1  1 -1  1  1 -1  1 -1  1  1
 1 -1  1 -1  1 -1 -1  1  1 -1  1 -1 -1 -1  1  1 -1  1 -1  1  1 -1
 1 -1  1 -1 -1 -1  1  1  1 -1 -1 -1  1  1  1 -1 -1  1  1 -1 -1  1
 1 -1 -1  1  1  1  1 -1 -1  1  1  1 -1 -1 -1 -1  1  1 -1 -1  1
 1 -1 -1  1 -1  1 -1 -1 -1  1 -1 -1 -1  1 -1  1  1 -1  1  1 -1
 1 -1 -1 -1  1  1 -1 -1 -1 -1  1 -1  1 -1  1 -1 -1  1  1  1 -1
 1 -1 -1 -1 -1  1  1 -1 -1 -1 -1  1  1  1  1  1  1 -1 -1 -1 -1  1
-1  1  1  1  1  1  1 -1 -1 -1 -1 -1  1  1  1  1  1  1  1  1  1  1
-1  1  1  1 -1  1 -1 -1 -1 -1  1 -1 -1  1 -1  1 -1  1 -1 -1 -1 -1
-1  1  1 -1  1  1 -1 -1 -1  1 -1 -1 -1 -1  1 -1  1 -1  1 -1 -1 -1
-1  1  1 -1 -1  1  1 -1 -1  1  1 -1 -1 -1 -1 -1 -1 -1 -1  1  1  1
-1  1 -1  1  1 -1  1 -1  1 -1 -1  1  1  1  1  1 -1 -1 -1  1 -1 -1
-1  1 -1  1 -1 -1 -1 -1  1 -1  1 -1  1 -1  1  1  1 -1  1 -1  1  1
-1  1 -1 -1  1 -1 -1 -1  1  1 -1 -1  1 -1  1  1 -1 -1  1 -1  1  1
-1  1 -1 -1 -1 -1  1 -1  1  1  1 -1  1  1  1  1  1  1 -1 -1 -1 -1
-1 -1  1  1  1 -1  1  1 -1 -1 -1 -1  1 -1 -1 -1  1 -1  1 -1  1 -1
-1 -1  1  1 -1 -1 -1  1 -1 -1  1 -1 -1 -1  1 -1 -1 -1  1 -1  1
-1 -1  1 -1  1 -1 -1  1 -1 -1 -1 -1  1 -1  1  1  1  1  1  1 -1  1
-1 -1  1 -1 -1 -1  1  1 -1 -1  1 -1  1  1  1  1  1 -1 -1  1 -1
-1 -1 -1  1  1  1  1  1 -1 -1  1  1 -1 -1 -1 -1  1 -1 -1 -1  1
-1 -1 -1  1 -1  1 -1  1 -1  1 -1  1 -1  1  1  1  1  1  1 -1  1
-1 -1 -1 -1  1  1 -1  1 -1  1 -1  1  1 -1 -1 -1  1  1 -1  1  1 -1
-1 -1 -1 -1 -1  1  1  1  1  1  1  1  1  1  1  1 -1  1 -1 -1  1
```

Each of the columns of this table represents one of the terms in the equation of the above base model. The first five columns represent the main effects of the five variables *G*, *V*1, *V*3, *DX*1, and *DX*3. The sixth column represents the [*V*1, *V*3] interaction, . . . , and the last column represents the [*V*1, *V*3, *DX*1, *DX*3] interaction. The order of vectors in the design matrix is the same as the order of main effect and interaction terms in the above equation.

In the application of the CFA program, the first five columns of this design matrix do not need to be typed in. The program generates these columns when told that the cross-classification is spanned by 5 dichotomous variables and that a first order base model is used. The remaining 17 columns must be typed in. The complete output from this run is not reproduced here. However, the CFA test data are given in Table 5.15 (see also Data Example 7 in Section 13.3).

Data Example 4: CFA Based on Fractional Factorial Designs: This section illustrates how to perform a CFA when a fractional factorial design was used for data collection. The unique situation we are in is that the table is smaller than it would be for a completely crossed design. We, therefore, have to type in a number of vectors.

In the following data example, we use the design matrix in Table 12.4 to reproduce the data reflected in Table 12.5. The five variables that span the table are social welfare reception in Years 3, 4, 5, and 6 of the study (variables $M3$, $M4$, $M5$, and $M6$), and depression in Year 6 ($D6$). Each of these variables is dichotomous. Completely crossed, these variables span a table with $2^5 = 32$ cells. However, only 16 runs were realized, using a Box-Hunter design with Resolution V.

The main effects part of the design matrix in Table 12.4 shows that the first four variables can be coded, as in a completely crossed table, from four dichotomous variables. The main effect for the fifth variable, $D6$, is coded as if it were the four-way interaction among $M3$, $M4$, $M5$, and $M6$. If we use only these 5 vectors for the CFA base model, the analysis is equivalent to a first order CFA, and types and antitypes can emerge from any combination of the 10 two-way interactions that can be specified for the five variables in the model.

In the application of the CFA program, we tell the program that four dichotomous variables span the table, which gives us the 16 cells that would result from completely crossing these four variables. The main effect of the fifth variable is typed in, in the form of a covariate. The following commands are issued.

• Click shortcut to CFA program: Starts CFA program; black program window appears on screen; the program asks whether data will be input via file (= 1) or interactively (= 2). For this example, we select interactive data input and type "2".

• The program responds by asking for the number of variables. We type "4". This is one fewer than the real number of variables. Later, we will type in the main effect coding vector for the remaining variable, $D6$.

• The program now prompts, for each variable, the number of categories. In this example, all variables are dichotomous. Therefore, we answer each question by typing "2".

• The program now prompts the frequencies for each cell. We type "45" for Cell 1 1 1 1, "0" for Cell 1 1 1 2, and so forth, until the frequency table is completed (for the frequencies, see the right-hand columns in Table 12.7).

• We now type "1" to indicate that we wish to save the frequency table. We name the file "Medicaid.dat".

• The program now needs to know which base model we are using. We type "1" to indicate that we use the base model for first order CFA.

• Following this, we type "2" to indicate that we are not invoking the Delta option. Thus far, the program still thinks we are using only four variables.

• Now, however, we type "1" to indicate that we are going to type in the scores of a covariate. These are the scores for the main effect of the fifth variable. We type "1" for the first score, −1 for the second score, etc., until the entire vector is typed in. The rest of the program specification is routine.

• By typing "4" we select the z-test, and by typing ".05" we set the significance threshold to 0.05. The Holland-Copenhaver procedure for the protection of α is selected by typing "3".

• We now indicate that the output file is named "Medicaid.out".

• By typing "2" we indicate that we do not wish to test hypotheses about composite types or antitypes, and by typing "1" we request that the design matrix be printed into the output file. This concludes the program specification. The program window closes.

The output file Medicaid.out contains the following, (slightly edited) lines.

```
                   Configural Frequency Analysis
                   ---------- --------- --------
           author of program: Alexander von Eye, 2002
                        last revision: March 2007

     Marginal Frequencies
     --------------------
     Variable Frequencies
     -------- -----------
         1        49.     67.
         2        51.     65.
         3        53.     63.
         4        56.     60.


   sample size N =        116
   the normal z-test was used
              with Holland-Copenhaver protection
   a CFA of order   1  was performed

                              Table of results
                              ----- -- -------
   Configuration      fo       fe   statistic       p
   ------------       ----    -------- ---------    -------
```

1111	45.00	9.285	11.7205	.000000	Type
1112	.00	.263	-.5132	.303913	
1121	.00	.293	-.5410	.294242	
1122	2.00	11.776	-2.8489	.002194	Antitype
1211	.00	.314	-.5603	.287631	
1212	.00	12.631	-3.5540	.000190	Antitype
1221	1.00	14.039	-3.4800	.000251	Antitype
1222	1.00	.398	.9537	.170110	
2111	.00	.337	-.5804	.280815	
2112	1.00	13.553	-3.4099	.000325	Antitype
2121	2.00	15.065	-3.3660	.000381	Antitype
2122	1.00	.427	.8762	.190459	
2211	7.00	16.158	-2.2782	.011356	
2212	.00	.458	-.6770	.249217	
2221	1.00	.509	.6875	.245899	
2222	55.00	20.492	7.6229	.000000	Type

```
        chi2 for CFA model = 260.3
         df =    10      p =  .00000000
     LR-chi2 for CFA model =  218.2
         df =    10      p =  .00000000
```

Descriptive indicators of types and antitypes
----

cell	Rel. Risk	Rank	logP	Rank
1111	4.846	1	16.4627	1
1112	.000	16	.000000	12
1121	.000	12	.000000	14
1122	.170	7	1.63290	6
1211	.000	13	.000000	16
1212	.000	15	.000000	15
1221	.071	10	2.75622	3
1222	2.511	3	.483597	8
2111	.000	14	.000000	11
2112	.074	9	2.60144	4
2121	.133	8	2.57424	5
2122	2.340	4	.458888	9
2211	.433	6	1.16393	7
2212	.000	11	.000000	13
2221	1.963	5	.399096	10
2222	2.684	2	9.67723	2

Design Matrix
------ ------
```
1.0   1.0   1.0   1.0   1.0
1.0  -1.0   1.0   1.0  -1.0
1.0   1.0   1.0  -1.0  -1.0
1.0  -1.0   1.0  -1.0   1.0
1.0   1.0  -1.0   1.0  -1.0
1.0  -1.0  -1.0   1.0   1.0
```

```
 1.0   1.0  -1.0  -1.0   1.0
 1.0  -1.0  -1.0  -1.0  -1.0
-1.0   1.0   1.0   1.0  -1.0
-1.0  -1.0   1.0   1.0   1.0
-1.0   1.0   1.0  -1.0   1.0
-1.0  -1.0   1.0  -1.0  -1.0
-1.0   1.0  -1.0   1.0   1.0
-1.0  -1.0  -1.0   1.0  -1.0
-1.0   1.0  -1.0  -1.0  -1.0
-1.0  -1.0  -1.0  -1.0   1.0
```

CARPE DIEM

This output file is unusual in two important respects. First, the number of variables is indicated as four, but we analyze five. The program does not display the marginal frequencies of the fifth variable, $D6$. Still, the program analyzes the data correctly, using the five vectors we placed in the design matrix. Without the vector for $D6$, the CFA-specific block of the output would have looked as follows:

Configuration	fo	fe	statistic	p	
1111	45.00	4.752	18.4637	.000000	Type
1112	.00	5.091	-2.2564	.012024	
1121	.00	5.648	-2.3766	.008736	
1122	2.00	6.052	-1.6470	.049774	
1211	.00	6.056	-2.4609	.006929	
1212	.00	6.489	-2.5473	.005428	
1221	1.00	7.199	-2.3104	.010434	
1222	1.00	7.713	-2.4172	.007821	
2111	.00	6.497	-2.5490	.005402	
2112	1.00	6.961	-2.2594	.011928	
2121	2.00	7.723	-2.0594	.019728	
2122	1.00	8.275	-2.5290	.005720	
2211	7.00	8.281	-.4451	.328116	
2212	.00	8.872	-2.9787	.001448	Antitype
2221	1.00	9.843	-2.8187	.002411	Antitype
2222	55.00	10.546	13.6884	.000000	Type

```
        chi2 for CFA model = 604.7
          df =   11     p =  .00000000
      LR-chi2 for CFA model =  351.1
          df =   11     p =  .00000000
```

Clearly, the variable Depression at Time 6, $D6$, plays a major role in the explanation of these data. This can be seen in the large cell-wise residuals and in the differences in the overall goodness-of-fit tests. The second difference between the above and a standard CFA output is that the design matrix that is reproduced at the end of the output contains four standard main effect vectors and one "covariate". This covariate, however, is not a covariate in the usual sense. Instead, it serves as the vector that represents the main effect of the last variable. Interpretation of types and antitypes can proceed as indicated in Section 12.3.

13.2   The cfa Package in R

R (R Development Core Team, 2009) is an integrated open source suite of software facilities for data manipulation, calculation, data analysis, and graphical display. R has an effective data handling and storage facility, a suite of operators for calculations on arrays, in particular matrices, a large, coherent, integrated collection of intermediate tools for data analysis, graphical facilities for data analysis and output on either the computer screen or in print, and a well-developed, simple, and effective programming language, called S (Becker, Chambers, & Wilks, 1988). This language includes conditionals, loops, user-defined recursive functions as well as input and output facilities. The term *environment* characterizes R as a fully planned and coherent system rather than an incremental accretion of very specific and inflexible tools.

R can be used as a vehicle for newly developing methods of interactive data analysis. It has developed rapidly, and now contains a large collection of packages. Within the community of computational statistics it can be considered as the lingua franca. R can be thought of as an environment within which many classical and modern statistical techniques have been implemented. A few of these are built into the base R environment, but many are supplied in the form of packages. There are about 25 packages supplied with R (called "standard" and "recommended" packages), and many more are available through the CRAN family of Internet sites (via http://CRAN.R-project.org). At these sites, users can also find task views that collect R packages for areas of interest. Many readers of this book might be interested in the Social Science and the Psychometrics Task View (Mair & Hatzinger, 2007). Another important development environment is the R-forge platform (http://R-forge.R-project.org).

There is an important difference in philosophy between R and other general purpose statistical software packages. In R, a statistical analysis is done in a series of steps, with intermediate results being stored in objects. Whereas SAS and SPSS give copious output from, for instance, a regression or discriminant analysis, R will give minimal output and stores the results in a fit object for subsequent processing by other R functions. In R, results are not some sort of "isolated islands" without any possibility for personal customization. Instead, results are objects that can be customized and plotted easily. In addition, the package source code is fully accessible.

In the R environment for statistical computing, the package `cfa` (Funke et al., 2008) has recently been developed, with more functions and arguments being developed. The most recent version of the `cfa` package offers the following functions:

- `cfa()`: Performs first order CFA of variable independence.

- `mcfa()`: Allows for two-group (or more) CFA.

- `bcfa()`: Bootstrap-CFA, which tries to replicate the pattern of significant configurations by resampling.

- `hcfa()`: Recursively eliminates variables in the cross-classification to generate all possible subtables, and performs a global chi-squared test on them.

- `fcfa()`: Performs Functional CFA.

- `kvcfa()`: Computes Kieser-Victor CFA.

Each function is implemented in an object-oriented manner, and, consequently, methods such as `print()`, `summary()`, and various `plot()` methods can be applied.

Performing CFA in the comprehensive R environment is a crucial benefit over stand-alone programs. The results, which are stored as R objects, can be processed toward performing additional customized statistical analyses and computations, and results, tailored to one's specific needs, can be exported into various formats. In addition, R provides a very powerful plot engine (see Murrell, 2005) that enables the user to easily produce customized plots. For visualizing contingency tables, the vcd package (Meyer, Zeileis, & Hornik, 2006) might be very useful within a CFA context. This package implements visualization techniques proposed by Friendly (2000).

Furthermore, the R system can be used with diverse operating systems: binary distributions are available for MS Windows (NT, 95 and later), MacOS, and various versions of Linux. Last but not least, R and all installable packages (about 1,800 user contributed and maintained packages at the time we wrote this book, covering most recent statistical technology) on CRAN are completely open source. The underlying GPL licence guarantees that users have also full access to the source code.

The R base distribution can be downloaded, free of charge, from `http://CRAN.R-project.org`. Once the base R is installed and started, the `cfa` package can be installed and loaded in the R command window by typing

```
install.packages("cfa")
library("cfa")
```

To obtain an overview of the options provided by the package, the user can type

```
help(cfa)
```

By using HTML-help, the user can navigate through the package functions listed above. Basic CFA can be performed by means of the function

```
cfa(cfg, cnts = NA, sorton = "chisq", sort.descending = TRUE,
format.labels = TRUE, casewise.delete.empty = TRUE, binom.test = FALSE,
exact.binom.test = FALSE, exact.binom.limit = 10, perli.correct = FALSE,
lehmacher = FALSE, lehmacher.corr = TRUE, alpha = 0.05, bonferroni = TRUE)
```

The arguments are the following (taken from the R help file):

- `cfg`: Contains the configurations. This can be a dataframe or a matrix. The dataframe can contain numbers, characters, factors, or Booleans. The matrix can consist of numbers, characters, or Booleans (factors are implicitly reconverted to numerical levels). There must be more than three columns.

- `cnts`: Contains the counts for the configuration. If it is set to NA, a count of 1 is assumed for every row. This allows untabulated data to be processed. cnts can be a vector or a matrix/dataframe.

- `sorton`: Determines the sorting order of the output table.

- `sort.descending`: Sort in descending order.

- `format.labels`: Format the labels of the configurations. This makes the output wider but improves readability.

- `casewise.delete.empty`: If set to "TRUE" all configurations containing a NA in any column will be deleted. Otherwise NA is handled as the string "NA" and will appear as a valid configuration.

- `binom.test`: Use z approximation of binomial test.

- `exact.binom.test`: Perform an exact binomial test.

- `exact.binom.limit`: Maximum n for which an exact binomial test is performed ($n > 10$ causes p to become inexact).

- `perli.correct`: Use Perli's correction for multiple testing.

- `lehmacher`: Use Lehmacher's test.

- `lehmacher.corr`: Use a continuity correction for Lehmacher's test (default setting).

- `alpha`: Alpha level (default setting = 0.05).

- `bonferroni`: Bonferroni adjustment for multiple testing (default setting).

Using Glück's spatial strategy data from Section 10.1.2, we now show how a first order CFA can be performed in R. First, we specify the observed frequency column vector:

```
ofreq <- c(30, 59, 304, 77, 1215, 141, 1462, 238)
```

Then the matrix containing the configurations

```
confmat <- cbind(gl(2, 4, 8), gl(2, 2, 8), gl(2, 1, 8))
```

The function `gl()` generates combinations of factor levels. For example, `gl(2, 4, 8)`, indicates that the first column vector of cell indices has two levels. Each of these levels is repeated four times, so that the total length of the vector is eight. Now, we can compute a first order CFA straightforwardly. Using the standard settings for the arguments, all we have to type is

```
cfa (confmat, ofreq, sorton="label", sort.descending=FALSE)
```

which gives us

```
*** Analysis of configuration frequencies (CFA) ***

  label     n    expected           Q      chisq      p.chisq sig.chisq
1 1 1 1    30  164.47953 0.040005565 109.951331 0.000000e+00      TRUE
2 1 1 2    59   28.13250 0.008824663  33.868395 5.896890e-09      TRUE
3 1 2 1   304  236.87328 0.020408675  19.022813 1.291649e-05      TRUE
4 1 2 2    77   40.51469 0.010467784  32.856664 9.921042e-09      TRUE
5 2 1 1  1215 1069.46687 0.059243299  19.804158 8.579583e-06      TRUE
6 2 1 2   141  182.92110 0.012539669   9.607305 1.938049e-03      TRUE
7 2 2 1  1462 1540.18032 0.039369294   3.968472 4.635982e-02     FALSE
8 2 2 2   238  263.43171 0.007794996   2.455178 1.171379e-01     FALSE
            z         p.z sig.z
1 -10.779168 1.000000e+00  TRUE
2   5.748365 4.505517e-09  TRUE
3   4.482200 3.693873e-06  TRUE
4   5.686283 6.491712e-09  TRUE
5   5.313288 5.383224e-08  TRUE
```

```
6   -3.221201 9.993617e-01   TRUE
7   -2.671478 9.962241e-01   TRUE
8   -1.660957 9.516390e-01 FALSE

Summary statistics:

Total Chi squared        =   231.5343
Total degreed of freedom =   4
p                        =   0
Sum of counts            =   3526

Levels:

V1 V2 V3
2  2  2
```

The results (based on the estimated expected cell frequencies) are the same as in Table 10.6. The two sets of type/antitype decisions differ from what was shown in Table 10.6, because different statistical CFA tests and different procedures for the protection of the family-wise α were used. In Chapter 10, the standardized Pearson residual test and the Holland-Copenhaver procedure were used. Here, Pearson's X^2-test (CFA Option 3) and the standard normal z-test (CFA Option 4) were used along with the Bonferroni procedure. In addition, here the type/antitype labels are replaced by true or false statements concerning the cell-wise CFA null hypotheses. Hierarchical and more-group CFA can be performed in the same way. F-CFA and Kieser-Victor CFA can be computed by means of the functions fCFA() and kvCFA(). Internally, both versions use the glm() function to fit the log-linear model within a GLM framework. Hence, we have to define the design matrix (effect coding) of dimension 8 times 4 as follows:

```
X <- matrix(c(1, 1, 1, 1, 1, 1, 1, 1, 1, 1, 1, 1, -1, -1, -1, -1, 1, 1, -1,
+  -1, 1, 1, -1, -1, 1, -1, 1, -1, 1, -1, 1, -1), ncol = 4)
```

In addition, both stepwise CFA functions require that the dimension of the table be given in the form of a vector. In our example, we specify

```
tabdim <- c(2,2,2)
```

To perform F-CFA, we call

```
res.fcfa <- fCFA(ofreq, X, tabdim = tabdim)
print(res.fcfa)
```

which gives us

```
Results of fCFA-fit:
        LR    X^2 df       p
```

```
Step 0 271.86 231.53  4 0.00000
Step 1  31.17  31.60  3 0.00000
Step 2   9.17   9.06  2 0.01018
Step 3   0.21   0.21  1 0.64649
```

```
        Excluded Cell Type/Antitype
Step 1              111      antitype
Step 2              121      antitype
Step 3              212      antitype
```

Note that we used standardized Pearson residuals for stepwise elimination. A more comprehensive output results from invoking the summary method.

```
summary(res.fcfa)
```

which returns

```
Results of fCFA-fit:

          LR    X^2 df       p
Step 0 271.86 231.53  4 0.00000
Step 1  31.17  31.60  3 0.00000
Step 2   9.17   9.06  2 0.01018
Step 3   0.21   0.21  1 0.64649
```

```
Final log-linear model:
Design Matrix:
     [,1] [,2] [,3] [,4] [,5] [,6] [,7]
[1,]   1    1    1    1    1    0    0
[2,]   1    1    1   -1    0    0    0
[3,]   1    1   -1    1    0    1    0
[4,]   1    1   -1   -1    0    0    0
[5,]   1   -1    1    1    0    0    0
[6,]   1   -1    1   -1    0    0    1
[7,]   1   -1   -1    1    0    0    0
[8,]   1   -1   -1   -1    0    0    0
```

```
Expected frequencies:
[1]   30.00   61.59  304.00   74.41 1212.41  141.00 1464.59  238.00
```

which adds the final design matrix and the vector of expected frequencies for the final model.

A Kieser-Victor CFA can be performed by calling

```
res.kvcfa <- kvCFA(ofreq, X, tabdim = tabdim)
```

The results that can be obtained by print(res.kvcfa) and summary(res.kvcfa) are the same.

To conclude, the cfa package within the R environment offers a powerful and flexible way to perform various forms of CFA. The results are returned as objects, and they can be further analyzed and visualized. Readers can find introductory R documents on CRAN. For an introductory book, we recommend Venables and Smith (2001). Further introductory and advanced books are currently published by Springer in their UseR! series.

13.3   Using ℓ_{EM} to Perform CFA

Vermunt's (1997) ℓ_{EM} is a general program for the analysis of nominal, ordinal, or interval level categorical data. ℓ_{EM} can be downloaded, free of charge, from `http://www.uvt.nl/faculteiten/fsw/organisatie/departementen/mto/software2.html`. A more advanced version of this program, named Latent Gold, is available for purchase. For the current purposes, we use ℓ_{EM} because it can be used to estimate any of the models discussed in this text. Based on our experience, ℓ_{EM} runs well under practically all versions of Windows, including XP and Vista Business.

In contrast to the CFA program that was illustrated in the last section, ℓ_{EM} is not interactive. It requires that a command file be written. For the following illustrations, we create command files in which we include the frequency tables. We perform all analyses, using the module for hierarchical log-linear models for manifest variables. For this module, ℓ_{EM} expects at least the following four elements of information:

- Number of variables,

- Number of categories of each variable,

- Model specification, and

- Frequency table.

As with the CFA program in the last chapter, the model specification does not require that a design matrix be typed when the base model is standard hierarchical. For nonstandard models, at least some of the vectors of the design matrix need to be specified in the command file. These vectors are presented as covariates. In the following sections, we show how to perform the data examples from Section 13.1, by using ℓ_{EM}.

ℓ_{EM} was not designed to perform CFA. Therefore, it does not provide a selection of cell-wise CFA tests. Of the nine tests available in the CFA program, it only provides the square root of the Pearson X^2 statistic, but not the corresponding tail probability. In addition, it does not allow users to protect α by using any of the procedures. These are elements of CFA that

ℓ_{EM} does not provide. The advantage of ℓ_{EM} over the CFA program is that it is more flexible and convenient when it comes to specifying models.

Data Example 5: Multiple, Multivariate Prediction CFA: For this first illustration of ℓ_{EM}, we use the example from Table 5.13. Repeating from Section 13.1.2, Violence at Time 1 ($V1$) and Time 2 ($V2$) is used to predict PTSD at Time 2 ($P2$) and Time 3 ($P3$). As was indicated in Section 2.1, the cross-classification $V1 \times V2 \times P2 \times P3$ is analyzed by using the P-CFA base model

$$\log \hat{m} = \lambda + \lambda^{V1} + \lambda^{V2} + \lambda^{V1,V2} + \lambda^{P2} + \lambda^{P3} + \lambda^{P2,P3}.$$

The following command file results in a P-CFA of the violence data.

```
* P-CFA of violence data using LEM
* A = V1
* B = V2
* C = P2
* D = P3
*
* Note: intercept implied
*
man 4
dim 2 2 2 2
lab A B C D
mod {A, B, C, D, AB, CD}
dat [82 7 47 13 3 3 0 11 0 0 12 7 0 0 2 17]
```

Reading from the top of the command file, we first see eight lines that begin with asterisks. These are lines that ℓ_{EM} interprets as commentary lines. Usually, these lines are used to describe the runs.

Command lines do not begin with an asterisk. The first of these states man 4. This indicates that four manifest variables are being analyzed. The second statement, dim 2 2 2 2, specifies that each of the four variables has two categories. The third command line, lab A B C D, assigns labels to the four variables. In the next line, the CFA base model is specified. Inside the curly brackets, we first find the labels of the four variables. This indicates that we wish to include the main effects of the four variables. The terms AB and CD specify the interactions included in the base model. ℓ_{EM} creates hierarchical log-linear models. This implies that all possible lower order effects of higher order interactions are part of the model, even if they were not explicitly included in the model specification. Therefore, in the present example, the result would have been exactly the same without including the main effects in the model statement. The last line of the command file contains the frequency table.

When the command file is complete, one starts the run by clicking *File* and *Run*. ℓ_{EM} places the results in a separate output window. In the present example, the output window contains the following, slightly shortened and edited file:

```
LEM: log-linear and event history analysis with missing data.
Developed by Jeroen Vermunt (c), Tilburg University, The Netherlands.
Version 1.0 (September 18, 1997).

*** INPUT ***

 * P-CFA of violence data using LEM
 * A = V1
 * B = V2
 * C = P2
 * D = P3
 *
 * Note: intercept implied
 *
man 4
dim 2 2 2 2
lab A B C D
mod {A, B, C, D, AB, CD}
dat [82 7 47 13 3 3 0 11 0 0 12 7 0 0 2 17]

*** STATISTICS ***

Number of iterations = 2
Converge criterion   = 0.0000000000

X-squared            = 109.3915 (0.0000)
L-squared            = 114.5127 (0.0000)
Cressie-Read         = 105.9638 (0.0000)
Dissimilarity index  = 0.2593
Degrees of freedom   = 9
Log-likelihood       = -426.91949
Number of parameters = 6 (+1)
Sample size          = 204.0
BIC(L-squared)       = 66.6496
AIC(L-squared)       = 96.5127
BIC(log-likelihood)  = 885.7477
AIC(log-likelihood)  = 865.8390

Eigenvalues information matrix
    292.2804   214.4182   211.3787   75.9852   70.3900   50.5419




*** FREQUENCIES ***

A B C D    observed  estimated  std. res.
```

```
1 1 1 1      82.000      62.083       2.528
1 1 1 2       7.000       7.304      -0.112
1 1 2 1      47.000      44.554       0.366
1 1 2 2      13.000      35.059      -3.725
1 2 1 1       3.000       7.083      -1.534
1 2 1 2       3.000       0.833       2.373
1 2 2 1       0.000       5.083      -2.255
1 2 2 2      11.000       4.000       3.500
2 1 1 1       0.000       7.917      -2.814
2 1 1 2       0.000       0.931      -0.965
2 1 2 1      12.000       5.681       2.651
2 1 2 2       7.000       4.471       1.196
2 2 1 1       0.000       7.917      -2.814
2 2 1 2       0.000       0.931      -0.965
2 2 2 1       2.000       5.681      -1.544
2 2 2 2      17.000       4.471       5.926
```

*** LOG-LINEAR PARAMETERS ***
* TABLE ABCD [or P(ABCD)] *

effect	beta	std err	z-value	exp(beta)	Wald	df	prob
main	1.7952			6.0208			
A							
1	0.4871	0.1033	4.714	1.6275			
2	-0.4871			0.6144	22.22	1	0.000
B							
1	0.5427	0.1033	5.252	1.7206			
2	-0.5427			0.5812	27.58	1	0.000
C							
1	-0.3092	0.0965	-3.204	0.7340			
2	0.3092			1.3623	10.27	1	0.001
D							
1	0.5949	0.0965	6.165	1.8129			
2	-0.5949			0.5516	38.01	1	0.000
AB							
1 1	0.5427	0.1033	5.252	1.7206			
1 2	-0.5427			0.5812			
2 1	-0.5427			0.5812			
2 2	0.5427			1.7206	27.58	1	0.000
CD							
1 1	0.4751	0.0965	4.923	1.6082			
1 2	-0.4751			0.6218			
2 1	-0.4751			0.6218			
2 2	0.4751			1.6082	24.24	1	0.000

At the beginning of the output file, the program identifies itself and its author. It then reproduces the command file. Results are presented, beginning with the *Statistics* block of information. After information about the number of iterations and convergence, we find the Pearson X^2, the $LR - X^2$, and the Cressie-Read X^2. Each of these suggests that the CFA base model be rejected. This is a precondition for types and antitypes to emerge. The tail probabilities of each of these statistics are included in parentheses.

We now move to the *Frequencies* block of information. This block is structured in a way similar to the CFA test block of the CFA program. Cell indices are listed on the left-hand side of the table, followed by the observed and the estimated expected cell frequencies and the standardized residuals (CFA Option 4: z-test). As was mentioned, the standardized residual is the square root of the Pearson X^2 statistic, or

$$\text{std. res.} = \sqrt{\frac{(m - \hat{m})^2}{\hat{m}}}.$$

To determine the tail probability for the standardized residuals, one can consult a z-table as it is included in introductory textbooks of statistics, or one can use one of the z-calculators that can be found on the Internet, for example at `http://www.stat.sc.edu/~west/applets/normaldemo.html`. The calculators give the probability to the left of a z-score for a normal distribution with a given mean and standard deviation. For example, the first standardized residual ($\mu = 0$, $\sigma = 1$) in the present output is 2.528. The corresponding z-score is 0.9943. Considering that the observed frequency is larger than the expected frequency, we calculate $1 - 0.9943 = 0.0057$. This value is the same as the one listed in Data Example 1 in Section 13.1.2. With reference to the Bonferroni-protected $\alpha^* = 0.05/16 = 0.003125$, this configuration does not constitute a CFA type.

The next block of the output presents the log-linear parameters. In most CFA applications, these parameters are not of particular interest. The same applies to the information in the last block of information. This block — it is not reproduced here — contains the conditional probabilities of the cells of the table.

Data Example 6: Predicting a Trajectory: In this section, we replicate, using ℓ_{EM}, Data Example 2 from Section 13.1.2, that is, the data example in Table 5.15 in Chapter 5. To repeat from Section 13.1.2, we predict the development of physical aggression against peers (*PAAP*1 and *PAAP*2) from aggressive impulses (*AI*). The base model for predicting the *PAAP*1-*PAAP*2 trajectory from *AI* is

$$\log \hat{m} = \lambda + \lambda_i^{AI} + \lambda_j^{PAAP1} + \lambda_k^{PAAP2} + \lambda_{jk}^{PAAP1,PAAP2}.$$

This base model can be contradicted only if one or more of the following interactions exist: $[AI, PAAP1]$, $[AI, PAAP2]$, $[AI, PAAP1, PAAP2]$. If types and antitypes emerge, they indicate trajectories that occur more likely or less likely than chance, conditional on AI. The following ℓ_{EM} command file produces the results we need for CFA.

```
* predicting a trajectory
* A = AI
* B = PAAP1
* C = PAAP2
*
* Intercept implied
*
man 3
dim 2 2 2
lab A B C
mod {A, BC}
dat [23 11 10 10 8 13 9 30]
```

Evidently, this command file has the same structure as the one in the last example. In the present case, we did not list the main effects of variables *B* and *C*. They are implied by the hierarchical nature of the *BC* interaction that is implemented in ℓEM. The output file, slightly edited and shortened, follows.

```
LEM: log-linear and event history analysis with missing data.
Developed by Jeroen Vermunt (c), Tilburg University, The Netherlands.
Version 1.0 (September 18, 1997).

*** INPUT ***

 * predicting a trajectory
 * A = AI
 * B = PAAP1
 * C = PAAP2
 *
 * Intercept implied
 *
 man 3
 dim 2 2 2
 lab A B C
 mod {A, BC}
 dat [23 11 10 10 8 13 9 30]

*** STATISTICS ***

 Number of iterations = 2
 Converge criterion   = 0.0000000000

 X-squared            = 17.2092 (0.0006)
 L-squared            = 17.9403 (0.0005)
 Cressie-Read         = 17.3609 (0.0006)
 Dissimilarity index  = 0.1634
 Degrees of freedom   = 3
 Log-likelihood       = -232.56102
 Number of parameters = 4 (+1)
```

```
Sample size          = 114.0
BIC(L-squared)       = 3.7317
AIC(L-squared)       = 11.9403
BIC(log-likelihood)  = 484.0668
AIC(log-likelihood)  = 473.1220
```

```
Eigenvalues information matrix
   143.3052    113.6860    107.6453      82.3101
```

*** FREQUENCIES ***

```
A B C    observed  estimated  std. res.
1 1 1      23.000     14.684      2.170
1 1 2      11.000     11.368     -0.109
1 2 1      10.000      9.000      0.333
1 2 2      10.000     18.947     -2.056
2 1 1       8.000     16.316     -2.059
2 1 2      13.000     12.632      0.104
2 2 1       9.000     10.000     -0.316
2 2 2      30.000     21.053      1.950
```

*** LOG-LINEAR PARAMETERS ***

* TABLE ABC [or P(ABC)] *

effect	beta	std err	z-value	exp(beta)	Wald	df	prob
main	2.6168			13.6919			
A							
1	-0.0527	0.0938	-0.562	0.9487			
2	0.0527			1.0541	0.32	1	0.574
B							
1	-0.0053	0.0973	-0.055	0.9947			
2	0.0053			1.0053	0.00	1	0.956
C							
1	-0.1221	0.0973	-1.255	0.8850			
2	0.1221			1.1299	1.57	1	0.210
BC							
1 1	0.2501	0.0973	2.570	1.2841			
1 2	-0.2501			0.7787			
2 1	-0.2501			0.7787			
2 2	0.2501			1.2841	6.60	1	0.010

In the *Statistics* block of this output file, we find the overall goodness-of-fit information, which, as it should be, is identical to the figures calculated by the CFA program. Accordingly, the estimated expected cell frequencies in the *Frequencies* block are the same also. The standardized residuals are smaller than Lehmacher's z statistics in Table 5.15. This is not surprising, considering that Lehmacher's test uses the exact variances for the calculation of the standard error of the statistics. Based on the results shown here, none of the configurations constitutes a type or an antitype (compare the std. res. with the critical value of $z = 2.497706$ for the Bonferroni-protected $\alpha^* = 0.05/8 = 0.00625$). In contrast, Table 5.15 shows that two types and two antitypes emerge from the CFA program.

Data Example 7: Auto-Association CFA with Covariate: For the following illustration of ℓ_{EM}, we replicate Data Example 3 in Section 13.1.2, that is, the example from the third panel of Table 7.4. Repeating from the earlier introduction of this example, the five variables Gender (G), Violence at Time 1 ($V1$), Violence at Time 3 ($V3$), Diagnosis at Time 1 ($DX1$), and Diagnosis at Time 3 ($DX3$) were crossed. Gender is the covariate. For the analysis of this cross-classification, we use the A-CFA base model as given in Section 7.2.2 (equation at bottom of p. 141).

There are 17 interactions in this base model. As was discussed in the last section, composite variables cannot be used. Instead, the interactions of the base model have to be specified as needed for a hierarchical log-linear model. In this section, we show how this can be accomplished in an economical way by using the program ℓ_{EM}. The command file is

```
* Auto-Association CFA
* A = Gender
* B = V1
* C = V3
* D = DX1
* E = DX3
*
* Intercept implied
*
man 5
dim 2 2 2 2
lab A B C D E
mod {AB, AC, AD, AE, ABC, ADE, BCDE}
dat [28 0 5 1 3 1 1 0 10 0 11 9 10 1 14 5 23 1 5 3 5 0 0 1 6 0 9 1 17 3
12 8]
```

The first part of this command file is parallel to the ones in the first two examples. Beginning with the model specification, this command file contains new elements. Considering that ℓ_{EM} creates hierarchical log-linear models, one can, in the present example, include the four-way interaction $[V1, V3, DX1, DX3]$. All lower order interactions among the variables in this four-way interaction are part of the base model. Specifically, these are the two-way interactions $[V1, V3]$, $[V1, DX1]$, $[V1, DX3]$, $[V3, DX1]$, $[V3, DX3]$, and $[DX1, DX3]$, and the three-way interactions $[V1, V3, DX1]$, $[V1, V3, DX3]$, $[V1, DX1, DX3]$, and $[V3, DX1, DX3]$. The base model also contains two- and the three-way interactions that include Gender. These are not covered by the four-way interaction $[V1, V3, DX1, DX3]$ and must, therefore, be specified separately. Specifically, these are the interactions

[G, V1], [G, V3], [G, DX1], [G, DX3], [G, V1, V3], and [G, DX1, DX3]. The resulting output file, slightly edited and shortened, is shown below.

```
LEM: log-linear and event history analysis with missing data.
Developed by Jeroen Vermunt (c), Tilburg University, The Netherlands.
Version 1.0 (September 18, 1997).

*** INPUT ***

   * Auto-Association CFA
   * A = Gender
   * B = V1
   * C = V3
   * D = DX1
   * E = DX3
   *
   * Intercept implied
   *
   man 5
   dim 2 2 2 2 2
   lab A B C D E
   mod {AB, AC, AD, AE, ABC, ADE, BCDE}
   dat [28 0 5 1 3 1 1 0 10 0 11 9 10 1 14 5 23 1 5 3 5 0 0 1 6 0 9 1
   17 3 12 8]

*** STATISTICS ***

   Number of iterations = 5
   Converge criterion   = 0.0000000057

   X-squared           = 11.5207 (0.2417)
   L-squared           = 13.4589 (0.1429)
   Cressie-Read        = 11.8062 (0.2245)
   Dissimilarity index = 0.0812
   Degrees of freedom  = 9
   Log-likelihood      = -560.63931
   Number of parameters = 22 (+1)
   Sample size         = 193.0
   BIC(L-squared)      = -33.9053
   AIC(L-squared)      = -4.5411
   BIC(log-likelihood) = 1237.0578
   AIC(log-likelihood) = 1165.2786


   Eigenvalues information matrix
      690.5117    484.5904    417.0929   393.6328   290.8560   281.9331
      233.1671    191.4042    189.7486   178.3932   146.0271   131.7933
      104.8420     75.8714     65.0764    42.7926    22.4045    19.5614
       15.9985     15.9303     15.0522    -0.0000

WARNING: 1 (nearly) boundary or non-identified (log-linear) parameters
WARNING: 2 zero estimated frequencies
```

*** FREQUENCIES ***

A B C D E	observed	estimated	std. res.
1 1 1 1 1	28.000	25.989	0.394
1 1 1 1 2	0.000	0.399	-0.632
1 1 1 2 1	5.000	5.458	-0.196
1 1 1 2 2	1.000	2.153	-0.786
1 1 2 1 1	3.000	3.667	-0.348
1 1 2 1 2	1.000	0.351	1.096
1 1 2 2 1	1.000	0.495	0.718
1 1 2 2 2	0.000	0.487	-0.698
1 2 1 1 1	10.000	10.112	-0.035
1 2 1 1 2	0.000	0.000 *	0.000
1 2 1 2 1	11.000	13.303	-0.631
1 2 1 2 2	9.000	6.584	0.941
1 2 2 1 1	10.000	11.231	-0.367
1 2 2 1 2	1.000	1.250	-0.224
1 2 2 2 1	14.000	11.744	0.658
1 2 2 2 2	5.000	5.775	-0.323
2 1 1 1 1	23.000	25.011	-0.402
2 1 1 1 2	1.000	0.601	0.514
2 1 1 2 1	5.000	4.542	0.215
2 1 1 2 2	3.000	1.847	0.849
2 1 2 1 1	5.000	4.333	0.321
2 1 2 1 2	0.000	0.649	-0.806
2 1 2 2 1	0.000	0.505	-0.711
2 1 2 2 2	1.000	0.513	0.680
2 2 1 1 1	6.000	5.888	0.046
2 2 1 1 2	0.000	0.000 *	0.000
2 2 1 2 1	9.000	6.697	0.890
2 2 1 2 2	1.000	3.416	-1.307
2 2 2 1 1	17.000	15.769	0.310
2 2 2 1 2	3.000	2.750	0.151
2 2 2 2 1	12.000	14.256	-0.598
2 2 2 2 2	8.000	7.225	0.288

*** LOG-LINEAR PARAMETERS ***

* TABLE ABCDE [or P(ABCDE)] * (WARNING: 1 fitted zero margins)

effect	beta	std err	z-value	exp(beta)	Wald	df	prob
main	1.0683			2.9105			
A							
1	-0.0143	0.1396	-0.103	0.9858			
2	0.0143			1.0144	0.01	1	0.918
B							
1	-0.5588	0.2070	-2.699	0.5719			
2	0.5873			1.7991	7.28	1	0.007
C							
1	0.2054	0.2304	0.891	1.2280			

2		-0.2216			0.8013	0.79	1 0.373
D							
1		-0.0428	0.2122	-0.202	0.9581		
2		0.0675			1.0698	0.04	1 0.840
E							
1		0.7844	0.2347	3.342	2.1911		
2		-0.7696			0.4632	11.17	1 0.001
AB							
1	1	-0.0412	0.1009	-0.409	0.9596		
1	2	0.0412			1.0421		
2	1	0.0412			1.0421		
2	2	-0.0412			0.9596	0.17	1 0.683
AC							
1	1	0.1357	0.0965	1.406	1.1453		
1	2	-0.1357			0.8731		
2	1	-0.1357			0.8731		
2	2	0.1357			1.1453	1.98	1 0.160
BC							
1	1	0.4703	0.1623	2.898	1.6005		
1	2	-0.4936			0.6104		
2	1	-0.3876			0.6787		
2	2	0.4541			1.5747	8.40	1 0.004
AD							
1	1	-0.0887	0.1293	-0.686	0.9151		
1	2	0.0887			1.0927		
2	1	0.0887			1.0927		
2	2	-0.0887			0.9151	0.47	1 0.493
BD							
1	1	0.3375	0.2004	1.684	1.4014		
1	2	-0.3375			0.7136		
2	1	-0.4015			0.6693		
2	2	0.3011			1.3514	2.84	1 0.092
CD							
1	1	-0.2511	0.2323	-1.081	0.7779		
1	2	0.1382			1.1482		
2	1	0.1884			1.2073		
2	2	-0.1382			0.8710	1.17	1 0.280
AE							
1	1	0.0598	0.1275	0.469	1.0617		
1	2	-0.0598			0.9419		
2	1	-0.0598			0.9419		
2	2	0.0598			1.0617	0.22	1 0.639
BE							
1	1	0.1125	0.1733	0.649	1.1191		
1	2	-0.0811			0.9221		
2	1	-0.0525			0.9489		
2	2	0.0281			1.0285	0.42	1 0.516
CE							
1	1	0.2084	0.1947	1.071	1.2318		
1	2	-0.2732			0.7609		
2	1	-0.2084			0.8118		

2 2	0.2049			1.2274	1.15	1 0.284
DE						
1 1	0.5197	0.1694	3.068	1.6816		
1 2	-0.5562			0.5734		
2 1	-0.5197			0.5947		
2 2	0.5504			1.7339	9.41	1 0.002
ABC						
1 1 1	-0.0844	0.0956	-0.883	0.9191		
1 1 2	0.0844			1.0881		
1 2 1	0.0844			1.0881		
1 2 2	-0.0844			0.9191		
2 1 1	0.0844			1.0881		
2 1 2	-0.0844			0.9191		
2 2 1	-0.0844			0.9191		
2 2 2	0.0844			1.0881	0.78	1 0.377
BCD						
1 1 1	0.0610	0.1498	0.407	1.0629		
1 1 2	0.0883			1.0923		
1 2 1	0.0410			1.0419		
1 2 2	-0.1162			0.8903		
2 1 1	-0.1948			0.8230		
2 1 2	-0.0577			0.9440		
2 2 1	-0.0046			0.9954		
2 2 2	0.0855			1.0893	0.17	1 0.684
BCE						
1 1 1	0.1008	0.2024	0.498	1.1060		
1 1 2	-0.1008			0.9041		
1 2 1	-0.1378			0.8712		
1 2 2	0.1378			1.1478		
2 1 1	-0.0492			0.9520		
2 1 2	0.0984			1.1034		
2 2 1	0.1349			1.1445		
2 2 2	-0.1349			0.8738	0.25	1 0.618
ADE						
1 1 1	0.0523	0.1272	0.411	1.0537		
1 1 2	-0.0523			0.9490		
1 2 1	-0.0523			0.9490		
1 2 2	0.0523			1.0537		
2 1 1	-0.0523			0.9490		
2 1 2	0.0523			1.0537		
2 2 1	0.0523			1.0537		
2 2 2	-0.0523			0.9490	0.17	1 0.681
BDE						
1 1 1	0.1085	0.2350	0.462	1.1146		
1 1 2	-0.1085			0.8972		
1 2 1	-0.1085			0.8972		
1 2 2	0.1085			1.1146		
2 1 1	-0.0841			0.9193		
2 1 2	0.2174			1.2429		
2 2 1	0.0841			1.0878		
2 2 2	-0.1087			0.8970	0.21	1 0.644

CDE								
1 1 1	0.1239	0.2652	0.467	1.1319				
1 1 2	-0.1144			0.8919				
1 2 1	-0.1239			0.8835				
1 2 2	0.1116			1.1180				
2 1 1	-0.1239			0.8835				
2 1 2	0.0572			1.0589				
2 2 1	0.1239			1.1319				
2 2 2	-0.1116			0.8944	0.22	1 0.640		
BCDE								
1 1 1 1	-0.0095	******	*****	0.9906				
1 1 1 2	0.0000			1.0000				
1 1 2 1	0.0095			1.0095				
1 1 2 2	0.0028			1.0028				
1 2 1 1	0.0095			1.0095				
1 2 1 2	0.0572			1.0589				
1 2 2 1	-0.0095			0.9906				
1 2 2 2	-0.0028			0.9972				
2 1 1 1	0.0095			1.0095				
2 1 1 2	******			0.00E+0000				
2 1 2 1	-0.0095			0.9906				
2 1 2 2	-0.0028			0.9972				
2 2 1 1	-0.0095			0.9906				
2 2 1 2	-0.0572			0.9444				
2 2 2 1	0.0095			1.0095				
2 2 2 2	0.0028			1.0028	0.00	1 1.000		

This output file can be interpreted similarly to the earlier examples. From a CFA perspective, the most important elements given in this file are the overall goodness-of-fit statistics and the frequencies table. From a modeling perspective, we note that only a small number of the effects in this model is significant, but the frequency distribution is explained very well. The model can, possibly, be made more parsimonious. From an estimation perspective, it is important to note that some of the frequencies are estimated to be zero (marked with asterisks). The estimates are correct. However, researchers interested in the substantive parts of this example may wish to replicate the study, using a larger sample.

Data Example 8: CFA Based on Fractional Factorial Designs: This section illustrates how to use ℓ_{EM} to perform a CFA when a fractional factorial design was used for data collection. As was explained before, the table that is being analyzed is smaller than it would be for a completely crossed design. We, therefore, have to type in a number of vectors.

In the following section, we use the design matrix in Table 12.4 again to reproduce the data example in Table 12.5. The five variables that span the table are social welfare reception in Years 3, 4, 5, and 6 of the study (variables $M3$, $M4$, $M5$, and $M6$), and Depression in Year 6 ($D6$). Each of these variables is dichotomous. Completely crossed, these variables span a table with $2^5 = 32$ cells. However, only 16 runs were realized, using a Box-Hunter design with Resolution V.

As was discussed in the context of the application of the CFA program in Section 13.1.2, 16 cells result when four dichotomous variables are completely crossed. Hence, we tell the program that the cross-classification is spanned by four variables, and we specify the main effect of the fifth variable in the form of a covariate. This is accomplished by the term cov(ABCD,1) in the mod line. In the parentheses of this term, we find all four variables listed. This implies that the covariate can assume different scores for each of the 16 cells. The 1 indicates that one covariate is specified. The values of the covariate are given using the des[...] command. These values are taken from the design matrix in Table 12.4 (last column in the main effects block). The ℓEM command file is

```
* CFA based on a fractional factorial design
* A = M3
* B = M4
* C = M5
* D = M6
* covariate = D6
*
* constant implied
*
man 4
dim 2 2 2 2
mod {A, B, C, D, cov(ABCD,1)}
des [1 -1 -1 1 -1 1 1 -1 -1 1 1 -1 1 -1 -1 1]
dat [ 45 0 0 2 0 0 1 1 0 1 2 1 7 0 1 55]
```

As was introduced in Data Example 3, covariates can be used to augment the design matrix. In the present case, the covariate is specified to capture the main effect of the fifth variable. The covariate vector, given in the des[...] line, is taken from the design matrix in Table 12.4. The slightly edited and shortened output that results from this command file is

```
LEM: log-linear and event history analysis with missing data.
Developed by Jeroen Vermunt (c), Tilburg University, The Netherlands.
Version 1.0 (September 18, 1997).

*** INPUT ***

 * CFA based on a fractional factorial design
 * A = M3
 * B = M4
 * C = M5
 * D = M6
```

```
* covariate = D6
*
* constant implied
*
man 4
dim 2 2 2 2
mod {A, B, C, D, cov(ABCD,1)}
des [1 -1 -1 1 -1 1 1 -1 -1 1 1 -1 1 -1 -1 1]
dat [ 45 0 0 2 0 0 1 1 0 1 2 1 7 0 1 55]
```

*** STATISTICS ***

Number of iterations = 61
Converge criterion   = 0.0000008303

X-squared   = 260.3030 (0.0000)
L-squared   = 218.1559 (0.0000)
Cressie-Read   = 233.5689 (0.0000)
Dissimilarity index = 0.6197
Degrees of freedom   = 10
Log-likelihood   = -252.39733
Number of parameters = 5 (+1)
Sample size   = 116.0
BIC(L-squared)   = 170.6200
AIC(L-squared)   = 198.1559
BIC(log-likelihood) = 528.5626
AIC(log-likelihood) = 514.7947

Eigenvalues information matrix
    118.3903   114.0995   113.3695   112.6715   11.7035

*** FREQUENCIES ***

A B C D	observed	estimated	std. res.
1 1 1 1	45.000	9.285	11.721
1 1 1 2	0.000	0.264	-0.514
1 1 2 1	0.000	0.293	-0.541
1 1 2 2	2.000	11.776	-2.849
1 2 1 1	0.000	0.314	-0.561
1 2 1 2	0.000	12.630	-3.554
1 2 2 1	1.000	14.039	-3.480
1 2 2 2	1.000	0.399	0.952
2 1 1 1	0.000	0.337	-0.581
2 1 1 2	1.000	13.553	-3.410
2 1 2 1	2.000	15.064	-3.366
2 1 2 2	1.000	0.428	0.875
2 2 1 1	7.000	16.157	-2.278
2 2 1 2	0.000	0.459	-0.677
2 2 2 1	1.000	0.510	0.686
2 2 2 2	55.000	20.492	7.623

```
*** LOG-LINEAR PARAMETERS ***

* TABLE ABCD [or P(ABCD)] *
```

effect	beta	std err	z-value	exp(beta)	Wald	df	prob
main	0.8106			2.2494			
A							
1	-0.1561	0.0940	-1.661	0.8555			
2	0.1561			1.1690	2.76	1	0.097
B							
1	-0.1209	0.0935	-1.292	0.8862			
2	0.1209			1.1285	1.67	1	0.196
C							
1	-0.0858	0.0932	-0.921	0.9177			
2	0.0858			1.0896	0.85	1	0.357
D							
1	-0.0330	0.0929	-0.355	0.9676			
2	0.0330			1.0335	0.13	1	0.723
cov(ABCD)							
1	1.8136	0.2923	6.204	6.1322	38.49	1	0.000

As in the first three examples, and as it should be, the overall goodness-of-fit results, the estimated expected cell frequencies, and the standardized residuals from the CFA program and from ℓEM are identical. ℓEM also indicates that the "covariate", that is, the main effect of the depression variable, has a significant effect (see the z-test or the Wald statistic in the last line of the output).

13.4 Chapter Summary

This chapter described three application programs that can be used for CFA. The first application involves using a specialized CFA program. This program uses a log-linear modeling module and offers a large selection of CFA tests and CFA base models. To use base models that are not pre-programmed, vectors of design matrices need to be determined and typed in.

The second option involves using the CFA module in the package R. This module contains a selection of CFA base models, and allows one to perform two versions of Functional CFA. This makes this module unique. In addition, this module is part of the R package, which allows users to use the CFA output as objects, and, thus, as input for other R modules, for further analysis.

The third option involves using ℓEM, a general purpose program for the analysis of categorical data. The downside to using this program is that specific CFA hypotheses cannot be tested directly. The main advantage of this program is that the specification of just any CFA base model is very easy, as long as it is log-linear. In this chapter, we present sample commands for a selection of the CFA models proposed in this book, using several programs. Our focus is on base models that are log-linear. CFA can be performed by using most of the log-linear modules in specialized or general purpose statistical software packages or using specialized CFA programs. In this chapter, we illustrate the application of three program packages, all of which can be obtained free of charge. The first package is a specialized CFA package (von Eye, 2007). It can be requested by sending an e-mail to voneye@msu.edu. The second program is the cfa package within the R environment (Funke et al., 2008). This program can be downloaded from the R website, http://CRAN.R-project.org, also free of charge. The third program is ℓEM, a general program for the analysis of categorical data (Vermunt, 1997). It can be downloaded from http://www.uvt.nl/faculteiten/fsw/organisatie/departementen/mto/software2.html, also free of charge.

References

Agresti, A. (2002). *Categorical data analysis* (2nd ed.). New York: Wiley.

Aickin, M. (1990). Maximum likelihood estimation of agreement in the constant predictive model, and its relation to Cohen's kappa. *Biometrics, 46*, 293–302.

Atkinson, A. C., & Fedorov, V. V. (1975). The designs of experiments for discriminating between two rival models. *Biometrika, 62*, 57–70.

Baron, R. M., & Kenny, D. A. (1986). The moderator-mediator variable distinction in social psychological research: Conceptual, strategic, and statistical considerations. *Journal of Personality and Social Psychology, 51*, 1173–1182.

Beaubien, J. M. (2005). Moderation. In B. S. Everitt & D. C. Howell (Eds.), *Encyclopedia of statistics in behavioral science* (pp. 1076–1082). Chichester, UK: Wiley.

Beck, A. T., Ward, C., & Mendelson, M. (1961). Beck depression inventory (BDI). *Archives of General Psychiatry, 4*, 561–571.

Becker, R. A., Chambers, J. M., & Wilks, A. R. (1988). *The new S language: A programming environment for data analysis and graphics*. London: Chapman & Hall.

Berger, M. P. F. (2005). Optimal design for categorical variables. In B. S. Everitt & D. C. Howell (Eds.), *Encyclopedia of statistics in behavioral science* (pp. 1474–1479). Chichester, UK: Wiley.

Bergman, L. R., & El-Khouri, B. M. (1999). Studying individual patterns of development using I-states as objects analysis (ISOA). *Biometrical Journal, 41*, 753–770.

Bergman, L. R., & Magnusson, D. (1997). A person-oriented approach in research on developmental psychopathology. *Development and Psychopathology, 9*, 291–319.

Bergman, L. R., Magnusson, D., & El-Khouri, B. M. (2003). *Studying individual development in an interindividual context: A person-oriented approach*. Mahwah, NJ: Erlbaum.

Bergman, L. R., von Eye, A., & Magnusson, D. (2006). Person-oriented research strategies in developmental psychopathology. In D. Cicchetti & D. J. Cohen (Eds.), *Developmental psychopathology* (2nd ed., pp. 850–888). London: Wiley.

Birch, M. W. (1963). Maximum likelihood in three-way contingency tables. *Journal of the Royal Statistical Association, Series B, 25*, 220–233.

Bishop, Y. M. M., Fienberg, S. E., & Holland, P. W. (1975). *Discrete multivariate analysis*. Cambridge, MA: MIT Press.

Blashfield, R. K., & Aldenderfer, M. S. (1984). The methods and problems of cluster analysis. In J. R. Nesselroade & R. B. Cattell (Eds.), *Handbook of multivariate experimental psychology* (pp. 447–473). New York: Plenum.

Bogat, G. A., Levendosky, A. A., von Eye, A., & Davidson, W. S. (2006). *The mental and physical health consequences of domestic violence for women and children receiving medicaid.* (Medicaid Administrative Services Grant)

Bortz, J., Lienert, G. A., & Boehnke, K. (1990). *Verteilungsfreie Methoden in der Biostatistik [Nonparametric methods in biostatistics].* Berlin: Springer.

Box, G. E. P., & Behnken, D. W. (1960). Some new three level designs for the study of quantitative variables. *Technometrics, 2,* 455–475.

Box, G. E. P., Hunter, J. S., & Hunter, W. G. (2005). *Statistics for experimenters: Design innovation, and discovery* (2nd ed.). Hoboken, NJ: Wiley.

Brennan, B. L., & Prediger, D. J. (1981). Coefficient kappa: Some uses, misuses, and alternatives. *Educational and Psychological Measurement, 41,* 687–699.

Bruwer, M. J., & MacGregor, J. F. (2005). Robust multi-variable identification: Optimal experimental design with constraints. *Journal of Process Control, 16,* 581–600.

Cheney, J., & Hinze, R. (2003). *First-class phantom types* (Tech. Rep. No. TR 2003-1901). Ithaca, NY: Cornell University Press.

Christensen, R. (1997). *Log-linear models and logistic regression* (2nd ed.). New York: Springer.

Christensen, R. (2005). Logistic regression. In B. S. Everitt & D. C. Howell (Eds.), *Encyclopedia of statistics in behavioral science* (pp. 1076–1082). Chichester, UK: Wiley.

Clark, D. B., Pollock, N. B., Bukstein, O. G., Mezzich, A. C., Bromberger, J. T., & Donovan, J. E. (1997). Gender and comorbid psychopathology in adolescents with alcohol dependence. *Journal of the American Academy of Child & Adolescent Psychiatry, 36,* 1195–1203.

Clogg, C. C., & Shihadeh, E. S. (1994). *Statistical models for ordinal variables.* Thousand Oaks, CA: Sage.

Cohen, J. (1960). A coefficient of agreement for nominal scales. *Educational and Psychological Measurement, 20,* 37–46.

Dodge, Y., Fedorov, V. V., & Wynn, H. P. (1988). *Optimal design and analysis of experiments.* Amsterdam: North-Holland.

DuMouchel, W. (1999). Bayesian data mining in large frequency tables, with an application to the FDA spontaneous reporting system. *The American Statistician, 53,* 177–190.

Euler, L. (1782). Recherches sur une nouvelle espce de quarrés magiques [Research on a new type of magic squares]. *Verhandelingen uitgegeven door het zeeuwsch Genootschap der Wetenschappen te Vlissingen, 9,* 85–239.

Everitt, B. S., Landau, S., & Leese, M. (2001). *Cluster analysis* (4th ed.). London: Arnold.

Fienberg, S. E. (1970). An iterative procedure for estimation in contingency tables. *Annals of Mathematical Statistics, 41,* 907–917.

Finkel, S. E. (2008). Linear panel analysis. In S. Menard (Ed.), *Handbook of longitudinal research: Design measurement, and analysis* (pp. 475–504). Amsterdam: Elsevier.

Finkelstein, J. W., von Eye, A., & Preece, M. A. (1994). The relationship between aggressive behavior and puberty in normal adolescents: A longitudinal study. *Journal of Adolescent Health, 15,* 319–326.

Finney, D. J. (1945). The fractional replication of factorial arrangements. *Annals of Eugenics, 12,* 291–301.

Finney, D. J. (1946). Recent developments in the design of field experiments III: Fractional replication. *Journal of Agricultural Science, 36,* 184–191.

Fleiss, J. L. (1975). Measuring agreement between two judges in the presence or absence of a trait. *Biometrics, 31,* 651–659.

Friendly, M. (2000). *Visualizing categorical data.* Cary, NC: SAS Publishing.

Funke, S., Mair, P., & von Eye, A. (2008). *cfa: Analysis of configuration frequencies (CFA)* [Computer software manual]. (R package version 0.8-5)

Glück, J. (1999). *Spatial strategies: Kognitive Strategien bei Raumvorstellungsleistungen [Spatial strategies: Cognitive strategies for spatial tasks].* Unpublished doctoral dissertation, University of Vienna, Austria.

Glück, J., & von Eye, A. (2000). Including covariates in configural frequency analysis. *Psychologische Beiträge, 42,* 405–417.

Gonzáles-Debén, A., & Méndez-Ramírez, I. (2000). Un nuevo concepto de tipo en el analisis de las frecuencias de las configuraciones de dos muestras. *Multicienica, 4,* 7–17.

Goodman, L. A. (1979). Simple models for the analysis of association in cross-classifications having ordered categories. *Journal of the American Statistical Association, 74,* 537–552.

Goodman, L. A. (1984). *The analysis of cross-classified data having ordered categories.* Cambridge, MA: Harvard University Press.

Goodman, L. A. (1991). Measures, models, and graphical displays in the analysis of cross-classified data. *Journal of the American Statistical Association, 86,* 1085–1111.

Greenberg, R. (2008). Causal analysis with nonexperimental panel data. In S. Menard (Ed.), *Handbook of longitudinal research: Design measurement, and analysis* (pp. 259–278). Amsterdam: Elsevier.

Gutiérrez Peña, E., & von Eye, A. (2000). A Bayesian approach to configural frequency analysis. *Journal of Mathematical Sociology, 24,* 151–174.

Haberman, S. J. (1973). The analysis of residuals in cross-classified tables. *Biometrics, 29,* 205–220.

Haberman, S. J. (1974). *The analysis of frequency data.* Chicago: University Chicago Press.

Hagenaars, J. A. (1990). *Categorical, longitudinal data: Log-linear, panel, trend, and cohort analysis.* Newbury Park, CA: Sage.

Hamada, M., & Wu, C. F. J. (1992). Analysis of designed experiments with complex aliasing. *Journal of Quality Technology, 24,* 130–137.

Hand, D. J., & Viniciotti, V. (2003). Local versus global models for classification problems: Fitting models where it matters. *The American Statistician, 57,* 124–131.

Havránek, T., & Lienert, G. A. (1984). Local and regional versus global contingency testing. *Biometrical Journal, 26,* 483–494.

Ho, M. H. R., Shumway, R., & Ombao, H. (2006). The state-space approach to modeling dynamic processes. In T. A. Walls & J. L. Schafer (Eds.), *Models for intensive longitudinal data* (pp. 148–175). New York: Oxford University Press.

Hoernes, G. E., & Heilweil, M. F. (1964). *Introduction to Boolean algebra and logic design.* New York: McGraw-Hill.

Holland, B. S., & Copenhaver, M. D. (1987). An improved sequentially rejective Bonferroni test procedure. *Biometrics, 43,* 417–423.

Holm, S. (1979). A simple sequentially rejective multiple test procedure. *Scandinavian Journal of Statistics, 6,* 65–70.

Hussy, W. (1991). Eine experimentelle Studie zum Intelligenzkonzept "Verarbeitungskapazität" [An experimental investigation of the intelligence concept of "processing capacity".]. *Diagnostica, 37,* 314–333.

Indurkhya, A., & von Eye, A. (2000). The power of tests in configural frequency analysis. *Psychologische Beiträge, 42,* 301–308.

Jackson, K. M., Sher, K. J., & Schulenberg, J. E. (2008). Conjoint developmental trajectories of young adult substance use. *Alcoholism: Clinical and Experimental Research, 32,* 723–737.

Jackson, L. A., von Eye, A., Barbatsis, G., Biocca, F., Fitzgerald, H. E., & Zhao, Y. (2004). The social impact of Internet use on the other side of the digital divide. *Communications of the Association for Computing Machinery, 47,* 43–47.

James, L. R., & Brett, J. M. (1984). Mediators, moderators, and tests for mediation. *Journal of Applied Psychology, 69,* 307–321.

Kales, H. C., Blow, F. C., Bingham, C. R., Copeland, L. A., & Mellow, A. M. (2000). Race and inpatient psychiatric diagnoses among elderly veterans. *Psychiatric Services, 51,* 795–800.

Kempthorne, O. (1947). A simple approach to confounding and fractional replication in factorial experiments. *Biometrika, 34,* 255–272.

Kenny, D. A. (2005). Mediation. In B. S. Everitt & D. C. Howell (Eds.), *Encyclopedia of statistics in behavioral science* (pp. 1194–1198). Chichester, UK: Wiley.

Kessels, R., Goos, P., & Vandebroek, M. (2006). A comparison of criteria to design efficient choice experiments. *Journal of Marketing Research, 43,* 409–419.

Kieser, M., & Victor, N. (1991). A test procedure for an alternative approach to configural frequency analysis. *Methodika, 5,* 87–97.

Kieser, M., & Victor, N. (1999). Configural frequency analysis (CFA) revisited: A new look at an old approach. *Biometrical Journal, 41,* 967–983.

Kieser, M., & Victor, N. (2000). An alternative approach for the identification of types in contingency tables. *Psychologische Beiträge, 42,* 402–404.

Klinteberg, B., Andersson, T., Magnusson, D., & Stattin, H. (1993). Hyperactive behavior in childhood as related to subsequent alcohol problems and violent offending: A longitudinal study of male subjects. *Personality and Individual Differences, 15,* 381–388.

Koehler, T., Dulz, K., & Bock-Emden, E. (1991). Headache syndromes as detected by configural frequency analysis. *Headache: The Journal of Head and Face Pain, 31,* 325–328.

Krauth, J. (2003). Type structures in CFA. *Psychology Science, 45,* 217–222.

Krauth, J., & Lienert, G. A. (1973). *KFA: Die Konfigurationsfrequenzanalyse und ihre Anwendung in Psychologie und Medizin [CFA: Configural Frequency Analysis and its application in psychology and medicine].* Freiburg, Germany: Alber.

Küchenhoff, H. (1986). A note on a continuity correction for testing in three-dimensional configural frequency analysis. *Biometrical Journal, 28,* 465–468.

Kutner, M. H., Neter, J., Nachtsheim, C. J., & Li, W. (2004). *Applied linear statistical models* (4th ed.). Boston, MA: McGraw-Hill.

Lautsch, E., & von Eye, A. (2000). Configural frequency analysis: New approaches and applications. *Special Issue of Psychologische Beiträge, 42.*

Lautsch, E., & von Eye, A. (2003). The development of configural frequency analysis as a statistical method. *Special Issue of Psychology Science, 45.*

Lautsch, E., & von Eye, A. (2005). The future of configural frequency analysis. *Special Issue of Psychology Science, 47.*

Lautsch, E., & von Weber, S. (1995). *Methoden und Anwendungen der Konfigurationsfrequenzanalyse (KFA) [Methods and applications of configural frequency analysis (CFA)].* Weinheim, Germany: Psychologie Verlagsunion.

Lawal, B. (2003). *Categorical data analysis with SAS and SPSS applications.* Mahwah, NJ: Erlbaum.

Ledolter, J., & Swersey, A. J. (2007). *Testing 1-2-3: Experimental design with applications in marketing and service operations.* Stanford, CA: Stanford University Press.

Lehmacher, W. (1981). A more powerful simultaneous test procedure in configural frequency analysis. *Biometrical Journal, 23,* 429–436.

Lerner, R. M., Taylor, C. S., & von Eye, A. (2002). *Pathways to positive development among diverse youth.* San Francisco, CA: Jossey-Bass.

Levendosky, A. A., Bogat, G. A., Davidson, W. S., & von Eye, A. (2000). *Risk and protective factors for domestic violence.* (Centers for Disease Control, Injury Prevention Center, Atlanta, RO1/CCR518519-01)

Lienert, G. A. (1968). *Die Konfigurationsfrequenzanalyse als Klassifikationsmethode in der klinischen Psychologie [Configural frequency analysis: A classification method for clinical psychology].* (Paper presented at the 26. Kongress der Deutschen Gesellschaft für Psychologie in Tübingen, September 1968)

Lienert, G. A., & Krauth, J. (1973a). Die Konfigurationsfrequenzanalyse VII: Konstellations-, Konstellationsänderungs- und Profilkonstellationstypen [Configural frequency analysis VII: Syndromes, changes in syndromes, and types of profiles]. *Zeitschrift für Klinische Psychologie und Psychotherapie, 21,* 197–209.

Lienert, G. A., & Krauth, J. (1973b). Die Konfigurationsfrequenzanalyse VI: Profiländerungen und Symptomverschiebungen [Configural frequency analysis VI: Changes in profiles and shifts in symptoms]. *Zeitschrift für Klinische Psychologie und Psychotherapie, 21,* 100–109.

Lienert, G. A., & von Eye, A. (1984). Multivariate Änderungsbeurteilung mittels Inkrementen-Konfigurationsclusteranalyse [Evaluating multivariate change using configural cluster analysis of increments]. *Psychologische Beiträge, 21,* 363–371.

Lindner, K. (1984). Eine exakte Auswertungsmethode zur Konfigurationsfrequenzanalyse [An exact test for configural frequency analysis]. *Psychologische Beiträge, 26,* 393–415.

Liski, E. P., Mandal, N. K., Shah, K. R., & Sinha, B. K. (2002). *Topics in optimal design*. New York: Springer.

Lobato, O. C., Martínez, J. M., Miranda, V. S., Rivera, H., & Serrato, H. (2007). *Diseño de la evaluación del índice Mexicano de Satisfacción del Usario del programa de abasto social de leche y del programa de estancias y garderías infantiles de la SEDESOL [Design for the evaluation of the Mexican Customer Satisfaction Index for the social milk distribution program for rural areas and nursery schools of the SEDESOL]*. (Unpublished project report)

Lord, F. M., & Novick, M. R. (1968). *Statistical theories of mental test scores*. Reading, MA: Addison-Wesley.

Lunneborg, C. E. (2005). Runs test. In B. S. Everitt & D. C. Howell (Eds.), *Encyclopedia of statistics in behavioral science* (p. 1771). Chichester, UK: Wiley.

MacKinnon, D. P. (2008). *Introduction to statistical mediation analysis*. Mahwah, NJ: Erlbaum.

MacKinnon, D. P., Fairchild, A. J., & Fritz, M. S. (2007). Mediation analysis. *Annual Review of Psychology, 58*, 593–614.

MacKinnon, D. P., Lockwood, C. M., Hoffman, J. M., West, S. G., & Sheets, V. (2002). A comparison of methods to test mediation and other intervening variable effects. *Psychological Methods, 7*, 83–104.

Mahoney, J. H. (2000). School extracurricular activity participation as a moderator in the development of antisocial patterns. *Child Development, 71*, 502–516.

Mair, P. (2007). A framework to interpret nonstandard log-linear models. *Austrian Journal of Statistics, 36*, 1–15.

Mair, P., & Hatzinger, R. (2007). Psychometrics task view. *R News, 7/3*, 38–40.

Mair, P., & von Eye, A. (2007). Application scenarios for nonstandard log-linear models. *Psychological Methods, 12*, 139–156.

Mann, S. (2008). Farm size growth and participation in agri-environmental schemes: A Configural Frequency Analysis of the Swiss case. *Journal of Agricultural Economics, 56*, 373–384.

Martinez-Torteya, C., Bogat, G. A., von Eye, A., & Levendosky, A. A. (2009). Resilience among children exposed to domestic violence: The role of protective and vulnerability factors. *Child Development, 80*, 562–577.

McCallum, R. C., Zhang, S., Preacher, K. J., & Rucker, D. D. (2002). On the practice of dichotomization of quantitative variables. *Psychological Methods, 7*, 19–40.

Meehl, P. E. (1950). Configural scoring. *Journal of Consulting Psychology, 14*, 165–171.

Mellenbergh, G. J. (1996). Other null model, other (anti) type. *Applied Psychology: An International Review, 45*, 329–330.

Meyer, D., Zeileis, A., & Hornik, K. (2006). The strucplot framework: Visualizing multi-way contingency tables with vcd. *Journal of Statistical Software, 17*, 1–48. Available from http://www.jstatsoft.org/v17/i03/.

Molenaar, P. C. M. (2004). A manifesto on psychology as idiographic science: Bringing the person back into scientific psychology — this time forever. *Measurement: Interdisciplinary Research and Perspectives, 2*, 201–218.

Mukerjee, R., & Wu, C. F. J. (2006). *A modern theory of factorial design*. New York: Springer.

Muller, D., Judd, C. M., & Yzerbyt, V. Y. (2005). When moderation is mediated and mediation is moderated. *Journal of Personality and Social Psychology, 89,* 852–863.

Murrell, P. (2005). *R graphics.* Boca Raton, FL: Chapman & Hall/CRC.

Osterkorn, K. (1975). Wann kann die Binomial- und Poissonverteilung hinreichend genau durch die Normalverteilung ersetzt werden? [Under what conditions can the binomial and the Poisson distribution be substituted with sufficient accuracy by the nomal distribution?]. *Biometrische Zeitschrift, 17,* 33–34.

Perrine, M. W., Mundt, J. C., Searles, J. S., & Lester, L. S. (1995). Validation of daily self-report consumption using interactive voice response (IVR) technology. *Journal of Studies on Alcohol and Drugs, 56,* 487–490.

Plackett, R. L., & Burman, J. P. (1946). The design of optimum multifactorial experiments. *Biometrika, 33,* 305–325.

Preacher, K. J., Rucker, K. D., & Hayes, A. (2007). Addressing moderated mediation hypotheses: Theory, methods, and prescriptions. *Multivariate Behavioral Research, 42,* 185–227.

Press, W. H., Flannery, B. P., Teukolsky, S. A., & Vetterling, M. T. (1989). *Numerical recipes: The art of scientific computing (FORTRAN version).* Cambridge, UK: Cambridge University Press.

Pugesek, B. H., & Diem, K. L. (1990). The relationship between reproduction and survival in known-aged California gulls. *Ecology, 71,* 811–817.

Pukelsheim, F. (2006). *Optimal design of experiments.* New York: Wiley.

R Development Core Team. (2009). *R: A Language and Environment for Statistical Computing* [Computer software manual]. Vienna, Austria. Available from http://www.R-project.org (ISBN 3-900051-07-0)

Reverte, C., Dirion, J. L., & Cabassud, M. (2006). Kinetic model identification and parameter estimation from TGA experiments. *Journal of Analytical and Applied Pyrolysis, 79,* 297–305.

Rovine, M. J., & Walls, T. A. (2006). Multilevel autoregressive modeling of interindividual differences in the stability of a process. In T. A. Walls & J. L. Schafer (Eds.), *Models for intensive longitudinal data* (pp. 124–147). New York: Oxford University Press.

Rudas, T., Clogg, C. C., & Lindsay, B. G. (1994). A new index of fit based on mixture methods for the analysis of contingency tables. *Journal of the Royal Statistical Society, 56,* 623–639.

Sanders, D., & Ward, H. (2008). Time-series techniques for repeated cross-section data. In S. Menard (Ed.), *Handbook of longitudinal research: Design measurement, and analysis* (pp. 621–637). Amsterdam: Elsevier.

Saunders, D. G. (1994). Posttraumatic stress symptom profiles of battered women: A comparison of survivors in two settings. *Violence and Victims, 9,* 31–44.

Schuster, C. (2001). Kappa as a parameter of a symmetry model for rater agreement. *Journal of Educational and Behavioral Statistics, 26,* 331–342.

Schuster, C., & von Eye, A. (2000). Using log-linear modeling to increase power in two-sample configural frequency analysis. *Psychologische Beiträge, 42,* 273–284.

Siegel, S. (1956). *Nonparametric statistics for the behavioral sciences.* New York: McGraw-Hill.

Simonson, L. G., McMahon, K. T., Childers, D. W., & Morton, H. E. (1992).

Bacterial synergy of treponema denticola and porphyromonas gingivalis in a multinational population. *Oral Microbiology and Immunology, 7*, 111–112.

Spielberg, C., Falkenhahn, D., Willich, S. N., Wegschneider, K., & Voller, H. (1996). Circadian, day-of-week, and seasonal variability in myocardial infarction: Comparison between working and retired patients. *American Heart Journal, 132*, 579–585.

Stevens, W. L. (1939). Distribution of groups in a sequence of alternatives. *Annals of Eugenics, 9*, 10–17.

Stigler, S. (1971). Optimal experimental designs for polynomial regression. *Journal of the American Statistical Association, 66*, 311–318.

Straube, E. R., von Eye, A., & Müller, M. J. (1998). The symmetry of symptom patterns in pre-post treatment designs. *Pharmacopsychiatry, 31*, 83–88.

Swade, D. (2002). *The difference engine: Charles Babbage and the quest to build the first computer.* Middlesex, UK: Penguin.

Swed, F. S., & Eisenhart, C. (1943). Tables for testing randomness of grouping in a sequence of alternatives. *Annals of Mathematical Statistics, 14*, 66–87.

Tanner, M. A., & Young, M. A. (1985). Modeling agreement among raters. *Journal of the American Statistical Association, 80*, 175–180.

Taylor, C. S., Lerner, R. M., von Eye, A., Bilalbegovič Balsano, A., Dowling, E. M., P. M. Anderson, P., et al. (2002). Individual and ecological assets and positive developmental trajectories among gang and community-based organization youth. *New Directions for Youth Development, 95*, 57–72.

Venables, W. N., & Smith, D. M. (2001). *An introduction to R.* Bristol, UK: Network Theory Limited.

Vermunt, J. K. (1997). *Lem: A general program for the analysis of categorical data* [Computer software manual].

Verotta, D., Petrillo, P., La Regina, A., Rocchetti, M., & Tavani, A. (1988). D-optimal design applied to binding saturation curves of an enkephalin analog in rat brain. *Life Sciences, 42*, 735–743.

Victor, N. (1983). An alternative approach to configural frequency analysis. *Methodika, 3*, 61–73.

von Eye, A. (1982). Statistische und methodologische Problemstellungen psychologischer Präventionsforschung [Statistical and methodological issues of prevention research in psychology]. In J. Brandtstädter & A. von Eye (Eds.), *Psychologische Prävention: Grundlagen, Programme, Methoden* [Prevention in psychology: Bases, programs, methods] (pp. 305–439). Bern, Switzerland: Huber.

von Eye, A. (2002a). *Configural frequency analysis: Methods, models, and applications.* Mahwah, NJ: Erlbaum.

von Eye, A. (2002b). The odds favor antitypes: A comparison of tests for the identification of configural types and antitypes. *Methods of Psychological Research Online, 7*, 1–29.

von Eye, A. (2004a). Base models for configural frequency analysis. *Psychology Science, 46*, 150–170.

von Eye, A. (2004b). The treasures of Pandora's box. *Measurement: Interdisciplinary Research and Perspectives, 2*, 244–247.

von Eye, A. (2007). Configural frequency analysis. *Methodology, 3*, 170–172.

von Eye, A. (2008a). Configural analysis of mediation. In M. Stemmler, E. Lautsch, & D. Martinke (Eds.), *Configural frequency analysis (CFA) and other nonparametric statistical methods: Gustav A. Lienert memorial issue* (pp. 1–18). Lengerich, Germany: Pabst.

von Eye, A. (2008b). Fractional factorial designs in the analysis of categorical data. *InterStat, 04/08.* Available from http://interstat.statjournals .net/YEAR/2008/articles/0804003.pdf

von Eye, A. (2010). Did you expect this cluster here? Distributional characteristics of clusters. *Bulletin de la Société des Sciences Médicales, Luxembourg.*

von Eye, A., & Bergman, L. R. (2003). Research strategies in developmental psychopathology: Dimensional identity and the person-oriented approach. *Development and Psychopathology, 15,* 553–580.

von Eye, A., & Bogat, G. A. (2005). Logistic regression and prediction configural frequency analysis — a comparison. *Psychology Science, 47,* 407–414.

von Eye, A., & Bogat, G. A. (2006). Mental health in women experiencing intimate partner violence as the efficiency goal of social welfare functions. *International Journal of Social Welfare, 15,* 31–40.

von Eye, A., & Bogat, G. A. (2009). Analysis of intensive categorical longitudinal data. In J. Valsiner, P. C. M. Molenaar, M. C. D. P. Lyra, & N. Chaudhary (Eds.), *Dynamic process methodology in the social and developmental sciences* (pp. 241–253). New York: Springer.

von Eye, A., & Brandtstädter, J. (1982). Systematization of results of configuration frequency analysis by minimizing Boolean functions. In H. Caussinus, P. Ettinger, & J. R. Mathieu (Eds.), *Compstat 1982: Short communications, summaries of posters* (pp. 91–92). Vienna, Austria: Physica.

von Eye, A., & Brandtstädter, J. (1998). The wedge, the fork, and the chain — modeling dependency concepts using manifest categorical variables. *Psychological Methods, 3,* 169–185.

von Eye, A., & Gardiner, J. C. (2004). Locating deviations from multivariate normality. *Understanding Statistics, 3,* 313–331.

von Eye, A., & Gutiérrez Peña, E. (2004). Configural frequency analysis: The search for extreme cells. *Journal of Applied Statistics, 31,* 981–997.

von Eye, A., & Lienert, G. A. (1984). Die Konfigurationsfrequenzanalyse XX: Typen und Syndrome zweiter Ordnung (Komplextypen) [Configural Frequency Analysis XX: Second order types and syndromes (complex types)]. *Zeitschrift für klinische Psychologie und Psychotherapie, 32,* 345–355.

von Eye, A., & Mair, P. (2008a). A functional approach to configural frequency analysis. *Austrian Journal of Statistics, 37,* 161–173.

von Eye, A., & Mair, P. (2008b). Functional configural frequency analysis: Explaining types and antitypes. *Bulletin de la Société des Sciences Médicales, Luxembourg, 144,* 35–52.

von Eye, A., & Mair, P. (2009). A functional approach to configural frequency analysis: Computational issues. In M. Stemmler, E. Lautsch, & D. Martinke (Eds.), *Configural frequency analysis (CFA) and other nonparametrical statistical methods: Gustav A. Lienert memorial issue* (pp. 84–94). Lengerich, Germany: Pabst.

von Eye, A., Mair, P., & Bogat, G. A. (2005). Prediction models for configural frequency analysis. *Psychology Science, 47*, 342–355.

von Eye, A., & Mun, E. Y. (2003). Characteristics of measures for 2×2 tables. *Understanding Statistics, 2*, 243–266.

von Eye, A., & Mun, E. Y. (2005). *Modeling rater agreement: Manifest variable approaches.* Mahwah, NJ: Erlbaum.

von Eye, A., & Mun, E. Y. (2006). Exploring rater agreement: Configurations of agreement and disagreement. *Psychology Science, 48*, 69–84.

von Eye, A., & Mun, E. Y. (2007). A note on the analysis of difference patterns — structural zeros by design. *Psychology Science, 49*, 14–25.

von Eye, A., Mun, E. Y., & Bogat, G. A. (2008). Temporal patterns of variable relationships in person-oriented research: Longitudinal models of Configural Frequency Analysis. *Developmental Psychology, 44*, 437–445.

von Eye, A., Mun, E. Y., & Bogat, G. A. (2009). Temporal patterns of variable relationships in person-oriented research: Prediction and auto-association models of Configural Frequency Analysis. *Applied Developmental Science, 13*, 172–187.

von Eye, A., Mun, E. Y., & Indurkhya, A. (2004). Classifying developmental trajectories — a decision making perspective. *Psychology Science, 46*, 65–98.

von Eye, A., Mun, E. Y., & Mair, P. (2009). What carries a mediation process? Configural analysis of mediation. *Integrative Psychology and Behavioral Science, 43*, 228–247.

von Eye, A., & Schuster, C. (1998). On the specification of models for configural frequency analysis: Sampling schemes in prediction CFA. *Methods of Psychological Research Online, 3*, 55–73.

von Eye, A., Schuster, C., & Gutiérrez Peña, E. (2000). Configural frequency analysis under retrospective and prospective sampling schemes: Frequentist and Bayesian approaches. *Psychologische Beiträge, 42*, 428–447.

von Eye, A., Spiel, C., & Rovine, M. J. (1995). Concepts of nonindependence in configural frequency analysis. *Journal of Mathematical Sociology, 20*, 41–54.

von Eye, A., & von Eye, M. (2005). Can one use Cohen's kappa to examine disagreement? *Methodology, 1*, 129–142.

von Eye, A., & von Eye, M. (2008). On the marginal dependency of Cohen's kappa. *European Psychologist, 13*, 305–315.

von Weber, S., Lautsch, E., & von Eye, A. (2003a). On the limits of configural frequency analysis: Analyzing small tables. *Psychology Science, 45*, 339–354.

von Weber, S., Lautsch, E., & von Eye, A. (2003b). Table-specific continuity corrections for configural frequency analysis. *Psychology Science, 45*, 355–368.

von Weber, S., von Eye, A., & Lautsch, E. (2004). The Type II error of measures for the analysis of 2×2 tables. *Understanding Statistics, 3*, 259–282.

Wald, A., & Wolfowitz, J. (1940). On a test whether two alternatives are from the same population. *Annals of Mathematical Statistics, 11*, 147–162.

Wallis, W. A., & Moore, G. H. (1941). A significance test for time series analysis. *Journal of the American Statistical Association, 20*, 257–267.

Walls, T. A., & Schafer, J. L. (2006). *Models for intensive longitudinal data.* New York: Oxford University Press.

Wood, P. (2004). The search for the syndrome that was there or the variable that wasn't: Configural frequency analysis, conditional independence, and tetrad approaches for categorical data. *Understanding Statistics, 3,* 65–83.

Wu, C. F. J., & Hamada, M. (2000). *Experiments: Planning, analysis and parameter design optimization.* New York: Wiley.

Wurzer, M. (2005). *An application of configural frequency analysis: Evaluation of the usage of internet terminals.* Unpublished master's thesis, University of Vienna, Austria.

Zelen, M., & Haitovsku, Y. (1991). Testing hypotheses with binary data subject to misclassification errors: Analysis and experimental design. *Biometrika, 78,* 857–865.

Author Index

Subject Index

About the Authors

Alexander von Eye, PhD, is Professor of Psychology at Michigan State University. He develops, studies, and applies methods for the analysis of categorical data (in particular, configural frequency analysis and log-linear modeling) and longitudinal data. He also works on and with classification methods and conducts simulation studies. Dr. von Eye has published over 350 articles in methodological, statistical, psychological, and developmental journals, and he is the (co)author or (co)editor of 18 books. He is Fellow of the American Psychological Association and the American Psychological Society, and he was visiting professor of statistics, psychology, human development, and education at a number of universities in Austria and Germany, as well as at Penn State.

Patrick Mair, PhD, is Assistant Professor in the Institute for Statistics and Mathematics, WU Vienna University of Economics and Business. He was a visiting scholar at the University of California, Los Angeles. Dr. Mair's research focuses on computational/applied statistics and psychometrics, including methodological developments as well as corresponding implementations in the statistical computing environment R. His publications appear in journals of applied and computational statistics.

Eun-Young Mun, PhD, is Assistant Professor of Psychology at Rutgers, The State University of New Jersey. Her research aims to better understand how alcohol and drug use behaviors develop over time, and to delineate mechanisms of behavior change in order to develop effective prevention and intervention approaches, especially for adolescents and emerging adults. She is also interested in extending existing research methodology by integrating and synthesizing distinctive methods together—in particular, pattern-oriented and person-oriented longitudinal research method—and by disseminating applications. She is coauthor of *Analyzing Rater Agreement* and publishes articles in developmental, clinical, and methodological journals.

306